Critique for What?

Great Barrington Books

Bringing the old and new together
in the spirit of W. E. B. Du Bois

∽ An imprint edited by Charles Lemert ∽

Titles Available

Keeping Good Time: Reflections on Knowledge, Power, and People
by Avery F. Gordon (2004)

Going Down for Air: A Memoir in Search of a Subject
by Derek Sayer (2004)

The Souls of Black Folk,
100th Anniversary Edition
by W. E. B. Du Bois, with commentaries by Manning Marable, Charles Lemert,
and Cheryl Townsend Gilkes (2004)

Sociology After the Crisis, Updated Edition
by Charles Lemert (2004)

Subject to Ourselves
by Anthony Elliot (2004)

The Protestant Ethic Turns 100:
Essays on the Centenary of the Weber Thesis
edited by William H. Swatos, Jr., and Lutz Kaelber (2005)

Postmodernism Is Not What You Think
by Charles Lemert (2005)

Discourses on Liberation: An Anatomy of Critical Theory
by Kyung-Man Kim (2005)

Seeing Sociologically: The Routine Grounds of Social Action
by Harold Garfinkel, edited and introduced by Anne Warfield Rawls (2005)

The Souls of W. E. B. Du Bois
by Alford A. Young, Jr., Manning Marable, Elizabeth Higginbotham, Charles
Lemert, and Jerry G. Watts (2006)

Radical Nomad: C. Wright Mills and His Times
by Tom Hayden with Contemporary Reflections by Stanley Aronowitz, Richard
Flacks, and Charles Lemert (2006)

Critique for What? Cultural Studies, American Studies, Left Studies
by Joel Pfister (2006)

Everyday Life and the State
by Peter Bratsis (2006)

Forthcoming

Thinking the Unthinkable:
An Introduction to Social Theories
by Charles Lemert

Critique for What?
Cultural Studies, American Studies, Left Studies

Joel Pfister

afterword by Charles Lemert

Paradigm Publishers

Boulder · London

Published in the United States by Paradigm Publishers, 3360 Mitchell Lane Suite E, Boulder, Colorado 80301 USA.

Paradigm Publishers is the trade name of Birkenkamp & Company, LLC, Dean Birkenkamp, President and Publisher.

Library of Congress Cataloging-in-Publication Data

Pfister, Joel.
    Critique for what? : cultural studies, American studies, Left studies / Joel Pfister ; afterword by Charles Lemert.
        p. cm.
    "Great Barrington books."
    Includes bibliographical references and index.
    ISBN-13: 978-1-59451-225-4 (hc)
    ISBN-10: 1-59451-225-6 (hc)
    1. Culture — Study and teaching — United States.   2. Culture —Study and teaching — Great Britain.   3. Americanization.   4. Criticism.   5. New Left — Great Britain.   6. United States—Study and teaching.   I. Title.
    HM623.P45 2006
    306.07'073—dc22

                                                                    2006001601

Printed and bound in the United States of America on acid-free paper that meets the standards of the American National Standard for Permanence of Paper for Printed Library Materials.

Designed and Typeset by Straight Creek Bookmakers.

10 09 08 07 06
1 2 3 4 5

For
Clive Bush, Richard Ohmann, Richard Slotkin, Alan Trachtenberg, Bryan Wolf

Contents

Acknowledgments

My "Cultural Studies and American Studies" seminar at Wesleyan University, which I have taught in one form or another since 1988, has been this book's laboratory. I am indebted to my lively students for our experiments. Previous classroom adventures set the stage for this project. James Shenton's seminar on radical history and Sacvan Bercovitch's course on American literature at Columbia, Alan Sinfield's and Peter Stallybrass's teaching at the University of Sussex, Eric Mottram's influence at the University of London, and much of my American studies work at Yale, with Alan Trachtenberg, Bryan Wolf, Dick Brodhead, Jules Prown, Vincent Scully, Fredric Jameson, David Montgomery, Jean-Christophe Agnew, and others, have enlightened me. I dedicate this book to five inimitable thinkers whose ideas, creativity, life force, decency, and friendship I have long treasured: Alan Trachtenberg and Bryan Wolf; one of my dear British friends, Clive Bush; and two Wes colleagues, Dick Ohmann and Rich Slotkin.

Sarah Winter and Dick Ohmann generously read and improved the book. Two other brilliant friends read most of it and made it better, David Lubin and Rich Lowry. Khachig Tölölyan, Henry Abelove, Laura Wexler, and Joseph Entin commented on and tightened parts of it. Paul Stephens, a terrific British friend from the University of London who now teaches at Stavanger University in Norway, sent me material on British politics that I found illuminating. Alan Sinfield kindly engaged in an e-mail exchange about the history of cultural studies at Sussex. Michael Denning, my former Yale classmate, spent about ten hours one day in 1990 discussing what's at stake in cultural studies. Then Hazel Carby, my former Wesleyan colleague, joined the fray. They later introduced me to Paul Gilroy, who offered more critical perspectives.

My beloved Lisa Wyant—full of ideas—got into the act and polished the introduction and final chapter. Her intelligence, passion, artistry, and politics have sustained me on both sides of the Atlantic. I wrote this book in New Haven, Brooklyn, Paris, and Branford. The Brooklyn site was my loving mom's warm home, where I grew up. Elizabeth Pfister, through her own example, inspired me to try to do some good in the world. I miss her. Jordan Pfister, my brother, gave me some good critical perspectives.

Wesleyan University, which provided me with several sabbaticals and leaves, as well as research funds to buy books, did much to make this project doable. A faculty fellowship at Wesleyan's Center for the Humanities in spring 2001 advanced my research and writing. The encyclopedic Henry Abelove was a most gracious and wise director of the center. As usual, the librarians at Wesleyan and Yale have been exemplary.

Numerous institutions have given me the opportunity to try out ideas, approaches, and questions. Priscilla Wald arranged for me to speak on American studies and cultural studies at Columbia's Center for American Cultural Studies in 1993. Maria Farland was responsible for my invitation to hold forth on the transnationalizing of American studies at Columbia's Humanities Center in 2000. Rachel Adams invited me to lecture on chapter 2 at Columbia's New York-area American studies seminar in 2002. A Yale American studies reunion in 1994 offered me the occasion to speculate about the future of American studies. In 2000 I previewed versions of chapter 4 at the European Collegium for African American Research (where Kimberley Phillips, Leigh Raiford, and Laura Yow responded helpfully) and at the University of Wisconsin (enlivened by Gordon Hutner and Dale Bauer). I then tried out some ideas that became chapter 6 at Colby College's American studies program, a delightful experience that featured my old friends David and Libby Lubin. At Wesleyan's Center for the Humanities I lectured on what would be chapter 5 in 2001. I further developed ideas that entered chapters 5 and 6 in a keynote address at a University of Chicago Society of Fellows conference on agency in 2001.

In the fall of 1989 I was lucky to bump into Jonathan Freedman, a founding editor of the *Yale Journal of Criticism*. Happily, he asked me to write a long review essay on either cultural studies or American studies. Wesleyan had hired me in 1987, after a two-year stint as lecturer in American studies at Yale, partly to help develop a doctoral program in cultural studies (which never materialized). So I had a keen interest in fusing Jonathan's options. The result was "The Americanization of Cultural Studies," *Yale Journal of Criticism* 4 (Spring 1991): 199–229. I had no idea then that that was the start of this book. I'll always be grateful to the journal for this chance. The essay, now chapter 1, is the seedbed for what follows. I am thankful to Johns Hopkins University Press for allowing me to reprint it in altered form. I kept writing about these matters. Gordon Hutner, founding editor of *American Literary History,* invited me to speak at a special conference his groundbreaking journal sponsored in 1999 and then published a version of the talk, "Complicity Critiques," *American Literary History* 12 (Fall 2000): 61–32. I have now significantly revised and retitled this contribution as chapter 4, "Complicity Critiques, the Artful Front, and Political Motivation." I appreciate permission from Oxford University Press to reprint this new version. And I am grateful to Yaroslava Mills for allowing me to quote from some of C. Wright Mills's unpublished letters and documents.

Dean Birkenkamp, president of Paradigm Publishers, and his colleagues, have been magnificent. It is an honor to be part of their noble venture and Charles Lemert's imprint.

I am certainly enmeshed in the web of contradictions I portray and offer these reflections in the spirit of humility and self-critique.

Joel Pfister

Introduction

For What and for Whom?

It is but lost time to converse with you whose works are only Analytics.
—*William Blake, "The Marriage of Heaven and Hell" (c. 1790)*

Who needs a socialist Heaven where everybody agrees with everybody else, where everybody's exactly the same? God forbid. I mean a place where we can begin the historic quarrel about what a new kind of civilisation must be. That's what it's about.
—*Stuart Hall, "Gramsci and Us" (1987)*

In the country I live in we can write whatever we want; nobody locks us up, nobody has to. Many of us lock ourselves up.... [American intellectuals] are abdicating the making of history.
—*C. Wright Mills, letter to his imaginary Russian correspondent, Tovarich (1959)[1]*

MANY OF MY AMERICAN STUDIES STUDENTS, PARTICULARLY THOSE WHO TAKE to cultural critique like birds to flight, are all too conscious that they will soon face what one of my teachers, Alan Trachtenberg, back in America's bicentennial year, called the long-standing American dilemma of "finding a vocation in a society one does not fully approve of."[2] My responses to their concern about having their wings clipped, as the chapters that follow demonstrate, are manifold and in process. Among my responses is a double fantasy that, though inadequate in so many ways, is meant to offer students some perspective on why it makes sense that at times they may feel frustrated by the very critiques they value. For their feelings of frustration are rooted in the social shaping and channeling of aspiration and opportunity they have begun to "unpack."

First, I tell them, try to imagine an American future in which something like a state-supported Institute for Social Transformation thrives. The imaginary institute's branches—in our equally imaginary Progressive America—recruit thousands of lively young citizens every year and invite them to serve as interns for a five-year term at a good salary. Interns form problem-defining and problem-solving groups that analyze and propose detailed national and international solutions for America's contradictions, inequalities, injustices, and conflicts. Many of them spend long periods beyond the institute's intellectual hothouses to learn—and unlearn—from people who need them. They ally themselves with lobbyists in Congress who endeavor to transform their proposals into realities. In this sort of America, students would likely view the critiques we debate as usable and appreciate that their country really values their efforts to do something concrete with "critical thinking."[3]

Now, I add, also imagine that this Progressive America has been made possible in part by the efforts of a party, or a movement that can sway parties. Suppose that this party or movement is consecrated to rebuilding a society truly by and for all of the people—in matters of economic opportunity, resource distribution, quality of education, political agency, welfare, health care, the natural environment, the built environment, and ethnoracial diversity. Its existence, too, would affect how students approach critique. For students would focus critique not only on criticizing but designing a better world. They would see themselves as creators and custodians of an unselfishly democratic—an ambitiously beautiful—society-in-progress.

Needless to say, my double fantasy is too vague, fanciful, unhelpful. No such institute, no Critique Corps, exists (though lavishly funded conservative think tanks are now developing such institutions, complete with apartments for interns).[4] American federal and corporate priorities lie elsewhere. And no such party or movement has yet been formed. But the point is that the absence of these kinds of supports, outlets, and incentives for critical thinking affects—limits—what is thinkable and imaginable.[5] Critique itself becomes a symptom of this lack. Hence teachers concerned with such matters must scramble to give students some sense of social direction and political possibilities as best they can. *Critique for What?* joins the scramble.

To be sure, there are many good reasons to study cultural and social critique. They include a desire to know what kind of power structure one is involved in, to be up front about who gets hurt often "legally" and systemically within social arrangements, to articulate and hence disrupt unquestioned ways of thinking, seeing, feeling, and valuing, and to better comprehend what social relations, institutions, roles, practices, and contradictions are correctable even if—especially if—they seem natural, inevitable, insurmountable. "The joke isn't cosmic, it's strictly man-made," one utopian character asserts in Aldous Huxley's final novel, *Island* (1962). "These things aren't like gravity or the second law of thermodynamics; they don't have to happen. They happen only if people are stupid enough to allow them to happen."[6] But when one gains some critical perspective on how and why this "stupidity" prevails, what next?

What does it mean, after all, for an intellectual to be "politically engaged"? In what respects does American "oppositional" critique do more than serve as public evidence of free speech? Might progressive scholars devote more time to developing not just cultural studies—or transnational studies—but social transformation studies, activism studies, political mobilizing studies, organizing studies? If so, to whom might such studies be worthwhile?[7] And what might they look like? Is it pressing to try to advance traditions of critique that—as Stuart Hall puts it—endeavor to shed light not only on "what a new kind of civilisation must be" but on how we might achieve it? The word "strategy" appears in many book and article titles of late, but in its academic postmodern guise "strategy" usually signifies theoretical preoccupations and not much more.

Fortunately, questions along the lines of *what is to be done?* are by no means new. Responses to these sorts of questions have long been formulated, debated, dismissed, displaced, suppressed, and forgotten in sundry ways. *Critique for What?* draws on the reflections of those who have taken up these matters to reissue a constructive and hopeful challenge to the now predominantly academic critique business. My book traces some key historical and thematic filiations linking American studies, British cultural studies, Left studies, historical studies, and literary studies, concentrating mainly on the postwar period to the postmodern present. The leitmotiv that runs throughout is my analysis of critical work that has produced knowledge about—including debates about—acting on these "studies."

Some scholars consider this a crucial production of knowledge. For them the grounds for thinking about agency, strategy, and organizing are not only ethical and political but demandingly and rewardingly intellectual. Others regard such subjects of study as the sole province of think tanks and advocacy institutes. Do these subjects warrant historical, cross-cultural, and theoretical analysis within the university? In exploring and advancing a tradition of thinking that takes up the *critique for what?* challenge, my book helps clarify what is at stake in these positions.[8]

Studies for What and for Whom?

My orientation is not substantively biographical. Yet some understanding of the lives of American intellectuals—Robert Lynd, C. Wright Mills, F. O. Matthiessen, Richard Ohmann, and others—as well as British intellectuals—Raymond Williams, E. P. Thompson, Stuart Hall, Raphael Samuel, and others—can highlight the historical pressures as well as the boldness, frustrations, hopefulness, and resilience that prompted reevaluations of the scope, style, and uses of critique. Such perspectives better illuminate what has been done and might be done. Below I draw thumbnail sketches of some of Lynd's, Mills's, and Matthiessen's concerns to better convey my book's concerns.

The impertinent query *for what?*, which structures my book title, originated in Columbia sociologist Robert Lynd's *Knowledge for What?* (1939), a polemic that engages its subject in ways worth remembering.[9] His audacious little book is a founding contribution to an American cultural studies whose transformative aspirations are at once academic and more than academic, beyond what William Blake termed "only Analytics." Lynd tries to make social science scholarship consecrated to progressive social change not merely reputable but prestigious, not marginal but mainstream, not only urgent but professional. He insists that an "appraisal" of America, especially its "elements of strain and disjunction," and a "critique" of the "focus and methods in social science research" must be grasped as symbiotic concerns rather than "independent lines of thought" (ix). Lynd prods his colleagues to rethink America not so much in the name of socialism, whose echoes reverberate through his arguments and references, but in "the spirit of science" (249). He tactically represents social science's mission not as radical, per se, but as "serviceable" (115). Lynd frames its knowledge more as a tool than a weapon, for its plan should be to "rebuild" (200) an "allegedly free" (194) America until that nation "make[s] real [its] claims of freedom and opportunity" (250).

Lynd knows well what social scientists are up against. He cites a host of contradictions—many of which still beset America—that social science must foreground and lobby to change: "business pressure-blocs ... prevent the passage of legislation manifestly in the public interest" (74); the American Medical Association sabotages "socialized medicine" because of self-interest (110); corporations crush decent labor policies (74); the rich systematically get richer (75). To grasp these contradictions, Lynd recommends supplementing disciplinary study with the study of "problem-areas" (166): "motivations in citizenship," "the relations between economic organization and political power," "the study of the family" (167), "incentives under private capitalism, as compared with other types of economy" (170). His analysis branches into strategy and social design. If scholars do their job properly, he contends, they should generate predictions, proposals, plans, policies, solutions. The constructive query that Lynd led up to and hinted but did not come right out and ask was: America for what?[10]

Not surprisingly, some of Lynd's reviewers found the thesis that social science should think through ways of designing a better America restricting and defended the pursuit of "knowledge for its own sake." Lynd's Columbia colleague Robert MacIver complained: "Would we have built up our knowledge of the civilizations of Egypt and Babylon if what we were really seeking was 'to know things about the past in relation to current institutional problems?'" Anthropologist Alexander Goldenweiser praised Lynd's institutional critique of university- and foundation-sponsored formulations of "knowledge" and "objectivity." Yet, like others, he too felt that "something should be left to the sheer passion for knowledge and wisdom" and feared that Lynd's unabashed "call to arms" would give ammunition to "detractors" of social science. Lynd rebutted that "far from denying free play to intellectual curiosity, [he wanted] social scientists to be more dangerously curious about some of the things that ... they find it convenient not to be curious about."

By contrast, Max Lerner's "Revolt against Quietism" hailed Lynd's "most spacious claims for the possibilities of social thinking—nothing short of the reconstruction of our culture." Even so, Lerner felt that Lynd had not gone far enough, having offered more cultural theory than "a theory of social change." Lerner advised synthesizing the study of power and of social change: "The pressing social iniquities today must be those turning on how power is captured and consolidated ... what revolutions are, why and how they occur, and how the revolutionary energies can be turned into humanist channels." (In the 1950s Lynd struggled to write a book analyzing American power.) Further, he implied that Lynd himself was stuck in some of the academicized limits he criticized in the work of others.[11]

However much that observation may have been true, the challenge embedded in Lynd's charge remains active today: "Our culture includes no positive philosophy regarding change and the techniques for achieving it" (111).[12] Lynd never lost this instrumental focus. In 1945 he wrote Dwight Macdonald about the potential of the new journal *politics*. He exhorted Macdonald not to allow the journal to degrade itself by sponsoring critics' "snipes" at fellow critics. Instead Lynd was more interested in attempts to devise plans of action. He cited the English journal *Labour Discussion Notes* put out by the Socialist Clarity Group: "They don't do the thing I want, namely develop over a period of time all major phases of a nation's life, but they approach it in their effort to meet segments of the problem with a constructive program. Why don't you set *politics* to this systematic job of blueprinting what is to be done?" Over the next three decades Lynd persisted in supporting "radical causes," but, bitterly alienated from academic sociology, never completed another book.[13]

In 1964, the year Lynd's book was reprinted, the sociologist David Riesman published his collection of essays, indubitably with Lynd's title and questions in mind, *Abundance for What?*[14] Almost two decades earlier Riesman had praised *Knowledge for What?* for rejecting the politically evasive "ethical relativism" that pervaded the social sciences, "a value-free attitude which might be thought of as the academic counterpart of popular cynicism." Riesman's 1950s and early 1960s studies of America's unequal distribution of wealth and power led him to voice another key question submerged in Lynd's queries, the second question whose framework has shaped my inquiries. His "Abundance for Whom?" might be extended: knowledge for whom? critique for whom? America for whom?[15]

If the *for whom?* concern prompts one to reconsider which groups or individuals might derive benefit and enlightenment from progressive critique, it also broaches another dicey issue: who cares about critique? Who is reading, viewing, or listening to critique in its manifold forms in critical and cultural production, besides those not receiving or giving grades? If it is crucial to make seemingly "progressive" critique legitimate and prestigious in academia, how, beyond academia, might it be generalized, popularized, as Hall is fond of saying, "hegemonized"?

The twin challenges *critique for what and for whom?* form an undercurrent that propels the writings of C. Wright Mills, another prominent Columbia sociologist who thought against the grain to imagine what decades later would be called American cultural studies. Robert Martinson made explicit the link between Lynd's *Knowledge for What?* and Mills's revisionary political intellectualism in his *Anvil and Student Partisan* survey of the latter's work in 1960.[16] Mills, perhaps more doggedly than Lynd and more radically than Riesman, was enraged by the discrepancy between America's reality and its rhetoric. Teaching in Copenhagen in 1956, he commiserated with two American friends: "It breaks your damned heart to think what America could do—or even more, what Americans—including oneself of course—might be." Referring to a book he was writing, Mills confessed: "I can't get what I want to say about America in it. What I want to say is what you say to intimate friends when you are discouraged about how it all is. All of it at once: to create a little spotlighted focus where the alienation, and apathy and dry rot and immensity and razzle dazzle and bullshit and wonderfulness and how lonesome it is, really, how terribly lonesome and rich and vulgar and god I don't know."[17]

Mills was satisfied with neither the American nor the Soviet molding of humanity and, like members of the British New Left he inspired, advocated the formation of a Third Way. Rejecting the "nationalist celebration" patent in much McCarthy-era American studies, historical, literary, and sociology scholarship, he regarded national borders as untenable intellectual borders and tried to enlist communist and socialist intellectuals around the world to promote strategic anti–Cold War dialogue. "With them we should make our own separate peace. Then, as intellectuals—also as public men—we should act and work as if this peace—and the exchange of values, ideas, and programs of which it consists—is everybody's peace, or surely ought to be." This entailed popularizing his ideas. *Listen, Yankee: The Revolution in Cuba* (1960) sold about half a million in the early 1960s. Yet he urged intellectuals "not to underestimate what even a small circulation of ideas can do."[18]

Mills, a former student recalled, was a "great teacher" who "shocked us out of our 'silent generation' torpor." What appears to be one of his early 1950s exam questions exhibits his effort to train students to think imaginatively about social transformation: "In terms of the scheme of character and social structure presented, design a study to determine, for the United States, the factors involved in 'the revolt potential' against prevailing economic and political institutions. Define 'revolt potential' as you will."[19] At times his dedication to teaching critique prompted him to wonder: teaching for what and for whom? For some students shocked him, especially when, as Mills might have put it, he challenged their "complacency." Once, when Mills returned to his office after class, he "burst back into the room tired and out of sorts ... [and] slammed down his books and said, referring to his students, 'Who *are* these guys?'" One of his concerns, like Riesman's, was: who notices critique? This absorbed him at least as early as 1944, at age twenty-eight, five years after Lynd framed the problem as "knowledge for what?" "The view that all that is needed is knowledge ignored the nub of the problem as the social scientist confronts it: he has little or no power to act politically and his chance to communicate in a politically effective manner is very limited."[20] Sadly, the price Mills paid for making critique more "politically effective"—analyzing the Bay of Pigs and the boycotts of Cuba as instances of U.S. imperialism—was that he spent the last year of his life, 1962, in the shadow of death threats, sleeping with a pistol at hand.[21]

Matthiessen endeavored to make the *critique for what and for whom?* challenge pertinent to the practice of American studies, a field he helped found in the 1930s and 1940s. Several of his Harvard students, including Leo Marx, Henry Nash Smith, and R. W. B. Lewis, did much to build this interdisciplinary venture in the 1950s and after. For several decades critics have taken Matthiessen to task for playing a formative role in diverting American studies from political and theoretical tracks they now value. I am tempted to suggest that some critics resent Matthiessen self-defensively because his career implies that one's "political" concerns cannot solely be a matter of theoretical "intervention" and professional disputation. More recently, postnational American studies scholars have criticized Matthiessen for his role in the institutionalization of nation-based American studies premised on the ideology of American exceptionalism. This criticism also obfuscates the academic, activist, and transnational concerns Matthiessen brought to his formation of American studies critique.[22]

Matthiessen's reviews of V. F. Calverton's and Granville Hicks's early 1930s Marxist rereadings of American literature suggest that the radical academic battle he felt compelled to take up vigorously was first to help show why American literature, not just English literature, was worth studying, and second to demonstrate that socialists could best engage the complexity of American literature.[23] He noted that at Yale of the 1920s and 1930s "literature . . . had still meant English literature" and recalled that "even as late as nineteen-thirty, the Yale library still catalogued [*Moby Dick*] under cetology, instead of under American literature."[24] Calverton and Hicks, Matthiessen felt, oversimplified literature, culture, and critique and did little to raise the intellectual and academic standing of either Marxism or American literature.[25] To counter this, Matthiessen endeavored to imbue a socialist-influenced American studies literary-cultural history with intellectual subtlety, legitimacy, and prestige. In evaluating Matthiessen's ever-developing efforts to devise more supple approaches than those he found in a 1930s Marxism he considered "mechanistic," Leo Marx compares some of his mentor's writings to the revisionary work of two of the most inspiring socialist contributors to British cultural studies: Raymond Williams and E. P. Thompson.[26] Matthiessen's articles, published not only in scholarly journals but in the *New Republic*, the *Atlantic Monthly*, the *Saturday Review of Literature*, and the *New York Times Book Review*, established him not simply as a literary critic but a public intellectual—a public socialist intellectual.[27]

Matthiessen, as an activist critic, took up causes that current American studies postnationalists now prize as inclusive. In 1935, for instance, Matthiessen traveled to Gallup, New Mexico, to report for the *New Republic* on the imprisonment of Mexican workers who tried bravely to unionize and defy both the mine owners (including the Guggenheims) and a politician who bought the land on which they lived so as to exploit them further. Matthiessen combined a socialist critique of worker and tenant exploitation (abetted by the state's gubernatorial, legislative, and police apparatus) with what would now be heralded as a border studies critique of the oppression of illegal migrant laborers. He labeled what these workers were up against state and corporate "terrorism." His piece is not only a critique of the political and economic system that relies on and legalizes such terrorism, it examines strategically the Mexicans' organization of their resistance. Matthiessen sounds not unlike his friend Carey McWilliams, who is now revered as a pioneer of socialist-influenced ethnic studies critique, and who, a few years after Matthiessen published his article, began to publish his important work on migrant laborers.[28]

In 1948 Matthiessen opined that "we in the United States have now reached the stage in our multi-national culture when some really vital educational experiments would take full advantage of the rich strains in our heritage." And in the pluralist tradition of Randolph Bourne, Horace Kallen, John Collier, and Louis Adamic, he continued: "Each [minority group] should be proud of [its] inherited culture. Our country has the greatest resources in the world to foster out of its own people this kind of internationalism."[29] He had a keen critical eye for difference as well as contradiction.[30] Not only did he deplore "discrimination against the Chinese and the Mexicans ... [in California and] against the Jewish people," Matthiessen was apprehensive about the American postwar treatment of the Japanese: "Whether we fulfill [our responsibilities] justly or as domineering imperialists will depend in large measure whether we take with us a doctrine of racial equality or racial superiority."[31] I suspect that Matthiessen would have been an avid reader of José David Saldívar's provocative *Border Matters* (1997).[32]

Irving Howe was right, when doing his utmost to eviscerate Matthiessen for "sentimental fellow-traveling" in 1948, to represent this radical as "one of the few literary intellectuals in America who, contrary to the current fashion, have continued to engage in active politics."[33] One might think that graduate students training to contribute to American studies—perhaps especially those who are gaining grassroots political and intellectual experience in campaigns to form graduate student unions and support allied university unions—would be inspired by Matthiessen's pivotal role in the founding and administration of the Harvard Teachers Union in the 1930s and 1940s. They might also find it significant that Matthiessen taught not only at Harvard but at the Sam Adams School of Social Studies (a school for adult workers he helped establish) during its brief life from 1944 to 1947.[34] One of his final publications is a contribution to *Monthly Review*'s forum, "Cooperation on the Left" (to which McWilliams also contributed). Matthiessen's commitments from the early 1930s until his death exemplify what he advises in that short piece, "Needed: Organic Connection of Theory and Practice" (1950): "The only kind of situation in which the Left can make any real advances is when theory and practice, discussion and action, are organically connected."[35]

There is every reason to hail the impressive contributions of contemporary scholars to a more activist American studies. In so doing it is worth remembering those of Matthiessen.[36] He was publicly assertive about his socialism when it was risky to be so. For Matthiessen political advocacy required more than theorizing: it had to extend far beyond the academic borders of critical reading, historicizing, and politicizing and could never substitute for organizing. He engaged politics in the union hall, street, and party convention as well as in the classroom, library, and study. Yet he grasped fully the politics of exegesis. His review of Van Wyck Brooks's *The Flowering of New England: 1815–1865* (1936) makes plain that he had little critical respect for belletristic American studies—even when it was based on considerable knowledge—and was unseduced by a nostalgic picture of the American Renaissance (or any other period) that was simplistically "elegiac" and evaded "the form and pressure of the time."[37]

Matthiessen helped make *Monthly Review* (1949–) financially feasible. In troubled times that journal sponsored not only national but transnational radical, socialist, and Marxist critiques. His posthumously published *Monthly Review* piece (quoted above) condemned the divisive "self-righteous nationalism generated by the cold war" and counseled the global "non-Communist Left" to foster "international cooperation" on "political, economic, and cultural" levels.[38] In chapter 2 I will make the case that Matthiessen wrote a founding transnational American studies book, *From the Heart of Europe* (1948), which voices outrage at America's attempt to establish cultural and economic as well as military hegemony over Europe. Matthiessen recognized that American power had in effect pushed people around the world to engage in forms of uninstitutionalized, often highly critical, "American studies." It was this book, Leo Marx remembers, that "made him a conspicuous target for red-baiting."[39] His speech seconding the nomination of Henry Wallace as the Progressive Party's candidate for president in 1948 asserts "that it is not our function to impose the blind will of an American imperial century upon the rest of the world." Conceptualizing American culture "in narrowly national terms," he held, "is to think in a test-tube and to fail to envisage men and women as growing to know what life is in an indivisible world."[40] Near the close of his life, not long after he wrote these words, Matthiessen was harassed with "threatening letters."[41] He committed suicide in 1950.

American Studies, Cultural Studies, Left Studies

If on one level *Critique for What?* is an extended question and complication, I want it to do more than question and complicate. I had the same impulse when I published "The Americanization of Cultural Studies" in 1991, the foundation of this project, preserved mostly intact as chapter 1. Subsequent chapters now elaborate, revise, clarify, and add to concerns and problems I registered in this initial foray. Among other things, there I suggested that as British cultural studies was becoming increasingly institutionalized and commodified in the U.S. academy as the latest sexy European theory import, it was being liberalized as a professional-managerial-class critique-for-critique's-sake project that overrated the radicalism of its academicized "interventions" and "interrogations."

I also compared the history of British cultural studies with that of U.S. American studies to contest the claim—made by some American cultural studies enthusiasts—that U.S. American studies never developed beyond some of its postwar manifestations as a purveyor of depoliticized interdisciplinarity.[42] Oddly, these critics of American studies targeted Tremaine McDowell's 1948 schematic monograph on the status of the emerging field. McDowell, a program builder, was no Lynd, Mills, or Matthiessen in intellectual power. But he urged American studies to educate Americans for peace rather than empire building, and to help them become cosmopolitan, comparative, and cooperative rather than ethnocentric and supportive of world Americanization, thus pointing toward transnational American studies. "Every group among us is now a minority group. . . . England rises in the fog just off the coast of Maine; France lies not far beyond the tip of Long Island; Spain replaces Cuba off the Florida shore; behind them all looms Russia." The "crash of the atomic bombs which from time to time we drop at our own heels" must accelerate the making of Americans' "critical self-knowledge." McDowell profiled postwar American studies programs that offered courses not only on history, literature, and art, but on sociology economics, geography, anthropology, foreign policy, and political science. Postwar American studies scholars, McDowell wrote, studied not just New England romanticism, but matters such as class stratification, race relations, the history of political parties, social movements, imperialism, labor history, and utopianism. He reserved special praise for a Barnard course on "Schemes for a Better World" and noted that the first American studies dissertation, submitted at Yale in 1933, was on "The American Cult of Success."[43]

Not long after I published my essay, the cultural studies publishing boom under way boomed louder (producing several books claiming the title *Cultural Studies,* such as one in a handy "Teach Yourself" series).[44] It is understandable why Fredric Jameson, the great Marxist theorist of modern and postmodern capitalism, felt compelled, in his astute early 1990s critique of cultural studies, to issue the disclaimer: "It's not my field!"[45] In the late 1990s this boom was accompanied by an American studies entrepreneurial boom. Over the past few years American studies—particularly in its Americanist Critical Theory guises—has become more visible in the academy than ever before.[46]

In part this is due to the efforts of some "practitioners" who hope to reconstitute American studies as a more theoretically engaged postnational studies that examines not simply the nation but the flow of power, ideologies, and resistances originating within, across, and far beyond America's borders. (Related criticisms had been leveled at British cultural studies a few years earlier.)[47] Migrating corporations, laborers, cultures, and critiques have indeed shaken up older concepts of what constitutes "territory." At its best this reconceptualization redraws the map of "American" studies concerns and helps globalize not only its knowledge base but its ways of thinking about how the impact of "America" has never been located geographically solely within the United States. Postnational critique also puts interesting pressure on national identification: it reassesses citizenship as an ideological construct and affiliation that humans may elect to subordinate to other affiliations. Some forms of postnational critique have roots in socialist workers-of-the-world-unite internationalism. Describing his "conversion" from capitalist individualist to socialist, Jack London's "plethoric national patriotism ... leaked out of the bottom of his soul" and left him caring "more for men and women and little children than for imaginary geographical lines." American studies postnationalists, inspired by cultural studies books such as Paul Gilroy's *The Black Atlantic* (1993), approach slavery, the modernisms, black musics, the German and Ghanian W. E. B. Du Bois, and the French Richard Wright as subjects of

Atlanticist studies (connecting the Americas, Europe, and Africa).[48] Parts of *Critique for What?* contribute to postnational American studies.[49]

During the past decade or so my historical, theoretical, and political interest in British cultural studies and American studies has remained strong. The queries *cultural studies for what?* and *American studies for what?*, however, have led me to think not only about recovering and building bridges between these interdisciplinary fields but to consider more expansively the wider range of political-intellectual initiatives within which some exciting work in these fields may be seen as developments and contributions. Put differently, I treasure my education in American studies and cultural studies and continue to be fascinated by their critical histories, but have become even more focused on probing some of the most important ideas, questions, problems, and ways of thinking that have helped make these fields vital to me. Hence this book draws on and contributes to the histories of cultural studies, American studies, and, broadly speaking, Left studies.

As my brief mention of Matthiessen's socialist interdisciplinarity suggests, this broader scope has long been a defining characteristic of American studies. One constructively self-critical American studies scholar, Gene Wise, acknowledged that numerous academic and nonacademic intellectuals outside the field have done what amounts to "American studies" more provocatively than many inside the field.[50] In graduate school I was taught to range far beyond books and articles written by scholars who identified themselves primarily within American studies. When Jameson published *The Political Unconscious* in 1980, for instance, it had a profound influence on how American studies graduate students in my era read cultural productions.[51]

An illustration of my more capacious reconception of emphasis may be useful. Decades ago, as a graduate student, I read with interest an American studies and a cultural studies analysis of the ideological significance of amusement parks. At first what intrigued me was their differences in approach. In more recent times I have been more attuned to their involvement in a common critical project with a complex transnational lineage.

I recall being dazzled back in 1979 by John Kasson's use of the Frankfurt school's "culture industry" theory in *Amusing the Million* (1978) to muse on the irony of machine workers distracting themselves at turn-of-the-century Coney Island on machine rides not so unlike the kind they ran on the shop floor. Kasson read this not as "liberation" but "subjection," an "amusement" that had become a "fantastic replication" and "extension of work." He situated his analysis in the history of carnival and concluded: "Rather than suggesting alternatives to the prevailing economic and social order, as carnivals have often done in other cultures, Coney acted as a safety valve, a mechanism of social release and control that ultimately protected existing society." Framed another way: Coney Island for what and for whom? "Its fantasy led not to a new apprehension of social possibilities, but toward passive acceptance of the cycle of production and consumption. The egalitarian spirit it fostered paradoxically served to reconcile visitors to the inequalities of society at large." The therapeutic ideological power of Coney's machinery, then, was its incorporation of fun and egalitarianism, its capacity to appear like a mass relief from—rather than another version of a source of—the capitalist-industrial contradiction. "Entertainers and customers alike appeared to be wearily going through the motions of amusement, quickening their interest only at the prospect of cruelty and danger."[52] Kasson's reading permanently revised my understanding of how mass-mediated work and play could operate in cahoots to keep a contradictory America running.

A few years later I appreciated Tony Bennett's cultural studies analysis of Blackpool's Pleasure Beach (1983), England's Coney Island. Bennett did not cite Kasson's book, but read Blackpool similarly as a machine refuge that "offered the working people of the industrial north a place in the vanguard of human development in their leisure analogous to that which the ideology of progress constructed for them in their work-places." Like Kasson, he suggested that "in releasing the body for pleasure rather than harnessing it for work, part of [the rides'] appeal may be that they invert the normal relations between people and machinery prevailing in an industrial context." Bennett's reading, however, differed from Kasson's in two ways. First, it was far more self-consciously theoreticist than historicist. Where Kasson used words like "fantasy," "ennui," and "subjection" to describe Coney consumers, Bennett saw Blackpool funseekers as readers of "sign ensembles" and the "intertextuality" of the different rides. If Kasson's narrative was more lucid and well told, Bennett took risks with a critical apparatus that he felt could help him describe and conceptualize power relations better than he could with everyday language. Second, Bennett, as a point of theory, held that consumers can never be wholly "interpellated" within Blackpool's top-down mass-industrial "regime of pleasure," but are capable of making their own bottom-up meanings and pleasures. Bennett's critical move seemed cool at the time (hooray for unpredictable consumers and rebel readers!), but, as I note in chapter 5, the 1980s produced too many gushing consumer re-encodings and "negotiations" that some critics, no doubt frustrated with a seeming dearth of political options, glorified as liberatory.[53] Chapter 1 quotes Bennett himself in 1990 mocking this as "sleuthing for the subversive." Now critics move more cautiously between both approaches.

Kasson's book—an American studies classic—is a synthesis of the history of mass culture, labor, and leisure that is indebted to German Marxist theory developed from the 1920s through 1940s. The Frankfurt School's Max Horkheimer and Theodor Adorno fled the Nazis and actually wrote their critique of the culture industry in America in the mid-1940s. Bennett's essay stands as an impressive British cultural studies analysis. His approach relies on French semiotics, structuralism, poststructuralism, and Louis Althusser's Marxist concept of "interpellation." As noted, Bennett, a sophisticated literary theorist, represents Blackpool as a text and its funseekers as meaning-making readers-encoders. These two works, then, exhibit some of the filiations linking American studies, cultural studies, radical history, progressive literary studies, and diverse Left studies. (Similarly, Jameson's writings inspire much work in cultural studies and American studies, though he can say of both: "It's not my field.") What many of these "studies" share, to employ Kasson's words, is an intellectual and political commitment to value the contemplation of "alternatives to the prevailing economic and social order" and the "apprehension of new [egalitarian] social possibilities." Kasson's post-Watergate and post-Vietnam American studies, like Bennett's Thatcher-era Marxist cultural studies, is geared to help one think critically about imagining a better world. "American studies" and "cultural studies" of this sort contribute to a more encompassing political-intellectual initiative with a long and varied history full of debates. It is aspects of the history and substance of this political-intellectual initiative—which points toward social transformation—even more than academic movements labeled "American studies" and "cultural studies" that most concern me.[54]

Anglo-American Transatlanticism

Throughout I maintain the Anglo-American perspective I took in "The Americanization of Cultural Studies," but in several chapters I focus on a political organizing moment of cultural studies whose origin preceded and partly promulgated its British academicization: the British New Left's political-cultural turn. One thing that draws me to the British New Left's cultural studies from the mid-1950s to the 1960s is the specificity of its response to and activist involvement in contemporary crises. Its critiques take the form not just of theory but of reportage and social planning. These critiques were not "interventions" in scholarly journals preoccupied with the "crisis of the humanities." As chapters 2, 5, and 6 explain, British New Left socialists examined culture in order to organize more effectively and imaginatively. They understood political engagement as more than theorists contesting theorists. As will be evident, in its postwar New Left phase cultural studies was often tantamount to revisionary socialist studies.

Generally, American interest in cultural studies has centered on its theoretical work. More attention must be paid to the intellectual, theoretical, and historical significance of its attempts to make political movement contributions, which appeared mostly in venues such as *New Statesman, Universities and Left Review, New Reasoner,* and *New Left Review.* These publications, as well as some key volumes of essays and books, feature Stuart Hall, Raymond Williams, E. P. Thompson, and Raphael Samuel writing as activists whose "cultural studies" necessarily is much more than cultural. Their socialist-cultural studies, like Lynd's and Mills's sociology, often made moving toward a more emancipatory social order—a project that Kasson valued but did not develop in his book—the political-intellectual aim. They "politicized" not only to expand their theoretical repertoires, reading practices, and historical inquiries—truly important aims—but to strategize about political agency, mobilizing, and organizing.[55]

What might be thought of as the British post–New Left also was active in the battle against Thatcherism in the 1980s, one of my concerns in chapter 5. While 1980s efforts to conceptualize and organize a new British socialism resonate with earlier endeavors of this kind, its political debates—published in magazines like *New Socialist* and *Marxism Today*—are more inflected by a range of theoretical concerns generated by academic cultural studies. What can Antonio Gramsci, Hall asks, tell us about "hegemonizing" that might help defeat Margaret Thatcher in current conditions? How can theory better develop a consumer-oriented socialism—not just a labor-oriented or citizen-oriented socialism—that makes use of popular pleasures? Chapter 5, in particular, contends that what progressive intellectuals and scholars need to develop more fully is not just hegemony studies but hegemonizing studies (this would include studying cultural and media tactics for popularizing critique). Two pragmatic responses to the *critique for what?* inquiry are: *critique for hegemonizing* and *critique for organizing.*

In chapter 1 I direct my critique at the U.S. academy's Americanization of British cultural studies. But in chapters 2, 3, and 5 I consider a partial Americanization of cultural studies that occurred in Britain, from the 1950s to the 1980s, before the American academy imported cultural studies as the latest style. This Americanization is not only far more long-standing, it is more complex than what I gleaned in 1991. As I observed then, some insightful critics have seen Americanization as synonymous with replacing Marxist and socialist critique with less potent substitutes. I now understand more clearly that the 1980s British academic cultural studies which the American academy sought to Americanize had already experienced waves of Americanization that had turned some of its radicalism into the "sleuthing for the subversive" consumer-revolution absorption Bennett ridiculed by 1990. Moreover, I grasp more than I did in 1991 that a historical analysis of the Americanization of British cultural studies must also signify the ways in which Americans—their politics, culture, approaches to organizing—radicalized British cultural studies in new theoretical and strategic ways. In 1991 more than a few American academics I knew who were excited about cultural studies reminded me a bit of 1960s American Beatlemaniacs. Many envisioned Americans as learning from the more theoretically sophisticated politically "authentic" British, yet they did not have the historical knowledge to see the British debt to American theorists such as Mills. Any argument that seeks to place American and British critiques in greater dialogue and debate must appreciate that they have been in mutually transformative conversations with one another for decades. Intellectuals on both sides of the Atlantic fathomed that they were grappling with some similar Cold War problems and also that they could learn from some of the differences in conditions that shaped the scope, subjects, and strategies of their critiques.

Chapters

At times I have imagined *Critique for What?* as akin to hosting a seminar with some—by no means all—of the political intellectuals, critics, scholars, and activists I most respect. I also pay heed to some of the movements, events, institutions, journals, and struggles that informed ideas and arguments about the possibilities of critique. Of course, the central question this book addresses could be approached productively from different perspectives and with a focus on different subject matter. Here I have little to say about ethnoracial studies, feminist studies, and queer studies, but find many of the critiques they have produced vitally important.[56] Moreover, many "cultural studies" insights that I find exciting originated in various guises—in literature, theater, art, humor, and memoirs as well as in criticism and political theory—long before "cultural studies" was named and institutionalized as an academic project.[57] My six chapters are thematic rather than chronological and are selective rather than comprehensive in coverage.

Part I is on British cultural studies and American studies. I have already suggested some of what chapter 1, "The Americanization of Cultural Studies," took up in its critique of the U.S.–sponsored formation of a professional-managerial-class, postpolitical, posthistorical, academic star-studded, often liberal cultural studies that I found disturbing. The 1990 University of Illinois Cultural Studies conference that I reviewed spurred me to think not so much of socialism but of postmodern academic critique as an *ism* (the explicit concern of chapter 6). Chapter 1 contemplates the kinds of British political-cultural critiques and commitments that U.S. academicization was repackaging for American consumption. As mentioned, this chapter also contests some American underestimations of U.S. American studies.

Chapter 2, "British New Left Cultural Studies' Transnational Critiques of the United States," is about how the early British New Left not only had to develop a cultural studies to rethink the substance of socialism and its organizing strategies, but had to devise a transnational American studies as part of its critical project because of the pressure the United States had placed on Britain to step in line in the Cold War. Some 1950s British New Left cultural studies transnational critiques of the United States resemble what U.S. American studies began doing more often in the 1990s when it more expansively examined the world outside and inside U.S. borders. At the same time, I consider the effects that American radicals, some of whom also developed transnational perspectives on America, had on the British. In addition, this chapter begins to revisit debates about electoral politics. Whatever one may think about the possibilities of electoral activism and movement activism, and about the relationships between them, it is vital to remember that these activisms have rich histories linked to the development of critique in Britain and the United States. This chapter begins to sift through some of these historical ties to propose that scholars interested in producing usable knowledge about social change rethink electoral as well as movement strategies.

Part II explores some of the relations among cultural studies, historical studies, and literary studies. Chapter 3, "On the History of Radical History and Cultural Studies," picks up on a concern I introduce in chapter 1: the vexed status of history writing in a cultural studies that typically hails the great historian Edward Thompson as one of its New Left founders. Here I trace some of the many provocative debates between cultural studies historians and theorists, on the one hand, and radical historians, on the other, about the place of theory in a history writing that some historians seem to sanctify as sufficient political practice. I review heated debates entangling Thompson, Hall, Richard Johnson, Samuel, and others recorded in the pages of *History Workshop* and connect these with debates about similar matters in America in sources such as *Radical History Review*. Again, the interchanges between

America and Britain are manifold. My many American English department friends who view historians as not notably inquisitive about theory may be surprised to find that historians were fighting about theoretical approaches years before similar squabbles absorbed English departments.

Chapter 4, "Complicity Critiques, the Artful Front, and Political Motivation" is a significant revision and expansion of an article I published not long ago. This chapter explains why it is important to reconsider a literary critical-literary historical trend that has become popular with critics over the past twenty-five years: the complicity critique. It is vital to understand how literary texts, cultural productions, and people are complicit with larger social contradictions. Yet if literary cultural studies is to be politically strategic, not only analytical, it must not stop there. I make the case that literary and aesthetic cultural studies is in a good position to retheorize how aesthetic culture can be used more affirmatively to better make and mobilize political agents invested not just in critically demystifying the present and naming guilty parties, but in imagining a future worth struggling and living for.

Part III criticizes critique for critique's and career's sake. Chapter 5 is about what I call popularism. Focusing on the 1980s, it examines Left tendencies in both Britain and America—in the reaction to Thatcherism and Reaganism—to place faith in popular culture as an engine for changing political consciousness. Especially in Britain, political hope for the popular almost became an *ism* that recast socialism as popularism. This critical-political development was less pronounced in America, where socialist critique was less prominent. Yet the British development of "consumer socialism" and popularism may be interpreted partly as a sign of Americanization. The larger question that persists is: How can progressive forces succeed in popularizing struggle? Or is more at stake than popularizing struggle? I survey the strengths and weaknesses of the shift to popularism in relation to a theme I broach in chapter 2: the decline of political parties as forces for progressive change. The British New Left of the late 1950s and early 1960s devised a cultural studies partly because it had become disenchanted with the Labour Party's surrender to America and with a Labour agenda that was only residually socialist. In the 1980s popularism magnified the weaknesses, strengths, delusions, and hopes of this revealing pop cultural turn.

Chapter 6, "Critique as Ism," is indebted to my students who, like Lynd Mills, and Matthiessen, want knowledge producers to formulate strategies and answers as well as questions and complications. Some versions of critique, like some sorts of popularism, supplanted socialism. I elaborate what I mean by critique as *ism* in chapter 6, but here I will characterize it in brief as the promotion of questioning far more than answering and as an emphasis on dismantling ideologies without giving due consideration to what kind of a world one might want to build in their stead. When Lynd counseled Macdonald not to publish critics' "snipes" at one another in *politics,* but to concentrate instead on formulating strategies, he was recoiling from a critique-for-critique's-sake pastime he found politically counterproductive. Cultural critics and theorists often have an individualistic curiosity about how they have been conned into being complicit with social contradictions and, as Mills would say, about how they "lock themselves up." But they might be more concerned about breaking beyond the imaginative and institutional confines of their critique production. Have forms of critique served as what Kasson calls a "safety valve"—an intellectual safety valve—playing a role similar to Coney Island's "Human Whirlpool"?[58]

Recently I received an arresting card bearing the moral and spiritual as well as political charge of Mohandas (Mahatma) Gandhi. "Be the change you wish to see in the world."[59] I wish I could say that most of the progressive academicians I know exemplify something like what Gandhi had in mind. And I wish I could say that I did. Many of us have perhaps been more consumed with epistemological radicalism, "interrogating" assumptions, and job advancement than with more communally exercising moral purpose and goodness. Academic institutionalization—its bribes, sanctions, and cultivations of envy—is powerful. Many scholars are inculcated to think of their work more as a profession than a calling, more as a career than a form of ethical stewardship and intellectual citizenship. Their critiques are mediated by the professionalization of the ego, aspiration, and affiliation. In such business conditions critique becomes a professional practice more than an expression of anything like love, grace, charm, or humor (apart from sarcasm and ironizing).[60]

My most challenging students—to draw on Mills again—have no wish to see critique become an academic compensatory form of "abdicating the making of history." They wonder if cultural studies, American studies, and a range of Left studies can realize their potential as social transformation studies. In this new millennium I offer some ruminations-in-progress with their agitation and our futures in mind.

Part I

American Studies and Cultural Studies

1

The Americanization of Cultural Studies

IN 1990 I ATTENDED A CONFERENCE TITLED "CULTURAL STUDIES NOW AND in the Future," sponsored by the Unit for Criticism and Interpretive Theory at the University of Illinois, Urbana-Champaign, and organized by Cary Nelson and Lawrence Grossberg. During his lecture, Stuart Hall commented critically on the proceedings and warned that cultural studies in the United States is in "a moment of danger." Shortly after he began to take questions, some members of the audience of several hundred erupted in protest, claiming among other things that the conference positioned them as "fans" who were meant to support a star-making (or star-polishing) machinery. Some who were infuriated with the event drafted and distributed a manifesto titled, "Hypocrisy in Cultural Studies," which posed the question: "Is there any point in establishing a radical voice which only duplicates those structures it seeks to displace?"

"Mixed impressions" describes my own take on the conference, and the term applies also, though for different reasons, to my reading of the first American book-length overview of cultural studies, Patrick Brantlinger's *Crusoe's Footprints*

(1990). In this chapter I hope to work out the implications of some of these impressions and place them in a clear theoretical and historical frame. Thus my aim is to return to and review some key contributions to the British tradition of cultural studies and, by examining the conference, Brantlinger's book, and other sources, to trace the forms that the "Americanization" of the field seems to be taking. In what follows I will situate one important school of British cultural studies in its political-intellectual setting; review the conference and *Crusoe's Footprints* as ideological symptoms of the "Americanization" of British cultural studies; discuss—and contest—the positioning of American studies by many of these critics as a cautionary example of an institutionalized cultural studies gone wrong; suggest continuities between British and U.S. cultural studies and work being done under the sign of the "history of subjectivity"; and close with some thoughts on cultural studies as a social practice, one undertaken by the academic wing of the professional-managerial class in this country.

Unlearning the Old Left:
The Political Work of British Cultural Studies

In his review of Raymond Williams's *Politics and Letters* (1979) Stuart Hall concluded, "It is not a book for the religious." At the Illinois conference Hall profiled cultural studies in the same way and underscored how crucial it is to keep the field "open." Hall learned how open its political project had to be in the mid- and late 1970s when feminism and concerns with race and racism "broke through the windows" of the Birmingham Centre for Contemporary Cultural Studies, while he served as its director. The center's Women's Studies Group published their anthology *Women Take Issue* (1978) as an "intervention" that would not only put women on the agenda but force a political-intellectual rethinking of the "field" and "object" of cultural studies. Next, *The Empire Strikes Back* (1982) and Paul Gilroy's *"There Ain't No Black in the Union Jack"* (1985) "intervened" as "correctives" to the "invisibility of 'race'" within cultural studies. Tony Fry has suggested that the class-stratified students and staff of the Birmingham Centre learned about the dynamics of class within as well as outside their own institution. Thus Richard Johnson, who took over as director when Hall left for the Open University in 1979, had good reason to describe the field not as a doctrinal "research programme for a particular party or tendency" but rather as a "political-intellectual stance" made "possible because the politics which we aim to create is not yet fully formed."[1]

Yet it is important to highlight that this understanding of British cultural studies as an open, though not pluralistic, project has its roots not in some pretence to "value-free scholarship," but in what Alan O'Connor has termed "political commitment." This is clear from both Hall's opening statement as founding editor of *New Left Review* (1960–) and his contributions to *New Times* (1989), a collection of essays most of which originated in *Marxism Today.* "We are convinced that politics, too narrowly conceived, has been a main cause of the decline of socialism in this country," he wrote in 1960. In arguing that the rebuilding of a Cold War socialist movement requires "cultural and social" as well as "economic and political" strategic critique, he stressed that the study of "the cinema or teenage culture in *New Left Review*" is not for purposes of appearing trendy but must be grasped as indispensable to a knowledge of "imaginative resistances of people who have to live within capitalism." Early anthologies published by the Birmingham Centre under Hall's directorship, such as *Resistance through Rituals* (1976) and *Policing the Crisis* (1978), joined by Paul Willis's *Learning to Labour* (1977) and Dick Hebdige's *Subculture* (1979), carried on this project.

Hall's focus on *culture* grew out of the pressing need to unlearn some of the assumptions, strategies, and goals of the Old Left: "There is no law which says that the Labour Movement, like a great inhuman engine, is going to throb its way into socialism." Under Hall's editorship (1960–61), *New Left Review* featured articles by contributors such as E. P. Thompson, Raymond Williams, and Richard Hoggart next to advertisements for Left cafés and listings of Left discussion groups around Britain.[2] The New Left's cultural studies was indivisible from the project of regrouping in response to the predicament of socialism within the crisis of Cold War capitalism.

British cultural studies has continued to rethink the possibilities of political critique and organization in magazines like *Marxism Today.* Stuart Hall and Martin Jacques's *New Times* collects essays whose object of study is not "culture" per se (for the interdisciplinary challenge it poses) but, more specifically, an epoch of advanced capitalism, a "post-Fordism" that supersedes what Gramsci labeled "Fordism." The strategic question for the contributors is how post-Fordism has altered "the world in which the Left has to operate." "If 'post-Fordism' exists," writes Hall, much as he did in *New Left Review* decades before, "then it is as much a description of cultural as of economic change." Here, too, Hall makes it clear that cultural study is driven by political necessity: "Can a socialism of the 21st century revive, or even survive, which is wholly cut off from the landscape of popular pleasures, however contradictory and 'commodified' a terrain they represent? Are we thinking dialectically enough?"

Dialectical thinking in "new times" must take for its critique "cultural and subjective dimensions" and must recognize, for example, not only that gender is constructed and "deployed politically" in ways that must be delineated but that "social practices," "forms of domination," and even the "politics of the Left" are "inscribed in and to some extent secured by sexual identity and positioning." A reluctance to acknowledge and study these intersections, Hall adds, is nothing less than a strategic failure, because without an understanding of them "we simply do *not* have a language of sufficient explanatory power" that illuminates both "the institutionalisation of power" and "the secret sources of resistances to change."[3] Richard Johnson's statement that British cultural studies is not in any doctrinal sense a "research programme for a particular party" is true, but it underplays the fact that cultural studies' New Left–inspired project has been, historically, "to create" or recreate a socialist politics "not yet fully formed."

As Hall and Johnson note in their essays on intellectual developments within the Birmingham Centre, the center was drawn early on to E. P. Thompson's *Making of the English Working Class* (1963) and Raymond Williams's *Long Revolution* (1961)—two important books emerging from the "first" New Left—precisely because these works recognized culture as a productive, determining force in its own right and not merely as a reflection or expression of the economic "base." But it was the translations of the work of the Frankfurt School, Louis Althusser, and Antonio Gramsci in the 1960s and 1970s—by the "second" New Left—that refashioned cultural studies at the Birmingham Centre. Althusser's concept of "overdetermination," for instance, challenged Old Left assumptions about "totalizing" and "totality" and the role of culture in causality: "A social transformation is not a 'totality' of the essential type, in which there is simple 'identity between levels,' with the superstructural levels the mere 'epiphenomena' of the objective laws governing 'the economic base,'" writes Hall. "It is, rather, a unity of the necessarily complex type—an 'ensemble' which is always the result of many determinations." The Althusserian structuralist "moment" of the 1970s prompted the Birmingham Centre to retheorize "culture" as a relatively autonomous "*signifying* practice" and "not so much the product of 'consciousness' as the conscious forms and categories through which historically definite forms of consciousness were produced." This theoretical perspective was more subtle and comprehensive than the Old Left's explanatory emphasis on what Richard Johnson has termed the "more brutally obvious 'determination'—especially mechanisms like competition, monopolistic control, and imperial expansion." The New Left challenge to the Old Left sets the context for Hall's observation that the Birmingham Centre always approached Marxism as a problem rather than the solution.[4]

Old Left constructions of "history," therefore, had to be rehistoricized and its categories retheorized, based on different concepts of totality, determination, and historical subjects. The Old Left labor history (for example, the work of Maurice Dobb and of Dona Torr) focuses on the category of class and on members of the working class as the universal subjects of history functioned, as Johnson notes, to classify both "a sphere of legitimate politics and a 'nonpolitical' realm." This "history" produced a "truth" that was both too narrow and unstrategic for New Left cultural studies in the 1970s, for their project had to acknowledge "new" historical agents (who were not new!).[5]

The influences of Roland Barthes, Althusser, Jacques Lacan, and Gramsci pushed forward a critique of assumptions about access to "lived experience" in Hoggart's *Uses of Literacy* (1961), Williams's *Long Revolution,* Thompson's *Making of the English Working Class,* and other histories and ethnographies. Thompson's *Poverty of Theory* (1978) retaliated by polemicizing against Althusser and the *New Left Review* policy of privileging "theory," which Thompson felt was seducing the younger Left in Britain away not only from "lived experience" but from "lived" political activity. As Hall put it in his exchange with Thompson, "experience" must be thought of as a category rather than an essence to be discovered in "the people," a category that must be "interrogated for its complex interweaving of real and ideological elements." Or as Johnson framed it, "Concrete social individuals are always already constructed as class-ed, sex-ed, and age-ranked subjects, have already entered into complex cultural forms, already have a complexly formed subjectivity."

At the same juncture, when history and theory were in danger of being perceived as separate or even antithetical enterprises, the Women's Studies group and the race and racism group pressed the Birmingham Centre to reevaluate its "theoreticist" (to use Hall's word) and historicist occlusions. The outcome was a commitment to a more theoretically informed history and historically informed theoretical practice, which was thought through in Birmingham Centre anthologies such as *Working-Class Culture* (1979) and *Making Histories* (1982): "The reintroduction of history is not a minimal aim," Paul Gilroy noted, envisioning a more complex and inclusive historicizing of "history": "Racism rests on the ability to contain blacks in the present." And as Hall asserts, "[The] term historical is taken, simple-mindedly, to refer to the past, but we have attempted rigorously to break with this disabling, inert definition."[6]

What is patent about these Birmingham anthologies is their political-intellectual-pedagogical commitment to enable their readers to think "dialectically enough." If cultural studies is at a critical juncture, what Hall termed a "moment of danger," I wonder if it might not also be the moment to make more of this Birmingham work available to a U.S. audience, as a crucial reminder of the breadth of activity British cultural studies has undertaken. Several republishing projects in particular would be desirable, certainly collections of Hall's and Johnson's essays as well as selected essays from Birmingham anthologies and working papers, especially *Culture, Media, Language: Working Papers in Cultural Studies, 1972–79*. If such publishing projects are undertaken, an effort must be made to situate these writings in the particular historical "conjuncture" (a term I discuss below) that produced their debates and that their debates sought to transform, rather than reifying them as "classic" or (even worse) "authentic" British cultural studies (the "real" way to do cultural studies). These debates and advances must be seen just as Cornel West profiled Hall, as examples, rather than as static models, of "how to keep political work alive in an age of shrinking possibilities."[7]

Americanization: Toward a Postpolitical Cultural Studies

At the Illinois conference, Hall raised three points to clarify what the "moment of danger" is for cultural studies on American shores. First, he pointed out that British cultural studies never underwent a "moment" of extreme professionalization and institutionalization like the one that is already a determining force in U.S. cultural studies. Second, he expressed concern that if the American academy does to cultural studies what it did to French poststructuralism, then "it would formalize questions of power" and constitute power solely as a problem of "textuality." Hall went on in good Foucauldian fashion to affirm that power is always already lodged in textuality, but the force of his admonition remained. Third, he commented diplomatically on the extraordinary "fluency" of some of the presenters, hinting that "fluency" should be a means to an end not an end in itself (more on this later).[8]

Others have voiced similar concerns. In 1988 Lawrence Grossberg, one of the conference's organizers, suggested that the selling (out) of U.S. cultural studies was well advanced and that its success story has "all the ingredients of a made-for-TV movie." Manuscripts easily solicited, books pouring off presses, and cultural studies job openings all suggest that the field in the United States "appears to be the latest signifier of what was called 'critical theory' in a variety of academic organizations." Grossberg is an American graduate of the Birmingham Centre who often writes about rock music (for instance, "MTV: Swinging on a [Postmodern] Star," in Ian Angus and Sut Jhally's *Cultural Politics in Contemporary*

America, 1987). He is perhaps the most active promoter of the cultural studies boom in the United States. His apprehensions about the future of U.S. cultural studies are featured in *It's a Sin* (1988).

Grossberg's promotion of cultural studies has centered on Stuart Hall and has targeted communications departments (where cultural studies is more frequently debated than in English departments). In *Critical Studies in Mass Communications,* a journal that has become a regular forum for debate over cultural studies, contributors have charged Grossberg himself with the "sin" of swinging on the (postmodern) cultural studies star. Alan O'Connor, whose work on Raymond Williams is exemplary, characterizes much of Grossberg's (re)construction of cultural studies as "postmodernist" "theoretical bricolage" and claims that Grossberg "has lost … [Stuart Hall's] sense of the rooted-ness of communication processes in social reproduction and politics." For O'Connor, Grossberg's work is of a piece with "conferences in the United States" that produce cultural studies as "various types of postmodern theorizing." Academics "who rarely have any connection to existing political and cultural movements and are somewhat surprised that this might even be possible" are institutionalizing U.S. cultural studies.[9] What O'Connor misses most in this (postmodern) cultural studies is political commitment.

Grossberg has in fact been attentive to the specific ways in which cultural studies might get depoliticized in the United States. For example, at the Illinois conference Tony Bennett succinctly caricatured the celebration-of-pleasure-as-resistance approach to consumers of popular culture as "sleuthing for subversiveness where one would least expect to find it." In *It's a Sin* Grossberg (citing similar critiques by Judith Williamson and Meaghan Morris) concurs: "The fact that specific cultural practices are pleasurable, even empowering, does not tell us anything about the political valences of such pleasures, or the possibilities of articulating such empowering moments to explicit political positions." Yet in *Critical Studies in Mass Communications* three communications scholars argued that Grossberg, as well as John Fiske (a British mass media critic who teaches in the United States), textualize and celebrate consumers' responses that are not discernably "oppositional," or if occasionally "oppositional," surely do not translate into "direct thinking about and behavior in politics." Todd Gitlin, in an indirect response to their critique, also registers skepticism about a cultural studies that frames "style" as resistance: "It is pure sloppiness to conclude that culture or pleasure is politics."[10]

Thus there is a growing uneasiness in communications departments with a U.S. cultural studies seemingly deracinated from politics in the narrow sense. In the British Labour Party and Communist Party context, Hall stresses that culture is a necessary political concern, but in the United States, with even fewer viable narrowly political alternatives apparently available, the apprehension is that U.S. cultural studies will turn into a depoliticized "politics" of the "cultural." What Hall and others witnessed in Illinois, in some of the presentations and discussions, seemed to be the production of a *postpolitical* cultural studies that fogged over the ground of contradictions that makes cultural studies imperative. The word "contradiction" was scarcely uttered in many of the talks.

Of course, the conference had strengths, especially its global emphasis: "Think globally and act locally," advised Gilroy (quoting one of my favorite bumper stickers). Graeme Turner, an Australian, and Bennett, who now teaches in Australia, made it clear that British cultural studies cannot be lifted from its context, universalized, and applied automatically to another national set of conditions and contradictions. Thus there was evidence in Illinois of an enabling cultural studies.

However, the emergence of cultural studies as interpretive performance also was apparent and reminiscent of poststructuralist interpretive performances, stylish in the early 1980s. Richard Johnson, in reconceptualizing cultural studies as the historical analysis of the production of forms of subjectivity, has referred to the need for a "post-poststructuralist" theory of subjective formations. The term "post-poststructuralist" has been picked up by American academics as a synonym for cultural studies. To be sure, cultural studies has much to learn from poststructuralism, not least of all because, as Bruce Robbins has noted, it has dragged "oppositional discourse into the field of fire" by making visible the "oppression of older categories like 'race' and 'woman' and 'the people.'" But what many viewed, on occasion, on stage in Illinois was akin to what Stuart Hall had seen at the Birmingham Centre years before when seminars had become overly "theoreticist": discussion "depended too much on prior knowledge, privileged access to the discourse and a false search for abstractions at a rarefied level." Hall's political-intellectual response to this circumstance in Illinois was a plea for "intellectual modesty" and a reminder that cultural studies is "deadly serious."[11] What was also obvious was that some (postmodern) stars-in-the-making were indeed "formalizing questions of power."

There was something else postmodern about the conference as well: an absence of a sustained engagement with the matter of history. The only panel devoted to the role of history in cultural studies featured Carolyn Steedman and Catherine Hall, and it was held in the evening of the last day.[12] Both panelists wondered about the significance of history being left until a time when about two-thirds of the audience had already departed. Catherine Hall began by voicing criticism of the "excess of textuality" manifest in some of the conference presentations and pleaded that history not be relegated to the status of backdrop. Her talk, "Positioning Missionaries: History and Theory," was an example of how to study a complicated historical "conjuncture"—Jamaica, 1830s–1850s. In this period, missionaries, discursive constructions of "Englishness," shifts in domestic ideology, and native Jamaicans intersected in complex ways to produce a new (not unresisted) form of racism. After the presentation, one person asked her to define what was "cultural studies" in her lecture (besides the "deconstruction" of Englishness), while another asked where the "politics" was in her analysis. Such questions betokened, in my view, a posthistory "presentism," a failure to see that history is inseparable from contemporary cultural studies. It would be hyperbolic to say that history was a thing of the past at the conference, but after the discussion following the final lectures the thought crossed my mind.

Marx's Footsteps to Crusoe's Footprints: The Liberalization of Cultural Studies

The wide-ranging bibliography in Patrick Brantlinger's *Crusoe's Footprints: Cultural Studies in Britain and America* will prove useful to anyone who wishes to learn more about this field and some of the debates that animate it. Brantlinger, who has been director of Victorian Studies at Indiana University for many years, has done much reading and research in cultural studies. I find the book to be of greater value as an elaborated bibliographic essay than as a critical statement on what is at stake in the field. It also will be of interest to readers as a symptom of how cultural studies may be "Americanized," as it is institutionalized and professionalized by the U.S. academy. Brantlinger's construction of cultural studies is not of the postpolitical speaking-in-tongues variety I occasionally viewed in Illinois; rather it is fundamentally a liberal packaging of the field. His liberalism can be best seen in his vision of multiculturalism, the humanities-in-crisis, and the English-department-in-crisis.

The Crusoe of Brantlinger's title is, I take it, the white, middle-class male professor who acknowledges that Friday's footprints are his own. The "main lesson" of cultural studies, Brantlinger tells us, is that "in order to understand ourselves, the discourses of 'the Other'—of all the others—is that which we most urgently need to hear." And the "goal of cultural workers" is "an authentically democratic mass culture uniting people through recognition of and respect for differences."[13] But Brantlinger should be reminded that there are different kinds of multiculturalism that require sorting out. In "Schooling in Babylon" (1982), an essay that Brantlinger knows, Hazel Carby's analysis of multicultural policies introduced to "liberalize" English secondary education in racially mixed communities led her to conclude: "Multiculturalism has reacted to racism as if it were limited to a struggle over forms of representation—a struggle over images—in an attempt to disguise the social relations of domination in which it is situated and which it reproduces." Brantlinger's humanist-in-crisis multiculturalism veers toward the "pluralistic model" of multicultural ideology that, Carby writes, "implies that racial prejudice and racial discrimination would come to an end through an education in cultural diversity." The racisms that Catherine Hall analyzes in "Positioning Missionaries" and that Gilroy examines in *"There Ain't No Black in the Union Jack"* are, however, not simply a matter of attitude that can be remedied by a more "humanistic" representation of diversity; the racisms they study are embedded in complex practices, domestic ideologies, and cultural formations.

Both Stuart Hall and Brantlinger see cultural studies as emerging, in part, from a "crisis in the humanities." But if Hall's cultural studies response to this crisis is, at the most fundamental level, a radical effort to explain and act upon the postwar predicament of British socialism in late capitalism, Brantlinger's interest in cultural studies seems more narrowly academic. Brantlinger, sounding a bit like a college promotional brochure, wishes to use cultural studies to make "the humanities disciplines . . . genuinely human, engaged, and engaging." The struggle is to make the liberal arts truly liberal: "The *liberal* arts—the humanities and social sciences, *must be* 'liberal'—even 'liberating'—or else degenerate into mere hypocrisy or obfuscation." This is closer to the pedagogical liberalism of William Cain or Gerald Graff (whom Brantlinger often cites in his first chapter) than it is to the politics of Hall. Brantlinger introduces the possibility of "the revolutionary overthrow of capitalism," but, revealingly, as "the only conceivable way of solving the ongoing 'crisis of the humanities.'"[14] That Brantlinger is a supporter of British cultural studies is unquestionable, but that he is often translating it into liberal terms is also clear. If the British constituency of cultural studies in the 1980s was, in part, composed of readers of *New Socialist* and *Marxism Today,* who will be the constituency of U.S. cultural studies, and what will they expect? It is likely that *Crusoe's Footprints* will help produce their expectations, and this makes me uneasy.

Cultural studies also appeals to Brantlinger as an interdisciplinary "critical theory"—the name change that Grossberg forecast in *It's a Sin.* Four out of his five chapters begin with literary references. In cultural studies Brantlinger sees the theoretically informed, multicultural English department of the future, where Frederick Douglass's *Narrative* (1845) would not "displace other great works of American literature" such as *Moby Dick* (1851) or *Walden* (1854), but would "certainly take its place alongside them." (Friday and Crusoe live happily ever after.) Stuart Hall, then, is a dialectical materialist who analyzes culture because it is politically pressing to do so. Brantlinger is mainly a literary culturalist with an intellectual appreciation for interdisciplinary cultural studies that has a materialist base.

What I find surprising is that this appreciation did not lead him to cite the work of scholars whose work really bridges cultural studies and Victorian studies, such as Catherine Hall, Nancy Armstrong, Mary Poovey, and Judith Walkowitz. Notwithstanding these omissions and other major ones (for instance, Janet Wolff, Joan Scott, Susan McClary, Stanley Aronowitz, Hal Foster, and Douglas Crimp), Brantlinger offers an informative sweep of who's who and who's doing what in cultural studies up till 1990.[15]

The Object of Study:
American Studies, Cultural Studies, and Marxist Discourse

Those who practice cultural studies usually try to be careful about making distinctions: the working class must not be misrepresented as a unified entity, American culture can only be read as American cultures, Marxism and feminism are really Marxisms and feminisms charged with internal debates and divergent tendencies. Yet, in some contemporary cultural studies criticism, American studies has been reduced to the "cautionary example" of how cultural criticism can be institutionalized and co-opted by the bourgeois U.S. academy. American studies should be examined critically, particularly if one is interested in the possible paths an academic "Americanization" of British cultural studies might take. But I shall argue that the "cautionary example" of American studies is more complex than it has been made out to be.

Brantlinger borrows the notion of American studies as "cautionary example" from Henry Giroux, David Shumway, Paul Smith, and James Sosnoski's "The Need for Cultural Studies" (1984). Part of what I find troubling about the criticism by both Brantlinger and Giroux et al. is the thin research they draw on to advance their arguments. Fredric Jameson's "Always historicize!" inspires much progressive work; however, to follow through on Jameson's counsel the theoretical reflex to "historicize" must not be reduced to a gesture; it must be empowered by actual historical work.[16]

Brantlinger paraphrases Giroux and his fellow authors as arguing that American studies was from the start "far less oppositional or critical than nationalist and celebratory," an expression of "academic and cultural chauvinism." What Giroux et al. wrote, to the contrary, is "that the nationalism which spawned American Studies and Canadian Studies was openly political," but that "American Studies books were critical of the ideological interests embedded in canonical documents of American culture." Brantlinger cites writing by Tremaine McDowell in 1948 (paraphrased as: "the ultimate goal" of American studies "is social harmony") as if his position was representative of American studies for about forty years, until Sacvan Bercovitch and Myra Jehlen (among others) somehow stumbled on the (non-Geertzian) concept of "ideology" and published *Ideology and Classic American Literature* (1986). McDowell's remarks contributed to ongoing discussions about interdisciplinarity in the 1940s. "The principles of Marxism remain at the basis of much of the best social thought of our country," wrote F. O Matthiessen. And in *The Cultural Approach to History* (1940), Caroline Ware pleaded for a study of "American history from the bottom up," a history that would delineate class and ethnoracial diversity rather than fabricating a "homogeneous unity."[17] American studies was founded neither as a radical nor as a conservative field. Rather, it was established by academicians many of whom considered themselves generally progressive, but who: had divergent notions of where they wanted the field to go, often demonstrated contradictory tendencies (as Matthiessen did) in their own work, and made contributions that must be situated in the context of the considerable conscious and unconscious ideological pressures of their particular historical moment.

The compelling criticism launched by Giroux et al. is that "interdisciplinarity became a means for practitioners to challenge a particular hierarchy, but it did not offer an alternative to the hierarchical order." The not-quite-named systemic "alternative" they have in mind, I take it, is socialism. Of equal import is Brantlinger's observation that while Hoggart, Williams, and Thompson developed a cultural studies rooted in an analysis of class, the American studies founders tended to elide class issues.[18]

Thinking about these criticisms, we would do well to keep in mind that British cultural studies developed in the late 1950s and early 1960s out of the New Left's efforts to challenge assumptions held by the Old Left. Especially in the 1970s, the Birmingham Centre consistently drew on material (Althusser, Gramsci, Benjamin, and Adorno) translated and published in *New Left Review*. American studies, by contrast, developed prior to the American New Left (which picked up steam in the early 1960s). Indeed, it took off institutionally in the late 1940s and early 1950s, that is, in the Cold War academy, purged by McCarthyism. "Marxism disappeared from the campus," writes one historian of the times. "Most of the main practitioners [of Marxism] were exiled from the academy and the tradition of left-wing scholarship . . . was broken."

Despite its chilly McCarthy-era institutional origins, however, the American studies tradition of "cultural criticism" is not so ideologically frozen as Brantlinger and Giroux and his coauthors have contended. In 1965, for instance, Alan Trachtenberg reviewed Leo Marx's *Machine in the Garden* (1964) in *The Nation*. After much praise for his mentor's study of nineteenth-century literature and society (Marx's book swiftly became an American studies myth-and-symbol classic), Trachtenberg argued that the historical process that Marx had yet to come to grips with was not simply industrialism (anxious middle-class representations of "machines" in gardens) but industrial capitalism. The "machine," like Brantlinger's humanities-in-crisis, functioned ideologically to displace capitalism as the central object of inquiry and locus of contradiction: "Industrial capitalism had other effects beyond its scars upon the landscape and its mechanization of values." Trachtenberg urged more comprehensive considerations of the relationship between industrial capitalism and the changing social structure, of the formation of a working class, and of the development of a market economy. "Marx's treatment of the dialectic within history," he concluded, "is not as strong or as convincing as his treatment of the conditions within consciousness."[19] The review is a nudge, asking: where's the other Marx?

Trachtenberg's *Incorporation of America: Culture and Society in the Gilded Age* (1982) acknowledges its "indebtedness" to Leo Marx rather than Karl Marx, but his book can be read on one level as a theoretical and historical corrective to what he found problematic about *Machine in the Garden*. A look at Trachtenberg's contents page exhibits the theoretical organization of his project. Trachtenberg builds from the ground up, beginning with lots of (already occupied) Western land, "Indian" removal, railroads, grain elevators, urban consumption of materials, federal gifts of land to corporations, tourism, and the mass publication and consumption of a mythic frontier. His next chapter, "Mechanization Takes Command," is about how command took mechanization, enabling the colonization of more new "frontiers" (modes and relations of production, markets, needs, tastes, perceptions). Subsequent chapters clarify the "corporate" transformations of social and cultural relations. Trachtenberg's movement from land to productive forces to productive relations to "super-structure" is materialist, but in every chapter the material, social, and cultural determinations, effects, and relations are understood *dialectically* as part of the same complex historical process. His debt to Williams's socialist concept of historical process goes beyond the "culture and society" in the subtitle.

Trachtenberg sees American studies in a radically different light than Giroux and his coauthors and Brantlinger do. He has long had an investment in recovering and often criticizing an indigenous, "usable" tradition of cultural criticism, as his anthology *Critics of Culture: Literature and Society in the Early Twentieth Century* (1976) makes evident. American studies, for him, gives voice to this "usable" past (with some European-sounding accents as well). The "theme" of American studies, he tells us in a recent defense of the myth-symbol school, is *dialectical:* a "firmer and more subtle grasp of the dialectical relations between consciousness and history." American studies is "critical cultural history," "pedagogical activism," and even "prophecy." Trachtenberg casts the cultural critics of American studies in the romantic, heroic mold of interdisciplinary banditti: "In the present climate of many American universities (the near-tropical eclecticism known as 'poststructuralism' and 'postmodernism') the American Studies scholar may seem less odd, less of a bandit." These banditti conduct their raids not only for "the sake of the subject" but in response to "the state and predicament of the culture-at-large." They are committed to contributing "somehow to the reshaping of the collective culture in the act of studying and criticizing it."[20] This "somehow," however, is not spelled out.

"Incorporation" is a critical concept that Raymond Williams introduces in *Marxism and Literature* (1977), in the context of his discussion of Gramsci's idea of hegemony. A hegemonic order can ignore elements of "alternative or directly oppositional politics and culture." However, "To the extent that they [the elements] are significant the decisive hegemonic function is to control or transform or even incorporate them." Incorporation is the manifestation of hegemonic power that "produces and limits its own forms of counter-culture."[21] Although he does not employ the word "incorporation," it seems to me that Michael Denning's 1987 critique of American studies, "'The Special American Conditions': Marxism and American Studies," views the field as an incorporated academic counterculture. Denning's article, published in the American Studies Association's *American Quarterly,* is particularly important to engage because some key overviews of the field that the journal published not long after Denning's piece appeared disregarded it, even in the endnotes. Brantlinger also missed it.[22]

Denning is concerned about establishing the analytical power and legitimacy of Marxism both inside and outside the U.S. academy. Thus he transforms Leon Samson's thesis, advanced in 1934, that "Americanism has

... served as a substitute for socialism" to one in which "'critical' American Studies"—in effect, an incorporated American Studies—must also be recognized "as a substitute Marxism." "Critical" American studies typically borrows "terms from a Gramsci, a Williams, a Benjamin—borrowings that too often ignore the context and role of the concepts in a larger conceptual system and tradition."

Denning sketches four main traditions of American studies scholarship and praises recent "critical" or "revisionist" works by Richard Slotkin, Michael Rogin, and Ronald Takaki for having "recast the 'special American conditions' of culture in an historical materialist way." He also lauds Trachtenberg's *Incorporation* as "perhaps the major revisionist synthesis to date." Yet Denning's interest in a cultural studies that makes explicit the strengths of the "larger conceptual system and tradition" of Marxism prompts him to compare the early American studies founders to those of British cultural studies, reaching the conclusion that "the work of Raymond Williams has proved richer and more prolific than any of the founding generation of American Studies, and the underfunded and understaffed Birmingham University Center ... has produced a body of work with greater range and political and intellectual influence than any American Studies program." Here Denning is simply claiming that, in intellectual terms, the work of British cultural studies is demonstrably "richer." When efforts to define an American studies "method" or theory, by Gene Wise, Jay Mechling, R. Gordon Kelly, and others are put next to similar cultural studies essays by Stuart Hall and Richard Johnson, Denning's argument has force. The subjects of British inquiry—"What is culture?" and "What are its forms and how is it related to material production?"—are theoretically richer than "What is American?" (Still, American studies projects have long been too heterogeneous to be reduced to this question.)[23] But if the British object of study is "richer," why didn't American studies acknowledge British cultural studies publications and engage in dialogue with them when they appeared?

Leo Marx began to do so in his 1961 review of Williams's *Long Revolution, Culture and Society,* and *Border Country* (which praised Hoggart's *Uses of Literacy* along the way). The tone of his essay, however, was one of despair as he expressed the British Left's and, one might guess, his own "profound uncertainty about the present rationale for socialism." "Reading the British left on this subject," he confessed, "one cannot help feeling that the whole stream of socialist thought in the West is drying up—running rapidly into a desert of abstractions and just plain words, words, words." The "loss of vigor" suffered by the British Left is "shared equally by the American left," leaving Marx to conclude that "the movement toward democratic socialism has bogged down, and the result is a futile churning of stale ideas." In response to what he represents as an American capitalism of profit and plenty, he proposes a moral rather than a materialist critique of capitalism: "What is needed, in short, is a socialist culture."[24]

Marx had elaborated this idea earlier in "Notes on the Culture of New Capitalism" (1959), published in the socialist *Monthly Review.* He rejects the claim made by Karl Marx that "social being ... determines consciousness." Such was undoubtedly true of "factory workers in Birmingham in the 1830s" but not, Marx felt, for Americans in 1959. Marx pinpoints "mass culture" as the new locus of a materialist critique since, he believed, in the age of affluence American capitalism no longer generates severe economic contradictions. (Johnson's liberal War on Poverty would, nonetheless, soon follow.) Materialist socialism—as opposed to "socialist humanism"—no longer appeared usable. In "The American Scholar Today" (1961) Marx would embrace Emerson's criticism as usable.[25]

At the same time, the American journal *Studies on the Left* (1960–1967)— inspired partly by C. Wright Mills's challenge to orthodox Marxism in *The Sociological Imagination* (1959) and partly by the radical history of William Appleman Williams—was in contact with *New Left Review* and kept abreast of theoretical debates in the British New Left. Mills's "On the New Left" (1961), for instance, was republished in *Studies on the Left* not long after it appeared in *New Left Review.* A review of Williams's *Long Revolution* and an article by Williams on "liberal tragedy" (1964) also were signs of an interest in transatlantic dialogue. The short-lived *Studies on the Left,* which published translations of Benjamin and Lukács, and which was guided by editors like Stanley Aronowitz, Warren Susman, Eugene Genovese, and Joan Scott, was an impressive contribution to the formation of a U.S. "cultural studies." Until Janice Radway took over as editor of *American Quarterly* in the mid-1980s, there were hardly any references in the journal to the Birmingham Centre, Williams, Eagleton, or even Jameson and Aronowitz. Gramsci and Althusser, whose writings were being translated in the 1960s and whose work transformed the Birmingham Centre, seemingly made no impact on writers theorizing about American studies in either *American Quarterly* or *Prospects.* Familiarity with Althusser might have enabled American studies to respond in a more complex way to the poststructuralist boom in the late 1970s and to engage its radical potential (as some literary theorists did), rather than simply dismiss it as "theory" (the spectre of a post–New Criticism) and retreat to affirmations of "context." The first *American Quarterly* article to record an indebtedness to the Birmingham

Centre was written by Elizabeth Long, whose title—"Women, Reading, and Cultural Authority: Some Implications of Audience Perspective in Cultural Studies" (1986)—explicitly classified her essay as cultural studies.[26]

The apparent dearth of politics in American studies led Robert Sklar, in a 1970 issue of *American Quarterly,* to challenge the "movement" to move with "the realities of America." An *American Quarterly* assignment in 1975 to comment on the "philosophy" of American studies offered Sklar the opportunity to assault the "poverty of theory" in the field and to blame it in part on its "reluctance to utilize one of the most extensive literatures of cultural theory in modern scholarship, coming out of the Marxist intellectual tradition." What Sklar had begun to do as early as 1970 was suggest that the American studies production of particular kinds of "contexts" had to be understood both historically and ideologically. The "emergence of civil rights and the war in Vietnam," as well as the women's liberation movement, were in the late 1960s and early 1970s beginning to break through the windows of American studies and shake its construction of "high cultural history." Sklar linked the 1950s and 1960s ideological production of "high cultural" context to "the needs of the new American empire to assert its cultural pedigree to older cultures which had become dependent on America." The postwar American empire had to convince the world that it had a culture, and so it launched, through American studies, an "international effort to make American literature and American ideas respectable and even significant to scholars in Europe and Asia."[27] Sklar's historical sense of the cultural production of an American studies "context," however, is itself structured by the text/context categories that are problematic.

While I have no wish abandon the terms "text" and "context," it strikes me as curious that at a moment when scholarship on American culture—especially Marxist scholarship—proliferates outside of American studies, one prominent "practitioner" seems to have inflated "context" itself into *the* American studies object of study; he has, in fact, transformed it into an "ism." Thus, in "A New Context for New American Studies?" (1989), published in *American Quarterly,* Robert Berkhofer maintains that the "disparate interests" of American studies are "about … contextual knowledge" or "contextualism." The distinguishing feature of the "new" "contextualism" is its "new" emphasis on "political critique," although, as Berkhofer acknowledges, this really "is not new," even though "its current vitality represents a new phase in American Studies." Berkhofer facilely equates Jameson's "always historicize" with "always contextualize," but what Jameson sees at stake in the dialectical concept of historicizing is not quite the same in this discourse of contextualism. There are isolated references to Jameson, Althusser, and Richard Johnson in Berkhofer's essay, but these references simply lend evidence to Denning's observation that such "borrowings" ignore the "large conceptual system and traditions" of Marxist theories. Indeed, the import of these "continental" ideas is funneled through the indigenous translations of Sacvan Bercovitch, who (for Berkhofer) makes such "new" criticism usable for American studies.[28] What concerns me about this construction of the new-that-is-not-new is that British cultural studies, as it does get acknowledged by a "new" American studies, might be absorbed or *incorporated* as a British contribution to the ongoing project of "contextualism."

British cultural studies often employs the Gramscian and Althusserian concept of "conjuncture" in its work rather than context (something Brantlinger might have elaborated on). Brantlinger does quote Alan Sinfield's astute warning that "to speak of text and context is already to risk separating the two."[29] In place of a conceptual privileging of texts-as-texts, the British cultural studies emphasis tends to be on forms. The inertly contextual is not the object of study; rather, the object is (drawing on Althusser and Gramsci) the cultural formation, the historical process, the "conjuncture." Thus in *Reconstructing Womanhood* (1987) Hazel Carby defines her project not as "a conventional literary history" (yet another study of texts-in-context) but rather as "a cultural history and critique of the *forms* in which black women intellectuals made political as well as literary interventions in the social formations in which they lived." She examines "individual texts," of course, but her underlying object of study is theorized as "the dominant ideological and social formation in which they were produced." "Conjuncture" puts the analytical spotlight on social contradictions. In *The Hard Role to Renewal* (1988) Stuart Hall defines "a conjuncture as the coming together of often distinct though related contradictions, moving according to different tempos, but condensed in the same historical moment." Gramsci associated "conjuncture" with a protracted crisis that makes visible "incurable structural contradictions" as well as the attempts of dominant "political forces ... to cure them within certain limits": "These incessant ... efforts ... form the terrain of the conjunctural and it is upon this terrain that the forces of opposition organize."[30]

As suggested above, American studies—rechristened by Kenneth S. Lynn, and sometimes by students, as Anti–American Studies—is not monolithic; like the programs in which it is taught in the United States and abroad, it contains—or fails to contain—divergent and contradictory tendencies. The theoretical emphasis on the conjuncture as the object of critical analysis is not new to American studies in practice, but the theoretical language—to abstract what one does—can help practitioners better communicate what they are practicing and why they are practicing it. Richard Slotkin's *The Fatal Environment* (1985) (which includes an introductory chapter on ideology—still rare for American studies at that time) and Trachtenberg's *Incorporation* both focus on the historical process—especially the coming together of contradictions within specific conjunctures—rather than on "inert" contexts-for-texts. Christopher Wilson's *Labor of Words* (1985), influenced by Raymond Williams and by the socialist Americanist literary historian William Charvat (whose work spanned the 1930s to 1950s), is a materialist study of the institutional and cultural production of "naturalism" and authorship. Evidence that cultural studies, Marxist theory, cultural history, and American studies are converging in exciting ways can be found in three of the most sophisticated, historically based studies of popular culture in the late 1980s and early 1990s, Lawrence Levine's *Highbrow/Lowbrow* (1988), George Lipsitz's *Time Passages* (1990), and Andrew Ross's *No Respect* (1989). These are materialist—not simply moral—critiques of the culture of capitalism.

Denning's own *Mechanic Accents* (1987) is surely the most self-conscious late 1980s theoretical effort to fuse the contributions of British cultural studies (especially Stuart Hall's "Notes on Deconstructing 'the Popular,'" 1978), Jameson's Marxist narrative concept of the "political unconscious," radical American labor history (David Montgomery, Herbert Gutman), American cultural history, and American studies (Radway, Slotkin, Trachtenberg). In making the cultural formation his object of study, Denning's approach is, if anything, not contextual but, in Althusser's and Jameson's style, *subtextual:* "to understand the way a culture's social and political unconscious determines its self consciousness."[31] Beyond this, *Mechanic Accents* can be seen as an effort to legitimize the explicit use of a fully developed Marxist theoretical framework within the American studies "movement."

It is not only important but timely for American studies to come to terms with the status of Marxist theories within the field, as Sklar and Denning have urged. Among other reasons, cultural studies in the United States will increasingly publish its own historical critiques of American culture, such as those collected in *The 60's without Apology* (1984) from *Social Text* and *American Representations of Vietnam* (1986) from *Cultural Critique*. But there are questions that must be raised about the future of a cultural studies that legitimizes academic Marxist criticism. If "critical" American studies can be considered a "substitute" Marxism, recent developments within Marxism suggest that some academic Marxist discourse is itself transforming into a "substitute" or at least an alternative (to) Marxism, as Ernesto Laclau and Chantal Mouffe's

"Post-Marxism without Apologies" (1987) exemplifies. In 1983, Jameson began his presentation at a conference on Marxism by acknowledging that "during this Marxist conference I have frequently had the feeling that I am one of the few Marxists left." The issue of legitimizing Marxist discourses has become complicated because, since 1960 (certainly since 1968), Marxist discourse has been legitimizing other radical discourses and also altering its objects and subjects of study. My questions are: Will Marxism, as it legitimizes these discourses, become all the more complexly radical and, in the process, gain greater academic legitimacy for socialist discourse, and thereby facilitate socialist transformation? Or, by shattering the descriptive label "Marxism," will this heterodox academic radicalism become all the more legitimized within the academy and the culture at large, thus clearing the path for a new, harder to label kind of social and cultural change? Or, by its very post-Marxist success, will it be paving the way for its liberal *incorporation*? These are thoughts to weigh in reference to the incorporation of British socialist cultural studies into a post–Cold War U.S. academy, which is now popularizing and commodifying it as cultural studies.[32]

The Subjective Tug: Toward a History of Subjectivity

In his preface to *Crusoe's Footprints,* Brantlinger mentions the forthcoming publication of books by Alan Sinfield and by Regina Gagnier on the history of subjectivity, although he does not devote much discussion to the historical study of the formation of subjectivities within cultural studies. The theorizing and historicizing of the cultural formation of subjectivities is one field where the contributions of British cultural studies, American studies, the history of gender and the body, and feminist poststructuralist theory are capable of converging in groundbreaking ways. I will limit myself here to sketching aspects of three approaches—from history, sociology, and theory—that might be placed in greater transatlantic dialogue with one another.

Leonore Davidoff and Catherine Hall's *Family Fortunes* (1987), Carolyn Kay Steedman's *Landscape for a Good Woman* (1986), Nancy Armstrong's *Desire and Domestic Fiction* (1988), Mary Poovey's *Uneven Developments* (1988), Mary Ryan's *Cradle of the Middle Class* (1980), Emily Martin's *The Woman in the Body* (1987), and Joan W. Scott's *Gender and the Politics of History* (1988) are, in various ways, concerned with reformulating approaches to the historically specific construction of gender, sexuality, affect, the body, motherhood, family life, and self-monitoring, and with rethinking the role these discursive constructions and ideologies play in class formation. Thus Davidoff and Hall, citing their debt to the Americanist historian Mary Ryan, describe their theoretical focus as "the gendered nature of [nineteenth-century British] class formation and the way sexual difference always influences class belonging." Armstrong's Foucauldian approach examines how late-eighteenth-century and early nineteenth-century middle-class, domestic British literature and conduct books discursively constructed femininity so that the emerging middle-class "feminine" domestic woman could be deployed ideologically to authorize "a whole new set of economic practices that directly countered what were supposed to be seen as the excesses of a decadent aristocracy." Along these lines, Scott argues that historians must attend to the ways in which gender difference becomes "one of the recurrent references by which political power has been conceived, legitimated, and criticized."[33] In several of these historical contributions, affect, gender, sexuality, "personal" life, "innerness," and subjectivity have been deprivatized and conceptually rehistoricized, not simplistically as reflections of or responses to "larger" "social" transformations, but as highly complex, socially based determinative forces in their own right.

A major contribution to the sociology and politics of family forms and privatized subjectivity is Michèle Barrett and Mary McIntosh's *Anti-Social Family* (1982), a work not often mentioned (unlike Barrett's *Women's Oppression Today,* 1980) in discussions of the contributions of cultural studies. Barrett and McIntosh study how particular kinds of family forms produce and naturalize specific sorts of subjectivities and how these subjectivities relate to historically specific structures of power. Perhaps the best American sociological work I know on the subject is Eli Zaretsky's *Capitalism, the Family, and Personal Life* (1976, revised 1986). Zaretsky argues that the "expansion of inner life" within the nineteenth-century middle-class privatized family was linked "to capitalist expansion," and thus psychoanalysis "speaks" to psychological "needs that have arisen historically."

Michel Foucault's historical contributions also belong in the theory of formations of subjectivity category, along with Birmingham-based works such as Rosalind Coward and John Ellis's *Language and Materialism* (1977) and Steve Burniston and Chris Weedon's "Ideology, Subjectivity and the Artistic Text" (1977). One of the most lucid expressions of theory's contributions to the study of the construction of subjectivities is Weedon's *Feminist Practice and Poststructuralist Theory* (1987).[34]

The Birmingham Centre's concern with pulling subjectivities into the field of cultural and historical critique originates from several sources. I have already discussed the circumstances surrounding the critique of the historians' category of "lived experience." The work of Barthes, Althusser, and Foucault also sparked criticism of Williams's concept of "structure of feeling," which Stuart Hall has referred to as "important" but "nonconceptual" and even "disabling." Althusser's structuralism, in Stuart Hall's words, helped one rethink the "I" not as "the seat of consciousness and the foundation of ideological discourse" or as "the integral Cartesian centre of thought," but as "a contradictory discursive category constituted by ideological discourse itself." Or, as Weedon put it, whereas liberal humanist discourse "assumes an already existing subjectivity which awaits expression," poststructuralist contributions view consciousness as "the fragmented and contradictory effect of a discursive battle for the subjectivity of the individual." Interest in these approaches yielded a more complex social understanding of the discursive relationship between cultural production and agency, reading, and authorship.[35]

Johnson's conception of cultural studies as the historical study of subjective *forms* owes much to Barthes, who recognized that "the more a system is specifically defined in its forms, the more amenable it is to historical criticism." Moreover, Barthes understood literature as cultural forms that function to "institutionalise subjectivity." What had been conventionally framed as narrowly "'literary' concerns," Johnson notes, can be reimagined more dialectically as the historical and ideological critique of "textual embodiments of subjective forms." Thus Williams's chapter on "Forms" in *The Sociology of Culture* (1981) offers concrete historical instances of the relationship between literary forms and the production of class-specific subjectivities. The work of Angela McRobbie and Janice Radway's *Reading the Romance* (1984) further develop the complexities of what Johnson terms the "wider social currency" of narratives-in-the-head-and-heart, specifically the capacity of "romance" to construct (and to be reconstructed by) "the subjective tug."[36]

Nancy Armstrong and Leonard Tennenhouse have edited important anthologies that contribute to the project of reconceptualizing literary concerns more culturally as political ones: *The Ideology of Conduct* (1987) and *The Violence of Representation* (1989). Bourgeois "literature," if I may put one aspect of their argument all too crudely, is produced as privileged texts because it reproduces subjective forms essential to class formation and through these forms naturalizes the exclusion of its designated "others." Thus the category "literature" becomes, particularly in the nineteenth century, the discursive site where the bourgeoisie "discovers" "truth" and the secrets of "subjectivity."[37] And so American literature—along with religion, psychology, film, theater, and art—can be retheorized and rehistoricized as a subjectivity industry, an "individuality" industry, an "inner self" industry.[38]

By the early twentieth century, the bourgeoisie began to "discover" the "truth" of its subjectivity in psychoanalysis, which took its discursive authority from both science and literature to colonize how the self is imagined. Over the past few decades cultural critique, in its engagements with psychoanalysis, has begun to historicize the ideological production of the "psychological" as a category within bourgeois class formation. Thus Jameson's Marxist *Political Unconscious* (1980) argues that the "symbolic possibilities" of psychoanalysis historically rely on "the preliminary isolation of sexual experience" and the "autonomization of the family as a private space in the nascent sphere of bourgeois society." And Mark Poster's *Critical Theory of the Family* (1980) identifies privatization as "the major structural condition" for the widespread appearance of the Oedipus complex in the bourgeoisie. In arguing that the "deployment of sexuality" that had begun in the mid-nineteenth century discursively produced "Freud" later in the century, and that the Freudian repressive hypothesis be reconsidered as a productive hypothesis (repression produces "sexuality"), Foucault reconceptualizes the discursive sexualization and psychologization of bourgeois subjectivity as a subtle "political ordering of life ... through an affirmation of the self."[39] Foucault, Jameson, Poster, Armstrong, and Tennenhouse help us understand a fascinating sleight of hand, a remarkable advance in class self-representation and compensatory self-absorption: bourgeois identity formation and significance production are now draped in "psychological" rather than class language. Hence class identity can be better reimagined as and experienced as strictly "psychological" identity in an ostensibly "classless" democracy.

Peter Stallybrass and Allon White's *The Politics and Poetics of Transgression* (1986) is one of the most lively and sophisticated cultural studies books to have rethought the historical situation of psychoanalysis within the ideology of bourgeois subjectivity. In one chapter the authors argue that Freud's narrative excision of the maid from his representations of the oedipal triangle be understood ideologically as his effort "to rewrite unconscious desires in closer conformity to the endogamous rules of the bourgeoisie." The specifically cultural studies nature of their project is apparent in how they theorize their object of study: they read Freud's writings not as the "discovery" of the "truth" of a universal self but rather as a symptom of a certain stage of "the formation of the cultural Imaginary of the middle class in post-Renaissance Europe." Furthermore, in academic criticism on their topic, they also see the "discursive mirroring of the subject-formation of the middle class."[40] The politics of such criticism and history writing is that it is often complicit in the historical and ideological project of reproducing the subjectivities of the professional-managerial class under the guise of the "humanities."

I suspect that cultural studies contributions to the history of subjectivities and the "subjective tug" will be well received in the United States. But I wonder, given the never to be underestimated grip of the middle-class ideology of individualism in this country, will what Johnson calls "radical constructivism" develop as an end in itself (to supplement or replace psychoanalysis) rather than as a means or an end connected to collective progressive social transformation? As Gayatri Spivak points out in *The Post-Colonial Critic* (1990), antiessentialism is a cultural activity of "people who are privileged enough to repudiate essentialism." Will a specifically "Americanized" antiessentialism shrink the political-cultural part of this project to occasional theoretical gestures? If this possibility seems worth entertaining, we would do well to heed Cornel West's reminder that "the structure of identity and subjectivity is important and has often been overlooked by the Marxist tradition; but forms of subjection and subjugation are ultimately quite different from 'thick' forms of oppression like economic *exploitation* or state *repression* or bureaucratic *domination*." My own optimism that the "subjective tug" will not become narrowly subjectivized lies in many of the works cited above, whose commitment to making connections between subjective forms and "thick" forms of oppression is strong.[41]

Romanticizing "Intervention": Professional-Managerial-Class Cultural Studies

I want to echo the emphasis of Richard Ohmann in *Politics of Letters* (1987) that those who practice cultural studies in the U.S. academy are members of what Barbara Ehrenreich and John Ehrenreich call the "professional-managerial class," a class "whose major function in the social division of labor" is historically "the reproduction of capitalist culture and capitalist class relations." It is crucial to think about how constructions and promotions of U.S. cultural studies will be complicit in this process of "reproduction." Which brings up the question: If cultural studies is practiced by the professional-managerial class, who is it *for*? At the Illinois conference, Cornel West, evidently drawing on Russell Jacoby's much debated *The Last Intellectuals* (1987), observed that the waning of the public sphere functions to displace political debate and cultural critique into the academy.[42] Will a U.S. cultural studies be primarily comprised of debates among academicians? Thus far, this is mainly the case.

As lucid and compelling as Stuart Hall's writing can be, it often veers into language familiar only to those with some background in critical theory. A curious and often powerful style of writing has emerged in the academic era of cultural studies: one that can be clear, engaging, conversational, and public, and yet theoretical or technical to the unitiated when "conjunctures," "negotiations," "interventions," and "interrogations" are suddenly dropped into sentences with little or no effort to define them and no shift in tone. Despite the praiseworthy let's-not-speak-in-tongues impulse, such language signals that the author has no doubt about who is going to be reading her or his writing. With whom are such "interventions" intervening? Several of my friends outside the academy expressed interest in reading this chapter to learn about "cultural studies," but they also asked if they would be able to understand it.

What I shall call the "discourse of intervention" should be seen as potentially problematic, particularly in cultural studies on this side of the Atlantic. Words like "intervention" and "interrogation" are meant to signify the cultural studies critic's serious "oppositional" stance toward hegemonic traditions of knowledge production. These two words carry some obvious militaristic and disciplinary connotations: armies intervene and spies are interrogated; police intervene and suspects are interrogated. "Intervention" and "interrogation" have given critical theorists in U.S. English departments a powerful self-image and sense of mission. I am delighted that literary critics are "intervening" in a literary criticism and "interrogating" a canon that have frequently been misrepresented as having no political agenda. But I am also bothered because this discourse of intervention seems to romanticize the critic's academic role as sufficiently "oppositional." Critics in the United States and those who visit the United States are able to command steep fees for lecturing or writing up their latest thoughts on oppositional practices and interventions. Yet when the implications of this professionalized "opposition" are thought through, the cultural studies approach suggests that a good deal more must be done than cultural *studies*.

The audience eruption at the Illinois conference made it clear to me that cultural studies is potentially explosive partly because those who do take its oppositional critiques seriously come to realize that studying culture in the academy is only one force that potentially contributes to changing culture. During his tenure as director of the Birmingham Centre, Hall understandably insisted on the importance of "studying seriously" rather than being "a good activist" because "what the movement needed from us as part of their struggles of resistance and transformation ... was what we had in our heads."[43] What is needed in the United States now is certainly not a postmodern romanticization of the "political-intellectual" but a greater historical understanding of the social, political, and academic conditions within which a discourse of "intervention" seemed to make sense for those British intellectuals who practiced cultural studies because it was unmistakably one necessary dimension of a larger intervention under way. Of course this "conjunctural" inquiry might also suggest that British cultural studies, faced with grim prospects of social change, has romanticized its own interventionist practices, capabilities, and concrete social achievements (see chapters 2, 5, and 6).

When I think back to the lists of Left discussion groups and advertisements for Left cafés that abounded in *New Left Review* during its first two years, I find it telling that, nowadays, there is little discussion of organizing in cultural studies publications and conferences. Much of the professional-managerial-class cultural studies work I read does seem distant from the contradictions and concerns that are written about in *In These Times* and books like Jeremy Brecher and Tim Costello's anthology, *Building Bridges: The Emerging Grass-roots Alliance of Labor and Community* (1990). In both 1960 and 1989 Hall was apprehensive about politics being "too narrowly conceived" by the British Left, and yet American communications sociologists, like Gitlin, when confronted with a very cultural style of U.S. cultural studies, caution that "politics in the strict sense" must not be forgotten. In *Another Tale to Tell* (1990) Fred Pfeil states his intention to contribute to "the *collective* project of imagining new ends, and coming together in new ways to reach them," and he regards his writing as just one arena of his political work.[44] How strategic does a U.S. cultural studies wish to be, and should its "oppositional" studies be channeled into writing about a collective project in more detailed ways? I think that we can interpret the muting of this concern within U.S. cultural studies as one symptom of its professional-managerial-class "Americanization."

In closing, I offer a restatement of my initial point that, as Stuart Hall has observed, a U.S. cultural studies must retain a strategic openness. This openness is neither simplistically pluralistic, nor is it merely an apparent pedagogical openness, layering over implicit or hidden agendas. The best cultural studies work is explicit about its positions and lucid about how its positions are located in debates, thus leaving those who engage with such positions free (as possible) to choose. That dual openness is worth practicing.

2

British New Left Cultural Studies' Transnational Critiques of the United States

> Of all the Western nations, we are the least class-stratified psychologi-
> cally and the only one without an active labor party.... . This is not
> because "the American way" is fundamentally different, but primarily
> because the American ideology as regards capitalism is less sophisti-
> cated than is that of any other Western nation.
>
> —*Robert Lynd, "The Structure of Power" (1942)*

> Omnivorous America can seemingly gobble up everything and
> celebrate it all.
>
> —*C. Wright Mills, "The Complacent Young Men" (1958)*

> "What job does [Pyle] do?"
> "Economic Mission, but that covers a multitude of sins." ...
> "[Pyle] was talking about the old colonial powers—England and
> France, and how you two couldn't expect to win the confidence of the
> Asiatics. That was where America came in now with clean hands."
> "Hawaii, Puerto Rico," I said. "New Mexico."
>
> —*Graham Greene, The Quiet American (1955)[1]*

E. P. THOMPSON'S POSTWAR CRITICAL STANCE TOWARD AMERICA'S DIGESTIVE power is patent in his satirical sketch of a professor of English employed by a small New England college, featured in the British Communist Party's *American Threat to British Culture* (c. 1951).[2] The professor is a hybrid of the hypocritical high-cultural dude and the vernacular show-me-the-money cowboy. In conversation with Thompson the professor regretted not having "'[made] good' in a big way in the postwar boom." After World War I he had taught in the Near East and saw the need for fresh meat. "Squar[ing] his jaw above his virile cowboy-style shirt with the decision of a J. P. Morgan" and "glower[ing] through his horn-rimmed spectacles," the professor said that back then he should have "'chucked all this Shakespeare stuff,'" purchased refrigerators, "'set up a *chain of slaughterhouses* throughout the Holy Land,'" and "'cleaned up!'" This "imperialist Babbitt," Thompson jibed, "was not pulling [his] leg": "The 'American Dream' really is as childish and as debased as this and its poison can be found in every field of American life" (25).

Here Thompson reasserts British high-cultural superiority and good taste: Britain's Shakespeare offers more than unprofitable "Shakespeare stuff," whereas America's dreams are mass-culturally immature and vulgar. Thompson recognized that the American repudiation of monarchy and aristocracy could operate as a pseudodemocratic cover. He quoted William Morris's scathing criticism of the United States just after the Haymarket anarchists were hanged, remarks germane to McCarthyite America: "'A country with universal [*sic*] suffrage, no king, no House of Lords, no privilege ... a society corrupt to the core, and at this moment engaged in suppressing freedom with just the same reckless brutality and blind ignorance as the Czar of all the Russias uses'" (26). It is not surprising, Thompson notes, that a mendacious *American* biographer alleged recently that Morris had become "disillusioned" with "revolutionary socialism" before his death (26).[3]

Thompson, whose mother was American, recommended combating America's imperial designs with "the biting edge of British humour ... [and] ridicule," a "moral offensive" (26), and historical perspectives on national identity. It was incumbent on progressives to redefine the discourses of "moral values" and "freedom and democracy," Thompson urged, because the "American capitalists and their British apologists" (28) have used them to cloud and legitimate their dominance. He prescribed popularizing Britain's history, "cultural achievements," and "revolutionary traditions" as bulwarks against American hegemony: "the only lasting victories will be where—whether in scholarship, or dance tunes, or philosophy—the American substitute is driven out by a development of the living British tradition." The British must use their whole culture to resist "the private fears and neuroses, the self-interest and timid individualism fostered by [American] pulp magazines and Hollywood films" (29).

Yet Thompson did not view the United States as a world-menacing cultural flop in 1946, when "a million informal [trans-Atlantic] transactions were going on ... which historians will never recover and which the hard-nosed Party organisers knew nothing about." That year Thompson, who had just published a story in England that the *New Masses* reprinted, ventured to New York to present himself as a writer and poet. He rhapsodized about a Manhattan "electric with life" and animated by an "internationalist consciousness." Thompson loved this "great anti-Fascist city, its diversity churning into a common torrent of solidarities." While screaming headlines demanded a Cold War freeze and "howl[ed] for an internal terror against Commies," other political formations pulsed with life and talent: "I attended a great rally in Madison Square Gardens [*sic*] and heard Robeson, Marcantonio, and communist councilman Ben Davis from Harlem. I saw the banners of the Ladies Garment Workers Union waved in defiance of the new Cold War." This war did much to "rupture" the "ordinary communications between members of the European and American Left." European Leftists found it more difficult to secure visas to visit the United States.[4]

So by 1951 Thompson saw Americanism principally as a threat. Some of the "morbid" ethnocentric and nationalist celebrations of England and Englishness that Paul Gilroy criticizes Thompson and Williams for contributing to can be contextualized partly as Cold War refusals to be American.[5] In place of "the American substitute," Thompson hoped that the British would take up not an already-formed socialism but "the question of Socialism" (29).

An "American" Future

In the late 1950s key intellectuals who spearheaded the first British New Left, including Thompson, Raymond Williams, and Stuart Hall, not only stressed the need to analyze cultural change to both reconceive and strategically advance the cause of socialism in Britain—a turn later academicized as cultural studies—they understood that they had to grasp the situation of Britain transnationally, and, more particularly, the multifaceted relations between Britain and the United States.[6] The political, economic, and cultural power that the

United States wielded over postwar Britain compelled the British New Left to transnationalize and, indeed, in many instances to Americanize its scope of critique and concern. Hall, like Thompson, feared that if a new socialism did not emerge "the [British] champions of 'me-too' [would] advance into the calm waters of an 'American' future."[7] He put "American" in quotation marks to signal that dominant American ideological tendencies, subjective formations, and values in varying degrees would take hold in Britain (Britishized Americanization). Hall, Williams, Thompson, and others on the New Left began to realize that they had to alter their conception of political organizing and the political because of changing mass-cultural representations of self-definitions that had a decidedly American tinge: mass culture persuaded members of the working class to read themselves more as psychological individuals, consumers, nationalists, and members of a vaguely expansive middle class. This seemingly nonpolitical shift in cultural identity formation, which some misconstrued as "classlessness," compromised Old Left political alignments and mobilizing tactics. Left critics recognized Anthony Crosland's importation of the idea of classlessness into Labour policy and strategy after 1957 as a liberal Americanization of perspective.[8]

For Williams, America provided yet another good reason to develop socialism, because it proved that "an increase in gross national product didn't necessarily ... abolish poverty" or usher in real democracy.[9] In 1962 he lamented that "the future of democratic culture in Britain, by the restriction of education both absolutely and along class lines, has left a vacuum which pseudo-Americanism seems to be rapidly filling."[10] And in 1968 Thompson, Hall, and Williams made it clear that the critique of America must be more than cultural: "If the rejection of U.S. influence remains at the level of distaste for cultural style and value, instead of an analysis and understanding of imperialism which can be given political embodiment, the realities of the situation are not likely to be changed."[11]

The more one understands this Atlantic power relationship, the more obvious it is why New Left cultural studies critics embraced and further developed Antonio Gramsci's concepts of hegemony and incorporation in the 1960s and 1970s.[12] Because America excelled at mass-cultural strategies to reproduce not only itself but its world position, the British Left needed a complex cultural studies to strategize resistance to U.S. hegemony. Thus Britain's bond with the United States precipitated the development of a theoretically and politically sophisticated British New Left cultural studies invention of what American studies only elaborated at the close of, not the outset of, the Cold War: a radical transnational American studies.[13]

Some Cold War American intellectuals also identified the need for such studies. In the late 1940s, for example, the Harvard socialist Francis Otto Matthiessen—a major builder of American studies in the United States and Europe—contributed his father's inheritance to underwrite not *American Quarterly,* the new American Studies Association journal, but the socialist-internationalist *Monthly Review.* An early typescript proposal for the journal, in Matthiessen's papers, foresees it as being "in form and content" similar to the British *Labour Monthly.* Paul Sweezy, founding coeditor (with Leo Huberman) of *Monthly Review* and Matthiessen's former colleague at Harvard, called this gift a "windfall."[14] At Yale College, Matthiessen had begun to be radicalized by the writings of British political intellectuals R. H. Tawney and Bertrand Russell as well as by the final campaign of Eugene Debs. When Matthiessen committed suicide in 1950, in agony over the dismal prospects for progressive thought and organizing under McCarthyism, *Monthly Review* dedicated an entire issue to him. It featured reminiscences and commentaries not only by eminent American Left intellectuals, but by some of Matthiessen's American studies students and friends who would go on to shape the interdisciplinary field in repressive times. But it was Matthiessen who saw the exigency of investing in *Monthly Review*'s socialist-internationalist critiques of the American Imperium. The final book he published in his lifetime, *From the Heart of Europe* (1948), read the Truman Doctrine and Marshall Plan as America's attempt to establish its economic, political, and cultural incorporation of Europe. What might Thompson have said about Matthiessen in the late 1940s if he had met him rather than the Shakespearean wanna-be meat magnate?[15]

Three events catalyzed the British New Left's development of cultural studies—and its transnational American studies—in 1956: Soviet Premier Nikita Khrushchev acknowledged Joseph Stalin's many crimes and executions of dissidents; Soviet invaders suppressed the Hungarian rebellion; the U.S. Sixth Fleet flexed its naval muscles and aborted Israel's, Britain's, and France's attack on Egypt's Suez canal zone because it did not suit America's world plan.[16] The news about the USSR convinced many British Left intellectuals that the Eastern bloc was not truly socialist. In 1968 Williams, Thompson, and Hall asserted that the USSR had been "hostile to socialist ideas." (And in 1990 Hall reaffirmed: "We have been waiting for [the fall of Soviet state rule] to happen for three decades.") They also held that the United States did not merit support. For while the USSR silenced its dissidents, America had endorsed McCarthyism and the execution of the Rosenbergs.[17] *New Statesman* editors regularly observed that America's postwar "dollar imperialism" targeted Britain as well as other countries.[18]

Such circumstances made it urgent to redefine and popularize what social-ism could be. The New Left's disenchantment with the British Communist Party matched its disillusionment with the Labour Party as an engine of modern progressive social change, a dual disappointment central to New Left reconceptions of politics.[19] This disenchantment was accompanied by a wide-spread enchantment with aspects of American popular culture. In 1957, for example, as the first New Left journals went to press, a teenager named John Lennon helped found the Quarry Men in Liverpool, a skiffle band that took its inspiration from American folk music and rock 'n' roll and that competed with local groups entranced by American jazz.[20]

The kinds of critiques the British developed were not unknown in America. *From the Heart of Europe* is one of the first great works of transnational Ameri-can studies. Matthiessen begins by explaining that he went to Europe—to teach in the inaugural Salzburg seminar in Austria and at Charles University in Prague—to think more critically about "some of the things it means to be an American today." (Similarly, for years *Monthly Review* published articles titled "What an American Needs to Know About ..." on various countries.) He recognized that "We Americans are the Romans of the modern world," and in many ways he defied "Rome." Critical of both U.S. and Soviet domination, in 1947 Matthiessen praised the alternative developments of socialism not only in Czechoslovakia but in Britain. His experience in Europe strengthened his democratic-socialist conviction that economic equality must accompany political equality.[21] Matthiessen believed that neither the United States nor the Soviet state helped make this combination possible in the Europe they fought over. Many of his 1940s concerns were later shared by the British New Left founders of cultural studies.

America's cancellation of the Suez invasion showed the world that the former British empire was now subordinate to the American empire. Dis-cussing the Left's electoral despair, Norman MacKenzie, an editor of *New Statesman,* admitted, in the late 1950s: "It is a painful process of adjustment, and it is often humiliating, as so many discovered for the first time in that final fling of imperialism at Suez.... Two world wars, punctuated by a great depression, have made it impossible for the British to compete on equal terms with America or Russia, or even hold what they have." America exacerbated the British Left's anxieties about its diminished domestic and international power. "One may deplore some aspects of American diplomacy—the flinty recalcitrance of Mr. Dulles, for instance, or the nonrecognition of Peking—or condemn the Soviet intervention into Hungary. But demonstrations in Trafalgar Square are not likely to have more than the most marginal effect on opinion in Congress." MacKenzie viewed the slogan, "Force America and Russia to give up the bomb," as indicative of the Left's "misunderstanding" of the new power relations. The fact that the United States turned Britain into an airfield for "American bombers armed with nuclear weapons" did not make the British Left feel more secure. So, unable to trust either the United States or the USSR, doubtful of the integrity of the Labour Party, and stuck with the American-sponsored Cold War demonization of socialism as Stalinism, the British Left took a New Left turn more toward broadly conceived cultural politics and analysis as seedbeds of social and political change.[22] Over the next few decades, cultural politics—responsive to the multiplication of cultural-political fronts in the 1960s—would sometimes supplant socialism. But in the late 1950s the British Left newly developed a socialist cultural politics as part of its project to reconceive, reenergize, and repopularize socialism.

America's managerial dominance over Britain took shape as early as the mid-1940s. William Appleman Williams notes that the United States withheld its wartime lend-lease support of Britain until it was weakened and agreed to open its imperial markets to American businesses.[23] The United States pressured the postwar Labour government to increase defense expenditures many times over, Alan Sinfield recounts, to the point where the cost "destroyed British economic reconstruction and threw the Labour government into confusion."[24] *Monthly Review* covered the continuation of this trend in the 1950s. As Sweezy interpreted it: "When [the United States] defeated the Axis powers, they wouldn't be a problem, but the British empire had to be dismantled. The British at that time were still considered the number two power, the other super power." So postwar America and Britain consolidated a "special relationship" that British New Left intellectuals dubbed "Atlanticism," the "American future," a "client" relationship.[25] Because New Leftists saw both the United States (NATO) and the USSR as threats, their efforts to reimagine, restrategize, and reorganize a more diverse British socialism were conjoined with their endeavors to conceptualize a "third way" for Britain and Europe that would place them in neither camp. In this enterprise they followed the French *nouvelle gauche*, from which they took their name.

Faced with what Williams, Thompson, and Hall characterized as the U.S. "penetration" of Britain, New Left intellectuals formulated interdisciplinary critiques not to institutionalize programs in universities and win battles for academic acceptance, as did post-Matthiessen American studies, but to rethink how the Left might reconstitute itself and respond to contradictions within and outside Britain.[26] Although key figures in British New Left cultural studies sometimes taught in extramural adult education programs and universities,

these political intellectuals tried to overcome the disciplinary "fragmentation" of knowledge not principally because it was a synthesis that made good
academic sense, but because they had to understand and resist "the new capitalism" centered in America.[27] "Our own first position," Williams, Thompson,
and Hall stated, "is that all the issues—industrial and political, international
and domestic, economic and cultural, humanitarian and radical—are deeply
connected." Their point was more than epistemological: "The problems of whole
men and women are now habitually relegated to specialized and disparate fields,
where the society offers to manage or adjust them by this or that consideration
or technique." They perceived the "fragmentation" of critique as a technique
of the new capitalism's "incorporation": "the discontinuity of Left and radical
opinion is a characteristic of the system as it is experienced." To redress this they
saw that "a new total description, however preliminary, is indispensable." While
both post-Matthiessen American studies and British New Left cultural studies
sponsored versions of interdisciplinary "totalizing," the latter pursued it out of
the political need to contest the new capitalism on behalf of a socialist "humanism" that would be elaborated "by and for ordinary men and women"[28]

Thus the New Left was pedagogical in intent, but wanted to bring a bracingly
self-critical socialist education not only to students and adult workers. Its critical activism, like that of *Monthly Review,* originated partly in the academy, but
thrived in Left culture and addressed a Left public.[29] Post-Matthiessen American studies was the university's child, sometimes an undisciplinized child,
that occasionally had to endure institutional sanctions, while British New Left
cultural studies started life as the university's prodigal child. American studies has been made up of scholars, and frequently, particularly in recent years,
conspicuously "politicized" scholars, while British New Left cultural studies
was largely founded by political intellectuals. Many New Leftists had doubts
about what Thompson called *"Academicus Superciliosus"*: "Academic freedom
is forever on their lips, and is forever disregarded in their actions."[30]

With these Cold War perspectives on Britain's "American" future in mind,
my purpose here is threefold. First, I will sketch some important British New
Left critiques of the United States—cultural studies versions of American
studies—in part to appreciate the power of their transnational perspectives
in the early Cold War years. I will show that Thompson, Hall, Williams, and
other New Leftists grasped America's managerial efforts "to internationalize
a new network of capitalism"—moves they believed should be effectively opposed.[31] They understood, as Fredric Jameson has framed it more recently, that
"'national' is now merely a relational term for the component parts of the world
system."[32] Britain was entangled, they explained, in "an international system,

economic, political, military, which in its own internal logic is continually overriding national interests."[33] This situation led them to expand their vision beyond the U.S. and Europe's contradictions to the "Western" exploitation of the "Third World."[34] Matthiessen's inquiry did not venture beyond Europe, but *Monthly Review* surveyed the U.S. influence on much of the world before and during the formation of the British New Left. The post-Matthiessen American studies that sought academic legitimation did not generally go in this transnational direction.[35] British New Left cultural studies had to take U.S. Cold War containment policies as its critical focus, whereas much early American studies scholarship was a symptom of this containment. Second, I will review some of what British New Left intellectuals learned from American intellectuals, culture, and protests. Third, I shall reflect on a similar set of conditions within which British and American critics have struggled since Matthiessen's death: the absence of major progressive political parties that might *use* radical critique.

Atlanticism Studies

In the British New Left Clubs of the late 1950s and early 1960s, as Hall put it, "the cultural debates and activities were considered as important as the more 'political' ones."[36] For Williams the cultural and educational projects of the New Left involved not just devising better ways to "bring the message" of socialism to "the people," but altogether rethinking socialism and the life it intended to make possible.[37] This focus on culture and what Gramsci called "civil society" as the site of potential political change, Raphael Samuel notes, was shaped by the New Left's distrust of "high politics" as a workable mechanism of social transformation.[38] Postwar Britain, MacKenzie complained, "incorporates much of the social machinery from the Socialist catalogue, but its motive power remains private gain." State "socialists," who administered "social-bureaucratic State capitalism," have become business-almost-as-usual "pillars of the Establishment." If socialism seemed unlikely to be voted in, culture still offered room to establish aspects of socialism in daily life. But what complicated the aspiration invested in this intellectual and cultural course of action was Britain's postwar position within an emerging "World America."[39] Still, the focus on reimagining socialism was the cutting edge of the New Left's refusal to bend to either the United States or the USSR.

Williams, Hall, and Thompson collaborated on *May Day Manifesto, 1968* (1969) not to assess the latest semiotic approaches to decoding advertising (they discuss this industry only for a few pages), but to analyze the global, Atlanticist, and domestic situation of Britain, and to formulate a "Socialist National Plan." They lamented the "incorporation" both of the Labour Party, which lost in 1955 and 1959, as a vehicle of corporate and American interests and of Europe itself "into an international economic system."[40] In 1960 Hall accused the Labour Party of moving into "the Second American Age."[41] Since the 1950s, New Left intellectuals have tried to persuade—and shame—the Labour Party to declare its independence from America. A *new* Left was requisite, they believed, because the established Left had become an "incorporated" Left.[42] "Atlanticism," Thompson wrote in 1982, "placed Western social democracy, the Labour Party itself, ultimately under the hegemony of the most advanced capitalist power in the world, in its military, diplomatic and even some of its economic options."[43] *Monthly Review* reported similar British views even in the early 1950s.[44] In part, then, cultural studies started out as incorporation studies. Thompson's "Revolution" (1960) proposed that Britain resign from NATO, though it might mean enduring "economic sanctions," "dislocation," and "hardship."[45] In 1981 the Labour Party radical Tony Benn speculated whether the United States would permit Britain to terminate its service as a launching pad, even if the British voted to withdraw American missiles: "The events of 1776 have been reversed, so that Britain has now to a large extent become a colony in an American empire."[46] (Terry Eagleton has mocked the current "coalition of the willing" Britain as "an off-shore U.S. aircraft carrier once known as the United Kingdom.")[47]

Thompson's "Outside the Whale," published in *Out of Apathy* (1960), the inaugural volume of New Left Books (now Verso), analyzed the apathetic and cowardly intellectual style ("accommodation," "adjustment") funded in *Natopolis*. This was Thompson's word for the military-economic-political-cultural-intellectual hegemonic web adhering the United States and western Europe.[48] In 1958 Thompson advised British progressives not to "think in terms of struggle within the American alliance," but instead to help initiate "in Europe a policy of active neutrality ... aimed at relaxing East-West tension, dismantling military blocs, and resuming economic, cultural and political intercourse between the communist and noncommunist world." For Britain was "still a major power," he believed, "not in terms of death-dealing fireworks, but in terms of world influence."[49] And in 1990 Thompson suggested that the Cold War benefited both the United States and USSR because the media attention that focused on their all-consuming rivalry obfuscated and frustrated liberatory impulses that wanted no part of their incorporative contest.[50]

Thompson identified the need both for a socialist nationalism and for an "internationalist conscience."[51] Here his emphases corresponded with those of Jean-Paul Sartre, who argued that "opposition to the Atlantic Pact should be the main criterion of left policy" and that "sovereignty must be won back ... to oppose [an] American imperialism which is everywhere breaking down national structures." Thompson viewed Britain as Sartre did France: as a "slave, subject to American authority."[52] Hence the New Left's American studies understood that more was at issue than culture in its linkage of cultural studies with Natopolitan studies.

Their American studies, like that published in *Monthly Review,* was partly a corporation studies: "Of the top 1,000 firms in the U.S. in 1965, 700 had branches or subsidiaries in Europe. Of the top 300, there are only a handful who do not have outlets, manufacturing plants, or sources of supply all over the world." In the 1960s Williams, Thompson, and Hall comprehended that U.S.–based multinational corporations, abetted by U.S. foreign policy, had the systemic "power to impose their logic on whole economies. The turnover of these giant companies exceed the national incomes of many countries in the poor world."[53] American corporate goals included the international consumerization of need, desire, and aspiration, the ongoing search for cheap labor, resources, and energy, and, as *Monthly Review*'s Paul Baran had shown, the strategic underdevelopment of some "Third World" countries. The price of competing with this "new kind of imperialism" was high: "Any other producer requires lower levels of wages until his technology catches."[54]

In short, Williams, Thompson, and Hall saw U.S. military, economic, and cultural might—conveniently ratified by pumped-up Cold War urgencies—combining to make the world safe for *corpocracy.* U.S.–based corporations, by exercising their power to influence the granting of American loans to countries and to install or remove their businesses, had become new "colonial governors" who preside over economic hostages.[55] *May Day Manifesto* describes Jamaica's failed attempt to build plants to process its bauxite deposits that a U.S. company had customarily shipped to Florida: "The extraction firm refused, and Jamaica was left with the choice of accepting the refusal or nationalizing the industry and initiating full Cuba-type sanctions from the U.S." Hall (a Jamaican), Thompson, and Williams concluded: "The smaller and weaker states are held within the control of United States strategies like iron filings within a magnetic field-of-force." They viewed America as Imperialism Inc., "In much of Latin America and Asia the process of incorporation has, it appears, gone too far for any moderate solution."[56]

Hall, like American intellectuals Sweezy, Huberman, C. Wright Mills, and Dave Dellinger, studied the U.S. response to Fidel Castro's revolutionary Cuba in the early 1960s. Hall coauthored "Notes on the Cuban Dilemma" (1961) with Norm Fruchter, an American radical and a member of Students for a Democratic Society, who assisted him in his editorship of *New Left Review.* Cuba resembled the New Left, they suggested, partly because it tried to establish a third-way "prototype of what is possible": it refused to ally and identify itself either with the American-Natopolitan bloc's version of the "free world" or with the Soviet bloc's rendition of socialism. "Social revolution in Asia, Africa, and Latin America is not in essence concerned with the Cold War," they wrote. "It is a revolution of the hungry countries against the industrially advanced: more especially, a revolution against the old structure of imperialism and therefore, profoundly hostile to capitalism as an economic system."[57] Cuba, like the New Left, strategically revised Marxism to suit current local conditions. "At almost every stage the revolutionary leadership has affronted orthodox communist theory." The Cubans eclectically synthesized "Sartre and Marx, Lenin and Marti and Democritus, looking through the Chinese Revolution to the Athenian City State!"[58] Hall and Fruchter's critique of President John F. Kennedy's imperialist New Frontier drew on Sweezy and Huberman's work in *Monthly Review* and on Che Guevara's "Notes for the Study of the Ideology of the Cultural Revolution" (1960), which was reprinted in their magazine's U.S. counterpart, *Studies on the Left.* They carefully qualified their criticism of Castro's tardiness in ensuring freedom of dissent, so dear to the New Left: "This is less a question—absurd as soon as it is posed—that Castro should himself set up and maintain alternative organs of criticism, than that he should define, more exactly within the rule of law, the freedom of criticism."[59]

Hall, Williams, and Thompson coauthored *May Day Manifesto* during the Tet offensive. They interpreted U.S. aggression against the North Vietnamese symbolically as a message "not to Hanoi, not to China, but to revolutionary movements from Southeast Asia to Latin America—[demonstrating] the consequences that will flow from any direct challenge to American hegemony."[60] Williams's biographer reports that he refused to lecture at the Massachusetts Institute of Technology because of its technological support for the war effort.[61] In 1965 historian Eric Hobsbawm implied, as did Hall and Fruchter about Cuba, similarities between the New Left's guerilla intellectuals and Vietnam's guerilla warriors: both refused "to fight on the enemy's terms." His appreciation of the Vietnamese, first published in *The Nation* and reprinted in *New Left Review,* was decidedly New Left: "Oppressed peoples do not want economic improvement alone." He concluded that the United States had overestimated the capacity of its nuclear arsenal to "stop people from making revolutions of which Mr. McGeorge Bundy disapproves."[62]

Thompson was drawn to the British Campaign for Nuclear Disarmament (CND) partly because it had the potential to bring a wide range of Natopolized subjectivities, afraid of annihilation, into organized protest. Aware of the single-issue limitations of CND in the late 1950s, he spotlighted the Aldermaston marchers' sense that they were protesting the "crooked attitudes of power which permit the Bomb to be used as an instrument of policy."[63] CND viewed both the United States and the USSR as deadly forces.[64] It kept its distance from the Labour Party.[65]

Universities and Left Review, which featured Thompson's piece, established clubs that helped popularize CND. For the New Left, Hall explained, CND was vital to engage and analyze because it was popular (it brought "ordinary people *into* politics"), was a movement ("a new kind of political mobilization—beyond ... the big party battalions"), and cut across class lines (while maintaining "an implicit 'anticapitalist' content").[66] Novelist Mervyn Jones too underscored this quality as essential to its appeal: "Most [CND members] were young, with a sprinkling of hardy survivors from the radicalism of the 1930s, but not many of the middle-aged generation.... Middle class rather than working class ... they exemplified—and CND helped to spread—a certain classlessness, or indifference to class, which was becoming manifest at this time and was reflected in novels, plays and films. For most of them, it was their first involvement in public activity."[67] In 1960 Hall's *New Left Review* published David Riesman and Michael Macoby's analysis of the Committee for a Sane Nuclear Policy (SANE), which sometimes seemed to echo Thompson: "This American equivalent of the Campaign for Nuclear Disarmament, confined as it has primarily been to asking for the cessation of nuclear tests and a successful Summit, has provided no adequate basis for a critique of American foreign policy, let alone of the domestic consequences of that policy."[68]

Decades later Thompson, stalwart in this resistance, edited *Star Wars* (1987) in support of the Atlanticist freeze movement. There he offered a satirical critique of President Ronald Reagan's "militarization of space" and the "Reaganaut" rhetoric that tried to make this escalation seem "self-evident." Thompson analyzed both the cultural production of American insecurity (his cultural studies) and the organizing and popularizing of dissent against the "star wars" nuclear "defense" system (his movement studies).[69] He was surely thinking of Suez as he described how Prime Minister Margaret Thatcher knuckled under when Reagan disapproved of her momentary concurrence with Soviet Premier Mikhail Gorbachov's "opposition to the arms race." Thompson suggested that the U.S. Cold War might be more about developing the state-subsidized technology to compete economically with Japan and

Europe than about stopping a Red Menace that advocated disarmament. He scrutinized Reagan as a "popular ideologist," salesman, front man, and public relations expert on Middle American stereotypes and fantasies capable of making Americans "feel both patriotic and altruistic about spending billions more dollars on military adventures." Thompson brilliantly turned the proposed Stars Wars satellite system into a metaphor for America's overarching hegemony: "The real message of Star Wars to West Europe is to get out from under America's hegemony—and umbrella—as soon as we can."[70]

In 1960 Thompson sized up Natopolis not only as a political-military establishment but a culturally produced state of mind, feeling, evasion, and preoccupation. Natopolitan apologists promoted "the politics of antipolitics," reveled in "disenchantment," "ennui," and "quietism," and psychologized dissent.[71] They elevated cynicism and apathy to an intellectual style: "No swearword is more devastating than 'romantic.'" Natopolitan culture's bribery was both economic and subjective: "Few are silenced by force and few are bought outright; but fewer still can resist the 'natural' economic interest and class power." Borrowing a term from Riesman, he added: "Its apologists are 'inner-directed.'" They did not grasp their "own nature" as "Natopolitan human nature."[72] Yet Thompson and his colleagues knew well that Natopolis was not monolithic and that protest was gestating in the belly of the whale.

The New Left Atlantic: Engaging American Radicalisms

Richard Hoggart, whose *Uses of Literacy* (1957) brought him to national eminence as a spokesman for British working-class culture, observed what he saw as an increasingly powerful trend toward cultural classlessness, a shift he associated with the Americanization of Britain. Before he became the first director of the Birmingham Centre for Cultural Studies in 1964, his essay for the groundbreaking New Left volume *Conviction* (1958) idealized American voices on the radio because they appeared "free of class overtones." Although some Britons recoiled at Americans' presumptuous "democratic *bonhomie*," Hoggart identified in this personality style the probable future of mass-cultural Britain: "To me the most chastening aspect of life [in the United States] is the realization that people at all levels of wealth and power really can, at times, look at each other face-to-face, that in a deep sense they can believe that each is as good as his fellow. When two Englishmen meet for the first time, by contrast, one can almost hear the built-in complicated fruit-machines of class-assessment whirring."[73] Hoggart failed to see that the American hegemonic system cultivates seemingly classless, informal interactions, accents, and attitudes partly as a means of establishing its class hierarchy and cultural image of economic freedom and democracy, a subject for a book that might be titled *Uses of Informality*. His homage, however, conveys the power of British class difference, encoded in classed bodies as well as classed minds—for which many American cultural productions doubtless spelled relief.

The British New Left engaged critically with manifold aspects of American culture and its developing radicalisms.[74] Some of its members interpreted and valued America as a site in which culture and social movements seemed to have a liberatory potential unsupported by—and undirected by—a self-proclaimed "vanguard" party. In the late 1950s and early 1960s New Left journals published an obituary in praise of Billy Holiday's "blood-curdling quality," a review of Vladimir Nabokov's *Lolita* (1955), critiques of avant-garde composer John Cage's alienated aesthetics of "noninvolvement" and of filmmaker Samuel Fuller's evasive "bourgeois romantic-nationalist consciousness," analyses of U.S. jazz musicians such as Ornette Coleman, a critique of bluesman John Lee Hooker's preoccupation "with sexual themes" and of Chuck Berry's rock 'n' roll "glorifica- tion of the American way of life."[75] *New Reasoner* published Arthur Miller's "The Freedom of the Writer" (1957), which lambasted the U.S. State Department's interference "with the circulation of American books abroad, American mu- sic and musicians, and American paintings."[76] Occasionally journals such as *Universities and Left Review* featured radical Americans' critiques of American arts and ideologies. Michael Harrington, for instance, bemoaned John Kenneth Galbraith's use of the word "affluence" to (mis)characterize 1950s America.[77]

The British New Left had many contacts with the U.S. Left. Its journals reprinted articles from, quoted from, or advertised U.S. publications such as *Monthly Review, The Nation, Liberation, Studies on the Left, American Social- ist,* and *Science and Society.* Raphael Samuel, coeditor of *Universities and Left Review,* referred to *Dissent,* established by Irving Howe in 1954, as its "sister publication in New York."[78] These journals did not tap *American Quarterly* for political or cultural insight into America. The first British New Left looked more toward American progressive intellectuals such as Mills, Galbraith, Ries- man, Dellinger, Harrington, Howe, Gabriel Kolko, and Dwight MacDonald than to American studies scholars such as David Potter.[79] In his obituary of Williams, published in *The Nation,* Thompson reminisced: "He told me once, in the late 1960s, that he felt closest to the American *Monthly Review.*" Williams had been a contributor to *Monthly Review.*[80]

Samuel argues that although the British New Left sometimes Americanized its critical categories, its "traditional socialist" impulse—"camouflaged" in

American "terminologies"—remained strong: "Capitalism—the 'system'—was still the main enemy, though we conceptualized it in terms of 'oligopoly' and our main line of attack was moral rather than economic." Hall too acknowledged the American debt: "Lacking much indigenous material to go on, the American analysts—Riesman, Galbraith, Wright Mills—who were at the cutting edge of these developments [consumerism, new political constituencies and sites and Left agendas] provided us with our main purchase on these arguments." The Students for a Democratic Society "Port Huron Statement," he added, broached "'quality of life' issues [that] constituted for us as significant an indictment of the present regime of capital as any other."[81] *May Day Manifesto* also praised American New Left "books and journals" and affirmed "solidarity" with the U.S. anti-imperialism movement's "internationalist objectives."[82]

Mills had a profound impact on the British New Left.[83] He lectured at the London School of Economics in 1957 and 1959 (broadcast by the BBC), subscribed to and commented on *Universities and Left Review,* and planned to contribute a chapter to the *Out of Apathy* volume. Near the end of his life Mills considered leaving Columbia for the new, experimental University of Sussex, where his friend Tom Bottomore would teach. "[Intellectuals] belong to something that's bigger than any government; we owe loyalty, if you want, to something higher than any one state," he stated in 1959, echoing Henry David Thoreau. Mills defined the Cold War intellectual's responsibility and orbit as transnational: "The minds of intellectuals have been formed by an essentially international process, and their work is essentially an international traffic."[84] In the estimation of one of his admirers, Mills "was more appreciated abroad" during his life.[85]

Mills's "The Complacent Young Men" (1958) comprehended that Britain's Angry Young Men literary movement and the British New Left, notwithstanding their differences, emerged from the same fault lines of frustrations and disillusionment. Mills read the desperation driving John Osborne's play *Look Back in Anger* (1956) as "unformulated" political resentment individualized as personal "trouble": "The young men have no political focus within which to express [their frustrations], so their anger turns inward." Osborne's protagonist enacts "a partial drama of not altogether understood symptoms": "If we suppose, for example, one difference in the situation of Jimmy Porter, Jimmy Porter as a character would no longer exist: a political movement which in its outlook and activities was alive to both the private troubles and the public issues in which he is involved." The other easy option, clear in Kingley Amis's *Lucky Jim* (1954), was to become a Complacent Young Man. Their "rejection

... does not stand on any alternative social basis in which they can really believe." Angry and Complacent "cultural workmen" in Britain and America "lock themselves up" before their dissidence can take political form. It is this self-incarceration, contextualized by Mills in 1958, that British New Left cultural workers analyzed and resisted in the *Out of Apathy* essays of 1960. The Left's political, cultural, and emotional challenge, in Mills's language, was to popularize options besides locking oneself up. This meant rethinking politics, culture, and how to unmake "political inactionaries."[86]

Mills saw that culture could be used to project a "halo" over power and dignify it as "authority" in multiple ways. The postwar American government, partly through U.S. Information Agency–sponsored renditions of American studies, disseminated representations of American culture around the world to better promote national prestige, legitimacy, and authority. Yet Mills contemplated the even more dominant American trend to make economic, political, and technological power into the preeminent sources of status, legitimacy, authority, and confidence. He observed ruefully that the Founding Fathers who treasured culture and learning as much as economic and political power—Benjamin Franklin, Thomas Jefferson, John Adams—would be anomalies in a modern America where money talks and progress is marked by the proliferation of "technological gadgets." While American cultural benefactors and philanthropists—the "sophisticated circles of the ruling elite"—existed, they were not prevalent. "Neither the very rich nor the politically powerful have generally been a durable and central public for live artists and intellectuals. Their sons have become lawyers, not sculptors; graduates of business schools, not writers; and these sons, the daughters of the very rich, have married." This was what Thompson not only detested but feared in the English professor who dreamed of meat markets. For, as Mills contended, the partially Americanized postwar Europe had become "increasingly subject to those tendencies." Mills speculated that the postwar "human mind as a social fact might be deteriorating in quality and cultural level."[87]

A. H. Halsey's overview of Mills's writing, published in *Universities and Left Review* in 1959, embraced the Texan as a model. Halsey argued that British academic sociologists lacked Mills's "socialist" "sociological imagination" and that this problem was serious because critique was becoming academicized: "the main responsibility for constructive analysis and criticism of society is passing increasingly to the universities."[88] Hall's editorial, "The American Scene" (1960), hailed Mills as having "contributed much to our approach." Michael Rustin's 1963 *New Left Review* retrospective on Mills asserted that "British sociology has yet to achieve the scope and depth of the best work of the classic tradition (or of the United States)" and linked Mills with work by Raymond Williams and by British radical historians.[89] "One of the excitements of the New Left—or anyway, the ULR," Samuel recalls, "was the discovery of new texts which allowed the socialist idea to be argued for in fresh terms. Wright Mills's '*magnum opus* on the American Power Elite' was one of the books which performed this function in our early days."[90] Alasdair MacIntyre's contribution to *Out of Apathy* lauded Mills as the "hero of radicalism," but also took issue with him for being too "submerged by the determinant image of man" and not focusing on "the resistances that men can and do offer under such pressures."[91]

Ralph Miliband's insightful *New Left Review* obituary, reprinted shortly after in *Monthly Review*, also framed Mills as the leading intellectual and moral light in New Left studies. Mills demonstrated that "commitment need not be dogmatic, and that radicalism need not be a substitute for thinking." What "angered" Mills, in the "frightened fifties," was not mostly the "Power Elite, Labour or White Collar," but "defaulting academics and intellectuals." Here Miliband's Mills sounds much like Matthiessen. Mills refused to allow his politics to be defined either by the NATO or communist bloc and insisted that critique should be about "help[ing] [to] make others free." He undertook his work on Cuba, as did the British New Left, in part because of his identification with its ideological predicament. His heart broke, Miliband inferred, because he came to believe that America would take decisive military action against Cuba.[92]

Mills's classic "Letter to the New Left" (1960)—which, as noted in chapter 1, was published both in *New Left Review* and *Studies on the Left*—addressed the British, whose journals he prized partly for their "emphasis on cultural affairs." It was Mills, after all, who had introduced the concepts of "cultural apparatus" and "cultural work." His "letter" posited an Anglo-American New Left "we": "Most of the time I am writing for people whose ambiguities and values I imagine to be rather different from mine; but with you, I feel enough in common to allow us 'to get on with it' in more positive ways. Reading your book, *Out of Apathy*, prompts me to write to you about several problems I think we now face." He criticized Daniel Bell's end-of-ideology ideology as an end-of-socialism Natopolitan wish that sought to legitimate and intellectualize political apathy. His perspective was global: "If the phrase 'the end-of-ideology' has any meaning at all, it pertains to selected circles of intellectuals in the richer countries.... The total population of these countries is a fraction of mankind." Intellectuals and the masses in Latin America, Africa, Asia, or the Soviet bloc, he suggested, would "shrug off" or "laugh" at Bell's assertion.

Mills advocated "ideological analysis" not as a fresh academic approach, but as Left intellectual responsibility. Yet for him Left critique entailed more than analysis: it merged "cultural with political criticism," encompassed "structural criticism and reportage and theories of society," and formulated "demands and programmes." Like Thompson, he saw utopianism as requisite: "Both in its criticisms and in its proposals, our work is necessarily structural—and so, *for us*, just now utopian." He envisioned a New Left studies that would do even more than always historicize, it would point the ways to "history-making."[93]

Mills appreciated Thompson's activist investment in trying to make as well as write history. In 1960 he wrote a supplementary letter to Fidel Castro, recommending Thompson for a teaching post in the Instituto Nacional de Reforma Agraria. He lauded Thompson's scope: "He can teach political theory or sociology of English literature or—given a month or so—anything that needs to be taught." And his intelligence: "one of the most brilliant young men in Britain." Mills also admired his independent stance and thought Castro would as well: "Until the Hungarian affair, he was, I understand, a member of the Communist Party of Great Britain, but now has no political affiliation. . . . There is no nonsense in this man about communism or anticommunism. He is an honest observer and straight thinker."[94] Thompson's application was turned down. Two sources claimed that "someone had told the Cubans that [he] was not politically reliable."[95] Later that year Mills wrote Thompson about the difficulties of anyone on the "noncommunist left" who tries to deal with the "hungry nation bloc" (here referring to Cuba, Mexico, and Russia).[96]

Thompson's "Remembering C. Wright Mills" (1980) admires Mills's hopeful sense that intellectuals—"cultural workmen"—could be formed into "a diffuse International": "Already West and East, South and North, the books were passing, the scholars, writers, and scientists were meeting, the students traveling, the technicians exchanging data." He praises Mills not just for his intellectual capacity to "build that house of theory between [Cold War] camps," but for his risk-taking character and courage, his "willingness to call ridicule upon oneself by exposing one's immature notions in public." While Thompson concludes that "the house of theory is not yet ready to receive the human race," he is grateful that the "no-man's-land" on which it is being built has become "a more friendly and more populated place since [Mills] has been at work there."[97]

Mills, as would Hall and others, focused less on the working class and more on "the young intelligentsia" as an "agency of change."[98] Even Thompson, Samuel, and Williams, who retained a strong emphasis on working-class issues, were attentive to emerging student activism. In 1969 Thompson, then teaching history at the University of Warwick, not only supported a student uprising there, he rapidly edited and contributed essays that defended the revolt, *Warwick University, Ltd.* (1970). (Thompson's critique of the new corporate-controlled British university resonates with Thorstein Veblen's 1918 study of the American business-run university and Mills's 1956 analysis of school ties forming the power elite.) Students learned through official files that the American visiting professor of U.S. history David Montgomery had been spied on by "an industrial 'security officer'" hired by the university, "perhaps with a view to criminal deportation proceedings." They protested the covert investigation of the Marxist labor historian and the managerial ethos of the university. Thompson expressed "solidarity with a zestful and courageous American radical student movement which (it is not clearly enough understood) operates within a very different culture, with different educational institutions, and with a sensibility seared by the absolutes of racial conflict and of direct, daily opposition to the Vietnam war."[99]

In the late 1950s and 1960s, British New Left journals published many articles by Americans as well as the British on what could be learned strategically from the widespread moral activism of American students around antiracist as well as anti-imperialist issues. "What was accumulating was not any kind of programmatic 'radicalisation,' it was a moral demand," Kenneth Rexroth asserted in *New Left Review* in 1960 (reprinted from *The Nation*). "The sit-ins swept the South so rapidly that it was impossible to catch up with them physically."[100]

Reminiscing about his emigration to England as a Rhodes Scholar in 1951, Hall noted: "There was no 'black politics' in Britain, postwar immigration had only just begun."[101] Early British New Leftists, however, studied anticolonial and neocolonial resistance movements in the "Third World" and American civil rights protests. *May Day Manifesto*, like *Monthly Review*, examined the systemic "relation between racial inequality, deprived communities and deprived countries."[102] In 1958 *Universities and Left Review* featured Jean Jenkins's chronicle of CIO efforts to organize black workers in the mid-1940s against the Jim Crow South's legalized "caste system" and peonage laws.[103] Reprinting work published in *Liberation*, it also paired Robert F. Williams's argument against black pacifism ("The Negro on the street who suffers most is beginning to break out of the harness of the nonviolent race preachers") and Dellinger's defense of nonviolence (which nonetheless acknowledged that "persons like Williams ... in many cases are the only ones who stand between an individual Negro and the marauding Klan").[104] 1956 was a benchmark for American as well as British radicalism, for in that year Rosa Parks refused to move to the back of a bus. Although Hall has testified that antiracism broke through the ideological windows of the Birmingham Centre in the late 1970s, he has also recognized that these foundational New Left concerns led to the London New Left Club's support for antiracist struggles connected with the Notting Hill race riots of 1958: "We participated in the efforts to establish tenants' associations in the area, helped to protect black people who, at the height of the 'troubles,' were molested and harassed by white crowds in an ugly mood between Notting Hill station and their homes, and picketed the Mosley and National Front meetings.... [and] stumbled across the powerful traces of racism inside the local Labour Party itself."[105]

Rexroth's sense that Americans were able to mount popular struggles against U.S. imperialism and racism because of "moral demand" more than "radical" ideology states a concern taken up in New Left discussions about how to fuel incentives to organize. In his introduction to *Out of Apathy,* Norman Birnbaum—an American sociologist who studied at the London School of Economics—generalized that *New Reasoner,* Thompson's venue, endeavored to develop a "socialist morality," whereas *Universities and Left Review,* coedited by Hall and Samuel, tried to imagine "what a socialist politics would be like." Respecting both approaches, Birnbaum assured readers that New Left Books was partly for those "who at the moment have no politics more complicated than a sense of moral unease."[106] As noted, Thompson has always lauded the traditions of British "moral revolt" and urged the Left "to go on the offensive on moral questions."[107]

Hall's take on the morality discourse and its "radical" usefulness is multidimensional. Like Thompson, he has been attuned to popular movements not catalyzed by party organizations. Hall appreciated CND as a new kind of *popular* political formation, unlike the "hard Left" Trotskyists who saw CND as a "movement dominated by misguided moral and religious enthusiasts" clueless about what constitutes "the nitty gritty of 'real politics.'" In 1960 Hall called for "a socialist movement" that would combine "the theoretical analysis which gives the movement perspective" and "the clarion call to moral principle, taken up in an unashamed way, which gives the movement guts."[108]

Thus the kind of strategic thinking about how to give the movement guts that one finds in the work of Williams, Thompson, Hall, Samuel, and others on the New Left was not only distinctively British. Their thinking had a significant Atlanticist component. If Natopolitan Atlanticism compelled the British New Left to take the United States as its object of transnational critique, the British also learned from some American political and theoretical concerns. By the late 1950s there were embryonic signs of a New Left Atlantic—a New Left Atlantic energy but also a New Left Atlantic despair—in formation.[109]

Postelectoral Politicking, the Americanization of Political Scope, and the Making of Unpartied Critique

Cold War socialist Atlanticism moved unevenly away from a vigorous engagement with debased electoral politics. To be sure, socialists were not the only constituency to become discouraged, sometimes cynically, with "democratic" electoralism. The progressive retreat from electoral activism, more evident in America, gradually became more manifest in postwar Britain. Below I consider briefly how resignation about electoral organizing and activism in America and Britain influenced critique, especially its "political" scope and aspirations.

In America the cliché that politics corrupts has become so accepted that it has long been taken not as criticism but as common sense. Allied to this is pessimism about the possibility that parties could ever initiate progressive change. Thus in Eugene O'Neill's *Hairy Ape* (1921), written just after the Red Purge, Yank, a worker, dismisses the socialist argument that he understand the conflicts he is experiencing as endemic to capitalism's class system and as alterable by electoral means: "Votes is a joke, see." A year later, referring to African Americans, W. E. B. Du Bois reasoned: "May God write us down as asses if ever again we are found putting our trust in either the Republican or the Democratic Parties." Thirty years later he thundered: "There are no two parties, just slaves of corporations." In 1925 the activist Mother Jones cast doubt on the suffrage movement: "The women of Colorado have had the vote for two generations and the working men and women are in slavery. The state is in slavery, vassal to the Colorado Iron and Fuel Company." Paul Simon's "Mrs. Robinson" (1967) hints that the way bored Cheeveresque suburbanites read the candidates' debate—"Every way you look at it, you lose"—is part of their class sophistication as well as alienation.[110] Many films, such as *Mr. Smith Goes to Washington* (1939), *The Candidate* (1972), and *Wag the Dog* (1998), equate politics with graft and the manipulation of the public. Recently a *New York Times* reporter summed up the popular apathy: "Why throw out the rascals for a new cast of rascals?" During the American-Anglo invasion of Iraq, *The Onion*, an American paper devoted to political satire, listed the "Top Anti-War Slogans," including: "I Oppose This War and I Vote. Wait, No, I Don't."[111]

Frances Fox Piven and Richard A. Cloward note not only that usually about half of the electorate vote in presidential contests and even less in other elections, but that "the United States is the only major democratic nation in which the less well-off, as well as the young and minorities, are substantially underrepresented in the electorate." Especially since Reconstruction, discriminatory registration requirements and access—not simply apathy—have *produced* nonvoters. In the late twentieth century the most impressive voter mobilizing efforts have been by corporations and activist right-wing groups that have targeted churches. Both parties, however, collude with one another by pitching their campaigns to the more "well-off" voters—and contributors. Piven and Cloward acknowledge that America's "weak party system penetrated by moneyed interest groups" gives demobilized voters "limited ability to affect policy." They make a persuasive case that only protest movements unbeholden to parties can put pressure on parties, remobilize voters, help sign up new voters, and achieve some change through electoral means.[112]

Historian Howard Zinn, like others on the Left, contends that voting is more of a parody than an exercise of democratic participatory citizenship: "we leave the house once in four years to choose between two mediocre white Anglo-Saxon males who have been trundled out by political caucuses, million dollar primaries and managed conventions for the rigged multiple choice we call an election." Historically, Americans have "voted" but have not been permitted to choose—that is, electorally—to alter the familiar pattern: "[Modern presidents] have taxed the poor, subsidized the rich, wasted the wealth of the nations on guns and bombs, ignored the decay of the cities, and done so little for the children of the ghettos and rural wastelands that these youth had to join the armed forces to survive—until they were sent overseas to die." Like Piven and Cloward, Zinn's knowledge of what catalyzes social change leads him to place more faith in organizing—and making a "commotion"—than in "voting."[113]

Michael Moore shares their sense of party intransigence and, extending Du Bois's criticisms, suggests that the Democrats-Republicans simply merge to make the one-party system official. Nevertheless, Moore urges his readers to run for office, offers strategies to do so, and lists so-called Democrats worth voting out as well as Republicans that can be toppled. He facilitates and tries to revive electoral activism.[114] And in *Changing the Powers That Be* (2003), G. William Domhoff proposes that the Left's "egalitarians" reinvolve themselves in electoral politics, abandon the third party strategy (which he regards as futile), establish Egalitarian Democratic Clubs throughout the country, and mute socialist "us" versus "them" class critique in order to capture the Democratic Party and win elections with liberal programs that can in the long run lead to progressive outcomes. While his electoral activism is conciliatory and liberal compared with the views of many on the Left, it asserts the importance of the *electoral front,* not only the cultural front and theoretical front.[115] Similarly, Todd Gitlin generalizes that the Right, unlike the Left, has no self-crippling ambivalence about winning political power. "On the Right are the Leninists of our time—ruthless, resolute, blunt. On the Left are more complicated, less disciplined folks with multiple, contradictory drives—purity, self-expression, guilt, resentment *and* power." Notwithstanding his consciousness of the "electoral cheating" of 2000 (he wrote this before the multifaceted electoral cheating of 2004), he pleads: "Don't be ashamed to seek some power." Gitlin, like Domhoff and Moore, does not embrace the Democratic party but sees it as the field of action.[116]

Substantive democracy should foster a level of citizen activism far beyond the narrow annual activity of voting. The holding of "free" elections in no way demonstrates that a state supports social freedom in a fuller sense. But that does not nullify the fact that voting can be a key instrument of social change—a fact that ruling Republicans certainly appreciated when they blocked voters from voting and invalidated other voters' votes in Florida, paving the way for the Supreme Court's presidential "selection" of 2000. I concur with historically grounded Left skepticism about party politics, yet am taken aback by the Left's long-standing promotion of resignation about the role that electoral organizing and activism might play in instituting social change. Below I want to think about why some Left intellectuals in Cold War America and Britain *promoted* the premise that significant social transformation through electoral means is probably impossible and consider the effects this resignation has had on the shaping of and investment in critique. What are the implications of the "unpartied Left"?[117]

In the 1920s, when Matthiessen returned from his stint as a Rhodes Scholar at Oxford to commence graduate study at Harvard, he "began to feel increasingly our [American] lack of a labor party." Although Matthiessen endorsed aspects of the New Deal Democratic Party, he felt that "this was not the same as having a party to belong to in the European sense—a labor party with a trade union base to which an intellectual could adhere with the realization that he could learn firsthand facts of economic organization from this contact, and could then, in turn, be of some use in helping to provide ideas for leadership."[118] He joined the Socialist party for a stretch in the 1930s. Matthiessen wrote angrily in 1948: "Progressives can no longer allow themselves to be deflected into delaying actions, into supporting the lesser of two evils. If you believe in a democratic socialism, you must act accordingly, and work for it." Two years later C. L. R. James lamented how much American intellectuals suffered by not having "a mass political labor party" to support, concluding "they are lost."[119]

Not everyone shared Matthiessen's sanguine view that Britain was engaged in a promising postwar socialist experiment. Even in the 1930s the great Oxford intellectual G. D. H. Cole and others had threatened to leave the Labour party because it was driving out socialists.[120] Updating such skepticism, C. L. R. James observed that British intellectuals "circulate in and around the Labour Party," though he did not rate Clement Attlee's postwar Labour government as truly socialist. On the same wavelength, in the late 1950s Miliband wrote a piece, published in both *New Reasoner* and *Monthly Review,* in which he reevaluated the Labour Party regime in the late 1940s and early 1950s not as a structural "transition to socialism," but as a capitalist experiment in "marginal collectivism" and "state intervention," something like the American New Deal. The Labour Party's real aim, he argued, was not to make a "socialist society"—a multidimensional economic, political, and cultural undertaking—rather, it was to give capitalism a more "socialized base."[121] Raymond Williams became convinced that the New Left had to extend "politics beyond the routines of the parliamentary process" and "define politics differently, in every kind of popular institution and demonstration, so that we can go on changing consciousness (our own included)" in substantively "democratic" ways.[122]

The Soviet invasion of Hungary and the admission of Stalinist crimes triggered mass departures from the Communist Party of Great Britain. When Thompson and John Saville criticized party dogmatism in *New Reasoner,* which they edited, they were suspended for three months. Both resigned not long after. This led to a New Left distrust of Old Left parties, to an emphasis on socialist critique, socialist morality, socialist humanism, and culture, and to a commitment to explore new nondogmatic forms of popular organization (inspired by CND). Organizational rethinking included experiments in journal politics and club politics in place of party politics and optimism about winning state control. (The *New Left Review* achieved a circulation of 10,000, while New Left club members reached about 3,000.) Much New Left activism and organizing took the form of publishing. The socialist morality and critique renewed the integrity that the Communist Party had lost; the emphasis on culture cultivated a plurality of concern and creative expression undominated by communist dictates; and the exploration of bottom-up rather than top-down modes of organizing prevented anything resembling Communist Party rigidity. "The Communist Party ... had frowned upon culture as a diversion," historian Victor Kiernan objected. "It was something to be dealt with after the Revolution. Instead, comrade, why aren't you out selling the *Daily Worker?*" The keen interest that Thompson, Hall, and others showed in William Morris became part of their effort to develop an independent British socialism that could intellectually, morally, and creatively liberate itself from the Soviet Communist Party model. Efforts to conceive of political agents beyond the working class also exemplified the New Left endeavor to imagine progressive social change uncomprehended within the Soviet paradigm.[123]

Much of Mills's writing addressed the decline of progressive party politics and electoral agency. The late 1950s Labour Party "seems to be in the process of the self-liquidation of one of the last (noncommunist) socialist parties in the western world." He considered America's "two-party state," subject to "corporate interest," to be just as effective as the Soviet Union's one-party state at undermining the "conditions of democracy" and substituting participatory politics with "administration." American, British, and Soviet political intellectuals, he argued, had to recognize that "in the absence of opposition parties, cultural activities become the only available form of opposition." Yet this recognition, he believed, calls for the conceptualization and organization of a "joint political-cultural struggle" that can "be waged in intellectual and moral ways rather than in a more direct political way." If parties and "voluntary associations" no longer function as "readily available vehicles for reasoned opinions and instruments for the national exertion of public will," new formations of "political-cultural struggle" would have to replace them.[124] This was not a cultural turn so much as a political-cultural turn.

And so the British New Left began to reimagine electoral recruitment as political-cultural socialist recruitment. In 1960 *Universities and Left Review* announced that it was preparing pamphlets titled "What Is the New Left?" (not "What Is Cultural Studies, Anyway?") and "You Should Be a Socialist in the Sixties" ("especially for use among Young Socialists and younger people").[125] Hall climaxed his opening *New Left Review* manifesto about New Left cultural studies with an emblematic quotation from William Morris's famous statement of 1885: "'The work that lies before us at present is to *make Socialists,* to cover the country with a network of associations composed of men who feel their antagonism to the dominant classes, and have no temptation to waste their time in the thousand follies of party politics.'"[126]

These themes—making socialists, remaking socialism, not wasting time in the follies of party politics—propel the writings of Thompson, Williams, and Hall. For all of the New Left's emphasis on culture, Hall assured his readers in 1960 that "the traditional task of socialist analysis will still remain. The anatomy of power, the relationship of business to politics, the role of ideology, the analysis of transitional programmes and demands, are all central to that discussion of the state, without which there can be no clarity, either of theory or practice."[127] In 1984 Williams called for a "radical reconstruction of all the main directions of social policy in the light of the most open and informed contemporary socialist analysis."[128] But Williams, Hall, Thompson, and others viewed socialism as so much more than policy reform. Williams explained that socialism is not just a "very complex set of ideas," but "an equally complex structure of feelings."[129] And as early as 1951 Thompson, like Williams, conceived of socialism as a formation of subjectivity as well as a system of moral value. Only the daily making of new socialists, he suggested, will bring a new socialism into being: "We do not wait for a new kind of person to appear until after Socialism has been won. . . . We must change people *now*, for that is the essence of all our cultural work."[130]

The New Left redeveloped socialism as a movement, not a party, and gradually more as an intellectual and political stance—later termed cultural materialism or cultural politics—than an organized electoral campaign. They theorized more for the sake of the cultural and critical movement than for their careers in the academy (Thompson's "career" lasted only a few years).[131] Particularly after 1956 they aimed to keep their fingers on the popular pulse.[132] The forms and styles of 1960s activism supported their late 1950s suspicion that what I term "movementism" was more effective at addressing popular discontents and cultural attitudes than either the Labour Party or the tiny British "revolutionary" parties such as the Socialist Workers Party.[133] New Leftists wanted the openness of their cultural and critical movements to "prefigure" a new, less structured, less centralized socialism—a taking-it-to-the-streets, schools, and art-theater-music scene cultural socialism whose popular energies would grow in strength in spite of the state.[134]

The impulse to reformulate political agency even more as cultural agency than electoral agency and the development of expansive political thinking even more than collective political action certainly did not obstruct the eventual American academic attraction to cultural studies. This more-than-electoralism posture had myriad strengths. New Leftists productively rethought socialist power not just as voting, controlling state administration, or redistributing wealth, access, and resources, but as something one thought, felt, and did outside the voting booth in what Gramsci termed "civil society."[135] In concentrating not just on socialist statism but on socialist culturalism, New Leftists stressed reconceiving how political agency and political imagination might survive and thrive apart from political parties. Eventually their critique of culture helped them better acknowledge the presence of a plethora of contradictions and beleaguered unpartied groups—a diversity of Lefts, potential Lefts, Left motivations, Left identities. They realized that even more needed to be changed than legislation and state power to make a better world: they also had to transform cultural perceptions and attitudes. Therefore British New Left intellectuals reworked narrowly conceived political party organizing more comprehensively as cultural and intellectual front organizing.[136]

The New Left was never a well-established oppositional group within the Labour Party. Hall notes that many New Leftists did not even belong to the party. [137] And yet Samuel acknowledges that they found themselves irresistibly "drawn within the orbit of Labour politics, even though we had constituted ourselves as its fierce critics."[138] Indeed, the inaugural issue of *New Left Review* in 1960 featured Ralph Miliband's critique of "the poverty of Labourism," Mervyn Jones's analysis of Labour Party failure, and Samuel's effort to explain the motivations, rationales, and identifications of "the working-class Tory" voter. [139] What Hoggart called the "imaginative inadequacy" of the Labour Left was especially vexing because the party possessed the mass-cultural power to conjure the dominant image of state socialism and tended to do so in bureaucratic terms.[140] In Hall's words, too often Fabian socialism's class of "professional patrician engineers" tried to install a "passive client class."[141] Williams also scoffed at the "Labour planner[s]" who feared real democracy.[142] Observing the Labour Party's relative abandonment of the miners during their 1984 strike, Samuel erupted: "As an electoralist party, it is bound to seek majority support for its platform. As a constitutionalist party, it is likely to be frightened by extraparliamentary action."[143]

So New Left engagement increasingly took on the character of an intellectual, critical, and cultural project, gradually for many mainly an academic project—"studies."[144] Winning hearts and minds became more like winning subscribers, club members, students, and consumers than winning voters to Left convictions. The more the Labour Party retracted its socialist commitment during the Cold War, the more the predicament of British New Left and post–New Left cultural studies critics began to resemble that of what C. L. R. James termed the "lost" American intellectuals: there was no well established party to which the Left's critiques and movements could optimistically appeal or lend support. Increasingly, British Leftists found themselves in a position similar to that of American Leftists loathe to practice what they called "lesser-evilism" (voting Democratic).[145]

This seemingly optionless predicament, "lesser evilism," had some peculiar effects on American minority party development. "The fear of being intellectually out of step, of belonging to a political party with no chance of immediate power," David Riesman reflected in 1947, "seems considerably greater here than in Europe."[146] In a *Monthly Review* debate on prospects for American socialism in 1956, one contributor urged his fellow "*Monthly-Review*-American Socialist[s]" to start a party, not to win elections—something deemed hopeless—but more generally to educate Americans and bring new readers to *Monthly Review*.[147] Here socialist practice became tantamount to reading—reading *Monthly Review*. This jump from electoral politics to journal subscription politics is a noteworthy shift in political value and aspiration. (Not long ago I received an envelope that blazoned Barbara Ehrenreich's endorsement of subscription activism: "Stop whining and subscribe to *In These Times*." *The Nation*'s resubscription envelope announces, "It's time to cast your vote," and prints "Yes" and "No" boxes.)

As Samuel affirmed, *Dissent* was much esteemed by members of the emerging British New Left in the late 1950s. It also exhibited the tendency to favor intellectual debate about socialism and pleas for journal subscriptions rather than a doomed socialist electoralism. The inaugural editorial made a case for *unpartied dissent*. The editors intended to "reassert the libertarian values of the socialist ideal," but this reassertion doubled as a post-McCarthy reassurance that the journal's founders do "not propose to become a political party or group. On the contrary, its existence is based on an awareness that in America today there is no significant socialist movement and that, in all likelihood, no such movement will appear in the immediate future."[148] *Dissent*'s socialism was a conceptual socialism, a critique socialism, an ethical socialism. The piece that followed this editorial was by Irving Howe, who underscored that the anti-Stalinist journal was interested in affirming "personal freedom"—an Americanized socialism in harmony with aspects of American individualism.[149] Then M. Rubel distinguished the socialism he advocated from "existing political programs," precisely because he opposed "exploitation" and upheld the "free unfolding of each individual."[150] A few issues after this, Lewis Coser, a *Dissent* editor, condemned "the radical sect" as "an obstacle, not an aid, in the development of a socialist movement in America."[151] Perhaps by detaching socialism from organized agitation and electoral campaigns, Howe, Coser, and their colleagues felt more able to attach an intellectual prestige to socialism that allowed socialist intellectuals to discuss it more seriously, substantively, and legitimately in academic and intellectual circles.

The journal entertained dissent against its championing of unorganized dissent-for-dissent's-sake. These critics defended the continued use of the word socialism to describe not just a critical but an organizing effort.[152] Gordon Haskell pointed out the oddity that some members of the Left, not just the Right, were now calling for the "liquidation" of socialist electoral opposition. He contended that the experience of organizing, not only theorizing, is an essential part of socialist education. Implicit in Haskell's concern seems to be the fear that *Dissent* was encouraging its readers to think like socialists and, in default, act like liberals (something not unknown in contemporary academic radicalism). "Is there no relation between the conscious, avowed ideas, purposes and programs of socialist groups and the organizational behavior of their members?" Haskell saw intellectual activity—journal socialism—as supplanting socialist activism. "Instead of a cause which can command their intellectual and emotional allegiance, [socialism] can hardly become more than a vague philosophy which demands no effort on their part, which leaves undisturbed the course of their personal and professional lives." In reply Coser mocked this insistence on "maintaining organizations that aren't organizations" as self-deluded and nostalgic. He preferred a socialism that invoked the need for social transformation without demonstrating its incapacity to organize and fight for it.[153] The following year *Dissent* self-critically published Harold Rosenberg's clarification that "Criticism . . . for Marx is an action. More exactly, it is the beginning of an action; one that demands completion by social transformation."[154]

The American Critique-Journal Left's antiorganizational impulse is understandable as a response to the rigidity of the U.S. Communist Party. In part it also may have been a reaction to the British Labour Party's policies and fall from power. From its first issue *Dissent* published disheartening critiques of the Labour Party and labour movement. By 1957 it introduced a "London Letter" column. In the journal G. D. H. Cole, who had an important influence on Hall, Samuel, and other budding New Leftists at Oxford, decried Labour's dilution of socialism in its postwar rise and decline: "What is the use of winning an election, except as a means to an end?" Other *Dissent* critics outlined similarly skeptical perspectives over the years during which the British New Left took shape. It may be that these reports reinforced the editors' sense that, given the circumstances, no party could well represent socialism and that the intellectual restoration of socialist debate was the best recovery that could be attempted in the Cold War conjuncture.[155] It would be too extreme to suggest that some critics began to value socialism as too precious to be warped by party politics, but there are hints of this.

In 1960, even as he promoted the enlistment of more socialist voters, Hall charged that Left organizing had been "too limited to transforming the Labour party from within ... [something] necessary but limited." He discouraged his New Left colleagues from backing Labour candidates simply to uphold "party unity." Instead, he advocated "the protest march or the boycott." Hall's concern over electoral struggles never faltered, but he and other New Leftists felt that those struggles constituted just one form of agitation on numerous political fronts.[156]

Over the last fifty years, British Left politics has come to look more like American liberal-Left politics not only because of despair over electoralism, but because of the diversification of political issues and constituencies.

Barbara Ehrenreich profiled the polyglot American Left in 1984: "There is a socialist left within this broad popular left [green, feminist, antimilitarist movements]. But it is painfully small by European standards, 'socialist' being the word that the right has fairly well succeeded in making synonymous with 'un-American.'"[157]

A few years after *New Socialist* published Ehrenreich's piece, that British Labour magazine featured an article by Scott Lash and John Urry on the American state of British politics. Reflecting on the political implications of an increasingly multiculturalized Britain, Lash and Urry equated some of those transformations with Britain's Americanization. Britain will continue to look more like the United States, they argued, but it will be much poorer because of U.S. dominance. Taking their cue from America, they contended that the Labour Party campaign against Thatcherism should not be based on socialism and class-oriented issues, but on pluralism and individualism. Their analysis reads like a caricature of some of Hall's anti-Thatcherism arguments and proposals. Like Hall, they support coalition building; unlike him, and more like Domhoff in 2003, they consider any socialist agenda a popular liability. "For many interests and groups, a Britain more like the United States would probably have been to their benefit. The position of black and other minority groups, that of women, that of various consumer and community groups, has changed much more positively in the United States than in most western European countries over the past couple of decades." Lash and Urry imagine Britain's "progressive" future within the borders of "American liberalism": "If the British social and political system is going to look more like the American—that is, without a working class with the powers to produce socialism ... then this may be merely the best that could be hoped for in such a pluralistic and disorganized society." While Hall still wanted to transform Britain into an independent socialist state—or culture—capable of distancing itself from American power, Lash and Urry proposed that the Labour-Left accommodate itself to the seeming inevitability of an Americanization of political scope and issues.

In America the socialist renewal that many British Leftists had dreamed of—"not simply winning and holding office [but] laying the basis for a whole new conception of life"—has often been academicized in scope as a theoretical and interdisciplinary renewal of a few relatively receptive departments in the humanities and social sciences.[158] Would "cultural studies" have been as trendy as it was in the U.S. academy—scholarly Beatlemania, for a time—if it had been labeled New Socialism Studies or New Left Studies? But even when Hall, Williams, Thompson, and their New Left colleagues announced their aim as "making" socialists, what these new socialists might actually *do* to bring new conceptions of socialism into being was often ambiguous. Hence in manifold ways the British socialist electoral predicament came to resemble the even more severe American socialist electoral predicament. British New Left cultural studies was founded as this predicament became apparent, as socialist critique became more detached from some traditional machineries of social change. New Left movementism may have been better at producing critical thinkers and cultural activists than voters and party lobbyists, a post-electoralism tendency that may be read as both a strength and a weakness.

In 1950, writing about America, C. L. R. James was grimly skeptical about the prospects of structural social transformation through conventional electoral means. Nevertheless, he argued for the importance not only of forming a party—a labor-based, membership-led party of the sort that Matthiessen yearned for—but of reconceiving the very concept of party: "This will be a party such has never been seen in the United States.... Though it will take a part in parliamentary politics, its inherent aim will be to break the practice of confining politics to merely voting for legislators." He considered two potential allies of this party to be potential enemies as well: "When this movement comes, it is the labor leadership and the intellectuals rallying to them who will strive with might and main to reduce it to a tame purely political party, to vote, go home and leave it to the leaders to build the most powerful welfaring of welfare states."[159] (His comment about "purely political party" brings the well-intentioned Domhoff to mind.) Like Hall, Thompson, Williams, and others, James rethought the field of what counted as politics. Perhaps less like them, in 1950 he wanted to step up what was perhaps an Old Left engagement with electoral politics, even while trying to reimagine what a "party" might be.

In this new millennium, one thing that cultural studies and American studies academics might do within the university is devise courses on electoral activism, courses that will build bridges rather than walls between the two words. Such courses might analyze not only the history of third parties and their occasional successes, but the instances in which movements, media institutions, lobbying, and protests of various sorts changed party policies. A key objective might be to investigate history to better formulate the ways in which electoral activism can be a significant exercise of political agency.

Coda

A knowledge of Atlanticism—and Left Atlanticism—is crucial to understanding the development and potential of cultural studies. The American pressure imposed on Britain compelled the New Left to transnationalize its critique and develop a contemporary transnational "American studies" in the 1950s and 1960s. If British New Left cultural studies intellectuals taught Americans much, especially in this early phase of their movement, they also learned much from Americans—some Americans, like Mills and *Monthly Review* contributors, who also internationalized their critical perspectives on America. It makes sense to compare the more academicized British cultural studies of the 1970s onward with American studies. But particularly in the first couple of decades of the Cold War, it makes even more sense to compare the formation of British New Left cultural studies initiatives with American critiques nurtured in American journals like *Monthly Review, Dissent,* and *Studies on the Left.*

In the late 1980s Hall affirmed "that the 'first' New Left, however mistakenly, thought of itself as a 'movement' rather than simply a journal." British cultural studies has its intellectual as well as political roots in a dwindling Left culture and weakened Left organizing efforts. One can imagine that Matthiessen the activist union organizer, the socialist, the internationalist, and the builder of U.S. and European American studies, would have been delighted with the elaboration of the British New Left cultural studies emphasis had he lived, the emphasis that Mills inspired. Yet over the decades, from postwar to postmodern, what Matthiessen may have found curious, and perhaps what we today should find noteworthy, is the relative detachment of such critical, political, and cultural initiatives from electoral organizing. Matthiessen, for all his acute disappointment over the failure of the Progressive Party's presidential campaign for Henry Wallace in 1948 (Wallace, formerly Roosevelt's vice president, won about 2 percent of the vote), may not only have found this relative detachment curious, he may have found it all too familiar, all too "American," all too self-protectively cynical.[160] Notwithstanding his likely admiration for aspects of postmodern culturalism and critique, he may have wondered, respectfully, constructively, and obstinately, as some of my students have on occasion: recruitment for what? prefigurative of what? critique for what?

Part II

Historical Studies and Literary Studies

3

On the History of Radical History and Cultural Studies

Our problems, however much conditioned by the past, *are in the present.*
> —*Robert Lynd, Knowledge for What? (1939)*

Memory and hope are the two qualities which blend into a Socialist conviction. That, too, may be why Socialism has been unfashionable among those who have grown up during and after the war: they have no memory, and no one has given them much reason to hope.... We must ... marry memory to hope again.
> —*Norman MacKenzie, "After the Stalemate State" (1958)*

This, then, is the point where the Left must not "give way": it must preserve the traces of all historical traumas, dreams, and catastrophes which the ruling ideology of the "End of History" would prefer to obliterate—it must become itself their living monument, so that as long as the Left is here, these traumas will remain marked. Such an attitude, far from confining the Left within a nostalgic infatuation with the past, is the only possibility for attaining a distance on the present, a distance which will enable us to discern signs of the New.
> —*Slavoj Žižek, For They Know Not What They Do (1991)[1]*

In 1990, when I reviewed the controversial University of Illinois conference memorialized in *Cultural Studies* (1992), it struck me as odd that only one panel out of dozens addressed the relations between cultural studies and history, for accounts of British cultural studies routinely name its founders as Raymond Williams, Richard Hoggart, Stuart Hall, and the radical historian E. P. Thompson.[2] One history panel speaker, Catherine Hall, portrayed herself as "a child of Thompson" (272), and the other, Carolyn Steedman, acknowledged having a "massive" "twenty-five year" "transference relationship to Thompson's classic, *The Making of the English Working Class* (273). Both of these British historians criticized the conference's underrepresentation of history. They wondered why the panel had been scheduled for the evening of the last day of the conference, when approximately two-thirds of the audience had departed. Some questions following their presentations made me worry that the status seemingly being assigned to history, at least on this occasion, was a postmodern sign of some of the changes cultural studies was undergoing in the liberal American academy—an American re-presentation of cultural studies as posthistory presentism.

One query put to Catherine Hall exemplified this posthistorical amnesia. The questioner acknowledged that her talk on early nineteenth-century Jamaica and imperial constructions of Englishness and race offered "good history," but asked skeptically: "What was specifically 'cultural studies' about your work?" (272). One of the reasons I found this challenge intriguing is that, superficially, it resonates with some of Stuart Hall's complex ruminations about history.

Since his late-1950s efforts to bring culture into the orbit of the New Left's strategic concerns, Stuart Hall, Catherine Hall's husband, has focused on analyzing *contemporary* cultural-political conditions. Stuart Hall has endeavored to reconceive the image, content, and purposes of socialism—to rescue it from outdated notions of its programs, constituencies, and strategies. "I'm a Modernist . . . not in an idiotic sense of abolishing the past, but unless socialism makes sense of the way in which people live their lives now, not only will no one vote for it, but why would anyone vote for it?"[3] Like a good historian, he has cited connections between some of the New Left's early positions and projects and those current in the Thatcher 1980s: "Socialist politics isn't just born again every day; it takes place within a set of traditions, within a formation." Yet he has consistently placed the accent on recognizing and analyzing change: "I'm four-square with Heraclitus: you can't step in the same river twice. . . . What matters is some sense of continuity through transformation—of political allegiances which won't go away, of bedrock reference points—which does allow us to say something about the present conjuncture.["]4 Francis Mulhern has criticized this as a "compulsive modernism, always announcing itself as if for the first time, shedding what it would otherwise have to assume as a formative, therefore limiting, history."[5] Hall in no way insists that cultural studies only be "about" contemporary conditions, but places pressure on "history" to deliver knowledge that will contribute to dynamic progressive struggles.

Many twentieth-century radical historians, of course, have assumed that an understanding of history opens rather than limits political options, analyses, and imaginations—a premise implicit in Catherine Hall's rejoinder to her questioner: "If cultural history isn't a part of cultural studies, then I think there's a serious problem." Curiously, as Fredric Jameson has noticed, she next asserted that this problem is in fact not new because cultural studies has long "neglect[ed]" history.[6] However, she added that in her own department of cultural studies—she then taught at the Polytechnic of East London—cultural history is regarded "as an integral part of cultural studies" (272). Steedman, who was concerned to expand the history of cultural studies beyond its manifestations in the University of Birmingham's Centre for Contemporary Cultural Studies to the polytechnics and other universities (all of them are now called universities) (617), observed that nine polytechnics and two universities offer B.A. degrees in cultural studies (620) and that in these locations pedagogy is "dramatically historical . . . in comparison with cultural studies in the U.S." (614). She criticized some Birmingham work on history, noting that it sometimes differed from cultural studies history done elsewhere: Birmingham's stress on group work and writing tended to preclude extensive and expensive archival work, usually undertaken by "the lone historian," while its emphasis on discourse theory contributed to an overwhelming focus on "the analysis of text" (618).

Hall and Steedman both made an intellectual case for the importance of sustained historical work, not just gestural "historicizing." "Many practitioners of cultural studies," Catherine Hall speculated, "have little interest in history and rely for their 'background' on secondary sources which they do not scrutinize with the textual eagle eye that is in use for their own objects of study" (272). In the hope that the cultural studies of the future would be rigorous, Steedman asked: "Will there be any room for detailed historical work; or are students of cultural studies bound to rely on great schematic and secondary sweeps through time?" (621).

Catherine Hall observed a couple of paradoxes that suggest that cultural studies and radical history have had quite a history, one that her word "neglect" does not convey. First, while history was not the central matter for the

Birmingham Centre—in terms of their publications—the most publicized event that drew international attention to the center was the heated History Workshop "history and theory" debate (December 1979) between Richard Johnson, the center's historian, and Stuart Hall, on the one hand, and E. P. Thompson, on the other. Second, noting the pervasive influence of Thompson's *Making of the English Working Class* (1963) and Raymond Williams's *Culture and Society 1780–1950* (1958), she concludes that "history was, and wasn't, at the heart of cultural studies in its Birmingham manifestations" (271).

Cary Nelson, one of the Illinois conference organizers, later coedited with Dilip Parameshwar Gaonkar, *Disciplinarity and Dissent in Cultural Studies* (1996), which includes Michael P. Steinberg's "Cultural History and Cultural Studies." This intellectual historian's piece is noteworthy for sundry reasons.[7] Steinberg calls for the making of a "Disruptive History" that will examine self-reflexively not "How We Got to Where We Are Now," but more complexly "Who We Are in Relation to How We Say We Got Here" (104). The British cultural critic John Berger rendered this concern somewhat differently in 1972: "History always constitutes the relation between a present and its past. Consequently fear of the present leads to mystification of the past."[8] Some of Steinberg's fears of the present resonate with those of Hall and Steedman: "Cultural studies's most disturbing potential is the denial of historicity and temporality, of existential subtlety, overdetermination, and the subsequent production of a uniform cynicism, all in the service of the alleged liberation from history" (104–05).

Steinberg moves toward, but never arrives at, analyzing cultural studies' "self-dehistoricization" (110) and its "alliance of exoticism and theoreticism" (110) as ideological expressions of the postmodern yearning to escape "from the past" into a "posthistorical world"—a "world" that is nonetheless "historically constituted" (127).[9] Although Steinberg acknowledges in passing the "largely British origins" of what is called "cultural studies" (110), one of the more refreshing aspects of his essay is its emphasis not on the Birmingham Centre or Hoggart-Williams-Hall-Thompson, but on Walter Benjamin and Max Weber as "founders" (114) of historical cultural studies. Steinberg's specialty, uncoincidentally, is European intellectual history.[10] He closes by examining examples of recent cultural studies histories, including Paul Gilroy's provocative *The Black Atlantic,* and suggests that the "syncretism of cultural studies and cultural history" (127) he has been "pleading" for is in formation.

I hope that much intellectually, theoretically, and politically exciting historical cultural studies work lies ahead. Still, I think that Catherine Hall, Steedman, and Steinberg, for all their insights, have underplayed the history of the productive if sometimes contentious relationships between radical history and cultural studies—cultural studies in its canonical British sense and cultural studies in a broader sense I will adumbrate. Those interested in thinking through the connections between cultural studies and radical history should be aware of this history as a resource. Because this is a multifaceted, extensive history, far more complex and voluminous than anything I can outline here, I offer only a few suggestive rather than comprehensive perspectives that contribute to the reconsideration of this history and of the concept of "cultural studies."

Thompson, Birmingham, History Workshop

In her introduction to the 1995 edition of E. P. Thompson's *Poverty of Theory* (1978), Dorothy Thompson, herself an established historian who taught nine-teenth-century British history at the University of Birmingham in the 1970s, called her late husband's book a "rarity": "[H]e concerned himself with [theoretical formulations] mainly in private reading and private discussion.... [H]e was concerned to examine particular problems rather than to enunciate overarching general principles. He approached his subject matter certainly with expectations—even assumptions—which were to be tested against the evidence" (ix). She adds that Thompson viewed his work as being within a "tradition of Marxist historiography," not as an outgrowth of a "system" (ix).[11] Here she verges on making public theoretical discussion sound inappropriate, beneath one's—I am almost tempted to say class—position as a historian of the "particular" and a developer of a "tradition."[12]

Even so, the relationship between theory and history much preoccupied Edward Palmer Thompson when he was interviewed by a representative of the American journal *Radical History Review* in March 1976.[13] Thompson raised the sorts of issues about politics and history one might expect: that the antagonistic conservatism of the history profession should spur radical historians to excellence and accuracy (7), that he learned more about politics and history from the Communist Party Historians Group than from his studies at Cambridge (13), and that *The Making of the English Working Class* was written not for academics but for students like those in his adult education classes (13). But he gave the interview a theoretical turn when he criticized the misconception that "you can have a methodology without a theory ... as if you can keep the theory inside a locked drawer in the desk," and affirmed that he has always been engaged "in a theoretical argument about the historical process" (15). The development of this (unspecified) historical argument operated dialectically with his efforts to "listen" (14) to historical evidence.[14] He also praised a 1974 essay by the Cambridge historian and *History Workshop Journal* editor Gareth Stedman Jones for "significantly modify[ing] some of the received wisdom that most of us offered as theory ten years or more ago" (16).[15]

Thompson's concern with theory—rapidly changing and proliferating theory of a kind he found unfamiliar, which he ridiculed as "Theory" in print—intensified over the next three years.[16] As Dorothy Thompson tells it, "When Althusser appeared on the scene he made little impact on practicing historians. For some reason, however, he suddenly became a major force among graduate students and some young historians and literary scholars.... Althusser's followers—even some of the historians among them—began to declare that history was a nondiscipline and that its study was of no value" (x). Major works by the French Marxist theorist Louis Althusser were translated and published in this period: *For Marx* (1969), *Lenin and Philosophy* (1971), *Reading Capital* (1971) (coauthored with Etienne Balibar), and *Politics and History* (1972). Close study of Althusser's "structuralist" books plus the translation of Antonio Gramsci's 1930s *Prison Notebooks* in 1971, which elaborated Gramsci's theory of hegemony, would bring the Birmingham Centre into its first real theoretical phase under the direction of Stuart Hall, who served as its acting director from 1968 to 1972 and as director from 1972 to 1979.[17] As Dorothy Thompson indicated, although scholars in several disciplines were interested in Althusser, this early turn toward theory did not yet alarm historians.

It was the British extension of Althusser's critiques of some Marxist notions of history, especially by two sociologists, Barry Hindess and Paul Hirst, that drove historians like Thompson to attack Althusser. In their *Pre-Capitalist Modes of Production* (1976), Hindess and Hirst criticized Althusser for not developing what they believed were the full "antihistorical" implications of his critique of Marxist historicism in *Reading Capital*.[18] In effect, they contended that history is no more than the particular "body of *texts*" (311)—limited representations—that historians have assembled to "constitute" an inaccessible past, yielding "thought objects" only, not reality. "The radical conclusion of Althusser's argument," they wrote, "would be that the supposed real object, 'history,' which the thought object is not, is not a real object. There is no real object 'history,' the notion that there is *real* history is the product of empiricism" (317). Having nullified history as discourse decorated with facts, they charged: "Marxism, as a theoretical and political practice, gains nothing from its association with historical writing and historical research.... The object of history, the past, no matter how it is conceived, cannot affect present conditions" (312). Politically, only the "current situation" (313) matters.[19]

Thompson decried their tomes as an academic theoreticism that advocated not simply posthistory politics but postpolitical politics. "What is being threatened—what is now actively rejected—is the entire tradition of substantive Marxist historical and political analysis, and its accumulating (if provisional) knowledge."[20] Raphael Samuel, a founding editor of *History Workshop Journal,* was sympathetic to theoretical debate. Yet he saw the work of Hindess and Hirst as "exalt[ing] theoretical practice to the point where it becomes an end in itself, arriving at formularistically irreproachable conceptual categories which are empty of usable content."[21] Thompson interpreted the tendency to invest explanations of history almost exclusively in structures as a historical sign that some Left intellectuals felt disempowered and forlorn in a Cold War scene dominated by two apparently immovable world powers ("structures").[22]

Richard Johnson took over as the Birmingham Centre's director when Stuart Hall left for the Open University at the close of the 1970s. Trained as a historian, Johnson, in the words of Stuart Hall, was "formed by Thompson's work."[23] Johnson contributed to and learned from the center's studies of Althusser, Gramsci, and new trends in British debates about the conceptualization of history. He endeavored to sort out what he thought were the theoretical and historiographical advances of Thompson's generation, which he termed "culturalist Marxism" or "culturalism," and those of the "Althusserian moment," which he called "structuralism," in what became an intensely controversial *History Workshop Journal* piece, "Thompson, Genovese, and Socialist-Humanist History" (1978).[24]

Three of his critical perspectives are particularly important. First, he argued that the "two traditions" of "culturalism" and "structuralism" are "in the end, complementary" and that it is productive to "take elements from both traditions" (79). But, as Thompson would later note in debate, Johnson's synthesis tilts toward Althusser's revisions. Johnson qualified what he had in mind: "to put it differently, [historians] will have to submit the best historical practices to an Althusserian critique" (79). Yet he applauded Thompson—who always placed great historical and political stress on foregrounding the agency of historical actors, especially the downtrodden—for the attention he paid to issues like "intentionality," "subjective experience," and the "'inwardness' of culture" (96). Second, Johnson used Hindess and Hirst, explicitly and implicitly, to contend that Thompson and Eugene Genovese had overemphasized class and culture in their work in such a way as to mute the "determination[s]" of the "mode of production" and the "rootedness" of the phenomena they studied in "economic relations" (81, 91, 92). Third, Johnson blasted Thompson and Genovese repeatedly, to quote again from Thompson's 1976 interview, for "keep[ing] theory inside a locked drawer in the desk." Johnson cleverly used Marx, even more than Althusser, to defend the practice of theoretical "abstraction" (89) from the particular: "Culturalism, preferring 'authenticity' to 'theory,' renders its own theoretical project guilty, surreptitious and only partly explicit" (97). In other words, a historian who "suppresses" his or her theoretical lens (and "debts") (85) does so in order to foster the illusion of "authenticity"—that his or her history actually captures past life and struggle as it happened.

Johnson's piece drew fire from Keith McClelland, Gavin Williams, and Simon Clarke, and a partial defense by Gregor McLennan (from the Birmingham Centre and later author of the highly theoretical *Marxism and the Methodologies of History* [1981]), and also numerous hostile letters, all published in subsequent issues of *History Workshop Journal*. In response to this largely critical outpouring, Johnson wrote a letter in which he employed one of Thompson's own words in reference to theory ("locked") to restate one of his main criticisms: "[*The Making of the English Working Class*] *is* an untheoretical book in that its conclusions, which are of great general import, remained locked up in historical particulars." Stedman Jones's letter deplored some of the acerbic caricatures of Johnson's arguments and observed that the critics of Althusserianism, including Thompson, had themselves used Althusserian analytical terms—such as social formation and overdetermination—in their diatribes.[25]

The translations of Althusser, British Althusserian work on history, Thompson's polemics, and historians' ardent defenses of Thompson all set the stage for the dramatic evening of December 1, 1979, ominously numbered History Workshop 13. Stuart Hall joined the much awaited debate between Thompson and Johnson in "St. Paul's church ... a crumbling neoclassical ruin near the Oxford University Press."[26] Hall's, Johnson's, and Thompson's papers were published in one of the most important British texts that has debated and outlined what is at stake in theoretically sophisticated historical practice, *People's History and Socialist Theory* (1981), edited by History Workshop's Raphael Samuel.[27]

Hall's "Defence of Theory," an intellectually compelling defense of theoretical complexity and lucidity, saluted Thompson's "history and political inspiration" (378). But Hall held that Thompson's recent polemics had failed to notice that Althusser had been subjected to revisionary criticism for some time not only outside but inside the ranks of Althusserians and that Thompson's ridicule risked sanctioning "a sort of mindless 'antitheory,' taking us back behind positions won in the last few years" (379). Hall offered his own criticisms of Althusser: some of Althusser's and Althusserian work is like a "self-generating theoreticist machine" (380) that can "terrorize" (380) graduate students; some Althusserians overdid the constructive critique of empiricism in their foolhardy rejection of concrete empirical historical analysis (380) (here it is easy to think of Hindess and Hirst); Althusser's writing on "Ideological State Apparatuses" can be too functionalist (381). Withal, Hall was appreciative of Althusser's efforts to reconceive the problem of "determinacy" more expansively in terms of "overdetermination" (380–81)—an interpretive stress on multiple causes of actions and phenomena.

Hall averred that both Althusser and Thompson share an interest in conceiving a "social totality" as made up of formations and practices—cultural, economic, political—that have a "relative autonomy" (381) from one another. However, Althusser endeavors to abstract and name his theoretical ideas—overdetermination, relative autonomy, social formation, and so on—and this makes these concepts potentially applicable to the study of different historical, cultural, and political situations. According to Hall, Thompson's sometimes similar notions of how one might conceptualize the relations of power structures, causality, contradiction, and cultural resistance in a specific historical conjuncture—to the extent that these notions remain embedded in narratives about historical particulars—may not be grasped and used so easily. This makes it more difficult for Thompson's readers to learn and act on the subtleties of historical, political, and cultural critique. Hall implied that Thompson's history writing was less "cultural studies" in its explicit instruction in critique than he would want it to be.

Next Hall focused on the category of "experience." Thompson's contribution to the comprehension of "lived historical experience"—a dimension of his stress on "agency and struggle" (384)—is exemplary: "This work stands as a permanent rebuke to those Althusserians who read their Master as saying that experience was *purely* ideological and unconscious and that a truly theoretical history was one which treated classes as mere 'bearers' of the historical process, without agency and historical process itself as a process 'without a subject'" (383). Nonetheless, Hall added, "experience," though not only subtextual, is not just waiting in the archives to be recovered; its "complex interweaving of real and ideological elements" (383) must be named and accounted for in the analysis and explanation of causality and agency. It is vital to investigate how historical "subjects" are formed and how their perceptions of their "experience" are constituted. Hall's assault on an undertheorized concept of "experience"—often working-class "experience" in the writing of many of the History Workshop historians who were in the audience—also was directed against what some historians seemed—or seemed to Hall—to assume about the political payoff of their excavations: "as if, simply to tell the story of past oppressions and struggles is to find the promise of socialism there" (384). That is, if a hermetic theoreticism can be an evasion not only from history but from the current political moment, so can a self-sufficient historicism that seeks a regressive or nostalgic political refuge in the resistance of past political actors: "historical reflection," like theoretical reflection, "can deeply inform, but not replace" a "real political practice" (384).

Thompson disputed Johnson's assertion that he was part of a founding "culturalist" group in part by differentiating his early 1960s allegiance to Marxism from Raymond Williams's highly critical stance toward Marxism, Richard Hoggart's lack of interest in Marxism, and what he took to be Stuart Hall's "sceptical ambivalence" about Marxism (397). Williams, Thompson observed, defined culture anthropologically as a "whole way of life," whereas his history conceptualized culture more explicitly in terms of politics as a "whole way of struggle" (398). The thrust of Thompson's rebuttal of Johnson was his charge that theoreticism is tantamount to political escapism and his reaffirmation that his and Genovese's work "had never been theoretically vacant" (401), just different from the "Theory" made chic in the Althusserian moment.

Johnson again upheld the conceptual usefulness of analytical abstraction, modeling, and labeling, while admitting that "intellectualistic and nonpopular" theoretical terms can segregate "intellectual debates from more popular located and common-sense understandings" (394). Johnson's and Hall's remarks attempt to sustain links between the critique of the present and the study of history in two ways. First, they insist that the historian must develop a critical consciousness of the conceptual assumptions, theoretical models, analytical language, and nexus of problems (for starters) that he or she brings to the tasks at hand both because the historian's lens—in part shaped by the present—will affect the historian's interpretation of history and because a consciousness of this lens will better enable the historian to think critically about this lens as one that is socially constituted. Second, Hall's and Johnson's commitments to the present are manifest in their pedagogical concerns: they favor theory, not to be pompous, fashionable, or "professional," but because students who work with it, or some forms of it, can better learn how to engage in political, historical, and cultural critique. A theoretically self-aware historical practice helps train readers as critical agents and political subjects because they are learning from the specifics of concrete historical case studies and from the theoretical abstractions, models, language, connections, and problems being "tested," to use Dorothy Thompson's word, in work on case studies. Paradoxically, this pedagogy of clarity entails helping students and readers digest some theory—what Thompson excoriated as "Theory"—that can be anything but clarificatory. Thus worthwhile theory—or "Theory"—must be made clear.

The Birmingham Centre's graduate students and faculty practiced theoretically complex history writing in the History Series of the center's "stenciled occasional papers," which were for sale. Sometimes these History Series papers focused on recovering neglected histories. Pam Taylor's "Women Domestic Servants 1919–1939" (No. 40 in the series, 1976) drew on extant historical research, "[p]ublished autobiographies, accounts written specially for me and (the largest proportion) oral evidence gleaned in fairly long interviews with 12 women in 1972" (1). Taylor's paper was revised and published with some other case studies in the center's *Working-Class Culture: Studies in History and Theory* (1979), edited by John Clarke, Chas Critcher, and Richard Johnson. Other History Series papers, such as Richard Johnson's "Peculiarities of the English Route: Barrington Moore, Perry Anderson and English Social Development" (No. 26, 1975), functioned as book reviews that illuminated theoretical approaches, terms, and models of explanation as well as specific historical developments. Still other History Series contributions, such as Gregor McLennan's "'Ideology' and 'Consciousness': Some Problems in Marxist Historiography" (No. 45, 1976), were even more explicitly theoretical throughout. McLennan compared economist, culturalist, and structuralist concepts of ideology and then offered a critique of historians' work that he maintained employed these concepts. History Series papers, such as Johnson's and McLennan's, demonstrate the pedagogical commitment of both graduate students and faculty to define, apply, and criticize theoretical concepts as straightforwardly as possible.

These stenciled papers were written and published at the University of Birmingham, which also housed a history department that featured noted historians such as Rodney Hilton and Dorothy Thompson—both were members, along with Edward Thompson, of the Communist Party Historians Group in the early postwar years. They believed in social and labor history as it had been practiced. Johnson, appointed to the center in 1974, had a half-time appointment in history—his office was next to Dorothy Thompson's.[28] As Johnson notes in his 1975 paper, he first gave it as a talk to the Social History Graduate Seminar in the School of History at Birmingham and later at the Theory Seminar at the center. "Criticisms and suggestions at both sessions," he added without detail, "were very useful (as well as being very different!)" (31). Johnson's 1974 presentations contained both praise and criticism of Edward Thompson. Considering Johnson's assessment of Thompson's "Peculiarities of the English" as "a fascinating essay and a formidable polemic [that] is not always addressed to the most important issues" (19), the question may arise: How might such double-edged evaluations have been received in-house?[29]

Papers such as McLennan's "'Ideology' and 'Consciousness'" mounted assaults on the work of Thompson and the "tradition" that shaped him that were often as cocksure in tone as they were daring in ideas. How might the Birmingham historians have discussed McLennan's epistemological critique—dismissal—of "the methodology of 'labour history' or 'history from below,'" or his assertion that "it is empirically clear that the existence of a substantial body of trade union or working-class history by no means produces a systematic Marxist history" (4)? And how might they have responded to McLennan's comparison of "younger" (2) Marxist historians, such as Gareth Stedman Jones and James Hinton, who are theoretically aware—that is, they show the influence of Althusser and Gramsci—to E. P. Thompson, whom he accused of using "literary sources" in place of "analytical argument" (5) and of being naive about the constructedness of "experience" (6)? The Birmingham Althusserian turn (2), in other words, was one that hit home for Dorothy Thompson, Edward Thompson, and some of their longtime colleagues.[30]

The Birmingham Centre's ambitious, sophisticated, and significant volume of essays, *Making Histories: Studies in History-Writing and Politics* (1982), edited by Richard Johnson, Gregor McLennan, Bill Schwarz, and David Sutton, should be read, especially with Richard Johnson's "Culture and the Historians" (1979) in the center's *Working-Class Culture,* to get a sense of how the Birmingham critics were reenvisioning "cultural studies" historical practice. In these writings several center faculty and student historians tried both to make visible the theoretical assumptions of British socialist historians from the early twentieth century, the era of Sidney and Beatrice Webb, and to historicize and develop the political implications of these historians' theoretical premises. Johnson's long essay "Reading for the Best Marx: History-Writing and Historical Abstraction" returns to Karl Marx's writings as examples of cultural studies history writing. Contributors also explore the politics of history production outside the academy (museums, advertising, film, television, theater) that helps form—or mystify—"popular memory" and discuss radical efforts to intervene in the making of those nonacademic histories.

As the editors of *Making Histories* framed it, a central aim was to create a flexible synthesis, one not constrained by the rigid (in their view) history versus theory battles of the 1970s: "The opposition between Althusser and Thompson [is] too stark and unproductive. The relation between theory and history is intrinsically uneven and difficult to finalize. Indeed the very distinction is ultimately hard to sustain" (9). Here again their commitment was pedagogical: to abstract in order to make history writing, historical consciousness, and political awareness more, not less, accessible to students and readers. Sometimes this meant the introduction and use of theoretical language to describe, analyze, and debate relationships, formations, and conflicts that would be less easy, or perhaps impossible, to grasp with quotidian commonsensical language.

The editors also elaborated on Stuart Hall's History Workshop critique of some historians' often tacit, perhaps even sacred, working premise about history writing's emancipatory payoff: not just that history writing is political, but that it is radical politics unto itself. "It is important," they admonished, "to be realistic about the political impact of history writing. Historical research and publication is necessarily slow. Its typical finished products—the book, the essay, the rejoinder—are the results of a painstaking process. Its audience, as it is constituted at the moment, is relatively small. There does exist a danger of *over*politicizing the intentions and effects of historical study. . . . [A] faith in the relevance of history can invite the belief that it is closer to real struggles, to real people—that the study of history spontaneously generates its own democratic politics" (9). The writing of history cannot liberate those in the past from the mystifications, interests, and contradictions that oppressed or bamboozled them. Histories of past struggles, conflicts, contradictions, dominations, and resistances must be written "in order to create a politics for the present" (8). And heeding this charge, it would be rewarding to study and teach the history of history writing that has helped change the course of history—not just prevailing intellectual trends within the academy, but the formation of popular opinion, the passing of legislation, the rendering of judicial decisions, the establishment of social movements—and to learn from and be inspired by this.

For all the achievements made by these conceptually explicit volumes, much of the work—not all of it—seems fixed in the theoretical mode: Birmingham cultural studies history is mainly writing about the writing of history and history writers. A more voluminous archive of theoretical engagements and historical case studies that contributes to an appreciation of the possibilities of cultural studies history can be found in the issues of *History Workshop Journal* (1976–). The debates and contributions published in this source and others in Britain—for instance, *New Left Review*—suggest that many members of the (radical) history profession in Britain, the United States, and elsewhere dealt with, argued about, and worked through concerns by no means unique to Birmingham's "cultural studies." A great deal of important theoretical and interdisciplinary work vital to the development of cultural studies lies outside the sphere of that which is conventionally designated, celebrated (or hyped), and consumed as official "cultural studies." Here I will discuss the first issue of *History Workshop Journal*, review some of Raphael Samuel's writings about theory, and sketch some theoretical directions the journal took.

The journal grew out of ten years of History Workshops—a "loose coalition of worker-historians and full-time socialist researchers" that originated at Ruskin College, Oxford. Ruskin, which employed Samuel as a tutor, was a "trade union college" founded, in Samuel's words, "as an attack on the examination system, and the humiliations which it imposed on adult students."[31] The workshops fostered collaborative research and published members' findings in thirteen pamphlets from 1966 to 1974, much as the Birmingham Centre did. This similarity is not all that surprising when one considers how closely Samuel and Hall worked together at Oxford in the "first" New Left.[32] In addition to organizing workshops and publishing the journal, the History Workshop collectives have sponsored or edited innovative anthologies of cultural, social, labor, gender, family, and intellectual history.[33]

The inaugural issue featured three important editorials. The first, by "the Editorial Collective," enunciated several crucial commitments: to publish clearly written, accessible, and "relevant" history that would be for the "ordinary" as well as professional community; to promote history writing that would function as a critical tool for understanding the present (an emphasis that Samuel elsewhere traced back to Marc Bloch's *The Historian's Craft* [1941], finished shortly before the author, a member of the French Resistance, was captured and executed by the Nazis); to resist the current academic fragmentation of history into subdisciplines; to expand the scope of history to neglected areas of social life; to use the journal as an organizing center for the formation of groups and the publicizing of meetings and events; and to make the theoretical presuppositions of history writing explicit and subject to debate.[34] Sally Alexander and Anna Davin's "Feminist History" editorial observed that social, labor, and political history had excluded considerations of women and that this resulted not only in too narrow a notion of history, politics, culture, and social agents, but also in a theoretically impoverished history that chronicled "the appearance of the world" without effectively scrutinizing its "fundamental order." Women had to be more than "tagged on" to history; their formation and the relations in which they were positioned and positioned themselves had to be "integrated into the overall understanding of a society."[35] The journal of socialist historians eventually changed its single adjectived subtitle to: *A Journal of Socialist and Feminist Historians.* Samuel's and Stedman Jones's "Sociology and History" editorial, which lauded the theoretical self-reflexivity of sociology, argued that history needed to become more expansively sociological in scope and more overtly theoretical in its discussions and debates.[36]

In the 1978 issue that featured Johnson's critique of Thompson and Genovese, Samuel contributed an insightful and controversial editorial on "History and Theory," a revision of which appeared three years later in *People's History and Socialist Theory* (1981). His editorial preface to this classic volume, "People's History," attributed the growing national interest in the field of history to "the vitality of social history journals—*Past and Present, History Workshop, Oral History,* and *Social History,*" "the regional labor history societies," "the labor and socialist press," and to "the large amount of material appearing in the form of cultural studies."[37] (In fact, this volume published Stuart Hall's groundbreaking essay, "Notes on Deconstructing 'The Popular'" along with Peter Burke's "The 'Discovery' of Popular Culture" in a section titled, "Cultural Studies.") Samuel's "Afterword: History Workshop, 1966–80" recalled the workshop's early phase in which its members "did not problematise Marxism—in 1966 there was rather little explicit Marxism in this country"—but did attempt, as "militant materialists," to "reestablish contact between Marxist thought and the reality it purported to address." He restated the workshop's commitment to clarity and to a readership including but also reaching beyond members of the academy: this meant "never taking a particular set of references for granted, explaining our terms, and attempting to create more open and accessible forms of historical dialogue," a practice that he contrasted with the new "university-based Marxism which makes little attempt to translate its work into a language which might be accessible to a larger socialist public."[38]

Samuel's "History and Theory" introduction also took new theoretical developments seriously. Samuel, like others, profiled historians as antitheoretical.[39] But he did so in a subtle way that presented their wariness as an intellectually sensible response based on their practice: they "are never so happy as when questioning received opinions, or multiplying exceptions to the rule" (xl). The understated point is that a historical practice that focuses on the analysis of particular events, agents, structures, and relations may have every reason to be distrustful of abstractions that may not help explain, name, or model a range of events, agents, structures, and relations. That is, an awareness of multiplicity or particularity can and should complicate any overconfident formulation of abstractions. He also began to historicize the historians' antitheoretical posture as an ideological response to Cold War pressures and the "witch hunt": mainstream historians professionalized themselves and celebrated "methodological individualism," while radical historians "tried to legitimise their work by removing theoretical prolegomena, softening Marxist terminology, and embodying their work in the form expected of scholarly monographs" (xli).[40]

Samuel observed that when the theoretical wave hit historians in the 1970s, there was yet another round of muting, though different from the early Cold

War version: the theoretical preoccupation with structures and victims—social construction theory as social subjection theory—muted the presence of agents and struggle in the new approaches. Although there was no lack of blatant contradictions to study, Althusserian theory, influenced by Sigmund Freud as well as Marx, assigned overwhelming hermeneutic and narrative significance to subtextual matters pertaining to the decoding of a social unconscious, an idea creatively developed by Pierre Macherey, Fredric Jameson, Pierre Bourdieu, and others (xliii). Theorists sometimes did so in "fashionable" (xliii) language, he argued, that seemed labyrinthine and hyperprofessional to a larger (socialist) audience of readers—as if these theorists wanted to evade the development of actual political organization and encode theory, especially subtextual inter-pretation, *as* politics.

Nonetheless, Samuel wrote, there were ideas contributed by the new theo-reticism that were "usable" (xliii), politically and historically: not only the idea that the historian's "explanatory" apparatus (xlix) should be displayed and debated, but the idea that the historian is an agent, an artificer, who in-escapably fabricates the "totality" or "false unity" he or she seeks to describe by using representation selectively to make historical or past representations into a product called history. "Periodisation, however convincing," Samuel admitted, "is always arbitrary; detail, however 'immediate,' is necessarily partial; while the choice of problematic is trimmed, in greater or lesser degree, to what the frame of reference will accommodate" (xliv). He countered these epistemological limitations with a pep talk, and in doing so perhaps allocated too much credit to the Hindess and Hirst approach: "If theory persuaded socialist historians to give up the ambition to comprehend the real world on the ground that the effort was epistemologically disreputable, the only effect will be to leave the terrain to the undisputed possession of those with no such qualms" (xlix).

Instead Samuel might further have developed an approach he heartily rec-ommended in his piece—not just to theorize history, but to historicize theory. "History and theory," he advised, "must be a two-way affair" (li). This "two-way affair" was precisely what Alexander and Davin endorsed in their inaugural editorial on "Feminist History": by working out the theoretical, historical, and political importance of both gender and family formation (their complex relational and structural social significance), one will see more aspects of a "social totality" than ever before, and, paradoxically, having learned these les-sons, newly recognize the difficulty—the impossibility—of imagining "total-ity." It was the social movements of the 1960s and 1970s, such as the feminist movement, and not simply Althusserian theorizing about representation, that made the idea of historical "totality" into an obvious epistemological problem, a problem that highlighted the artifice of a too narrow and uncomplex history. If Samuel had been more historically concrete in his analysis of why Althusserian critiques of history—as a necessarily circumscribed representation or narrative construction—made political sense to some, particularly younger, historians in this period, he might have argued the following: because the theoretical attacks on the epistemological limitations of imagining a social "totality" were rooted in real historical and political problems that had hitherto been too invisible to certain groups, even political groups like British Marxists, then the new political challenge for historians is not really how to keep from feeling immobile in the face of epistemological constraints made philosophically apparent, but rather how, with greater energy and commitment than ever, to best write new histories to help make these groups, these movements, and the contradictions affecting them more visible, compelling, and comprehensible to social agents in schools, factories, offices, homes, and Parliament.

Stuart Hall moved in the direction of historicizing cultural studies in this way at the 1990 Illinois conference, when he described the feminist movement and the antiracist movement as "exterior forces" breaking "in through the window" of cultural studies. History and its agents broke through these Birmingham windows and reformed theory. As Hall admits, the increasingly de-centered "center" had to contend with this invasive history of social movements, often more so than some people involved with the center were ideologically disposed to do. "As a thief in the night," Hall said, "[the feminist movement] broke in; interrupted, made unseemly noise, seized the time, crapped on the table of cultural studies."[41] But this history was breaking through windows in many sites of various sorts in Britain, the United States, and elsewhere not only during but long before this "cultural studies" cataclysm, and was compelling, even forcing, the development and consideration of new theory writing, history writing, law writing, medical writing, and so on. Historical agents who operated in many social arenas in many geographical areas collectively, and in most cases unknowingly, revised what counted as "the cultural" and "the political" in "cultural studies."

In his 1990 *History Workshop Journal* obituary of C. L. R. James, Stuart Hall, in sketching James's critical thinking, showed the theoretical usefulness of historical or "conjunctural" thinking. James, he observed admiringly, "wrote of literary giants like Shakespeare and Aeschylus as figures whose 'genius' with language was created by the tumultuous historical upheavals in the conjunctures in which they were writing."[42] Hall puts the historically Romantic and ideologically individualizing category of "genius" in quotation marks not because he denies the brilliance of certain intellectual achievers or their achievements, but because, like James, he understands intellectual and artistic work as an ineluctably social practice that is part of the historical process (Aeschylus and Shakespeare could not have thought of themselves as "geniuses" since the material and ideological conditions that produced that category would not exist for many years). The Birmingham Centre had a certain "cultural studies" "genius" during the 1970s. Much of its published work was written by graduate students. But this "genius," like the works of Aeschylus and Shakespeare, was partly "created by the tumultuous upheavals in the conjunctures in which" the center developed its sometimes heavily embattled intellectual practice. The same must be said of the "genius" of *History Workshop Journal:* Jeffrey Weeks's "Foucault for Historians" (1982), Eric Foner's "Why Is There No Socialism in the United States?" (1984), Terry Lovell's "Knowable Pasts, Imaginable Futures" (1989), Raphael Samuel's "Philosophy Teaching by Example: Past and Present in Raymond Williams" (1989), and his two-part "Reading the Signs" (1991, 1992) are just a few pieces thoroughly hit by late twentieth-century social changes that tell readers much about the possibilities of history, socialist theory, and cultural studies.

The United States and Cultural Studies

History hit American history writing too.[43] In a 1973 interview Eric Foner, then a young American radical historian, framed history as "a political subject . . . a fact which many historians do not, I think, want to acknowledge." Historical thinking and writing, he insisted, are invariably conditioned by the present and must themselves be historicized: "History is written with one eye on the past and one eye on the present. . . . Changing interpretations mirror the changing political nature of society" (44). To illustrate this he observed that as African Americans, Latinos and Latinas, feminists, immigrant Catholics, and other politically, socially, culturally, and economically disempowered groups forge a sense of political identity and interests and fight for social power, they win roles in the narrative of "history" (44). Foner identified his radical writing and teaching of history as a critical practice attentive to contradiction, oppression, resistance, and ideology. He also saw it as a productive practice—a necessary construction of significance, meaning, and narrative. Foner's pedagogical aim, to teach students "how to think critically" (44), was not narrowly professional. Furthermore, he underscored that history, especially a history of radical protest movements, can inform the strategies of student antiwar protestors: "Radical movements ... [are] cut off from the working class; whereas previous move-ments had a base in sections of the working class.... Radicalism has never succeeded in a big way in America, but there were times when radical move-ments had a lot more massive support than they do now" (43). Indeed, many American radical historians learned more from what had recently happened in Birmingham and Selma, Alabama, than in Birmingham, England.

In his reminiscences about his undergraduate stint at Yale in the mid- and late 1960s, Gerald Bruck overgeneralized, "Ours was the first generation since the abolitionists' to grow up with some sense of the racist burden of American history."[44] The freshman found himself moved by the moment to write an on-the-scene report for the *Yale Daily News* on the civil rights protest march from Selma to Montgomery, Alabama, in 1965. In Alabama he encountered "businessmen, officials, community leaders, well-dressed men who didn't look much different from our fathers [but who] behaved with a viciousness I would never have believed at second hand," and in Jackson, Mississippi, he saw "blacks ... scoot at my approach, from the sidewalk to the gutter." But he also witnessed how "a motley crowd's passive resistance worked a kind of magic in the world. It was as if a crack was opening in reality, and the adrenalin of all our favorite songs could rule the future." At the same time he observed "racial" (49) tensions in the movement among different groups.

Back on campus, Bruck realized that if he wanted to explain and grasp the significance of what he had witnessed he would have to study history: "Staughton Lynd admitted me to his survey of Southern history" (50). Lynd was a radical historian, son of the famous sociologist Robert Lynd and interdisciplinary scholar Helen Merrell Lynd, coauthors of *Middletown: A Study in Contemporary American Culture* (1929), a classic study of the social experience of everyday life and conscious-ness in middle America. Lynd spent the first three years of his academic career teaching at Spelman College, the noted black women's college in Atlanta, Georgia, and served as director of the Freedom Schools in the 1964 Mississippi Summer Project.[45] Bruck describes him: "He argued the existence of a moral code to which everyone everywhere was accountable.... Demands of the state could not dimin-ish personal responsibility" (50). Lynd trespassed beyond the official boundaries of history and this inspired students: "One of his extracurricular preoccupations was encouraging the poor and illiterate to record their stories, filling a perennial gap in the primary sources for future historians" (50). His students learned to see themselves as social agents and came to understand the practice of history as being tied to the future of a larger community.

Soon "Assistant Professor Lynd" would go to Hanoi, North Vietnam, as part of an unofficial American peace mission of radicals (including historian

Herbert Aptheker and Tom Hayden of the Students for a Democratic Society), and he was in the first group of academics and others to protest the war in front of the Pentagon. He then contended with nonrenewal at Yale, despite having written several books. On relocating to Chicago, as Lynd tells it, he "was offered a job by the history departments at five Chicago-area institutions (Northern Illinois University, University of Illinois Circle Campus, Roosevelt University, Loyola University, and Chicago State College), only to have appointments vetoed by the five administrations."[46]

Bruck wound up writing his senior thesis with the distinguished historian C. Vann Woodward, a "patient and forgiving man" (55). Woodward achieved great fame for his role in assisting the National Association for the Advancement of Colored People (NAACP) with historical evidence for their landmark case against school segregation, *Brown v. Board of Education* (1954), and soon after published his historical critique in *The Strange Career of Jim Crow* (1955), which Martin Luther King, Jr. nominated "the Bible of the civil rights movement."[47] Yet, according to Bruck, Woodward had done this work for the NAACP "reluctantly and refused credit for his role. He wanted it understood that he would never compromise the web of curiosity and suspicion that partly formed his craft for the sake of serving the present. Not on purpose, anyway." One day Woodward asked Bruck, "Why study history?" Bruck, sounding like the dismissed Lynd, replied, "Well, to show where we've gone wrong, to find the reasons beneath it, to help keep it from happening again." Woodward retorted, "Nonsense." Bruck then queried Woodward why he studied history. Woodward asserted, "Because I like to" (55).[48]

Lynd wrote that he studied history partly because he was intrigued by the writings of Marc Bloch and R. G. Collingwood on historical practice, by the work of the radical American historian of the early Republic Charles Beard, and by the contributions of Progressive historians like Carl Becker. Mainly his interest was driven by contemporary pressures: "As one considerably alienated from America's present, I wanted to know if there were men in the American past in whom I could believe."[49] His experience teaching at a black college in the South propelled him to rethink his own Revolutionary era research, conducted under the spell of Beard and Becker: he, like them, "had tacitly assumed that white artisans and tenant farmers were the most exploited Americans of the late eighteenth century, overlooking the one fifth of the nation which was in chains."[50] Lynd's participation in the civil rights movement increasingly pushed him to reject the idea that the historian serves as an ostensibly noninvolved, "objective" observer. He accepted instead the dictum of Karl Marx, substituting historians for Marx's philosophers: "The historians have interpreted the world; the thing, however, is to change it."[51] His historical and pedagogical practice entailed viewing the historian as playing a civic role in the formation of a critical and self-critical citizenry.

Lynd, as did his father and mother, and E. P. Thompson, came to stress agency—"human energy and striving"—in historical accounts and posed the question and the challenge: "How would the work of the historian be different, if man's existential freedom to choose became the historian's point of departure?"[52] This concern developed into an increasing wish to use history in numerous ways: Lynd advocated not only that historians take the "events of [their] own lifetime" as the subject matter of historical practice (also a "contemporary cultural studies" concern), but that they probe the "past as a source for forgotten [social and political] alternatives," and, based on this investigation, that they propose "alternative scenarios for the future" (a pragmatic political purpose articulated as boldly as any similar statements I have read in "cultural studies" work).[53] Behind this historical search was an American New Left question that also gripped British New Left intellectuals such as Thompson, Williams, and Hall, especially after the disillusioning Soviet admission of Stalinist atrocities and the Soviet invasion of Hungary in 1956: "[N]ew societies [not based on private property] may not be more humane than those they replace. Still, the interesting question of our time will appear to future historians as that one—namely, Is a humane socialism possible?"[54]

Lynd regarded Thompson as "the most influential historian writing in the English language during the second half of this century."[55] He linked Thompson's freedom of thought to the fact that he spent most of his life as a historian-activist writing on the fringes of or altogether outside the academy.[56] Lynd embraced several aspects of Thompson's project: Thompson's critique of a theoreticist brand of Marxism that (quoting Thompson) "'allows the aspirant academic to engage in harmless revolutionary psychodrama, while at the same time pursuing a reputable and conventional intellectual career'"; his unswerving belief that (in Lynd's words) "the working class mattered, not because it was destined to overthrow capitalism, but because it kept alive among the Satanic Mills an ethic of mutuality that prefigured a better society"; and his efforts to build a "political culture" with a range of social groups through his writing and lecturing.[57]

Yet, in his one conversation with Thompson, at Genovese's New York apartment in 1966, Lynd found himself in fundamental disagreement with Thompson's contention that one cannot be "doing history" and "doing politics" at once. "Surely," Lynd wrote, "[this premise] falls short of what Marx called a unity of theory and practice. I wonder if the difficulty Thompson found in connecting theory and practice was related to something else: that the focus of his scholarly inquiry shifted further and further back in time, from William Morris (late nineteenth century), to the formation of the English working class (early nineteenth century), to studies in seventeenth- and eighteenth-century popular culture."[58] What Lynd did not quite verbalize, but only hint, was that politically conscious history writing can serve as a temporary refuge from the present rather than a practice to grasp and change it. Still, he may have underestimated Thompson's sophistication and motive. Reading Thomas McGrath's poetry, Thompson stepped back from his American friend's occasional wistful and perhaps wishful Cold War tendency to focus on if not quite romanticize the "'unexploited forces'" of the "unrealised past" (327). Thompson warned against "fall[ing] back on the incantation of the past ... in place of a more arduous resolution."[59]

Howard Zinn, like Lynd, his peer and former colleague at Spelman, is a prominent activist-historian who writes, if not historical "cultural studies," then a critically explicit form of historical social change studies or historical protest studies.[60] He rejects "safe history" and repudiates history writing conceived as "private enterprise."[61] Zinn has been an organizer of shipyard workers, a civil rights activist, a playwright, and principally a professional historian.[62] One of his favorite quotations is George Orwell's "Who controls the past controls the future."[63]

Zinn's reminiscences of his seven-year stretch at Spelman (1956–63) exhibit his self-historicizing efforts to integrate narratives of his activities with students, accounts of larger historical transformations in race relations taking shape, and strategic insights into how to foster progressive social change. Much of his Columbia graduate school research had focused on class, but American issues of race had been crashing through his windows years before he moved to Spelman. Zinn writes of attending a Paul Robeson and Pete Seeger concert in Peekskill, New York, in 1949, and trying to leave in the thick of a racist crowd: "My wife [six months pregnant] and daughter crouched down in the front seat. A fusillade of rocks smashed every window in the car.... A rock smashed the head of a young woman who was riding with us, fracturing her skull."[64]

At Spelman Zinn was radicalized in new ways, partly by the racist and antiracist whites he met (because of his employment he was unable to find an apartment off campus), partly by the conservative black administration, partly by the students whose urge for activism was being awakened by the emerging civil rights protests. His students, including Alice Walker, taught him "that it's easy to mistake silence for acceptance."[65] On numerous occasions

Zinn helped his students organize protests. The first was a "modest campaign to desegregate Atlanta's libraries"—his students kept requesting copies of the *Constitution* and the *Declaration of Independence* in whites-only libraries. He learned that "the tiniest acts of protest in which we engage may become the invisible roots of social change."[66] Legal reforms such as the Voting Rights Act that made southern politicians take blacks more seriously and bus desegregation legislation do prompt people to change and discard "long-held habits."[67] Zinn's work shows that history writing can produce casebooks—documenting the fact that organized resistance happened and analyzing its successes and downfalls—which can serve as resource books, "how to" books of strategies.[68] His vigor in encouraging his students to overthrow such habits led to his dismissal as a tenured professor in 1963 (he was then hired by Boston University to teach political science; Staughton Lynd quit his post at Spelman in protest and was hired by Yale).

Zinn, like his friend Lynd, writes history-as-overt-critique, best exemplified perhaps in his revisionist bestseller, *A People's History of the United States* (1980), and best conceptualized in his *Politics of History* (1970). One of Zinn's most famous essays, "Marxism and the New Left" (1968), is both a defense of theory (harking back to the intellectual gains of the Old Left, which sometimes became too rigid and theoreticist rather than effectively activist) and a defense of New Left grassroots pragmatism (which nonetheless, he pleaded, could benefit from "both testing and reworking theory"). Zinn made a case for dialectical, historical thinking: "A dialectical approach, in the Marxian sense, suggests that we evaluate a situation not as fixed but in motion, and that this evaluation affects that motion. Dialectical materialism asks awareness that we are creatures of limited vision, ocularly and intellectually, and therefore must not assume that we see or perceive everything—that conflicting tendencies often lie beneath the surface of events."[69] Like the British cultural studies historians of the 1970s, Zinn has for several decades been keenly cognizant that history is produced in several mass-cultural spheres—not just schools—and that its hegemonic power must be contested in diverse sites. And like the theoretically astute British cultural studies historians, Zinn is well aware that history writing is a fabrication, an insight that has long mobilized rather than immobilized him. Objectivity, he holds, is neither "possible" nor "desirable": "It's not possible because all history is a selection out of an infinite number of facts.... It's already biased in the direction of whatever you, as the selector of this information, think people should know."[70]

Jessie Lemisch, like Lynd and Zinn, is part of a heterogeneous contingent of New Left radical and activist historians trained during the 1950s to early 1960s period. Like Lynd and Zinn, he was fired for protest activity—antiwar work at the University of Chicago in the mid-1960s. He had theoretical concerns similar to theirs. Much of his early historical work contributed to a "bottom up" history of the American Revolutionary period. He acknowledged the influence of work by Thompson and Eric Hobsbawm on "subpolitical" or "prepolitical" peasant or working-class movements.[71] In 1969 Lemisch delivered a controversial lecture at the American Historical Association on "objectivity" and "politics" in the profession, a lecture that, in its extended form, the American Historical Association refused to publish—Lemisch reveled in naming names of powerful "objective" historians. An enlarged version of this piece, which had become an underground classic among radical historians in its unpublished form, was finally published by a small Canadian press: *On Active Service in War and Peace: Politics and Ideology in the American Historical Profession* (1975).[72]

In this theoretically conscious monograph, Lemisch takes conservative and liberal historians' antiradical fulminations against "present-mindedness" and "political activism" in history writing and turns their charges on them. Lemisch reviews history writing, historians' professional speeches, and historians' media statements to demonstrate that many celebrated conservative and liberal historians deployed their own "present-mindedness" and "political activism" on behalf of America's Cold War military, political, economic, and cultural policies, and in support of an idea of degraded "human nature" that would legitimate such repressive policies (54). Doing so he contributed to the historical understanding of American history writing as ideological and, more specifically, he expanded the concept of "the political" to include political history writing that hid under the cloak of "objectivity." "We exist," Lemisch concluded defiantly, referring to radicals, "and people like us have existed throughout history, and we will simply not allow you the luxury of continuing to call yourselves politically neutral while you exclude all of this from your history.... You cannot fire us for activism without having your own activism exposed. You cannot call apologetics 'excellence' without expecting the most rigorous and aggressive of scholarly replies" (117). Lemisch did not write what Zinn calls "safe history."

Whether or not Foner, Lynd, Zinn, and Lemisch discussed concepts like relative autonomy, overdetermination, and ideological state apparatuses in their writing and teaching in the 1960s and early 1970s, their concerns were political and theoretical in ways that can be recognized in the work of the British "cultural studies" historians of the 1970s and early 1980s. These American New Left–era historians responded to some of the same Cold War social transformations that galvanized the British New Left and provided the intellectual and social foundation for the making of "cultural studies."[73]

Another member of this New Left generation of historians, Eugene Geno-vese, who was paired with E. P. Thompson in many of the *History Workshop* debates, used Gramsci's concept of hegemony in his history writing on slav-ery before the Birmingham Centre began exploring the 1971 translation of Gramsci's *Prison Notebooks*. Genovese defined hegemony very basically as "the seeming spontaneous loyalty that a ruling class evokes from the masses through its cultural position and its ability to promote its own world view as the general will."[74] As we will see, for Genovese the keywords in this working definition are "cultural position."

Richard Johnson cast, and partly caricatured, Genovese and Thompson as "theoretical twins" in his 1978 *History Workshop* critique: "*Roll Jordan Roll* [1974]" (surely to date Genovese's masterpiece) is a kind of *Making* of the black nation, very clearly influenced by Thompson's early work with the same epic scope, the same emotional commitment to its main object—the culture of the slaves—and . . . the same theoretical and epistemological position." He also acknowledged: "Thompson's later work . . . seems to owe something to Genovese's early discovery and use of Gramscian concepts in understanding the relations of master to slaves. 'Hegemony,' in the shape of the slaveholders' paternalism, is the main organising idea of *Roll Jordan Roll*, but it is important in Genovese's history as early as *The Political Economy of Slavery* [1965]" (82). Johnson pointed out that Genovese had responded to criticisms, similar to those launched against Thompson, in the American journal *Radical History Review* (1977) (83). It was Genovese's theoretical innovations, not only his pathbreaking empirical recovery of lost histories, that attracted the notice of cultural studies critics, historians, and American studies scholars.

Genovese had read parts of Gramsci's untranslated works as well as the first slim English translation by the American radical Carl Marzani, *The Open Marxism of Antonio Gramsci* (1957), and Gywn Williams's classic es-say "Gramsci's Concept of *Egemonia*" (1960). His extended discussion of the importance of Gramsci to the American New Left appeared as a review essay in the University of Wisconsin–based journal that William Appleman Wil-liams helped sponsor in 1959, *Studies on the Left*.[75] The intellectual, political, and strategic issues that Genovese's "On Antonio Gramsci" (1967) broaches resonate with later writings by Raymond Williams and Stuart Hall on Gramsci. Genovese's arguments are more sociologically grounded, pedagogically clear (especially when compared with Williams's brilliant but at times turgid com-mentary), self-historicizing, and politically wide ranging.[76]

Among the issues he raises about Gramsci's concepts, three are particularly seminal. First, Genovese asserts the importance of theory not only for scholarly work, but for political work directed toward the emancipatory transformation of America. Matters that have concerned him in his historical practice—causality, agency, culture—are identical to those that preoccupy his political thinking. Gramsci appeals to Genovese—in his roles as a historian and a theorist of social change—because Gramsci's work emphasizes the causal significance of culture (398) and, while never ignoring "bread-and-butter" economic pressures that can help trigger social transformation, runs counter to the "mechanism and determinism of official American Marxism" (420). Genovese uses Gramsci to underscore the point that revolution does not happen automatically as a result of severe economic and/or political crises.

Second, Genovese writes, perhaps somewhat patronizingly, that workers must be educated to understand that they are fighting not solely for their own class interests, but for a more egalitarian cultural, economic, and political production of life and relations. Therefore a "superior world order" must be conceptualized so that people will no longer give their "consent" to the old "irrational" (dis)order (400). "The cultural front" will assist people critically so that they can articulate their "discomfort or oppression" and go on to imagine a better future (407).

Third, the problem with initiating any of the social changes in consciousness that Gramsci has in mind in the United States is that there is no effective party that can organize and inspire "the cultural front." The absence of a viable party can breed symptoms in radicals such as theoreticism or abstractionism: "Until socialists have a party within which to test their doctrines, the doctrines must remain abstract and undeveloped. Until we have an organization capable of demonstrating that we can live and work as well as think in ways foreshadowing a better society, there is no reason for any skeptic ... to believe us" (420–21). Finally, Genovese sees this party predicament historically in the context of the emerging New Left, a heterogeneous movement that he both acclaims and criticizes: "The New Left has been primarily a moral rather than political (in the narrow sense of the word) movement.... Those who have criticized them from a Marxist viewpoint have failed to impress them with the argument for a new party because that demand has been advanced as a political-administrative solution to what seems to them, quite correctly, to be a moral and broadly social problem" (419–20). Gramsci is the theorist who speaks to the concerns of the New Left, according to Genovese, because Gramsci, like many members of the diverse New Left, grasps that political struggle is necessarily also a cultural struggle which must be waged in many spheres of socially organized life.

Thus if Genovese, at this stage in his thinking, can be dubbed a "culturalist," he is a Gramscian cultural frontist who insists on keeping "bread-and-butter" issues and the imperative for political organization—party organization, not only social movement organization—on the agenda. Genovese's essay offers some indication of how his historical cultural studies serve as resources for strategic contemporary political studies. He entertained a certain ambivalence about a tendency among some historians on the multifaceted New Left to "confuse the two roles" of "ideologue" and "historian," and indeed lambasted Staughton Lynd for doing this. But the contemporary political relevance of Genovese's own Gramscian-influenced historical critique of the determinist concept of class interests—a determinist reading that he claimed Lynd recycled in his work—is manifest: "Today, the best radical scholars agree that such forms of vulgar Marxism should be replaced with serious research on the nature and role of social classes, considered not only as representative of specific material interests but as complexes of goals, cultural assumptions, and social and psychological relationships. In this way, these scholars are moving from a concern with mechanistic details to the mainsprings of social and political behavior."[77]

Radical History Review (1974–), like its British counterpart *History Workshop Journal* (founded two years later), is one of the richest resources for theoretical discussions about history. It was established by the mid-Atlantic historians organization (MARHO). Among other things, the journal provides provocative examples of the new cultural history that emerged in part out of intellectual history and social history and in part out of the cumulative effects of the larger historical social movements and transformations that shook up the New Lefts in Britain and the United States.

The two obituaries the journal published in 1997, commemorating the life and work of the exuberant Raphael Samuel, convey the strong intellectual, political, and comradely links between *Radical History Review* and *History Workshop*.[78] This bond was most evident perhaps in a special issue on *Marxism and History: The British Contribution* (1978–79). In the "Editors' Introduction" members of MARHO's Boston Collective acknowledged a deep debt: "Since the appearance of Edward Thompson's *The Making of the English Working Class* (1963), radical historians of the United States have drawn more heavily than ever before on the long tradition of Marxist scholarship in Britain—for theoretical inspiration, for methodological guidance, and, perhaps most important, for a model of the kind of engaged and critical socialist history we would like to establish on this side of the Atlantic." Yet the editors registered some intellectual reservations about their own enthusiasms worth contemplating: "But we have not yet thought enough about where to draw the line between constructive emulation and self-deluding mimicry. To what extent have we ignored the peculiarities of the English? How often do we ask British questions of non-British sources, and hear only British answers?" (3).[79]

The already distinguished young American editors of a *Special American Issue* (1986) of *History Workshop Journal*—Susan Porter Benson, Jane Caplan, Ellen Ross, and Sean Wilentz—were even more revealing in their discussion of their intellectual and political tie to the British radical historians. Explaining the struggle of modern American radical historians to do critical work, they cite "the chilling effect of McCarthyism" in the 1950s and hold that it "effectively wiped out almost all traces of radical inquiry among practicing historians"—a radical inquiry that was rekindled, they say, as a result of social movements in the 1960s. "Yet relatively few would-be revisionists had more than a passing familiarity with radical political theory of any kind. Thus the few radical spirits who, by dint of talent and persistence had succeeded in the academy, quickly became our own official (and unofficial) teachers. Among them were such diverse minds as Eugene Genovese, Herbert Gutman, Gerda Lerner, and William Appleman Williams." To redress this scarcity of informed radical historicism, the young historians "began to take an interest in kindred spirits abroad, especially in England and France where traditions of left historical thought were far better developed than here.... Often this led to further incursions into the classic writings of Marx, Gramsci, Adorno, and others."[80]

Hence young American radical historians, according to this narrative of adoption, looked to Britain to learn how to think politically and historically in complex ways. The United States, they regret, lacked the political culture that would have nurtured them in a similar manner. Yet during the Cold War era, U.S. radical critique had been fostered by Paul Baran and Paul Sweezy, Herbert Aptheker, Philip Foner, John Hope Franklin, Warren Susman, James Weinstein, David Montgomery, Gabriel Kolko, Victor Navasky, Harry Braverman, and others, and by journals such as *Studies on the Left, Socialist Review* (originally *Socialist Revolution*), *History and Theory, Telos, Radical America, Liberation, International Labor and Working-Class History, Feminist Studies,* and by older radical journals that weathered the early Cold War such as *Masses and Mainstream, politics, Monthly Review, Dissent,* and *Anvil and Student Partisan,* and by Left intellectuals such as C. Wright Mills, Dwight Macdonald, Paul Goodman, Harvey Swados, Herbert Marcuse, Hannah Arendt, Malcolm X, Angela Davis, Amiri Baraka, and Noam Chomsky.[81] In the late 1940s Irving Howe was in dialogue with Theodor Adorno on how to theorize mass culture; in the mid-1950s Carl Marzani was translating Gramsci (and establishing an important radical press); and in the early 1960s Hans Gerth (Mills's coauthor for two books) and Don Martindale were translating Walter Benjamin for *Studies on the Left.*[82] Not too bad for an American Intellectual Left.

Thompson's preface to Staughton Lynd's *Class Conflict, Slavery, and the Constitution* (1967) contributes an evaluation of U.S. radicalism and history writing that differs from the assessment in the *Special American Issue*.[83] Thompson expresses appreciation both for the "moral toughness, which comes from older Puritan timber" (ix) that strengthens Lynd the activist and for the insistence upon "essentials," the "discipline of context" (x), and the attentiveness to the "contradictoriness" of "culture" (xi) that inform the work of Lynd the historian. He contrasts Lynd's work with that of vulgar radical historians who fight and write with "blunt instruments and bandaged eyes," erase "every wart and wrinkle" from the "all-holy-common-people," and handle "historical problems as if they were settled theorems for which proof only was required" (xi). Thompson places Lynd in the frame of intellectual and political developments within American history writing. "Professor Lynd is one among a large, and growing, group of younger scholars who combine the old zest with a professional excellence and human maturity which are ridding the radical tradition of the bad intellectual habits into which it fell so often in the past. Those parts of the established professional ascendancy which are somewhat comfortable, somewhat fashionable, and somewhat conservative, are coming under a criticism very much more searching than anything to which they have been accustomed" (xii). These Americans are "unwriting other people's history" and as part of that enterprise they must both rehistoricize the history that has been written and the moments in which that history was written: "Seeing events, both as they occurred and as they were refracted with changing emphases, in the historical memory, enforces the realisation that as we argue about the past so also are we arguing about—and seeking to clarify—the mind of the present which is recovering the past" (xii).

What the American editors of the *Special American Issue* termed the "radical inquiry among practicing historians" that was dying out in the McCarthy era constituted a robust project for historian David Montgomery's collegiate circle. Montgomery, after World War II, studied at Swarthmore College. His education, like that of many veterans, was funded by the GI bill. "Our [seminar] discussions were oriented not simply toward understanding the world, but toward changing it, in contrast to the celebration of 'cultural freedom' in the 1950s, which favored minds that purred like finely tuned engines, while the gears that might connect them to popular struggles remained in neutral. We devoured books, stuffed many carbons into the typewriters on which we banged out papers late into the night, and argued incessantly about economic planning, civil rights, labor's new power and the Taft-Hartley Law, the United Nations, and the triumphs of the Chinese Red Army." By "us" Montgomery seems to mean both faculty and students: "Although no student then cringed before the authority of professors, to say the least, our instructors had just returned from government agencies that investigated the concentration of corporate power or administered economic controls. Capitalism, socialism, and the quest for the future that might borrow wisely from all existing systems were matters of immediate, practical concern to us."[84] That last sentence seems much like one that a student in a probing "cultural studies" seminar might write in the 1970s or today. Presumably many of those students and faculty still pursued their "radical inquiry," in some cases less publicly, even during the chilliest of the McCarthy Cold War years. During this freeze *Monthly Review* and *Dissent* were founded.

Some of the young American radical historians of the 1970s and 1980s responded to British radical history in the ways that American scholars from several fields—English, communications, sociology—have reacted to British cultural studies in the late 1980s and 1990s: as bearers of the real politics, the real theory, the real thing. Of course, if one is concerned with developing progressive history writing, then one should study the range of resources that have been and are currently available. Intellectual and professional connections between British and American radical scholars have been legion.[85] American social change studies historians and British "cultural studies" historians such as Thompson and Johnson have shown equal interest in studying how subordinated groups forged self-consciousness and resistance.

U.S. Historians and Cultural Studies

If any American historians worthy of the name had the impression that history writing was simply a window on the past rather than a "construction" whose organizing narratives change over time, then John Higham's classic essay "The Construction of American History" (1962) should have disabused them of such an illusion.[86] Since then Michel Foucault's syntheses of history and theory, Hayden White's historical critique of nineteenth- and twentieth-century genres of narrative in history writing, Dominick LaCapra's critiques of "totalizing" assumptions built into much history writing, Joan Scott's integration of feminist-poststructuralist theory and historical thinking, historical work published by American journals such as *Radical History Review* and *History and Theory*, and books and journals produced in other countries (a tiny portion of which I have discussed or merely alluded to above), are some of the intellectual sources that have prompted many contemporary American historians to grapple with political-theoretical questions in their research, writing, and teaching. Historians can be discriminating in their selection of theory. Hence Bryan Palmer's polemic, *Descent into Discourse: The Reification of Language and the Writing of Social History* (1990), which identifies itself as a poverty of discourse theory successor to Thompson's *Poverty of Theory,* is certainly not without its own theoretical predilections and complexity.[87]

It is no trade secret that historians can sell books to fairly large general audiences and succeed in having their books "adopted" in undergraduate courses in part by avoiding "jargon" (a consideration their publishers seldom let them forget). However, if one were to hazard a guess that many of the most intellectually exciting American historians do attempt to think critically about theory, sometimes theory that falls under the banner of "cultural studies," then the sixty-six-page "Symposium: Intellectual History in the Age of Cultural Studies" (1996), published in *Intellectual History Newsletter,* would lend support to this speculation.[88] Casey Blake, the journal's editor, invited "over seventy scholars in the fields of intellectual history, cultural history, and cultural studies" to contribute to the symposium, and to his "great surprise" about half accepted the challenge (3). The diverse responses shed light on the sometimes uncertain position of the intellectual historian. Is intellectual history, which has traditionally concentrated on the work of intellectuals (typically "dead white males"), in the process of being engulfed or rendered unfashionable by cultural history, the history of meaning, cultural studies? Or is the scope of this field being expanded and clarified in its dialogues with new theoretical and historical work on culture?[89] The symposium suggests that many of the history-and-theory debates that absorbed contributors to *History Workshop Journal* and *Radical History Review* in the late 1970s remain active in new versions.

Several contributors welcomed the cultural studies and poststructuralist stress on "antifoundationalism," which the historian Joyce Appleby described aptly as the "rigorous assertion of the ungivenness of the given" (5). Histories of the ideological making of what come to seem like "givens" tend to multiply the historical questions one brings to culture as a fabrication and tend to broaden one's understanding of the compass of "the historical." The literary historian Mary Kupiec Cayton further developed some implications of antifoundationalism for historical and political inquiry: "There is no truth in the positivist sense, only truths that make sense within a system of other cultural truths" (54). Thus the historian can investigate what Foucault termed histories of "truth" or "truth" production—skeptical histories that challenge the historian to try to step back self-reflexively from his or her "givens" or "knowledge" or aims and trace their historical production and perhaps also their collusion with systems of power.[90] This centering on culture as the human production of meaning, "truth," significance, and value complicates and relativizes the assignment of aesthetic value and moral value because hierarchy is desacralized as a construction, often a construction of the powerful, rather than taken for granted. As Appleby recognizes, a critical awareness of the production of values, categories, and hierarchies can be liberatory precisely because it opens the door to their dismantling, rearrangement, or redefinition.

Yet several symposium contributors contend that the implications of the political critique of the cultural production of meaning, significance, knowledge, truth, and value have created distortions that intellectual historians are well placed to expose. Martin Jay, for example, is critical of "Bourdieu, Foucault and Co.'s reduction of knowledge to power" (6). Is the production of all knowledge always relationally inflected by and thus molded by what Foucault abstracts as "power," as if power is an all-controlling force whose presence is always already wholly incursive?[91] A critical and epistemological "privileging" of the category of "the political" is itself a cultural production of significance and value that at times may conceivably reduce rather than expand one's perception of cultural relation, value, and achievement. Indeed, recently achievement and appreciation have not been very "cultural studies" words.[92] George Cotkin, like Jay, expresses reservations about the cultural studies focus on "domination": "Repulsion with the colonialist or hegemonic aspects of every text often seems to be the master key that unlocks all the doors of cultural studies" (11). Richard Wolin acknowledges the intellectual usefulness of following Gramsci in exploring how knowledge can be shaped by hegemony and of following Foucault in assessing how knowledge can be infused with power. Yet he protests, sounding like some of Robert Lynd's reviewers in 1939: "If ideas were only valuable in terms of their status in a [Gramscian] 'war of position,' then they certainly were not worth studying intrinsically or for their own sake.... As long as there are aspects of the 'will to knowledge' that transcend the 'will to power,' there will remain a place for intellectual history as an autonomous sphere of scholarship" (17, 18). The cultural studies politicized skepticism of "knowledge," especially "knowledge" produced by elites, Wolin claims, has tapped into an American "anti-intellectualism" (16).

What seems clear, then, is that some intellectual historians—who may be in basic agreement with cultural studies critics that social contradictions should be transformed through political practice and not be self-servingly evaded in one's consciousness and one's work—are at the same time wary of overestimating politics as the allegorical key that opens all aspects of and governs all questions brought to the historical explanation, textual interpretation, and intellectual evaluation of cultural phenomena, behavior, and relations. If the "privileging" of "the political" is at times tantamount to a mode of allegorical reading (recall the older socialist allegorical emphasis on uncovering class interests, and the newer [post] Althusserian allegorical stress on decoding the subtextual "social unconscious"), have some intellectuals, radicals, and critics installed this allegorical style as a hermeneutic "given"?[93] Might this allegorical tendency be seen both as a potential intellectual problem and as a highly principled intellectual achievement?

In considering this matter, it is important to bear in mind that if critical detachment can be painfully disillusioning, it can also be pleasurably engaging and empowering. Recently both James M. Loewen and Lawrence Levine voiced concern that students turned off by history may not be turned on to a social imagination capable of scrutinizing their society as a transformable process, an ongoing collective project. Levine cites James Atlas, who in 1990 anxiously reviewed new curricular proposals for New York elementary and secondary schools, from which Atlas quotes disapprovingly: "From now on it won't be enough to know the capital of Idaho or who Pocahontas was; seventh graders will be expected to know why they should know these facts and not others: 'The subject matter content should be *treated as socially constructed* and therefore tentative—as is all knowledge.' Deconstruction comes to P.S. 87." Levine retorts unnostalgically: "I can't refrain from commenting that if this be 'deconstructionism,' I wish it had come to Junior High School 115 when I was a student there in the 1940s. We had no idea *why* we were learning what we learned, no clue to how and to what end the facts fed to us were chosen. It was this ignorance of why that made history such a perennially dreary subject to legions of students."[94] Likewise, F. O. Matthiessen regretted that his prep school rendered history uninteresting and unimaginative in the 1910s.[95] Matthiessen, Levine, and Loewen assume that a critical history of how individuals and groups choose—or are prevented from choosing—to fabricate their social world and its power structures can motivate rather than automatically deflate and disenchant students.

Not unexpectedly, *Intellectual History Newsletter*'s symposium contributors reworked the critique of what was termed the "structuralist" bias in the 1970s—its tendency to gloss over historical accounts of agency and motivation. "Like all functional inquiries—and cultural studies is linked to functionalism—it can explain the replication of thought and behavior better than novelty," Appleby writes. "It can pinpoint how cultural systems of representation and communication function, but not why they break down or even take a different turn" (5).

As Cayton frames it in her critique of the discourse-made-me-do-it school, the "cultural models of meaning-making ... . are less suggestive as to how any individual can make choices that can have a telling impact on those cultural/linguistic milieus.... [W]e get the big picture—bigger than us all—but it is discourse and culture themselves that finally run the show, and knowing something about the way they structure experience for us is not the same thing as empathetically understanding experience itself" (54).

These are serious concerns for any historian interested in the dynamics of social change as well as agency. As I have been suggesting, such concerns are by no means wholly new within cultural studies: Thompson has not been the only scholar associated with cultural studies who has been dismissive of facile functionalist explanations and advocated the theorizing and historicizing of agency. The best cultural studies scholars have emphasized the study of structures, systems, hegemony, ideology, discourse, and "interpellation" to better learn how to educate more critical social agents.

Several intellectual historians disparaged literary studies—the American location of much cultural studies today—and the "jargon" that pervades much poststructuralist and cultural studies literary work (such disputes have long obsessed social scientists). Martin Jay, however, defended the formulation of "specialized vocabularies" (6) that are used to "make, interpret, and criticize meaning" (6). And Dominick LaCapra upheld critical theory, suggesting that too much recent cultural studies theorizing was not sophisticated enough—"thin soup" (10). The ongoing jargon debate reminded me of a *History Workshop Journal* editorial, "Language and History" (1980), in which the editors expressed sympathy for those socialist readers who responded with frustration to the "mannered use of words" and "elitist use of language" patent in writings by historian-theoreticians. "But," they added, "not if it leads us to mystify ordinary language as self-explanatory, and certainly not if it implies that the existing stock of language contains all that is necessary or desirable for new thought.... Plain speech runs thought on tramlines which are even harder to break out of than elaborate jargons or codes. Indeed the tramlines of plain speech may be harder to break away from because they seem part of common sense itself."[96]

Cultural studies is partly a historical response to and expression of the widespread—not just academic—expansion of the understanding of the scope of "the political." History shows that intellectuals, critics, and people from numerous walks of life elaborated expansive concepts of "the political" long before the 1960s. But since that decade, social movements, mass culture, and education have played formative roles in popularizing, institutionalizing, and commodifying forms of broadened political consciousness. Cultural studies, in the spirit of its New Left influences, contributes to a heightened and expanded perception that, in Wolin's terms, "the real political battles to be fought" (16) have multiplied rather than diminished. A fundamental cultural studies challenge is to consult history—histories of cultural, intellectual, artistic, economic, and political critique, histories of social protest, histories of progressive political parties—to better learn how to promote a critical awareness of all of the battles and of these battles' relationships with one another. If cultural studies concerns are here to stay—even if such concerns are not labeled "cultural studies"—it is because history makes such concerns pressing. I began my work on this chapter with the sense that cultural studies concerns were now filtering into numerous kinds of disciplinary, interdisciplinary, popular, and political projects. However, I conclude it with a clearer appreciation that numerous kinds of disciplinary, interdisciplinary, popular, and political projects helped make cultural studies historically imaginable and exigent.[97]

4

Complicity Critiques, the Artful Front, and Political Motivation

Art Saves Lives.

—*Bumper sticker (2003)*

We will produce no more for profit but for *use*, for *happiness*, for LIFE.

—*William Morris, quoted by E. P. Thompson in 1951*

"Cultural politics" often seems to imply a contrast with some other kind of politics, usually "real politics": that is, electoral and party politics.... It remains characteristic of the Labour Party and the labour movement, as of British life in general, that it represents culture ... as having little or nothing to do with the serious business of politics and practical life. This separation ... has had the result not only of depoliticizing culture but also ... of "deculturizing" politics.... [This] segregates [politics] from the lives and interests of "ordinary people," who are in turn induced to accept the representation of themselves as incapable of, and bored by, political reflection and action.

—*Janet Batsleer et al., Rewriting English (1985)*[1]

In 1991 Stanley Aronowitz observed the curious paradox of an American English department-based conception of "politicizing" that in its more extreme renditions renders literature and literary criticism ideologically suspect. "I have been told by more than one superbly trained literary critic that they rarely, if ever, read novels or poetry," he writes. "Poetry and mainstream fiction genres [have] become for them a suspicious form that partakes in processes of social and ideological reproduction."[2] Critics who have given up on Tainted Literature—or even more so Tainted Lit. Crit.—often turn to media studies, cultural history, or critical theory.[3]

Antecedents of postmodern critical devaluations of literature and literary criticism flourished in the postwar Workers Education Association that employed E. P. Thompson and Raymond Williams for many years. Thompson had once aspired to be a poet and insatiably turned to William Blake, William Morris, and other authors for guidance and inspiration. He rejected as preposterous the supposition that literary study is politically frivolous. The great historian "read" English as well as history at Cambridge, taught literature—not history—for the first few years he instructed adult workers, and wrote literary criticism as well as poetry. Williams wrote several books on literature and drama that served as fertile theoretical seedbeds for his later wide-ranging cultural studies. But to write them he had to combat "the sense of guilt which most [Workers Education Association] literature tutors [had] that theirs is not a really useful subject and that it must be made to resemble social history or philosophy or logic before it can be fully accepted in adult education."[4]

Contemplating these tensions, I also appreciate Stuart Hall's complex political choice. His uncompleted Oxford dissertation on Henry James explored the Atlanticist "theme of 'America' vs. 'Europe,'" but with a theoretical focus on James's tendency to overrun "the capacity of the narrative 'I'" (a trend that James Joyce's dissolution of the narrative "I" advanced). In the 1990s Hall still maintained that "these two questions ... have major cultural studies implications." Hall's thesis, based on his brief description, probably would have helped literary studies move toward a broader comparative history of the cultural formation of subjectivities. But the pressing political events of 1956 (see chapter 2) made him uneasy about continuing to formulate "cultural questions in 'pure' literary terms." Although the Birmingham Centre inspired some important theoretical and historical work on literature, Hall never focused much on literature again. His interest was more in the way literary theory could be developed as cultural theory. He chose to cultivate signifying practices studies, cultural representation studies, and political discourse studies rather than explicitly revise literary studies.[5]

At different times over the last three decades I have related to all of the positions sketched above and find it challenging to articulate, no less resolve, the tensions within them. Many talented critics, not a few trained in my generation, approach literature as a complex field of ideological forms, codes, narratives, mystifications, displacements, and crosscurrents, even more than as a theoretical and historical resource that might contribute artfully to a more expansive understanding of what constitutes politics, political motivation, and the bases of political organizing. They politicize literature-as-ideological-symptoms, but often can be less attuned to thinking through how literature and the arts might teach us how to repoliticize politics. Some of these critics have been affected by the premise, frequently circulated tacitly in American studies, that the real "political" subject is history and that historicizing literature is the next best "political" thing a literary critic can do besides writing history. Many such critics have excelled at scrutinizing how texts are "complicit in the power arrangements of a dominant culture"—a trend I label *complicity critiques*—a key theme below.[6] Especially in literary studies, cultural theory has often taken the form of complicity theory.

Here I will outline not only why it is strategic to consider the complicity of literature—and its authors, institutions, teachers, readers—but also the affirmative capacity of culture to help produce incentives, energies, feelings, and ideas that promote progressive social change. This entails reevaluating the concept of *affirmation* and its relevance to an artful front. Literature can be illuminating politically—even when it does not try to be or seem "political"—because it often reminds "politicizers" that the category of politics, however capacious, does not encompass the full range of literature's—and life's—value, pleasures, and concerns.

Traditions of Complicity Critiques

Complicity critiques are historically specific, changing in response to changing conditions. They have not always been in agreement about what constitutes the contradictions with which one's behavior, work, thinking, seeing, and feeling may be complicit. The expansion of the critical imagining of the category of "the political," especially since the 1960s, has also broadened critical understanding of how social actors can be complicit in a range of oppressions and exploitations.

Perhaps the *locus classicus* that exemplifies seminal aspects of some well-known complicity critiques, a passage whose significance reverberates throughout the work of critics such as Raymond Williams, Terry Eagleton, Fredric Jameson, and Alan Sinfield, is Walter Benjamin's statement about the task of historical materialism in his "Theses on the Philosophy of History," written not long before he committed suicide to escape capture by the Nazis in 1940. The "historical materialist," he asserts, must try to view the "cultural treasures" or "spoils" that he or she may love and admire as a "distanced observer": "For such cultural riches, as he [or she] surveys them, everywhere betray an origin which he [or she] cannot contemplate without horror. They owe their existence, not merely to the toil of the great creators who have produced them, but equally to the anonymous forced labor of the latters' contemporaries. There has never been a document of culture which was not at one and the same time a document of barbarism." The historical materialist, unbribed by beauty, wealth, comfort, status, or spurious transcendence, must "brush history" and perhaps his or her own ways of seeing "against the grain" by never losing sight of the conjunctural relationships between the "treasures" and the structures of power and contradictions that make their production possible or predictable. In the spirit of Benjamin, Eagleton exhorts critics to "remind culture of its criminal parentage."[7]

Benjamin's oft-cited passage is not without problems. His abstraction, "cultural treasures," seems to pertain to high culture. He does not speculate on how some nonbourgeois or non–ruling class observers might view, repudiate, or redefine the value of some of these "treasures." His abstraction appears to recycle a victimology in its tacit assumption that the "prostrate bodies of . . . victims" of the "victors" do not or cannot develop a resistant, complex culture of their own.[8] Benjamin does not foreground what he well knew: documents of high culture can themselves advance—albeit, sometimes in contradictory ways—materialist critique. Culture's "parentage" can be enabling and liberating rather than "criminal." Nevertheless, the force of Benjamin's passage is that it importunes readers not to be taken in by "cultural treasures" whose ideological power resides in their capacity to appear untouched by ideology and power relations.

Bourgeois and ruling class constructions of "individuality" over the past two centuries have often exhibited the same teflon-like ideological qualities as Benjamin's "treasures." Eagleton, again following Benjamin, stresses relational self-reflexivity and ethical responsibility: the ostensible autonomy and "freedom of any particular individual is crippled and parasitic as long as it depends on the futile labor and active oppression of others."[9] Benjamin's historical materialist makes such premises and linkages visible by reading allegorically: the analysis of every aesthetic, cultural, or subjective form, and of every institution, is reopened with allegorical keys constructed out of a knowledge of social contradiction, conflict, and oppression.[10]

In 1937 Herbert Marcuse, also a Frankfurt School materialist critic, developed another example of the complicity critique—his concept of the cultural and literary production of affirmative culture and subjectivity. Marcuse observes that affirmative culture evades the recognition of social contradiction often by using literature and the arts to displace the problem onto the self—it represents "humanity" as "an inner state" rather than a social production. "Freedom, goodness, and beauty" are mystified as spiritual qualities. Affirmative culture "thus exalts the individual without freeing him from his factual debasement."[11] For Marcuse, this affirmative survivalist subjectivity, in its fabricated transcendence, spirituality, and "depth," colludes with the reproduction of the very social contradictions that fuel the ideological need for therapeutic transcendence, spirituality, depth, or autonomy. Affirmative culture, a complicitous culture, often fosters the individualizing, familializing, psychologizing, and aestheticizing of what Marcuse envisions as a necessarily collective project of liberation. (It may be worth bearing in mind, when considering this critique of affirmation, that the Frankfurt School kept its distance from working-class and radical movements during its founding decade in Germany, 1923–33.)[12]

Over the past few decades Benjamin's and Marcuse's Marxist contributions to the formulation of complicity critiques have been elaborated productively to historicize the ideological work that literature performs. Yet it is essential not to forget that there is a rich tradition of complicity critiques that was developed by nineteenth- and twentieth-century American authors who, like Karl Marx and other social thinkers who would influence the Frankfurt School, responded critically to the expansion of industrial and imperialist capitalism and its division of labor, class stratification, and racialized and gendered relations. Some of the most trenchant cultural theorizing and oppositional criticism America has produced can be found in its literatures.[13]

In "Man the Reformer," a lecture written for the Mechanics' Apprentices Library Association in 1841, Ralph Waldo Emerson veers from his usual idealism to invite his audience to survey the origins not of cultural treasures but of tainted commodities that "implicate" their consumers: "It is only necessary to ask a few questions as to the progress of the articles of commerce from the fields where they grew, to our houses, to become aware that we eat and drink and wear perjury and fraud in a hundred commodities." Posing such questions involves thinking about where the sugar that sweetens both the tea and the worldview in cozy middle-class New England homes comes from: in Cuba,

Emerson acknowledges, one slave in "ten [dies] every year ... to yield us sugar." The taken-for-granted practices and habits of daily life and trade often make one's complicity in an exploitative process seem invisible or if seen at all seem simply unalterable. "One plucks, one distributes, one eats..... [Y]et none feels himself accountable. He did not create the abuse; he cannot alter it; what is he? an obscure private person who must get his bread. That is the vice—that no one feels himself called to act for man, but only as a fraction of man."[14] In "New England Reformers" (1844) a similar class critique led Emerson to ask: "Am I not too protected a person? I begin to suspect myself to be a prisoner, though treated with all this courtesy and luxury."[15] To be complicitous is to be an accomplice.

Over the last decade, students in the antisweatshop movement have not only gotten the point, they have organized and acted on it. The movement is empowered by its heightened sense of complicity. Its student activists, as did Henry David Thoreau, have thought through their relationship not only to those who make their clothes but to those who control their corporate universities. "Harvard pays more than a thousand workers poverty wages while sitting atop an endowment of almost $20 billion. Janitors, security guards, and dining hall workers earn as little as $6.75 an hour and work up to ninety hours a week," according to one Harvard protester. Many have understood the existence of sweatshops not as unfair capitalist aberrations but as contradictions systemic to capitalism's class and economic structure. "By 1999," antisweatshop activist Molly McGrath points out, "the wealth of the world's 475 billionaires was greater than the combined incomes of the poorest half of humanity." She also recognizes self-critically that students "were able to build this movement because of our [class] privilege ... the real heroes—the garment workers themselves—will never receive the kind of attention we have." For some activists this education leads to careers as organizers for unions and community groups.[16]

Because the web of responsibility is global, the web of complicity is global. When studying at the Frankfurt School in 1963, Angela Davis was horrified to learn that racists had blown up four young girls she knew in her hometown, Birmingham, Alabama, while they were in Davis's church. She found that her "protected" fellow students felt too disconnected from the social conditions that made this carnage possible to fathom her rage and grief. Davis's lucid formulation of complicity and accountability is probably still incomprehensible—and inadmissible—to many Americans and Europeans: "They could not understand why the whole society was guilty of this murder—why their beloved Kennedy was also to blame, why the whole ruling stratum in their country, by being guilty of racism, was also guilty of this murder."[17]

Those who practice complicity critiques have long been dismissed by many of the accused as grim, strident, ungrateful, impolite violators of the code of middle-class respectability. Edward Cavan, a socialist English professor at Harvard, interrogates his complicitous position in May Sarton's novel *Faithful Are the Wounds* (1955), which reputedly is based partly on episodes in F. O. Matthiessen's life leading up to his death.[18] Cavan, the protagonist who becomes the target of a witch hunt by the House Un-American Activities Committee, is a brilliant teacher who not only inspires his students to pay "intelligent homage" (97) to the formal complexity of literature, but urges them to investigate what members of his department discount as "the periphery of literature—economics, history, all that could be rolled up in the term 'cultural historian'" (104). He refuses to play the role of the "safe" (191) academic who, in his words, "is only considered responsible as long as he is *not* responsible" (121). Cavan is relentlessly accusatory partly because he has begun to comprehend that the field of English is complicit in the shaping of politically quiescent citizens who will universalize and individualize social problems as "life" and will then adorn their misreading with literary, psychological, and spiritual "depth." One of his colleagues, in conversation with Cavan's sister Isabel, objects: "One can talk to you. And one couldn't talk to Edward." She replies: "Because I don't make you feel guilty.... I'm nobody's conscience, and Edward, it seems to me, was" (192).[19]

Richard Ohmann began graduate study in English at Harvard not long after Matthiessen committed suicide. His critiques have shed much light on the Cold War complicity of English.[20] Ohmann's classic *English in America* (1976) helped raise the profession of English to a new level of political self-critique. Protests against the Vietnam War radicalized him to the point where he, like Cavan, felt unbearably hoodwinked by Cold War English. He remarks in 1996 that "the anger of [his book *English in America*'s] tone [in 1976] [was] closely linked to a feeling of having been deceived and of having collaborated in the deception." He called this deception "the big lie." And "that," he adds, "explains the repeated trope of unmasking."[21] Cold War English at Harvard and elsewhere, Ohmann notes, sponsored a self-righteous post-Arnoldian critique: critics merely saw consumers, McCarthy's witch hunters, businesspeople, and warmongers as philistines who had not yet realized that Literary Culture could redeem materialistic society and inspire it to transcend its sordid concerns for more humane ones. This posture led to a sometimes smug, sometimes ambivalent detachment from most political movements that noisily agitated for systemic social transformation. But by the late 1960s radical scholars' sense of the linkages between the corporate university and the social contradictions that had become more visible yielded the Thoreauvian conclusion that "'Who ruled Columbia?' and 'Who ruled America?' turned out to be two forms of the same question."[22]

Ohmann began to see that English had been in subtle ways drafted to boost the Cold War effort. English taught skills requisite for the performance of (often alienating) clerical and managerial labor: "punctuality, good verbal manners, submission to authority, attention to problem-solving assignments set by someone else, long hours spent in one place."[23] From its fund of cultural capital, English supplied the professional-managerial class and the ruling class and those who aspired to cultural as well as economic membership in these classes with some of the cultural references, narratives, and codes that could adorn their self-presentation and self-image. English also distributed a compensatory, often romantic or, in Marcuse's language, affirmative subjective capital that helped managers and professionals to encode and read their individuality, their personal conflicts, their family histories, and their psychological rebellions as endlessly complex, by implication far more complex than forms of selfhood and self-expression available in socialist and communist countries. If the social sciences, the sciences, and the business schools taught Cold War warriors knowledge of the marketplace and battlefield, the humanities helped these warriors constitute their "soul," their "innerness," their "depth," and possibly even a beguiling self-illegibility that they might exhibit as their autonomy from a liberal corporate state that made this interiority so desirable and commodifiable.[24]

It is not surprising to me that many of my students have been energized by complicity critiques in literature, the new literary history, and historical scholarship on the institutionalization of English as they begin to become critically conscious of their own cultural, economic, and political involvements within systems of power. Yet other students, perhaps in part because of their class interests and conditioning, retreat from the asperity of some complicity critiques and find relief in discounting literary cultural studies as "oppression studies" and "cynicism studies." I take this dismissal seriously as an intellectual and political loss and do not write it off as simply ideologically self-protective. Still other students, who grasp the importance of complicity critiques, express a need for something more constructive.

Such responses raise questions about the strategic efficacy of a concentration on complicity as general critical practice. Patricia Penn Hilden (Nez Perce) holds that many American Indians, while under no illusions about the power relations that surround them, "tend to" eschew "aggressive" "guilt-eliciting accusations about the past" as culturally, spiritually, emotionally, and politically counterproductive. And when Stuart Hall, in the late 1980s, found himself and other members of the "first" New Left indicted in public by younger intellectuals for not initiating a gender, racial, and sexual politics in the late 1950s and early 1960s that looked like the politics that developed out of the late 1960s and 1970s, he objected that such "riot[s] of moralizing"—the "easy option"—were better at producing unproductive guilt than practical strategy. Hall stepped back from the complicity critique, which here took the form of an "anachronistic" "moralism of blame and sectarian rectitude and self-righteousness," not to evade it, so he pleaded, but to be more tactical. "That just demobilizes people.... We still have a great deal to learn, collectively, about how we can engage in such a discussion without taking people off the hook, but so that we can collectively learn from it in order to transform our political practice." By the same token, might one "politicize" one's reading of literary authors not simply by examining how authors and their texts are complicitous with larger social contradictions, but—"without taking [authors] off the hook"—by asking how authors and their texts might help "transform our political practice" and galvanize our political agency?[25] The political aim, presumably, for Hilden, Hall, and others, is not just to criticize but to sustain and mobilize.

Recently Alan Trachtenberg, an astute American studies historicist and cultural critic, has lamented the "scandal mongering" proclivities of some historicist critics to expose "writers for their complicity in bad discourses of gender, race, class" *solely* to condemn them.[26] This "retro-punishment," Trachtenberg suggests, may not be nearly radical or intelligently adversarial enough in its sometimes oversimplified contribution to the study of the cultural dynamics of historical and political self-understanding and self-misunderstanding. If critique only searches for evidence of complicity, other evidence of the dynamics of cultural power and its political possibilities may be unnoticed or underestimated. Ohmann proposes the caveat: "Human activity [is] always political, if not *only* political."[27] Taking a cue from students, Hilden, Hall, Trachtenberg, Ohmann, and others I discuss below, it may be politically and critically strategic to begin to think through the *not only political powers of culture.*

Cultural Rescue(?):
Rethinking the Social and Political Value of Affirmation

C. Wright Mills was a master of the complicity critique. He read the efforts of "cultural workmen" to excise politics from their work as a complicitous "pseudo withdrawal," a "political act ... [whose] effect is to serve whatever powers prevail if only by distracting public attention from them."[28] And he hammered "moral[ly] fright[ened]" liberals for only defending civil liberties while turning a blind eye to "any left-wing or even any militantly liberal position." For Mills negative critique entailed an appraisal of what needed to be rejected and what needed to be struggled for. "To really belong, we have got, first, to get it clear with ourselves that we do *not* want to belong to an unfree world. As free men and women we have got to reject much of it and to know why we are rejecting it." Yet, as one of his former students reminisced, Mills's "withering critique" was never "simply negative"—it held out the "promise of something better."[29]

Mills often reflected not only on the necessity of negative critique and struggle, but on the affirmative value of culture. Censorious of the "lazy escapes" manufactured by mass-distraction industries, he offered eloquent affirmations of some "escapes" as educative, empowering, and fun. "Everyone with any liveliness does a great deal of escaping, and is continually planning future escapes from which he hopes to learn something more about himself and about the world." The Mills who wrote critique as a weapon to "fight against other ideas and arrangements of ideas and images that you are against, morally, logically, or factually," also rejoiced in his writing as a life-giving process: "You come to know how altogether alive you can be when you're in the middle of the big flow." In 1952, corresponding with an old friend, he tried to describe what was worth getting "keyed up" about and sounded far more like Walt Whitman and the Depression-era John Dos Passos than like Max Weber or Thorstein Veblen. "Long weekends in the country and snow and the feel of an idea and New York streets early in the morning and late at night ... and yes by god the world of music .... That's what the hell to get keyed up about." Art, architecture, music, literature, and nature, he implied, could more movingly convey what was worth *living for*—not just worth *struggling for*—than much "critique": "The trouble with you and what used to be the trouble with me is that you don't use your goddamned *senses;* too much society crap and too much mentality and not enough tactile and color and sound.... You've got to coax the sight and sound back, carefully tease it to life again and it will fill you up."[30] Sensual value informed his conception of *not only political value.* Neither ideas nor "politics," he hinted, suffice to breathe life into life.

Cornel West, like Emerson, Matthiessen, Mills, and Ohmann, knows well the force of complicity critiques. But he also offers a moving consideration of the life-affirming powers of culture and by implication broaches political concerns not addressed by Marcuse in his late 1930s European eve-of-World

War II take on the category of "affirmation." West, clearly shaped by America's 1960s culture and its legacies, highlights the power of cultural agents, especially oppressed agents, to use culture to prevent violence, specifically the violence born of social frustration and desperation that is directed against the self. He said in 1990: "When I talk about Sarah Vaughn—and I could talk about Baby Face or Marvin Gaye or a host of others—I'm talking about people who keep me *alive*" (my emphasis). In its power to sustain "human bodies," culture "in part" "convinces you not to kill yourself, at least for a while."[31]

Here West did not indict Vaughn as a pawn of an industry that commodifies ideologically distractive, compensatory, or therapeutic culture. He did not suggest that in order to establish her political value she should have recorded songs whose lyrics promoted explicit social critique and revolution. As Tricia Rose observed recently, popular music's political values and effects are often messy to assess partly because music can help build community and group identity "without addressing a specific political agenda."[32] Vaughn's music—its performance, sounds, rhythms, collective makers, contexts—nourished the resources of its admirers to *live* in the face of the social obstacles they encountered.

Cultures of joy and of hope, West believes, rather than being evasive, can empower one to go "back into [the] struggle." And by hope he means something more life-sustaining than unreflective American optimism. On this distinction he quotes Czech president Vaclav Havel: "'Hope has to do with being certain that what you're doing is just, regardless of whether things get better or not.'" West finds cultural and spiritual joy, hope, and power not just in Duke Ellington's "artistic genius," but in "his way of being in the world."[33] The impulse to fight for progressive social change is nourished by more than critique.

With this impulse in mind, Lawrence Levine recovers some of the achievements and dynamics of slave *culture,* mostly an oral culture, composed of spirituals, adaptations of African religious traditions and Christianity, secular songs, work songs, tales, dances, creative language development, jokes, rituals of insult, and narrative innovation.[34] Levine contests historians who write off these cultural formations as "therapeutic" palliatives that substitute for emancipation. "The slaves' expressive arts and sacred beliefs were more than merely a series of outlets or strategies," Levine explains, "they were instruments of life, of sanity, of health, and of self-respect. Slave music, slave religion, slave folk beliefs—the entire sacred world of the black slaves—created the necessary space between the slaves and their owners and were the means of preventing legal slavery from becoming spiritual slavery" (80). Slave culture, according to

Levine, sought to invent a "necessary space" of life, identity, and self-reflection not wholly defined by or produced in relation to oppressive conditions.

In an article on 1930s Depression culture, Levine expands on his defense of the social value of therapeutic affirmation: "to 'escape' a reality one cannot change is one way of altering that reality, or at least its effects." Levine explains that two sources particularly inspired him to favor this position: his earlier work on slave culture and his interpretation of Preston Sturges's classic, *Sullivan's Travels* (1941). In the film John Louis Sullivan is a Hollywood director who, like Sturges, makes his millions by creating feel-good movies. But Sullivan, like Emerson, is pricked by his conscience and begins to ponder how his movie contributions to the laughter industry—the therapeutic amnesia industry—are complicit with a hegemony that sanctions poverty. Thus Sullivan—tramping in the ideological footsteps of Jacob Riis, Stephen Crane, and Walter Wyckoff—sets out incognito to "discover" how the "other half" lives and costumes himself as a hobo among the poor and homeless. In his sociological "travels," however, he temporarily loses his memory and is imprisoned on a chain gang (for real) and there is no escape.

The movie giant's incarceration marks the commencement of his true learning experience. Cut down to size, he rediscovers the social efficacy of escapism. He and the other prisoners are brought to a black church one evening where, instead of hearing a sermon, they see a Walt Disney Mickey Mouse cartoon, full of slapstick violence—an unreal violence—choreographed to provoke laughs (Levine does not describe the cartoon). The dog Pluto—like Sullivan, his fellow prisoners, and perhaps even some of the parishioners—is caught in fly paper and chases his own tail in his futile efforts to free himself. The prisoners and parishioners laugh, and Sullivan, observing this response, undergoes a religious conversion to laughing—to culture's safety-valve capacity to help people laugh it all off for awhile. Soon after Sullivan regains his memory and cleverly (and symbolically) confesses to his own murder (it is the only way he can get into the public eye). Once reporters descend on Sullivan's "murderer," they recognize the director, and he is released. He abandons his Steinbeckian realist film project (*O Brother, Where Art Thou?*) and resolves instead to make more movies ("with a little sex" in them) that bring consumers therapeutic relief, affirmation, and laughter. Levine, in sync with the ostensible moral of the story, cites Depression-era testimonies by consumers who wrote letters to radio shows to thank them for playing songs that helped sustain them in seemingly untransformable conditions ("they make life seem more like living"). He concludes: "If we become too obsessed with power, we risk losing sight of the culture itself."[35]

The radical historian, playwright, and activist, Howard Zinn, registers a similar concern in his autobiography. Zinn recounts his decision to conclude one of his courses at Boston University with the performance of a Mozart quartet that featured several classical musicians enrolled in the class. "Not a customary finale to a class in political theory," he admits, "but I wanted the class to understand that politics is pointless if it does nothing to enhance the beauty of our lives.... Political discussion can sour you. We needed some music."[36] Suggesting that art must give pleasure as well as raise social consciousness, Zinn places emphasis on the former service as particularly requisite. "To accomplish the first alone is not something to be scorned (Stalinism would not allow it), because we should always be acting out those delights of the good life—humor, music, poetry, excitement, adventure—that we hope will be available to large numbers of people in the world when freed from sickness, war, and suffocating work conditions."[37]

Similarly, Lindsay Anderson's film that chronicles antinuclear protest in England, *March to Aldermaston* (1958), includes a scene showing young people dancing to jazz in which the voice-over muses: "It's no use being against death, if you don't know how to enjoy life when you've got it."[38] On one level, Levine, Zinn, and Anderson may be suggesting that it is crucial for agents of political change to remind themselves that there is more that is worth fighting for and living for than politics. As Giles Miller, one of my students whom I asked to elaborate on West's statement and Levine's slave culture thesis, wrote eloquently several years ago: "Culture is a source of human agency even as it limits that agency, and we seek its life-affirming properties even as we manipulate its ideologies to naturalize relations of inequality to construct and subjugate 'Others.' Understanding how human agency works is as important as understanding how oppressive human relations are perpetuated because those relations can only be addressed (outside of academia) through that agency."[39] Contrasting the tendency of American Indians who "know they are oppressed and don't feel powerless" with American whites who "don't feel oppressed but feel powerless," Winona LaDuke (Anishinabe [Ojibway]) testifies to the importance of cultivating cultures and communities that dispel the "mythology ... they've been teaching you ... that you have no power."[40]

I admire the work of West and Levine, and the movement of their thinking in this direction—toward strategies of affirmation—is provocative. Large-scale affirmation industries can, through their commodities of affirmation, energize and empower consumers—they can function as agency technologies. But it is vital to ask always: *What is being affirmed?* West notes that the music of Sarah Vaughn and others can convince one not to kill oneself. But what is one keeping oneself alive for? Or what is one being kept alive for and in what conditions? Jackson Lears has argued that Levine's analysis of slave culture and his recent work on 1930s Depression culture are too therapeutic in their survivalist affirmation of cultural formations that help one merely cope or "muddle through."[41] Is the culture that keeps some of us alive only a blessing, or is it sometimes complicit with larger social oppressions and contradictions?

In 1989, the year before West cited the power of Vaughn and others, Señor Love Daddy of We Love Radio in Spike Lee's film *Do the Right Thing* acknowledged the contributions of Vaughn, Gaye, and many other black musicians to the black community: "We want to thank you for making our lives just a little bit brighter, here on Love Radio." Love Radio provides "cool" often romantic music—it doesn't seem to include Radio Raheem's favorite militant in-your-face attitude-affirming anthem, Public Enemy's "Fight the Power"—to help the residents survive a "heat wave" manifested not only as sizzling temperatures but as tense social, economic, gendered, generational, and racialized relations. (Note that Lee did not title his film, *Fight the Power.*) Music, for both Love Daddy and Raheem, is a form of self-definition, an assertion of racial value, an experience of temporary relative autonomy. In 1987 Allan Bloom's conservative paean to Great White Books, *The Closing of the American Mind,* voiced a curiously similar sentiment—though in reference to the power of White Western Culture, not Vaughn and company: "A value is only a value if it is life-preserving and life-enhancing."[42] West, Love Daddy, and Bloom all pay tribute to the life-affirming aspects of culture—*different* cultures (which occupy different and unequal positions in the U.S. power structure). Affirmation is by no means necessarily a progressive effect in its own right. As critic Joseph Entin has observed: if Vaughn helps keep West alive, her music also may have helped keep Clarence Thomas alive. Yet West and Thomas aim to produce very different kinds of social and political worlds.[43] Affirmation may well function as part of the cultural machinery of domination—cultural products that may affirm antiracist positions, for example, may still be sexist.

Hegemonic domination does not operate in late capitalist culture simply by oppressing. It may work best when it animates and fascinates those it subordinates with doses of what will be construed as "liberation." Complex domination works in multiple ways to produce subjectivities that will not "feel" oppressed (except by their "individual" failings) and some subjectivities that will not "feel" that they are participating in the systemic oppression of others.

Sturges's *Sullivan's Travels,* which moves toward a dialectical understanding of the dynamics of complex oppression, is more politically polyvalent than Levine's affirmative reading of it suggests. Sturges is self-reflexive, but he is not

Sullivan. In part Sturges is critical of a privileged complicity critic, Sullivan, whose romantic experiment with The Impoverished was never really intended to help transform the social structure responsible for the unequal distribution of wealth and well-being. Sullivan testifies to his reconversion to therapeutic entertainment on a private airplane flight high in the clouds with no ground in sight. Yet the unemployed aspiring actress with whom he falls in love makes clear that laughter too is part of the power structure when she confesses that because Sullivan—disguised in hobo drag—isn't a casting director she doesn't have to laugh at his jokes. Of course, the hobos with whom Sullivan fraternizes in search of "suffering" cannot afford to see his movies (they must put up with self-righteous sermons in soup kitchens). And the only movies the prisoners enjoy are those that the black church invites them to view. The cloudy ending leaves these contradictions and others—for instance, the unjust legal system that protects movie directors from prison farms—in plain sight even as Sullivan seems to want to cloud them over. The capitalism that Sullivan labels a "cockeyed caravan" is patently rigged in favor of its "directors." Still, the film hints that Sullivan has reached some new insight into what he does, not based on what he calls "sticking" his "head in the sand" (or the clouds).

Sturges's film may be interpreted as being critical of an affirmation management that is meant to contain, deflect attention from, or compensate for the social discontents of those able to consume movies. Though other aspects of *Sullivan's Travels* may be judged as "complicit" insofar as they seem to affirm the fundamental inability of the (ostensible) social critic (Sullivan) and his or her institution (Hollywood) to grasp the effects of domination and use cultural productions to contest structures and processes of domination. Sturges makes such divergent readings possible in order to place them in productive tension with one another. Doing so, he produces a film—romance and screwball comedy, social critique and realism—that is far more ideologically complex, self-critical, and self-questioning than any of the film projects that interest Sullivan.

Literary Cultural Studies and Agency Studies

My own work on the ideological effects that literary formations have on the cultural formation of subjectivities has relied on aspects of complicity critiques conceived by authors and critics. It would be dreadful if this critical orientation were encoded as a mere stylistic "phase" that some American literary historians were passing through in the late twentieth century. This phase has helped bring much social critique, old and new, into mainstream debates and discussions in higher education and is rooted in continuing social contradictions and oppressions.

Yet it may be that one can deprive oppressive social power of some of its power not only by fostering the explicit critique of that power. It may be politically smart to be able to move in and out of complicity critiques to think more strategically and pedagogically about the not only political dimensions of (always political) human activity and art. A politically self-conscious literary cultural studies might reconceptualize its objectives not just as literary inclusion studies or meaning production studies or historicizing studies or complicity studies or subjection studies, but as a revitalized and pragmatic agency studies capable of reconceiving the transformative power of cultural affirmation.[44] It is crucial to focus not only on how culture contains, incorporates, or prevents progressive social change, but on how literature, the arts, and literary and aesthetic studies may help spark the social agency that will attempt social transformation in creative, egalitarian, and democratic ways.

This has been an important concern of some on the Old Left, New Left, and beyond. In his reflections on his first weeks as a working-class undergraduate at Cambridge, Raymond Williams writes of the *kinds* of relief and affirmation he valued in the university's Socialist Club, an organization that provided an "alternative and viable social culture, as well as political activity. It had a club room, it served lunches, it had film shows, it was a way of finding friends—it was not like just joining a political society." In 1961 Williams would write, in the spirit of William Morris, and perhaps with experiences such as joining this club, reading and writing fiction, and teaching drama to working-class adults in the back of his mind: "It has been the gravest error of socialism, in revolt against class societies, to limit itself to the terms of its opponents; to propose a political and economic order, rather than a human order.... [T]he alternative society [socialism] has proposed must be in wider terms, if it is to generate the full energies necessary for its creation."[45] Williams, Hall, and others associated with New Left cultural studies sought to remedy this in varied ways. In the 1980s Hall employed Gramsci's theory of hegemony to battle Thatcherism and rethink the presentation and contents of a democratic socialist movement. He approached the project not simply as the task of critique but more comprehensively as the "task of renewal."[46]

Hall had been thinking about the union of cultural and political renewal as an agency-making force for several decades. He characterized the New Left clubs of the late 1950s and early 1960s—which, like Williams's Cambridge Socialist Club in the 1930s, sponsored cultural events as well as political debates—as "not only symptomatic of our politics, but a sign that for us and for the left, the 'question of agency' had become deeply problematic." The cultural turn—the agency turn—that the "first" New Left developed was a tactic to comprehend more accurately what had to be done to cultivate and popularize new sorts of socialist commitment and motivation. Hall observed that the edge of the "second" New Left, spearheaded by Perry Anderson, was that it launched "a much more rigorous theoretical project committed to a more orthodox, less 'revisionist' reading of Marxism." But, he charges, "it was not a project which constituted the question of political agency as in any way problematic, either theoretically or strategically."[47] For the earlier New Left, one historian concludes, "commitment, alignment, and allegiance and even affirmation were in effect all part of an effort to confirm in the present the attempt to take socialism at full stretch."[48]

Employing key passages from West, Williams, Hall, Zinn, Nathan Huggins, and others, and with Levine's essay and others as their points of focus, I asked one of my recent "Cultural Studies and American Studies" seminar groups to compose an "Agency Studies Handbook" for their final assignment. Generally, the students emphasized the importance of both critique's analyses of systemic oppression and culture's power as a force that can generate energy, incentive, fascination, and identities as means of developing progressive critical consciousness and collective agency. Several sought to sketch the sociality of agency. Michael Levenson underscored: "Every site of cultural control and subjugation is also a potential site of agency and change." But Levenson, like others, did not romanticize this two-way relationship as intrinsically revolutionary. Several students reconfigured Nathan Huggins's concept and critique of "soft rebellion" (bourgeois white bohemians of the 1920s who migrated to Harlem to watch blacks perform "primitiveness" on stage indulged in a chic feel-good or *soft* rebellion).[49] Josh Morgenstein formulated the idea of "soft agency"—hegemonic brands of preferred agency that "obfuscate hegemony by allowing people to believe that they are [simply] individual actors serving [only their] 'personal' interests." Modern literary ideologies that individualize and psychologize selfhood—and interest—have often played a significant role in purveying versions of "soft agency."

Most students were interested in envisioning an agency studies that would contribute to mobilizing organized resistance to structural oppression and help conduct what Gramsci termed a "war of position" in the struggle to shape popular consciousness. They sought to counter the production of resignation foregrounded by West: "Large numbers of people in the world, especially in American society, don't believe that they make a difference."[50] Levenson found

Eagleton's concept of the critic's task quoted above to be too limiting in the formation of progressive collective agency: "Agency Studies must not only, in the words of Terry Eagleton, 'remind culture of its criminal parentage,' but show examples of resistance to this criminality and of the power that culture has to promote social equality."[51]

Those who wish to develop a more strategic literary cultural studies might contemplate what roles it might play in a more encompassing American cultural studies that might retheorize itself more explicitly as a social transformation studies, an activism studies, a mobilizing studies, an organizing studies. Indeed, complicity critiques that only dismantle and do not focus on agency and counterhegemony building might be viewed as complicit in maintaining the contradictions they purport to oppose. Complicity critiques, if limited in this way, might be compared to the Puritan jeremiads that Perry Miller and later Sacvan Bercovitch viewed as conveniently "incorporated" self-critiques that funneled Puritans back into their lucrative patterns of sinning.[52] At their hermetic worst, complicity critiques can be historically decorated forms of a self-liberatory therapeutic confessionalism that partly purges the professional-managerial-class complicity critic as the critic announces his or her guilt and complicity. This discourse forms part of what Pablo Morales (one of my seminar students) skeptically disparaged as the academy's "soft, wine [whine?] and cheese rebellion."[53]

Some narrow complicity critiques conform to what Sinfield, in his analyses of some new historicist and cultural materialist work, calls an "entrapment model" in which "power seems to head off dissident activity even before it is conceived." His work on the emergence of sixteenth- and seventeenth-century English Protestant "inwardness" has led him to criticize some literary historians for depicting hegemony as "too total," its "effects" as "too unitary," and its system of operation as "too coherent." Sinfield represents the activation of Protestant interiority as a "high stakes, high risk strategy," which both "produced acquiescent subjects" and "stimulated a restless self-awareness, one that might allow, in some, a questioning of the system." The politics of a literary cultural studies that is tantamount to an entrapment studies is often retrograde and mystifying in its inadequate historicism.[54] Carolyn Porter also criticizes certain new historicist critiques, which revel in complicity to the point of "neutraliz[ing] opposition," as being "complicit in the cultural operations of power [they] want to analyze and resist."[55] This contamination theory writes off any resistance tainted by what it resists.

Ohmann has sounded a related cautionary note about assigning hegemonic power too much seamless power. Two decades after the publication of *English in*

America, the diverse reviews of his controversial complicity critique taught him that English by the late 1970s had more room for dissent than he had suspected. To have allowed for this ideological multidimensionality, he jests, "would have raised complicating difficulties for the book's central thesis about humanistic subservience to institutional logic and corporate power." Ohmann goes on to point out that in the mid-1960s "many early activists against the Vietnam war [were] students and teachers of the humanities."[56] Likewise, radical Michael Albert, a founder of South End Press, warns that "our negative/critical messages don't generate anger and action, but pile up more evidence that the enemy is beyond our reach.... For some leftists, it is as if celebrating progress or even admitting progress somehow falsified our purpose."[57]

It is useful to bear in mind West's 1985 critique of the American professional-managerial-class institutionalization of critique, which centers on Foucauldian critique. He argues that "Foucauldian" "postmodern skepticism" seeks to dismantle "regimes of truth" and "power-laden discourses in the service of neither restoration, reformation, nor revolution, but rather of revolt." West then notes how this limited "revolt" critique "provides [critics with] a sophisticated excuse for ideological and social distance from insurgent black movements for liberation." "Revolt" critique, in this restrained theory-for-theory's-sake form, affirms the critic (a feel-good through feeling bad exercise): "By conceiving intellectual work as oppositional political praxis, it satisfies the leftist self-image of black intellectuals, and, by making a fetish of critical consciousness, it encapsulates black intellectual activity within the comfortable bourgeois academy."[58]

Can cultural studies, occasionally demonized by some students and professors as "oppression studies," more constructively and pragmatically expand its social transformation studies dimension? Such a study might strive not to be structured as a response only to the oppression it opposes. Contributors to a constructive literary cultural studies might consider how such a project might be conceived.

To close, I will offer just one cluster of suggestions. It may be enlightening for teachers to devise courses not only on literary activism—on the work of authors such as Jack London, Upton Sinclair, Meridel LeSueur, Tillie Olsen, Adrienne Rich, Amiri Baraka, and others—but on literary critical activism—on the work and careers of Matthiessen, Ohmann, Kampf, Paul Lauter, Bruce Franklin, and others. Moreover, literary cultural studies might more self-consciously produce and teach cultural and literary histories that study the affirmative possibilities of culture as a regenerative, adhesive, organizing, alliance-building force. Daniel Aaron, George Lipsitz, Lizabeth Cohen, and

Michael Denning have contributed books that take this path—each analyzes the emergence, dynamics, and effects of organizing cultures.[59] This historical and analytical work would profit from being supplemented by an analysis of the contemporary scene. In *Rainbow at Midnight* (1994), Lipsitz concludes: "If we are to confront the materialism, greed, and selfishness unleashed by the enterprise economy of the 1980s, we need to have the instincts of an organizer."[60] The analytical emphasis must be placed not only on how culture shapes consciousness, but on how it enables us to organize.

Todd Gitlin has suggested that the "protestors" who enacted the sit-ins and teach-ins of the 1960s be reconceived as citizens engaged in "an affirmation," a "prefiguration" of a "superior way of life." He warns that activists and organizers on the Right, unlike those on the Left, are not overwhelmed—or cramped—by the "emotion" of "complicity." The Left's feelings of guilt, he claims, can easily transform into a counterproductive "rage" that "tries to choke off the sense of complicity, but always fails." He concludes: "Affirmation not only feels better, it does better, more consistent enduring work—it has more pride."[61]

Barbara Ehrenreich emphasizes how indebted "solidarity" is to "passion": "People want concrete things, like more money and better benefits and so forth, which draw them into the labor movement or the progressive movement, but nothing really takes off until they are fired up in some way by a different kind of vision.... . A good organizer realizes that there are emotional dimensions that go beyond rational interests that everybody brings to a movement."[62] So too Williams prized *energy* not psychologically but as a political agency-building and critical concern. In 1958 he wrote that the people who most desired democracy in England were those who did not have it: "There, as always, is the transforming energy, and the business of the Socialist intellectual is what it always was: to attack the clamps on that energy—in industrial relations, public administration, education, for a start; and to work in his own field on ways in which that energy, as released, can be concentrated and fertile."[63] Such energy thrives on more than opposition.

This point is worth elaborating. Recently, Stanley Aronowitz has associated agency with the capacity to see oneself as the subject of "social struggle."[64] Decades earlier Thompson laid the groundwork for this position. In his famous criticism of Williams's *The Long Revolution* in 1961, alluded to in chapter 3, Thompson challenged Williams's idea that progressive critique should analyze culture in the anthropological sense of "whole ways of life." Literature is often more "anthropological" than expressly "political" in its "cultural studies" scopes of concern. Thompson viewed Williams's "ways of life" emphasis as too passively analytical, too politically unfocused. Thus he aimed to modify Williams's project with a more activist project: he contended that progressive historical and cultural critique should be written more instrumentally to illuminate "whole ways of struggle." Thompson helped make radical history synonymous with ways of struggle studies.[65]

I value Thompson's explicit "politicizing" of Williams's formulation. And yet, as I have argued, it is wise for the "strugglers" not only to focus on ways of struggle, especially when contemplating how liberatory agency and political motivation may be cultivated. Struggle and discontent, as well as analysis, certainly help produce agency and motivation—the resolve to sacrifice, fight, campaign. In conjunction with this, a vision of how "life" can be cultivated and enhanced—not simply criticized—can also inspire the resolve to struggle. As Hall put it in 1987: one lobbies for socialism not just to win office, but to lay the "basis for a whole new conception of life."[66] What is worth pondering—as an insight that sheds light on the goals of critical thinking, the foundations for organizing, and efforts to "unclamp energies"—is British New Left novelist Mervyn Jones's late 1980s perspective on the New Left's marginalization of writers, dating back to the late 1950s and early 1960s: "The left has not really overcome a certain attitude which regards the arts as peripheral rather than central to politics, or—something far more important than being central to politics—central to life."[67] We politicize to live, not live to politicize.

Part III

Beyond Critique for Critique's and Career's Sake

5

Popularism

If it's not fun, why do it?
        —*Jerry Greenfield of Ben and Jerry's Ice Cream, bumper sticker (2001)*

Once it becomes hip to be a Freedom Fighter among young people,
it's a new world.
                        —*Cornel West, Restoring Hope (1997)*

From actors to musicians, comedians to athletes, Rock the Vote
harnesses cutting-edge trends and pop culture to make political participation cool.... Regardless of whether youth are signing petitions,
running for office, contacting their elected officials, or taking up a
sign in protest, they are all rocking the vote.
                        —*www.rockthevote.com (2003, founded 1990)*
(visit the rockthevote on-line store, featuring Rock Star Babydoll, Rock
                        Star Tee, and Script Logo Beanie)[1]

"WHY MUST THE LEFT DRESS IN WORKERS' GARB," THE RADICAL HISTORIAN
Jesse Lemish griped in his polemic on "pop front" culture, "I Dreamed I Saw

MTV Last Night" (1986). The Left should wise up, like the avant garde, he protested, and learn the "language" of mass culture, so that it can better popularize its "important messages." Maybe then it might figure out how to "talk to Americans." He recounted how he had been dragged to a Pete Seeger concert to rehearse his generation's obsolete "ritual of affirmation" and also complained how bored he had become with contemporary didactic documentaries of Left history marred by the "ancestral visual language" of 1930s realism. Lemisch, born in the "ancestral" thirties, exhorted Lefties to (post)modernize their consuming enthusiasms and affirmations as he had. Thus he raved over the Artists United against Apartheid "Sun City" video because it exemplifies what rock critic Robert Christgau terms "'the essential rock and roll equation between celebration and revolt.'"[2] The Left, he forecasted, would look (and see) much better if it tuned into MTV's constructions of feelings, fashioning of fascinations, and forms of self-identification. His article is a plea to rethink the style as well as the substance of the Left. To further this cause, he adopts the role of a Left public relations manager eager to *use* the allure of the popular. A cooler, hipper, more entertaining media- and youth-conscious Left, he stressed, is more likely to disseminate dissent effectively in Reagan America.[3]

Lemisch's case for cool Leftism drew fire in *The Nation*'s letters column—mainly from some of his fellow radical historians. They criticized him for ignoring the corporate management of the popular culture industries, for effacing cultural-historical links between Pete Seeger and other musicians he praised, and for overlooking the diversity of music that has nourished peoples' progressive hopes in the United States and elsewhere.[4] In feisty rebuttal, Lemisch specified in what way the Left was now playing the wrong cultural game—the class struggle "game," in which the capitalist exploitation of the working class is focused on as the preeminent contradiction: "This game has always been played on a tilted board, with all the pieces inevitably tumbling toward the corner marked 'class analysis.' But the movements emanating from blacks, students, women, gays and others could not be predicted by class analysis—suggesting that we need a more flexible approach to the game, or maybe that we should throw the board away." A multi-Left, Lemisch urges, should "organiz[e] people where they live."[5]

A study of what's popular is necessarily a study of the range of social groups that make things, views, and people popular. Lemisch is right in his insistence that organizers must recognize what "turns on" their potential constituencies. But to do so must they consider the multiplicity of what these potential constituencies turn on? Do most Americans dream of MTV? Can all Americans afford cable television—or own a television? Are Americans who do not dream of MTV politically significant? Lemisch in no way suggests they are not. Still, how do these Americans qualify as players and pawns in Lemisch's new unboring board game of political inclusiveness? Do those Americans who watch MTV have a range of concerns, including political concerns, not addressed even by MTV's most progressive videos?[6] Is Lemisch's imagined MTV-watching Left a Reagan-era pop cultural Left clinging to the rejuvenating hopefulness of what might be termed its 1960s youthism? And yet can one ignore the fact that on average most Americans watch television for over four hours daily?[7]

The Allure of Transforming the Popularizing Apparatus

Lemisch's pop front polemic is a contribution to a long-standing debate about how best to mobilize progressive forces. Harvey Swados's epigraph for *A Radical's America* (1962), borrowed from Anton Chekhov, is one slant: "There ought to be, behind the door of every happy, contented man, someone standing with a hammer, continuously reminding him with a tap that there are unhappy people."[8] John Lennon seconded the hammer thesis in theory: "The idea is not to comfort people, not to make them feel better but to make them feel worse."[9] Guilt-tripping is a venerable strategy. In 1903 Mother Jones, tactically rearticulating the popular, staged a march of children from Philadelphia to President Theodore Roosevelt's home in Oyster Bay, New York, to refocus "public attention" on child labor. The cracked Liberty Bell had been on tour, so why not child laborers? She used sentiment and theatricality to stir up consciences, shame, outrage, sympathy, and support, even in the corporate media. At Philadelphia's city hall she "put the little boys with their fingers off and hands crushed and maimed on the platform. I held up their mutilated hands and showed them to the crowd and made the statement that Philadelphia's mansions were built on the broken bones, the quivering hearts and drooping heads of these children." She orchestrated public disclosure and exposure: "President Wilson said that this strike must be eventually settled by public opinion. It's about time we aroused a little." Such struggles were risky, but Mother had a blast: "Get it straight, I'm not a humanitarian—I'm a hell-raiser."[10]

The challenge is to be an effective hell-raiser in a country within which—as Robert and Helen Merrell Lynd put it in 1929—"the American citizen's first importance ... is no longer that of citizen but that of consumer."[11] America's chief identity product is that of the consumer-individual. Inspiring *citizens* that it is their ethical responsibility to be hell-raisers may be hard enough. How does one convince *consumers* to "buy" hell-raising?

The usual incentive to consume is enjoyment—or what passes for enjoyment. If one strives to become conscious of the contradictions, oppressions, and exploitations with which one is sometimes avoidably and sometimes unavoidably complicit, and if one develops what E. P. Thompson terms an "internationalist conscience," is it possible to enjoy oneself? Or can one's conscience and one's enjoyment be mutually sustaining? If so, what might radicals learn from this possible union?[12] Terry Eagleton has praised Eric Hobsbawm as "a politico who has survived the most bloodstained century known to humanity, yet who has managed to relish his life in the process." Hobsbawm loves "parties, debate, travel and ideas."[13] C. Wright Mills, hard on contradiction and complicity, soft on fun, held that enjoyment was not only possible but necessary: "To be disgruntled with the way the world is going is not necessarily to be a disgruntled person." He treasured "comical and inane ideas," for "men of power are grim, and our chief weapons in times like these are audacity and laughter"[14] Notwithstanding his commitment to making people feel worse, recall that in practice Lennon sang not all we need is critique but *all we need is love.*

Lemisch's MTVism brings up another strategic concern: might twenty-first-century consumer-individuals come to identify Mother Jones's sort of hell-raising not just as moral but as *cool*? If capitalist mass culture has the capacity to make its distractions seem cool, can progressive forces rearticulate mass culture so as to make the deflection of attention from contradiction seem uncool? Cameron Crowe's film, *Almost Famous* (2001), posits the existence of a "buzz" that makes people love rock music, quite apart from the ways in which this "buzz" is distorted by the music industry, the star hype, and the social contradictions that intensify the yearning for a buzz. Could it be that the pursuit of progressive social change also has a "buzz"—that sometimes gets distorted?

In considering such matters it is helpful to place Lemisch's manifesto in dialogue with Warren Beatty's *Bulworth* (1998). This film is yet another example of the cultural and critical tendency to make heightened skepticism about progressive electoral change commonsensical, a trend I discussed in chapter 2. It begins with the information that the March 1996 California Democratic primary is under way, and the "populace is unaroused." As usual, party politics is as boring as it is rotten. Democratic Senator Jay Billington Bulworth, a former liberal who has sold his soul to neoliberal conservatism to get reelected, is on the verge of cracking up. Wracked by his 1960s conscience, no doubt lined with the images of Martin Luther King, Malcolm X, and Robert F. Kennedy framed on his wall, Bulworth hires an underworld contact to have him assassinated in the next couple of days. An insurance lobbyist bribes him with a $10,000,000 insurance policy—made out to his daughter—on condition that the senator block the passage of a bill to guarantee that poor people can get health insurance (Bulworth has arranged to be killed before he can do this). Relieved that his end is near, Bulworth experiences a bout of real freedom of speech. On a campaign stop at a black church, he shocks everyone by comically and unapologetically baring the truth about the corrupt political system he serves. At the church he is attracted to Nina, a black woman who later takes him to an all-night hip-hop disco where he falls in love not only with her but with rap. Through rap—which is represented as synonymous with truth-telling—he finds his voice and becomes what can only be described as a postmodern hip-hop politician who discovers that the best way to win public support is to blow the whistle on the system.

Thus hipness becomes tantamount to a real politics that addresses structural contradictions. In a television debate, Bulworth raps: "We got a club, right? Republicans, Democrats, what's the difference? Your guys, my guys, us guys—it's a club." As his distraught assistant surreptitiously disconnects the lights on the set, Bulworth is symbolically silhouetted in black. And when the assistant announces, "power failure," it is clear that Bulworth's "black" behavior is just that—no longer can he be bribed to be silent. In another speech, Bulworth raps: "Come on now let me hear the dirty word—socialism!" Bulworth falls for Nina, enjoyment, rap, social realism, and finally life itself, and tells the insurance lobbyist that their deal is off and also tries to cancel the assassin's contract on him. He embodies a postmodern version of Norman Mailer's 1950s "white Negro"—the white "hipster" who emulates black hipness—in the final scene when he has won both the primary and Nina, who reassures him: "You're insecure because you're white.... You know you're my nigger." Nina had been hired to help kill him, but instead becomes his savior, converting him to hip (hop) politics and epistemological "blackness."

On the one hand, *Bulworth* exhibits extraordinary hopefulness about the power of popular culture to seduce politicians to see and speak social truth. Bulworth wins the primary by a landslide and momentarily sparks a new trend of honesty in politics (the voters, like their senator, are now "aroused"). By implication, popular cultural politics may yet make America a cool, enjoyable, just, and responsible place where one's libido and social conscience are both fulfilled. On the other hand, the film sends the message that just about all politicians are indeed crooked and that if they buck the system, they are bound to be assassinated (like the Kennedys, King, Malcolm X). After Nina anoints Bulworth her "nigger," the enraged, resentful insurance lobbyist, perched on a rooftop, shoots and apparently kills Bulworth. The forces that keep U.S. politics systematically corrupt seem to triumph over truth-telling, public health, economic justice, sane race relations, enjoyment, popular music, and love, thus appearing to confirm Bulworth's prediction in church: "You're never gonna get rid of somebody like me." Yet the film presents rap and the gritty politics it popularizes as coming closer than anything else America has to do the trick. *Bulworth* closes enigmatically, perhaps hopefully, with Amiri Baraka—who plays a kind of Shakespearean fool or seer—chanting outside the hospital: "We need a spirit, Bulworth, not a ghost." "You got to sing, Bulworth." "And the spirit will not descend without the song."

I am intrigued by Lemisch's polemic and Beatty's *Bulworth* partly because in chapter 4 I argued that U.S. cultural studies critics should think more expansively not only about developing critiques of cultural producers and cultural productions that foreground their complicity in the mystification or reproduction of social contradictions—a requisite critical project—but also about the ways in which culture has the affirmative power to energize agency and engage resistance to injustice. That is, how have deployments of the affirmative aspects of culture helped, directly or indirectly, incite and organize political incentive and energy? Alan Wald links his pre-1960s teenage social alienation with his love for "the cool jazz scene." And his college's "classical[ly] Marxist" Young Socialist Alliance was even more fun because it was "culturally sophisticated with a touch of beat/bohemianism." Yet he recognizes that this fusion of culture, politics, and cool was not new, for the Old Left was "just as intelligent, just as devoted, and just as cool when they were young."[15] Culture can be used to rationalize, disguise, deflect attention from, and sometimes illuminate social contradictions. It can also excite and inspire agents—by politicizing, but perhaps *not only* by politicizing—to organize to combat contradictions.

Antonio Gramsci engaged these concerns in prison in the 1930s when he developed hegemony theory. Dominant social forces use cultural hegemony to win popular "consent" to their rule. Yet the hegemonic goal is often more ambitious: a sophisticated cultural hegemony strives to socialize citizens, workers, and consumers not just to be resigned to, but to be exuberant about "competing" and consuming (in socioeconomic systems that distribute wealth, power, and access unequally). Thus the Left must interest itself in the hegemonic ways in which incentives, interest, and forms of subjective potency are produced so that it may intervene in and become a force in shaping them. Lemisch asks a Gramscian question (without citing Gramsci): Can the U.S. Left tactically learn more about what makes popular culture popular in order to *hegemonize* resistance and organizing as compelling—perhaps also as fun? stylish? fascinating?

The British New Left has also generated some extremely complex debates about cultural-political tactics. The "first" New Left substituted the Fabian, Labour Party, and labor movement preoccupation with capturing state power—what Stuart Hall called "statism"—with their own analytical (and sometimes celebratory) focus on "the political and cultural life of ordinary people."[16] Many postwar consumers identified more with pop cultural roles, categories, aspirations, and fantasies made available to them within civil society than with state politics.[17] "What we need are not only discussion groups," Hall recommended in 1960, "but *centres of socialist work and activity*—rallying points of disturbance and discontent within the local community, the nerve centres of a genuinely popular and informed socialist movement." He urged that the Left clubs develop "their own initiatives" rather than adhere to what some may have construed as "the tables of Socialist Law."[18] In the 1980s the Greater London Council's (GLC) accomplishments materialized some of what the 1950s New Left had envisioned. At its best, Hall attested, the GLC had been able to draw on the "popular energies" of movements (organized by blacks, women, the disabled, the homeless), acknowledged their "autonomy," and with their support initiated changes in government and cultural administration. This process drew the "sites of daily life ... into the orbit of politics."[19] New Leftists made central the question of how ideas, ideologies, perceptions, and structures of feeling became and could become "popular."

Hall noted in 1960 that socialism had to regain the support of youth in order to popularize itself.[20] From the 1950s through the anti-Thatcher campaigns of the 1980s, the cultural studies Left, like Lemish, saw youth culture as a key arena of social change.[21] New Leftists linked the turn toward youth and their enthusiasms with their criticism of the Labour Party: youth were not "under the constant watchful eye of the Parliamentary whips!"[22] Hall worried that political parties failed to grasp popular culture as an effective organizing tool: "The old people will want to organise the young: will they take it? The younger people will want to play jazz and show films: will the old stagers let them?"[23] New Leftists had begun to see the capability of youth culture to catalyse boycotts, protest marches, and new kinds of political organizations. In short, youth cultures were not only reenergizing, but reinventing postwar understandings of what politics might encompass and how it could be organized.[24] New Leftists came to appreciate that politicking had to be more than electoral—it had to be popular, cultural, and invested in the practices, perceptions, and structures of feelings of daily life. They reassessed the cultural apparatus as the *popularizing apparatus*.

Youth rebellion exemplified the possibility that capitalism's popularizing apparatuses could be turned against it: "It is significant that the liveliest revolt against the existing system," Williams contended in 1960, "particularly among the new young generation, is in precisely these cultural terms." The "cultural questions," he claimed, illuminated how "change in our society" takes place and what changes need to take place.[25]

Williams's interest in studying popular culture was first and foremost strategic: to learn how to transform it "on its own ground."[26] He had described the "long revolution" as a process whereby progressive forces struggled to achieve "popular control" to bring about political, economic, social, and cultural changes.[27] Similarly, even in 1960 Hall espoused a cultural politics because of politics, not because of a fascination with popular culture: "The purpose of discussing the cinema or teenage culture in *New Left Review* is not to show that, in some modish way, we are keeping up with the times." His "Notes on Deconstructing 'the Popular'" (1981) is even more emphatic (echoing Rhett Butler's farewell to Scarlet O'Hara in Margaret Mitchell's *Gone with the Wind* [1936]). Although popular culture is the site of resistance and consent to hegemony, he writes, "it is not a sphere where socialism, a socialist culture—fully formed—might be simply 'expressed.'" Nonetheless, "it is one of the places where socialism might be constituted.... That is why 'popular culture' matters. Otherwise, to tell you the truth, I don't give a damn about it."[28] And in "The Culture Gap" (1984) Hall makes no bones about why he studies culture: he wants the Left to "expropriate" it.[29]

Key founders of British New Left cultural studies sustained versions of this early New Left project in their support of counterhegemonic battles against Thatcherism in the 1980s. Margaret Thatcher's cultural as well as political successes—as much as Gramsci's theories—fueled their interest in redeploying the popular. They debated how a knowledge of popular culture—not just of parties or of the state—might aid the Left.

I want to revisit these debates for three reasons. First, they demonstrate something that U.S. cultural studies scholars should be more aware of—much cultural studies theorizing was done as responses to and attempted interventions in political campaigns and Labour Party policy.[30] Gramsci was vital to many British New Left critics not so much because they wished to make theoretical "interventions" in academic journals, but because they hoped to influence the political and cultural strategy of the parties, movements, and bureaucracies that sought to oust Thatcher. Second, the debates get at the heart of some New Left and post–New Left cultural studies tendencies to place culture in competition with traditionally conceived "politics" as the key to political transformation. They amplify a critical orientation in cultural studies that invests—perhaps overinvests—much political stock in popular culture as the motor of social change. Third, I will reflect on this particular trend not only because of its enduring political-intellectual significance, but because I believe that it made a certain style of British cultural studies even more tantalizing to the Reagan-Bush era U.S. academy as the latest "sexy" theory import. When some American advocates of cultural studies tried to make it a force in the "culture wars," it was already looking far more pop cultural than socialist. Many U.S. academics were interested not in *Socialist Hegemonizing Studies* but in what they took to be a postsocialist cultural studies. In America "cultural studies" evoked not intellectual work produced to catalyze a revisionary socialist movement, but a more complexly theorized, interdisciplinary, multidisciplinary, and postdisciplinary academic popular culture studies, gender and sexuality studies, multicultural studies. To consider the timing of this Americanization, my analysis, as it has in the previous chapters, criss-crosses the Atlantic.

Cool Aid?

As Jesse Lemish's MTVism suggests, the American efforts to popularize the Left through popular culture were often linked with two related concerns: representing the Left as pleasurable and as hip. In the 1990s several things happened that drew my attention to a cultural studies tendency toward ludic hipness. One incident occurred at the University of Illinois "Cultural Studies Now and In the Future" conference in April 1990. It was not recorded in the tome that published the conference papers. As noted in chapter 1, audience members criticized the conference in conversation, verbal protest, and a broadside printed and distributed on the scene. The conference, dissenters argued, reproduced social and academic power relations that cultural studies presumably opposed, in part by staging the lecturers as celebrities and casting the audience as fans.

This performative dimension became explicit when Homi Bhabha and Meaghan Morris took the stage. Bhabha was about to deliver his talk on "Postcolonial Authority and Modern Guilt" while Morris sat on stage. As Bhabha began, a bass guitar could be heard booming rhythmic funk riffs elsewhere in the large building. The conference organizers dispatched representatives to squelch the soundtrack. Before they succeeded, Bhabha, with good humor, began to move his body to the rhythm. Soon he turned to Morris and asked her to dance on stage. Morris, who declined, may have viewed their dancing on stage as a confirmation of their status more as hip critical theory performers than as would-be intellectual agents of social change—though the two roles are not necessarily mutually exclusive. (Some cultural studies theorists cultivate the aura of rock stars and, interestingly, some have borrowed the titles of hit rock songs for their books.)[31]

At times the Illinois stage seemed like a chic critique fashion show. Numerous conversations I had with young academics in this period induced me to posit connections between the importation of cultural studies and the formation of what bore some signs of an academic subculture.[32] American studies never had such subcultural or bohemian "oppositional" prestige and glamour. I mused: What purposes would cultural studies serve in the U.S. academy as a subculture? During America's late-twentieth-century "theory" decades, was cultural studies expanding political critique and making it usable in new ways, or was it reducing critique to compensatory culturalist hipness?[33] Were professors experiencing Bulworth's hip(-hop) epiphany?[34]

Could it be that the political potential of a glossier, more popular American cultural studies is precisely its capacity to make some aspects of politics glossy and thus less easily glossed over? Can this kind of postmodern pedagogy and scholarship, drawing on Lemisch's interests in MTV, help give students from various classes and social groups the incentive to invest in political and cultural critique and transformation? At the Illinois conference, Hall, reflecting on the dangers of the institutional Americanization of cultural studies, felt the schoolmasterish need to remind the audience—and the lecturers—that cultural studies is "deadly serious." I welcomed his warning. That said, as we will see, for several decades Hall and company have asked in all seriousness: can a ludic social movement and critique make it "cool" to get involved in a range of "deadly serious" political fronts?

Mills certainly wrote "deadly serious" books, articles, and lectures that the British and American New Lefts admired. At the same time, scholarly and popular commentaries on him, in his day and ours, suggest that his enduring mystique is partly beholden to the fact that in the gray-flannelled 1950s and early 1960s this leather-clad professor "came roaring into Morningside Heights on his BMW motorcycle, wearing plaid shirts, old jeans, and work boots, carrying his books in a duffel bag strapped across his broad chest."[35] Riding a motorcycle is not inherently "cool." The arch-conservative William F. Buckley, like Mills, enjoyed riding his motorbike in New York City. Mills's bike solved his problem of parking near Columbia. Yet in the 1950s Mills's students knew that their professor's motorcycle and sartorial idiosyncrasy constituted a symbolic refusal to go along with the politics and organization of value that many of the gray-flannel "suits" tried to symbolize as normal, respectable, and rational. "We cannot expect to create a Left with mere slogans," Mills admonished in 1959, adding significantly, "much less with the tired old slogans that bore us so."[36]

Shooting from the Hip at Oxford

Hall and several of his Oxford confrères on the British New Left-in-formation were absorbed with concerns about political-cultural style as well as substance in the mid- and late 1950s. The editorial collectives of *Universities and Left Review* (which included Hall and Raphael Samuel) and of *New Reasoner* (which included E. P. Thompson) were influential in directing the look of the New Left. The *New Reasoner* group was shaped by the struggles of the 1930s and war in the 1940s. While the younger *Universities and Left Review* contingent, composed of members of what Hall termed "the 'Oxford left,'" was especially molded by the pressures and alienation of the early Cold War.[37] Hall describes their differences not oversimply as age, but as arising from different political formations.[38]

Samuel is forthright about how the *Universities and Left Review* group cultivated an avant garde political counterculture—and a not-only-political counterculture—as a means of establishing group identity and confidence as well as broadening their political and cultural concerns and sympathies (42). They defined Britain's problem not just as capitalism, but, in more bohemian terms, as the uncool "Establishment" (42).[39] Their heroes included abstract artists, filmmakers, and playwrights as well as C. Wright Mills. They sponsored jazz and poetry readings as well as protest on behalf of the Campaign for Nuclear Disarmament. And with the translation of Karl Marx's *Economic and Philosophical Manuscripts* (1844), the young radicals gave Marxist "alienation" the attention that "exploitation" once enjoyed among socialists (43). "'Alienation,'" Samuel elaborates, "involved a whole set of displacements in socialist thought. It transposed the two-camp division of society from the field of production to that of civil society. For the 'Mr. Moneybags' of Marx's *Capital* it substituted such more indeterminate totalities as 'the mass persuaders.'" Alienation authorized a cultural and subjective turn in their political interests. Exploitation suggests the need for defensive organizing, whereas one may not at first think of organizing to combat "alienation." Yet the Oxford New Left did indeed use "alienation" to organize young professional-managerial backing for the New Left.

Universities and Left Review saw its mission not only as enlarging the scope of Left critique, but as reorganizing the professional-managerial class Left. The journal tapped into and shaped the cultural interests of its supporters to better succeed in this remobilizing project. It sponsored the formation of *Universities and Left Review* clubs throughout Britain (the London clubs were especially popular), and these clubs provided stages not only for political debates, but for cultural performances. They made socialism *fun*. In particular, the magazine appealed to young socialists and not, in the words of one young New Leftist, socialist "squares" (44). "'*ULR*-ers' dressed sharply and danced coolly," Samuel recalled. "In the idiom of the day, they were 'hip'—a term or fantasy of self, coined by Norman Mailer, writing on 'The White Negroes' in *Dissent,* our sister publication in New York.... They discovered in working-class adolescents the rebels and outsiders of our time." "Hip" (in the know) and "cool" (in style) were current argot in jazz circles even in the 1940s (OED). Mailer's White "hipster" of 1957 emulated what Mailer took to be a black subjective survival style or, in contemporary parlance, *attitude*. The hipster's cultural interests and style enabled him to develop a critical and subjective distance from social authority and the past—he would not grow old gracefully. He achieved imagined potency through transgressive marginality. Samuel adds that the term "hip," "which spread like wildfire" through their circles, "made some of us uncomfortable" (44), but does not explain why. We "conceptualize[d] political issues in terms of 'Ancients and Moderns' and ... treat[ed] our adversaries as by definition 'old-fashioned' and 'out of date'" (44). Yet taking account of the omissions in the early New Left's development of a political counterculture, Samuel includes on his list individual rights, women's rights, gay and lesbian rights (51–52). He attributes this to the New Left's still somewhat orthodox "socialist unconscious" (51).

Hall perceives the New Left, particularly the Oxford *Universities and Left Review* circle, as making more of a "modernizing" departure from an older Left. He suggests that this break was conditioned by the site of its rather elite institutionalization. Musing on the magazine's Oxford origins, he contrasted the politics and (counter)cultural hipness of the editorial collective with the "brittle, casual self-confidence of Oxford's dominant tone" (18) and the sexist, masculine "'Hooray Henries' of its time, attempting to relive *Brideshead Revisited*. I 'hear' that Oxford now principally as a particular pitch of the voice—the upper-middle-class English male commanding attention to confidently expressed banalities as a sort of seigniorial right" (19). Against the "willed triviality" (18) that Hall detested, the magazine's group debated how the "broad left" was responding to "consumer capitalism" (18) and identified with the university's minority population of "young veterans and national servicemen, Ruskin College trade unionists, 'scholarship boys' and girls from home and abroad" (19). Nonetheless, both he and Samuel suggest that their boldness in setting up *Universities and Left Review* partly derived from the Oxford confidence they reviled. "The very idea of four Oxford graduates setting out to teach socialism to the world comes from the particular vanity of this university," Samuel asserted. "We wouldn't have had the arrogance to embark on this project if we had not been the beneficiaries of a century of accumulated moral, symbolic and cultural capital that this university had." Hall acknowledges: "The degree to which we were totally unreflective about [Oxford's class influence] really terrifies me in retrospect."[40]

Michael Rustin, a slightly younger member of the New Left, also reads this Oxford countercultural New Left as class-based. He proposes this as an explanation for the relative lack of political engagement imagined or attempted by the magazine's collective in the policies of the Labour Party or in the orientation of the labor movement. The subcultural Oxford New Left, he maintains, had little truck with working-class struggles. [41]

Let Them Eat Culture;
Or Designer Socialism as Designer Popularism

Several British New Left cultural studies intellectuals tried again to reestablish a political counterculture in the 1980s. Gramsci's concept of hegemony as a cultural and ideological struggle for "hearts and minds" achieved not just intellectual but political prominence as Left intellectuals debated one another throughout the decade on how best to wage the fight for hegemony against Thatcherism and recapture what Gramsci called the "national popular." Two major magazines, *Marxism Today* and *New Socialist,* featured these debates. An intellectual, cultural, and political movement nominated "designer socialism" emerged as the locus of controversy. Designer socialists drew on a limited understanding of what Stuart Hall and *Marxism Today* editor Martin Jacques in 1988 termed "New Times." Some designer socialists perceived a transition toward (what Hall and Richard Hoggart in the 1950s thought of as a popularized semblance of) "classlessness." Classes still existed in the 1980s, Hall explained, however, many workers were doing different kinds of work in the service rather than industrial sector, and they often identified not primarily with their class but with their gender, ethnoracial, or sexuality group. Thus Hall and others endeavored, as Lemisch later did, to persuade the Left that it now had to update its awareness of its actual and potential political constituencies. The Left, Hall warned, echoing his 1950s admonitions, had entered New Times that demanded new strategies that hinged on using the new powers of culture.

These Gramscian strategies moved toward reconceiving socialism as *popularism*.[42] Radical historian Eric Hobsbawm expressed the romance and excitement of a Left that had at long last begun to recognize the exigency of rethinking itself as a mass-cultural Left. "The advance to socialism," he implored, "depends on mobilizing people ... who remember the date of the Beatles' break-up and not the date of the Saltey pickets." The cultural studies New Left wanted to learn how to appeal not just to voters, citizens, or workers, but to fans and consumers. If the Beatles, Rolling Stones, and other rock stars seemed to make pseudopatriotic deference uncool, why couldn't rock make Thatcherism uncool? And if fans had the incentive to queue up all night to buy tickets for a Stones concert, imagine if that incentive was channeled in the service of social(ist) transformation? The Beatles and Stones, after all, were far more successful at selling and popularizing some antiauthoritarian attitudes than the Left in both Britain and America. In the United States such supergroups commercially staged the "British invasion" and did much to demilitarize youth culture and discredit U.S. imperialism in Vietnam not just as morally unjust, but as a machinery of Establishment conformism.

David Widgery saw alliances between rock and a more expansive "socialist politics" as electric fusions that might well prevent the Labour Party from "boring a generation to political death by its narrow definitions of what is political."[43] The playwright David Edgar, writing for *New Socialist*, indicated the debt this cultural strategy owed the 1960s "culture of insubordination" and "vocabulary of protest": in the "great industrial struggles of the 1970s ... the rediscovery of the sit-in and the squat were transformed—pumpkin-like—into the industrial work-in and the factory occupation."[44] Scott Lash and John Urry observed that the 1960s and 1970s shop-floor militancy of young Britons was inspired not so much by class consciousness, but by "popular music, the changing styles of dress ... and radical individualist opposition to authority and especially to the deference accorded to the age."[45] Widgery warned that if socialism makes its "emotional appeal ... to a working-class sacrifice and middle-class guilt, and if its dominant medium is the printed word and the public procession, it will simply bounce off people who have grown up this side of the sixties watershed."[46] Some Labour tacticians actually tried to refashion aspects of party politics as partying politics.[47] Labour Party election campaign vans boomed: "The Labour Party is the fun party, the good time party, come and enjoy yourselves."[48]

At times, Hall, Widgery, and others—well before Lemisch took a stab at it in the United States—seemed to aspire to become not just theorists of a new politics, but public relations strategists of the Labour Party, labor movement, and the less organized socialist Left. Hall repeatedly offered the Labour Party lessons in how to hegemonize. "The style of propaganda, party political broadcasts, of much educational and agitational material," he explained, "locks us into very traditional and backward-looking associations. Our political imagery is even worse in this respect. We virtually fought the 1983 election on the 1945 political programme." His solution? *Always popularize!* "Developing a real popular historical consciousness on the Left is *not* the same thing as thinking the present in the language and imagery of the past."[49]

Another related characteristic of this redesigned socialism is the discourse of the new and the obsolete. The problems and contradictions addressed by the Labour Party, the argument went, had lost their popular appeal. Britons were more diverse than ever and now looked to culture even more than to class politics for their incentives (in America, this was Lemisch's new board game). Hall lectured: "Why should socialism be a popular political force when it is not a force in popular culture and aspirations of the masses?"[50] Apparently, "the masses" no longer wanted to consume Labour.

Hall, like Widgery and others, was excited about the hegemonic potential of rock and pop music. In "People Aid: A New Politics Sweeps the Land" (1988), Hall and Jacques waxed rhapsodic about the "unparalleled mobilizing power" of trans-Atlantic media events like the Live Aid concerts: "The combination of culture and politics, altruism and fun, was irresistible." The mega-concert provided an example of the "cultural languages" the Left had to learn in order to reach youth. Hall and Jacques's premise was that popular culture, exemplified by rock, could mobilize faster and more effectively than traditionally conceived party appeals. They hoped that those who had only wanted to be entertained by a "charity rock" fund-raiser would wind up mobilized by a cause.[51]

At its most extreme, *pop socialism* turned into a questionable *pop stylism* in the hands of journalists like Robert Elms, editor of *Face* magazine, who published his polemic "Ditching the Drabbies" after the ill-fated National Miners Union strike of 1985. The miners, and the working-class politics they represented for style agitators like Elms, were chucked into the category of "drabbies." Elms proposed that the Left reglamorize itself to reach beyond the traditionally conceived socialist public. His prose reads like ad copy for a new Left wardrobe and makeover: "Style and the Left were once synonymous.... Throughout its international history socialism has understood the power of style.... From basque berets to beatnik boots, any creed which cherishes both the individualism of the free thinker and the solid bond of unity should have a surfeit of style." Elms placed the "mass desire for style" at the center of the masses' aspirations for "mass improvement." If Widgery and Hall elaborated the popular as political strategy, for Elms what truly mattered was grasping the social magic of style and glamour: "Style is a shorthand for the way you do things—everything." He represented style—not organizing—as the developer of agency. More extremely than Hall, he believed: "The anachronistic image and imagery of much of the trade union movement has been an important part of our massive failure of presentation." But presentation for whom? Was the (changing) working class still part of the audience Elms had in mind?

For strategic inspiration Elms turned not to Marx, but to Oscar Wilde, who advised: "'Only fools do not judge by appearances.'" Out-of-style socialists misunderstood the problem of Thatcherist Britain as pertaining to the unequal distribution of wealth, employment opportunities, and political power. Elms set them straight: "In a Britain where there are more video recorders and home computers per head than anywhere in Europe, vague promises of wage slavery and bread for all simply will not move anybody." Consumer-voters, Elms cautioned, will not buy sales pitches that stress complicity and responsibility: "Until we throw off the shabby yoke of middle-class guilt and the rigid conservatism of old-style socialism, we will not win the style wars." And so Elms and others tried to reoutfit Gramsci's war of position as a war of style.[52]

Marxism Today waged the style wars with advertisements for *Marxism Today* credit cards, underwear with Aeroflot insignias, and Spanish Civil War shirts. It featured strategic articles on choosing the right wines. For some, no doubt, the attention lavished on popular culture, fun, performance, style potency, and commodity acquisition made this New Left seem less threatening and more upscale in its enthusiasms. Glossy Left identity and commodity fetishization moved in tandem, unbothered by vulgar haranguing about redistribution and exploitation. Consumer-socialists embraced popular diversions as potential subversions—that is, as individual expressions of popular pleasures and consumer agency that no commodity could ever wholly script.[53] To the extent that this consumer emphasis can be associated with the spread of American capitalism, then British consumer cultural studies was partly Americanized before it was awarded fashionable status in the U.S. academy in the mid- and late 1980s.

One can "consume" intellectuals as well as Aeroflot underwear. In the 1980s the designer Left sought to rally its forces and win new adherents by staging Left intellectuals as celebrities (and celebrators). "Join the fun at Left Alive," one advertisement entreated readers in *Marxism Today*. Being "Left Alive," the copy announced, was not so bad. The magazine sponsored an "extravaganza" that included "discussion, politics, sports, dance, and drama ... live music in the bar, swimming, jazz, dance, jogging, children's entertainment." Williams, Hall, author Angela Carter, and Ken Livingstone, head of the Greater London Council, topped the list of celebrity speakers.[54]

Critiques of Designer Popularism

Designer socialism stirred up heated debate in major Left publications.[55] Judith Williamson's "The Problems of Being Popular" (1986) challenged the sometimes unstated designer socialist premise that citizens were capable of being fascinated only by what had been mass produced as popular. "I can't say this too strongly, people's lives are *transformed* by the discovery of radical ideas, and it is a terrible abdication on the part of the left if we cannot continue to develop these."[56] This criticism on behalf of criticism has merit. Writing about the relative successes of the *Universities and Left Review* and *New Left Review* clubs established throughout Britain in the early 1960s, Rustin observes that critical thinking was in demand: "[They] had amazing success in attracting weekly audiences of hundreds of people to meetings.... Suddenly, the political agenda was completely redefined and opened up. Literature (especially that of commitment), history (especially that of the 1930s and of communism), art and architecture, social theory, youth culture, class neutralism and the Cold War, and the more 'conventional' political issues of poverty, economic planning and education, succeeded one another as the week's topic."[57] One might object that *New Left Review* never filled Wembley Arena with tens of thousands screaming Left fans frantic to hear Williams or Williamson explain how one might best decode advertisements. Still, Williamson is rightly concerned about the ideas and issues that animate Left public pedagogy—far more is at stake in teaching than popularity.

Williamson also challenged designer socialism's celebrations of "popular pleasures" by probing the power relations built into the construction of and social need for particular kinds of (often compensatory) "pleasures." She describes the "pleasure" she took as a teenager from reading paperback romances as "masochistic," and makes the more general point: "Surely we can try to understand that pleasures are had from mass culture and how personal and social needs feed into these pleasures without jumping to the conclusion that they are a 'good thing'?" The dialectical tension "between the way we are constrained to live—which of course can be made to yield pleasures—and the way we would like to live . . . . is starting to slip away in left debate, as if there were really quite enough that's radical in what's already there—as if change were no longer a priority." Popular tastes are *made* popular. The Consumer Left, she objected, underestimates the cultural as well as the political and intellectual range of interests and concerns of its constituencies.[58]

In its efforts to win attention for itself and be accepted, she holds, the Pop Left has become too timid to imagine and promote alternative structures of value, meaningfulness, relationship, and fascination. "The way to tackle a popular subject now is apparently to show how unalternative you are," Williamson complains. "Hence a fashion seminar at *MT*'s Left Alive '86 conference involves top designers and fashion writers—a session on pop TV means writing advertisers and promo directors—and why not throw in Armani, Vidal Sasson and Steven Spielberg while one is about it?"[59] Williamson viewed designer socialism as a contraction rather than an expansion of Left social vision and ambition—and as a symptom of Left despair. Over a decade later, writing about America, Barbara Ehrenreich also expressed concern about the Left's "deluded populism," and suggested that it should get "used to being in a minority—a small minority—for some time to come." She added: "You don't just drop things because they are unpopular."[60]

Stuart Cosgrove, a radical cultural historian, contributed a satirical piece to *Marxism Today* on how the cultural studies—or consumption studies—post–New Left was making Left critique synonymous with popular culture studies that celebrate consumer reencodings of commodity codes. He started his university career by reading Bertolt Brecht, his satire went, but was then swayed by popular culture courses and textbooks and soon found himself "glued" to the television show *The Two Ronnies*: "I had spent the last four years of my life watching unadulterated shit, convinced that the analysis of popular television was a radical act. . . . You know I've worn through the soles of three pairs of Frank Wright loafers trudging around university refectories to talk about 'Top of the Pops' and the future of Consumer Socialism." Activism, he implied, entails more than being a fan and inciting students to consume subversively and outrageously.

Simon Frith and John Street's "Party Music" (1986) scrutinized the Labour Party's music campaign. Red Wedge, for instance, was a band of celebrated musicians who toured the country performing as cultural mobilizers on behalf of the Left. The group "shrugged off the notorious reluctance of musicians to organise; they're prepared to discuss policies rather than states of mind and being, the usual concerns of rock thought." Nevertheless, Frith and Street recalled Abbie Hoffman's experience at Woodstock—he was kicked off stage by The Who's Pete Townsend for giving a political speech rather than simply grooving in Woodstock's aura (the millionaire rock star's "we won't get fooled again" line apparently precluded explicit political opposition). Thinking about the tenacity of corporate-formed rock-consumer expectations, Frith and Street wondered if Red Wedge was succeeding "in politicizing youth. . . . Its position is muddled on this, on the one hand claiming to represent youth, on the other to educate them. Red Wedge's audiences themselves appeared to reject both models for a more familiar one—the Red Wedge stars were there to entertain them." (One also may wonder how many of Live Aid's millions of worldwide viewers who sought entertainment were mobilized.) Frith and Street made the sort of distinctions that Williamson called for in evaluating the political contents of popular culture: "The market pursuit of the good lifestyle may be utopian," they cautioned, "but it is not utopian socialism." They also recognized that the Labour Party itself was no supporter of utopian socialism—or perhaps any substantive socialism—and concluded: "The important question Red Wedge asks (and hasn't yet answered) is how to move from the recruitment of young consumers and *voters* to the empowerment of young producers and activists (and the nagging suspicion is that the Labour party leadership would prefer to keep people in a consuming and voting niche anyway)."[61]

In celebration of its thirtieth anniversary in 1987, *Marxism Today* published comments on the magazine by Left luminaries—assessments that testify to the magazine's openness to sometimes barbed criticism. Several writers pointed both to the trendy London-centered politics that the magazine represented and to its class profile. "*MT* to me," quipped author Michael Ignatieff, "is like an extremely bright, cheerful little rodent, with bright-rimmed glasses and bow tie, leaping off a sinking ship." Journalist Ann Leslie proposed retitling the magazine *Socialism for the Thinking Yuppie*. Some of the magazine's articles parodied this class appeal. The authors of "What Will You Wear to the Revolution" (1987) noted candidly that "Stalinist chic" clothes are purchased "by hip, young apolitical dudes in Covent Garden, not those gathering at Blackpool and Brighton." One correspondent dissented: "As a Communist Party member, I frankly find statements like 'the pleasure of purchase . . . should not be a ritual of guilt' insulting, and I would find it very difficult to defend or explain such bad taste to an unemployed or low paid person for whom a spending spree is an unknown pleasure." Other criticisms included the charge that designer socialism was really a form of guilt-free and complicity-free designer individualism—encouraging designer Lefties to be comfortable not only with consuming, but with individualizing their commitments.[62]

One of the most powerful critiques of designer socialism focused on what some perceived to be its abandonment of the miners in the grueling National Union of Miners strike of 1984–85, which the miners lost. Two months before the strike was declared—in response to the announced closing of mines—Hall again exhorted the Labour Party and the Left not to think in "anachronistic cultural terms": "This is not an argument for abandoning the traditional Labour constituencies or those particularly hard-pressed and disadvantaged minorities with whom the labour movement now needs to forge real alliances in action at the grassroots level. . . . It is an argument for recognising the complexity and diversity of cultural experience in Britain today and developing strategies which address the mass common experience."[63]

Samuel's "Doing Dirt on the Miners" (1986)—published in *New Socialist* a few months after Elms's piece in that same journal pooh-poohed the miners as unstylish—observed angrily that "during the strike itself it seems that there was a repressed rage [registered in London-based designer socialist publications] at having to support a cause which many only half-believed in" (14). The "metropolitan intelligentsia" settled "accounts with their radical past," embraced pragmatic "electoralism," eschewed "direct action," and adopted "a politics of survival"—not the miners' survival, but their own. Their "postradical chic" advocated "a politics built out of a negation of the past, both their own and that of others." Samuel cited Vera Britten's censure of socialists who "'don't like the smell of the proletariat.'" Male industrial laborers, he suggests, having failed to live up to Marx's revolutionary hopes, have been punished by the designer Left: they have been rendered subordinate as subjects of political interest. Overlooking the female feminists who supported the young and older miners, Samuel overgeneralized: "To feminists, or those who (though men themselves) borrow and manipulate a feminist vocabulary, [the male worker] is a representative of 'male' politics. For the young or would-be young ('Mutton dressed as lamb'), he is denounced for being 'middle aged,' a recent addition to the lexicon of political abuse which seems to be sweeping London labour circles."

Samuel's insight into the symptomatic significance of this denial is on the same wavelength as Williamson's analysis published just one month earlier in *New Socialist*. He wrote: "The strike is serving as a displaced object of the left's discomfort with itself, of a Communist Party, which is no longer certain what it exists for, of a Labour Party which is no longer sure what it believes in, of a New Left which has lost its taste for the streets." The response to the strikers also exhibited the extent to which some designer socialists and Labour Party leaders had given up on the economic restructuring once deemed essential to the socialist project.[64]

Williamson, Cosgrove, Samuel, and others believed that the power of truth-telling would in itself compel attention—a traditional socialist hope. In the early 1950s, Thompson quoted Morris on not pulling back: "If you tell your audiences that you are going to change so little that they will scarcely feel the change, whether you scare anyone or not, you will certainly not interest those who have nothing to hope for in present society, and whom the hope of a change has attracted toward Socialism."[65] As forthright as Williamson and others wanted to be, under Thatcherism, many Leftists became convinced, and understandably so, that the Left's strategic role had to entail more than confidently disseminating radical analysis and that, like it or not, facing the music had become a complicated ideological endeavor.

The Competition between Culture and Politics to Be Political

Here I will again elaborate on aspects of the Bulworth trend I first broached in chapter 2: the Left tendency to represent progressive social transformation through electoral means as unlikely and the belief that electoralism is naive. Recently several British and American critics offered critiques of the politics—perhaps the antipolitics—of some formulations of cultural politics, cultural opposition, and cultural agency. I want to assess some of these critiques by first relating them to an observation that James Kavanagh made in 1990: U.S. culture, he notes, is adept at establishing consumer interest in sports competitions, cable TV, Hollywood films, popular literature, and other cultural productions that "make every effort emphatically to disavow 'politics,' to avoid thinking about who should control the power of the state." Many consumers are more preoccupied with consuming popular culture and commodities than with listening to political speeches or political news (sex scandals are the exception) even when they are miniaturized into digestible sound bites. What Kavanagh omits from his account is the considerable electoral choice conservative voters enjoy in America. Yet he provocatively reads the cultural "depoliticization" of (more progressive) citizens not as a failure of the democratic capitalist system, but as one reason for its reproductive success.[66] Several critics have asked whether some forms of cultural studies have lent support to this mass-cultural machinery of (traditionally defined) "political" disengagement.

Both Todd Gitlin and Francis Mulhern pick up on the thesis that the popular electoral decline of the Left since the 1960s motivated the intellectual Left's compensatory turn toward popular and youth culture as the site of social change and potential insurgency. Mulhern has advanced the argument that cultural studies has substituted work on popular culture for more traditional Left concerns, such as "the old concepts 'class,' 'state,' 'struggle,' 'revolution.'" I would contend that the most complex critiques in U.S. cultural studies that focus on popular culture examine these categories and other expansive Left categories (working out relationships among class, racialization, gender construction, and popular culture). Yet Mulhern's thesis is provocative: "From the beginning, cultural studies has tended to dissolve politics into culture. Even Raymond Williams, who remained politically engaged and active outside the field of culture proper, in retrospect conceded that he had inflated the possibilities of cultural politics, and never quite escaped this tendency in his theoretical work."[67] Mulhern, however, acknowledges that the Left has split into many cultural, single-issue, identity-based Lefts, and that intellectuals sympathetic with these developments have increasingly paid greater heed to popular culture because the orthodox Left has tended to undervalue the presence, power, and worth of these political constituencies. Eagleton laments that this diffusion has produced a situation in which broad-based solidarity is often no longer headlined as a goal among Lefts that prize their difference from and differences with one another.[68]

In the mid- and late-1980s, Williamson, Cosgrove, and Rustin suggested that designer socialism's celebratory absorption with popular culture, fashion, and consumption should be understood as both a class project and an odd mirror-image-of-capitalism project—what Rustin characterized as a "politics [based] wholly on the interests of the middling strata" and a "tacit accommodation to the values of resurgent capitalism, in order (they hope) better to fight it."[69] Some British cultural studies critics, Mulhern stresses, seem more committed to experiencing "the secret pleasures of everyday capitalism" and to embracing consumer agency as subversive than to thinking through culture as a route to political organizing (Hall's 1960 conception of the New Left cultural-political project). And some, he adds, have overinvested their appreciations of popular culture and its commodities with a "deflated utopianism" that amounts to conformism.[70] The criticisms of Williamson, Cosgrove, Rustin, Mulhern, and Gitlin, viewed as a set, move toward suggesting that the sort of cultural studies that celebrates popular culture, even when it preserves the language of socialism, seems more like capitalist cultural studies. Such studies are too much a symptom of that which they hope to transform.

Gitlin in particular bemoans the power of some cultural studies to make electoral and governmental politics seem so untrustworthy, so unworthy of one's involvement, so uncool, so boring—for suckers. "The right may have taken possession of 10 Downing Street or the White House or Congress—and as a result of elections, embarrassingly enough!" Gitlin writes sarcastically, "but at least one is engaged within the English department" (33). He advises cultural studies aficionados to "learn more about politics, economy, and society, and in the process, appreciate better what culture, and cultural study, do *not* accomplish. If we wish to do politics, let us organize groups, coalitions, demonstrations, lobbies, whatever; let us do politics" (37). Contrasting the affiliations of political intellectuals in the United States, Britain, and Australia (three bases for cultural studies) with those in continental Europe, Gitlin notes: "In varying degrees, left-wing intellectuals in France, Italy, Scandinavia, Germany, Spain and elsewhere retain energizing attachments to Social Democratic, Green, and other left-wing parties" (34).[71]

Gitlin would not deny that teaching and learning in the university—itself a type of social organizing—has manifold political effects. But he counsels: "Let us not think that our academic work is already that [organizing, coalition building, lobbying]." George Lipsitz—a more optimistic advocate of culture-supported activism and organizing—concurs: "Taking a position is not the same as waging a war of position." He continues: "Students"—and teachers, I would add—"sometimes seem to feel that once they have changed themselves they have changed society." Yet how much of society must change in order to count as "changing society"?[72]

There are several problems with these kinds of critiques. Even the cultural studies that informed designer socialism did not always focus with bloated buoyancy on popular culture—many critiques of Thatcher were grimly focused on election results and dedicated to rethinking propaganda strategies. The popular culture versus electoral politics–economic issues divide that Gitlin and Mulhern posit as a defining feature of cultural studies is inaccurate as a description of much cultural studies work by Hall, Williams, Thompson, and others. Cultural studies has not been and is not monolithic.

It is extremely difficult to gauge the "political" effects of cultural politicizing. Must "real" politicizing establish formal and organized political constituencies to be effective? "Organizing" and "real politics" can take myriad forms. Gitlin, who came of political age in the 1960s Students for Democratic Society, is aware of this. Even so, at times he may be too distanced from the cultural politics he writes off: "Are the communities of African Americans or Afro-Caribbeans suffering? Well they have rap (Leave aside the question of whether all of them want rap in equal measure)" (33). More glib sarcasm: "Attend to popular culture, study it with sympathy for the rewards that minorities at least attempt to find there" (34). But sometimes there may be more to grooving than just grooving: Gitlin sampling hip-hop in his office, and 30,000 people, largely Afro-Caribbean, listening to hip-hop at a mid-1980s Greater London Council concert in a climate of systemic police brutality may be two vastly different cultural and political experiences.[73]

What Gitlin calls "doing politics" is easier said than done. Since the 1950s, for example, the British New Left has indeed made intermittent efforts—not hugely successful ones—to have some effect on Labour Party policy. Both Hall and Gitlin would concur that the Lefts are certain not to have any impact on electoral, legislative, and judicial politics unless they organize themselves to try to do so.[74] At the same time, what Gitlin fails to credit is the recognition that it is not possible to vote in or legislate all the "political" changes needed to transform social life in America. Culture—which produces habits, ways of seeing, structures of feeling, patterns of significance, systems of value—is a *political* site of much that needs to be transformed.[75] Popular culture is more complexly political than simply what "diverts" people from "real politics" with evasive compensations. An unfortunate shortcoming of some debates about cultural studies and cultural politics—manifest in Gitlin's work—is their contribution to setting up a binary opposition—a competition—between the politics associated with culture and identity (sometimes termed "soft politics") and the politics associated with parties, elections, economic policies, and governments (sometimes called "hard politics").

Why (Is) Cultural Studies?

The Left often tends to characterize—sometimes glamorize—itself as op- positional, adversarial, radical, dissident. While identifying oneself as radical certainly can give one a resistant subjective potency and a transgressive air of political defiance, it is also a way of announcing that one or one's group stands apart from the hegemonic crowd and, unlike them, has not been bam- boozled. Paradoxically, the Left often makes a virtue out of its marginalized in-the-minority identity, even as it strategizes to hegemonize and become the majority. As the founders of early Cold War cultural studies well knew, Left bids for majority support did not always take this tack. Not long before cultural studies was established, the organized Left styled itself as the obvious *majority* choice. As the Labour Party's prime minister of Britain from 1945–51, Clement Attlee ushered in some fundamental structural reforms, including the National Health Service and the nationalization of key industries. One commentator described his cultural "style": "It suited him to be thought a dull little man, and to sound rather like a suburban bank manager. Such people can make revolutions and no one will be frightened." Attlee conveyed reassuring respectability, not if-you-were-as-clever-as-I-am-you'd-be-radical hipness.[76] The encoding of certain political beliefs as cool and others as uncool can of course alienate groups—branded uncool—whose support the Left would like to win. Nevertheless, Attlee's own appeal was by no means timeless. He exemplified the postwar Left program and style that Hall argued was in need of New Left revision in the 1950s and long outmoded by the 1980s. Hall and his colleagues were right—the Left had to acknowledge new constituencies, issues, forms of economic power, contradictions, and understandings of what constitute "politics."

Likewise, the Reverend Jesse Jackson, founder of the Rainbow Coalition in the mid-1980s, had to negotiate American New Times. It is fascinating to wonder whether Hall noticed any similarities—not just the many obvious differences—between Attlee's older reassuring Leftism and Jackson's approach when he interviewed him in 1986 to discuss strategies for popularizing the Rainbow Coalition. In one revealing exchange between Jackson-the-political leader and Hall-the-political intellectual, Jackson rejected Hall's description of his foreign policy proposals as "radical." Jackson preferred a different vocabulary—his foreign policy proposals, he insisted, were "moral," not radical, and fundamentally in America's best "interests." (Nowadays the accent on the critical often supplants the stress on the moral, while many in the New Left era were at home with the idea of a critical morality, a socialist morality.) Whatever strength and confidence American progressive forces might gain by billing themselves as "radical," Jackson, by implication, seemed to view this tactic as self-limiting and impolitic if the goal is to win majority support.[77] The Reverend Jackson instead attempted to reappropriate discourses of righteousness—rooted in the Civil Rights movement—that the New Right had used to attract an electoral majority.

How might one label progressive forces if one's aim is to popularize them in the new millennium? Which label and which history that goes with the label work best in which conditions: common sense, moral, reasonable, democratic, egalitarian, civic, dissenting, radical, Left, socialism? Manning Marable stands by socialism, a label I discuss at greater length in chapter 6, as "a project of radical participatory democracy." Here Marable's choice is in sync with the decision Hall and others made in the late 1950s. Yet even in the 1930s the term "socialist" was under fire in the Labour Party. Radical, as Jackson suggests, connotes positions beyond what most people could possibly adopt. As for Left: "I am not too happy about terms like 'the left,'" Noam Chomsky, that great exponent of clear thinking, admits. "And I don't use it much. Take the solidarity movements of the '80s. Were they on the left?"[78]

Michael Moore's populist style, as well as his intelligence and humor, make his filmed and written critiques accessible. His baseball caps, flannel shirts, and jeans cast him as ordinary.[79] If Raymond Williams stressed that culture is ordinary, Moore shows that *politics is ordinary.* He wants his exposés, satires, and criticisms to seem not only accessible but commonsensical. Moore's point is that when one confronts the contradictions produced by America's unequal distributions of wealth, power, and access, one is taking neither an especially radical nor a particularly righteous or moral stance—one is simply acknowledging the obvious, the truth. And for Moore this is what "The Big One"—the United States—should be all about. This isn't an *ism,* he would have viewers believe, it's just opening one's eyes to who is hurting others and who is getting hurt—and to what might be done to publicize and stop it.

Debates about progressive strategy, definition, and labeling should continue. It may be that the American and British Lefts can pick up considerable support in some groups partly by representing themselves as hip, glamorous, stylish, pleasurable, and in tune with pop culture. (Of course, what's "cool" and even what's deemed pleasurable often changes rapidly in corporate-consumer capitalism—most young people today neither remember nor care about either the date of the Saltey pickets or that of the Beatles' breakup.) Organizing around enjoyment surely sounds more affirming—more consumer-friendly—than organizing around critiques of one's complicity with the reproduction of social contradictions. And yet religion has long popularized conscience and confessions of guilt as motivating forces, often through song and ritual. Reflecting on the Civil Rights movement, the challenge may be not only to establish an organizing culture based on critical clarity, moral confidence, affirmation, or style, but a culture of courage.[80]

Recently an organization called Avenging Angels established itself as a public relations, advertising, and marketing organization for the "causes and candidates of the Left." Their inaugural announcement in *The Nation* does not cite hipness, pleasure, joy, morality, complicity, or culture. Like Williamson, it boldly touts the transformative power of analysis and wit. "To improve your style, said Nietzsche, improve the quality of your ideas."[81] Progressive academics, rather than focusing only on theoretical and historical "politicizing," might take their cue from Avenging Angels and design courses on how dissent and critique have been popularized: Who succeeded and how?[82] To consider this is to move from hegemony analysis—important in and of itself—to hegemonizing analysis—the next step.

The Avenging Angels' "liberal" concentration on what some cultural studies intellectuals dismiss as electoralism is noteworthy. Should voting be a politically crucial issue to consider, not because the major political parties have miraculously decided to offer progressive initiatives, but because voting is a political activity accessible to (most) citizens? What cultural studies might do more concretely is contemplate how people may better gain access to political power and how to better *organize organizing.* Left organizing strategy—not just theory—could be at the heart of cultural studies.

The American Right is pondering such matters on campus. Over the last few years Republican mobilizers have altered their image to win postmodern recruits and reorganize organizing. Since the World Trade Center slaughter on September 11, 2001, increasing numbers of student Republican activist groups have emerged that want to "boogie" while fomenting a conservative revolution, having been "influenced as much by the mood and mores of MTV as ... by the musings of Allan Bloom." One major right-wing funding agency has printed an organizing handbook, "Start the Presses!," which, a reporter observes, "explicitly counsels its conservative charges to 'loosen up,' to, in effect, get in touch with their inner Abbie Hoffman." More and more campus activists are discarding blue blazers and "paleos" such as Pat Buchanan and Strom Thurmond to make over conservatism as hip, cool, and youthful. A group called "Hip-hop Republicans" exists at Howard University, while some conservatives at Bucknell sport spiked hair and "full-goth" metal wear. This Hunter S. Thompson rendition of Republican fervor often appeals to libertarianism even more than morality—or blends them as self-righteousness. "Start the Presses!" recommends no-holds-barred media strategies: "As a media outlet, you have the power to transform a minor event or fact into a major embarrassment.... If the school persecutes you, send out press releases, notify alumni and give the administration a public black eye."[83]

A far larger group of students, however, have joined the antisweatshop movement and have gained educations in popularizing contradictions, complicity, and organized resistance. Some of their protests have mounted critiques of the hipness designed to obfuscate exploitation and oppression (commercialized hipness, they realized, often involves one in rather than absolves one of complicity). Hence students have "rallied against Guess Jeans," which paid off the progressive rock band Rage Against the Machine to anoint their product as "hip." One student responded: "We have been told we needed to buy these clothes to be sexy, to be popular.... We felt used." As the antisweatshop and living wage movements have taken on dimensions of anticorporate and, for some, anticapitalist movements, increasing numbers of student activists concerned with social justice have rethought what deserves to be made popular. The killings that occurred on September 11, 2001—and the killings that followed—have prompted many students not to embrace Republican clubs as cool, but to commence antiwar organizing as ethical.[84]

The Rolling Thunder Down Home Democracy Tour, organized by progressive radio host, Jim Hightower, strives to make political engagement not just cool but fun for all ages and social groups. Inspired by the late-nineteenth-century Chautauqua Circuit project to bring religion, art, music, and educational lectures to the small towns of America, the Rolling Thunder tour—featuring local activists and artists as well as nationally known progressive artists (rap groups, folk groups, actors) and spokespersons (such as Moore, Molly Ivins, Studs Terkel)—bills itself as a "citizenship fair." Its "fun-loving" blend of politics, music, and entertainments are meant to reexcite citizens about a democratic participation that includes, though goes well beyond, voting. They offer a *How to Chautauqua* manual that tells potential organizers how to get their own versions of Rolling Thunder events rolling and publicized. This organizing initiative—organizing a real party, if not a political party—weaves critique and celebration into cultural events set up to popularize not only the ethical necessity for but the festive possibilities of a participatory democracy-under-reconstruction.[85] Rolling Thunder's stress is not on "cultural politics" only but on cultural-political mobilizing.

When thinking about the range of protesting and organizing that matters, it would be a grave error to underrate "cultural politics" as simply a fad or symptom that arose because there was no party or candidate worthy of one's vote. After the 2004 presidential election, pundits concluded that George W. Bush had gained ground not by focusing on policy, but by actively shaping and tapping into the "cultural issues": moral values (antiabortion sentiment, protests against gay marriage), identities (Americanness), and fears (terrorism). Conservative think tanks specialize in cultural-political mobilizing: setting the terms of debate, managing the media, influencing what's popular.

In 2005, former Governor Howard Dean, the new head of the Democratic National Committee, demonstrated some of what he has learned from these strategies by reframing the Democratic Party not as defenders of the post-Roosevelt welfare state but as the party that champions individualism and opposes government interference with fundamental rights and choices (for instance, countering "invasive" Republican efforts to outlaw women's rights to end pregnancy in certain cases). Interestingly, Dean wrote the foreword to George Lakoff's *Don't Think of an Elephant!: Know Your Values and Frame the Debate* (2004). For Lakoff, a progressive linguist and cognitive scientist, an understanding of the structuring and deployments of the "cultural civil war" is crucial to winning the political civil war. Lakoff's recent books are hegemonizing manuals that advance the imagining of "powerful progressive stereotypes" and tactics for "framing" not just issues and policies, but cultural identities and values. Formulating the cultural-political problem much the way the British New Left did in the late 1950s, he holds that the analysis of culture, language, stereotypes, and representations is essential not only to explaining why "a significant percentage of the poor and middle class" voted "against their economic interests," but to reversing this trend. Intellectuals such as Lakoff and Thomas Frank maintain that twenty-first-century progressives need not simply more earnest organizing commitments, but more savvy cultural tactics.[86]

When cultural studies was being Americanized in the 1980s and early 1990s, the question commonly put forth was: What is cultural studies? In danger of getting lost was the historical and fundamentally tactical question: *Why (is) cultural studies*? That question remains pressing.

6

Critique as Ism

I know a lot of fancy dancers....
They move so smooth but have no answers.
                    —*Cat Stevens, "Hard-Headed Woman" (1970)*

[Our theorists] exhort, plead, persuade, and harangue; but they have
not been conspicuously successful in suggesting practical expedients.
They take, moreover, too limited a view of the problem.
                    —*Carey McWilliams, Brothers under the Skin (1943)*

Even [C. Wright] Mills, the angry man of American social letters, may
ultimately expect to hitch a ride on the American gravy train, against
his personal will, as one of its most celebrated critics. For criticism
too is a saleable commodity, as long as it remains professional and
sharpens no movement of protest.
                    —*Philip Rieff, "Socialism and Sociology" (1956)[1]*

HERE I RETURN TO THE CHALLENGE—HELPING STUDENTS WHO TAKE CRITIQUE
to heart—with which I began. When Janice Radway was nominated for the

175

presidency of the American Studies Association, which she won, she had to write a statement and suggest what her objectives as president might be. It was eerie for me to read this, because I found that a scene she sketched was so familiar. Radway narrated an encounter with one of her cultural studies undergraduates, Kevin, who was frustrated because he did understand the critiques she was teaching and did not know what to do with them: "It makes me feel hopeless and depressed.... If everything is so determined, and racism and sexism and homophobia are so much a part of our culture, how can I ever do anything to change things? And besides, what alternatives are there? How am I supposed to know how to construct a good society?" Her well-intentioned counsel was much like my own response in such situations, something along the lines of bumper-sticker encouragement to think globally, act locally. At the same time she "stressed," as I have with students, that "coalition-building and collective action [are] essential to success." Her statement was not more specific about possible courses of social action. Radway does not relate how effectively her "counseling" addressed "Kevin's quiet plea for hope and his desire to find something concrete to do."[2] Such advice is salutary, but it is easy to infer that some of Radway's students, like some of my own, have been less than inspired by it.

Can American political intellectuals give more substantive responses to help students fired up by some of the field's "interrogations" and "interventions"? Or should "academics" simply turn the full responsibility for figuring out what their students might do to them, insisting piously, perhaps evasively and self-protectively, that they want them to read the books and write the papers they assign on time, but wouldn't dream of "telling them what to do"? Kenneth Rexroth's reaction to student queries similar to Kevin's in 1960 simultaneously recognizes and recoils from the need for a response: "I have been asked by some well-dressed, unassuming, beardless student, 'I agree with you completely, but what shall we, my generation, *do*?' To this question, I have never been able to give but one answer: 'I am fifty. You are twenty. It is for you to tell me what to do. The only thing I can say is, don't do the things my generation did.'"

Rather than passing the buck, or passing the critique, it might be more constructive, as Richard Ohmann advises, to acknowledge "that for all our efforts to connect our teaching with the world outside—to insist that there really was no *inside*—many, many students who now learn to demystify power, injustice, male supremacy, capitalism, you name it, have little idea how to change any of these things or much hope that it's worth trying." The "worth trying," thankfully, has a history and some strategies attached to it.[3] I explore episodes in this history and some of these strategies below.

Unassimilated Curiosity

Critique is partly a self-critical endeavor that at its best breaks from rigid, predictably patterned thinking, feeling, and perceiving. It presses beyond conceptual boundaries to think what had been unthinkable. In Susan Glaspell's *The Verge* (1921), Claire Archer, the feminist-botanist who challenges stereotypes of the "natural," evokes this spirit in her aim to deviate from "the old pattern, done again, again and again. So long it doesn't even know itself for a pattern."[4] Critique often entails making apparent not only the presuppositions, conventions, categories, paradigms, images, and language through which one apprehends the world and oneself, but the history and power relations that produced them. It can help rescript not simply what is imaginable, feelable, and doable, but what or who one can be. For Michel Foucault, historical critique is about cultivating curiosity, "not the curiosity that seeks to assimilate what it is proper for one to know, but that which enables one to get free of oneself."[5] Stanley Aronowitz attempts to persuade his students to scrutinize their knowledge and tries to question what he thinks he already knows in order to produce "what we both do not know."[6] Paul Sweezy underscores that Karl Marx's "major historical essays" eschew "formulaic" or "textbook" thinking: "They're critiques of the work of his contemporaries. Every major work that Marx ever wrote has 'critique' either in its title or subtitle."[7] In homage to C. Wright Mills, Ralph Miliband writes: "He never made the vulgar mistake of taking seriously only those who shared his view of the world.... The basic requirement was not shared opinions, but honesty and knowledge, scholarship and relevance."[8] Similarly, Leo Marx applauds F. O. Matthiessen's impatience "with ideologically bound students who tried to tailor the evidence to fit a priori schemes.... Everything that [he] wrote was part of his lifelong project of discovering what he himself believed."[9]

The critical study of power, habits, and training, like the study of anything else, can become conventional to the point where waffle-iron questions mold waffle-shaped answers.[10] Theoretical concepts—ideology, hegemony—must not obfuscate or oversimplify relationships so that we see only categories. Hence I was grateful when two of my "Cultural Studies and American Studies" students, Linda Rodriguez and Adayna Gonzalez, sought to qualify our seminar's use of Antonio Gramsci's concept of "consent"—what hegemonic groups seek to secure from those they dominate.[11] To classify America as a "consent"-winning hegemony, they insisted, may elide the ways in which dominant groups and the system that benefits them use coercion to enforce compliance (Gramsci himself theorized about "consent" in a fascist prison).

And often there is a good measure of socially produced resignation and ignorance of potential alternatives mixed into "consent."

Once students begin to question their questions, their answers, their premises, the categories they think through, and where, how, and why they got them, and to demystify the ways in which they have been bamboozled—by national, gender, sexual, class, and racial discourses—and to work out the implications of what seems unfair, they often become as morally outraged as they are intellectually excited. Raymond Williams terms this the "first terrible realisation that what we are thinking is what a lot of other people have thought"—an insight that dispels the "illusion of freedom." But, he adds, "beyond it, under pressure, there is a very high kind of freedom. This is when you are free to choose, or to choose to try to alter, that which is really pressuring you."[12]

More is at stake here than therapeutic critical self-reflection and self-realization, or "unpacking" how one has been hoodwinked by taken-for-granted patterns. My most astute students know that politics is more than "theoryhead" clashes and that the Left must be more than a Theoretical Left. For Mills critique meant trying to write the "what's-it-all-about book" with "not a line of bullshit in it." He associated critical thinking not only with the effort to reach a new level of "self-consciousness we call intellectual," but with the Tolstoyan drive to try to "find out how to live" and to act on those findings.[13] Students frequently value making judgments about what we are involved in. But when the academic production of knowledge does not encompass considering what we might do about what we are involved in, students can feel guilt-tripped, betrayed, and trapped, and reencode criticism as theoretically informed cynicism. Then cultural studies and American studies may seem more like cynicism studies. Cynicism often revels in caricaturing and discounting much needed analysis as a mere academic exercise. I try to prevent this by asking my students to think about how they want to define and use American studies.

It seems to me that nowadays much American studies teaching and learning take four basic forms that merit scrutiny. First, American studies is often taught as historicizing and contextualizing studies. Teachers usually encourage students to embrace two of the great academic isms: historicism and contextualism. Whether the American studies historicizer is confronted with literary texts, political movements, civil institutions, social attitudes, rock songs, sexual conventions, or clocks, he or she is instructed to attempt to fathom their historical conditions of possibility and causes. American historicism and contextualism sometimes stand in place of another ism, one that explicitly champions historical and contextual analysis in the service of economic, political, and quality-of-life transformation: socialism.[14]

Second, postmodern American studies frequently takes the form of a historicized version of social construction studies, cultural fabrication studies, meaning production studies, intellectual premises studies, moral assumptions studies, discourses of feelings studies.[15] This kind of American construction studies focuses on how American "life" is assembled. "Oppositional" construction studies must be more ambitious than simply teaching students to realize: "I'm constructed; you're constructed"; or "I'm interpellated; you're interpellated."[16] Historicized construction studies may speculate more dialectically on how socially made ways of feeling and seeing—and the ideological encodings that make them seem natural, universal, or psychologically given—might be transformed through critical, cultural, and political agency.

Third, since the postwar period American studies has legitimated and advanced interdisciplinary—even antidisciplinary—scholarship in the academy. In recent times American studies has provided a space for the development of outright postdisciplinary studies. This undisciplinized work entails refusing to be intellectually or institutionally colonized by departmentalized subject matter, methodologies, questions, and assignments of value or significance. Even in this new millennium, nontenured scholars and graduate students who generate postdisciplinary and nonprofessionalized public scholarship often risk their careers to do so. Some administrators favor programs such as American studies mainly because they see them as infusing established departments with new intellectual energies. Usually these departments still call the shots.

Fourth, in many universities American studies has aided in the institutionalization of inclusion and exclusion studies—diversity studies. What might be labeled exclusion studies involves investigating who and what are missing from this picture, this narrative, or this historical account, and restoring considerations of gender, race, ethnicity, class, sexuality, and then expanding canons accordingly. The less trenchant versions of inclusion and exclusion studies have a crude checklist quality and imply that a fully checked list ameliorates the social problem. More incisive versions of this critique ask questions not only about inclusion and exclusion, but about the systemic contradictions and reproductive strategies of the dominant culture that prejudicially regulates inclusions and exclusions.

These American studies efforts to broaden our understanding of that which is historical, social, and political—and thus potentially alterable—are important critical developments. But postmodern American studies historicists, constructionists, and inclusionists have been better at equipping students with habits of historical reflection and an inclusion morality than at enabling them to develop usable perspectives on political strategizing. It has been more adept at helping students cultivate critical agency than political agency, though the two are conjoined in manifold ways. My students have wondered: If critique dismantles, is it not also important to build, to imagine new social possibilities and ways of achieving them? If not, do some "critiques" sustain the systems of contradictions they seemingly seek to understand and change? If on one level critique must not be intellectually straightjacketed as a means to an end, on another level it may be revealing to "interrogate" the production of critique for critique's sake. Assessing the recent progress of the Left, Michael Albert has much praise for its effect on "ideas and behaviors," but regrets that it has had less success in changing "institutional setting[s]," creating organizations, and offering "vision and strategy." The question progressives seem unprepared to answer, he suggests, is: "What are you for?" Similarly, Winona LaDuke objects: "Many so-called progressives or leftists spend all their time criticizing. What is the solution?" And as Carlyne Sainphor, an antisweatshop student protestor at Penn State, puts it: "We want answers."[17]

Several years ago, during the final session of my "Cultural Studies and American Studies" seminar, I jokingly asked my students if they really wanted me—expected me—to give them some sense of "counterhegemonic" occupations they might pursue after graduation. They replied: *YES!* During the break, I retrieved two letters written to me by former students who had taken the seminar and read them to the class. One alum worked both for a tenants' rights organization and for a pregnant women's refuge in San Francisco, and the other was temporarily employed by a community organizing and betterment group called City Year in Boston. The students were grateful because they learned something about graduates who had tried to put what we had learned and unlearned in the classroom into social practice.[18] Since then I have established a dialogue with my university's Career Resource Center to educate myself in what students might do while they are in college and after they graduate—besides reading American cultural studies books—to contribute not only to social "service" organizations, but also to political organizations that agitate for specific social changes (options include a range of career activities from becoming an AFL-CIO union organizer [www.organize.alfcio.org] to working for Amnesty International [www.amnestyusa.org] to participating in the Green Corps Environment Leadership Training Program in advocacy and organizing [www.greencorps.org] to being employed by public service organizations sponsored by the government, the United Nations, university consortia, and corporations).[19]

From Somehow Critique toward Usable Critique

Many intellectuals have argued for the importance of forging links between critique and the organization of progressive forces. In his oft-quoted final thesis on Feuerbach, Karl Marx asserted: "The philosophers have only interpreted the world in different ways, the point is to change it."[20] Bertolt Brecht maintained that the aim of the social critic should not just be to write "the truth," but "to write it for and to somebody, somebody who can do something with it."[21] In 1948 Mills gently but firmly rebuked his coauthor's, Hans Gerth's, academic detachment in a letter. While Gerth valued "debunking" and "good journalist accounts and analysis of what the setup is," Mills also stressed the need to address "what to do": "Do you think that now one should not advance any 'programs,' not even *articulate* some idea, even if they can't and won't be realized so far as one can see? ... Isn't it possible at all to state 'programs,' even when we don't have any going movement or power which might carry them out?"[22] Aronowitz holds that "one may be a radical sympathizer without belonging to a radical organization, but you can't be a radical without a collective practice." Such practice "provides a context for dialogue among intellectuals and activists about the *how* as much as the *what* of transformation."[23] The tendency of sympathizers to overlook the how of transformation agitated Alan Wald when he reviewed several books in 1988 that advocated a "radical pedagogy" (including one by Paolo Freire): "strangely lacking in each case," he lamented, "is a substantive consideration of the problem of implementation: the precise means by which our cultural work—whether in the form of scholarly writing or in the creation of critical consciousness among students—expresses itself in organized collective political activity that *concretely* leads to the restructuring of the U.S. social and economic order" (my emphasis).[24]

For these intellectuals, theory is not only about how to analyze, but how to organize. "Politicizing" is not the equivalent of politics. Yet in most American studies, historical studies, and even cultural studies scholarship, what this "politics" might look like or how it might come about has remained amorphous. This often takes the form of what I term the *somehow critique*. Such critiques are written so that somebody somewhere will use them somehow to do something good someday for someone. Some of the best works I know have exhibited this tendency.

On the same wavelength, Gregor McLennan, a cultural studies historian, asked in 1984: "Why is it that the 'so what do we do now' sections of acute analytical articles feel like the air has leaked out of a bright balloon?"[25] Likewise, Paul Buhle praised George Lipsitz's *Time Passages* (1990) for its impressive recovery of the "collective memory" and "political sensibility" of some of America's many "hybrid" or "bifocal" cultures, but his review asked about something more: "To trace such cultures back to their origins, and draw out their subversive contents for the present day, suggests (although Lipsitz doesn't quite say so) something like a Transitional Programme for socialist cultural transformation."[26] In general, American studies has not "quite said so."

Critiqueists

The *somehow critique* is one aspect of a more general tendency, particularly prominent in America: the making of critique itself into an ism. This might be nominated *critiqueism*. I would add this ism to the other three popular American academic isms—historicism, constructionism, and inclusionism—that are too often unhinged from any organized movement like socialism. The postmodern academy trains students, especially graduate students, to be not just historicists but professional reproducers of critique who write within and for an academic "public." Critiques proliferate with the assumption that they are somehow prefigurative of some better world.

This tendency is by no means new. In the early 1950s, when E. P. Thompson was still in the British Communist Party, he urged his colleagues not to "let any of our opponents be given a chance to sneer that the Communists and their friends have found one more thing to be *against*" rather than more "positive[ly]" explaining what they are for.[27] Critiqueism is better at being *against* power structures than *for* a new world. It makes figuring out the problem or highlighting the contradiction the whole concern. Hall has had to remind socialists that pointing out social contradictions in no way means "that the world will collapse as a result of logical contradiction."[28]

Some forms of critique foreground blame as the primary objective. This can generate more moral guilt-tripping than knowledge designed to help effect specific forms of social transformation. As discussed in chapter 4, Hall withstood this self-righteous moralizing a few years ago when some younger critics indicted the New Left for omitting certain social groups—rather large groups, such as women, gays, lesbians, blacks—from their "new" vision of what's Left. Hall decried an unproductive blame historicism that simply "demobilizes" rather than unites progressive forces.[29]

A related aspect of critique is exhibited by Left critics who relentlessly attack other Left critics—witness Irving Howe's profile of Mills below, and one could cite his "Stalinophobic" (Howe's term) fury unleashed at Matthiessen in 1948.[30]

In the introduction I quoted Lynd's epistolary counsel to Dwight MacDonald not to have his journal *politics* sponsor "snipes"—advice that Macdonald often ignored (particularly in his acerbic *Partisan Review* review of Mills's *White Collar* [1951] and in his subsequent, brief correspondence with his former friend, Mills).[31] Perry Anderson, invoking "socialist fellowship" and the "duties and decencies of critical dialogue on the Left," has taken E. P. Thompson to task for his assault on Louis Althusser: "The harmfulness of this style of polemic to the possibilities of rational or comradely communication on the Left can be in no doubt. The long and disastrous tradition that lies behind it is sufficient reminder of that."[32] Though Anderson occasionally apologizes for his own militant efforts to correct Thompson's history writing and political positions, *Arguments within English Marxism* (1980)—his "comradely" critique of Thompson—is punctuated with snipes at the historian. Notwithstanding Anderson's brilliance, one may wonder about the role he has played in transmuting Marxism into arguments (mainly arguments). This competitive zeal to achieve not just intellectual excellence but intellectual dominance is often a more politically disabling than enabling form of critique.

Another characteristic of critique is a laudable commitment to questioning that, paradoxically, can sometimes function to fence in the critical enterprise. This tendency has old roots. Commenting ironically on literature professors who decline to contaminate art with politics, Leo Marx quipped, in 1950, that "they have so admirably catholic a spirit that they can entertain all ideas without endorsing any." If some students demand solutions, other students—and many of their teachers—are consistently, sometimes downright aggressively, skeptical of solutions and regard anyone presumptuous enough to propose solutions as dogmatic. They seem to value critique first and foremost as an intellectually ludic question-generating game that should in no way interfere with their effort to make up—or not make up—"their own" minds. This question-proliferating play can itself be a rigid manifestation of what Mills recoiled from as "doctrinaire" liberalism.[33]

Political Embodiment Studies

From its inception, members of the British New Left proclaimed that its cultural and theoretical turn was geared not only toward rethinking the "socialist project" but toward giving it "political embodiment."[34] The political expectations they attached to socialism, however, have been varied. In 1987 Raphael Samuel testified that although he has been a "lifelong socialist," he "lost faith in socialism about thirty years ago"—not coincidentally, when he helped found the New Left—and has not "wanted to live in a socialist society since sometime about the mid-fifties." He suggested that he would be suspicious if Britain actually adopted a government it packaged as "socialist." Samuel came to revere socialism not as a concrete program but a "metaphor for solidarity."[35] His remarks exemplify and perhaps exaggerate a sometimes healthy, sometimes defeatist New Left skepticism about the efficacy of organized political change.

Many on the Anglo-American Left have long recognized that a major obstacle to "embodying" socialism is even mentioning socialism (what Warren Beatty's Senator Bulworth ironically calls the "dirty word"). As noted in chapter 2, it is unlikely that the U.S. academy would have invested in a cultural studies named *New Left Studies* or *Socialist Studies.* In the late 1940s Matthiessen felt that the New Deal had assigned diffuse and conflicting meanings to the term "liberal" and criticized several magazines for deploying it as "a rather evasive gesture to stall off definition of a more clear-cut position to the Left." He also found the term "progressive" inadequate, "since out of its Populist context it also can become too vague." Then he recalled fondly a speech by Governor Floyd Olson of Minnesota in 1933 in which Olson embraced the self-description "radical." Matthiessen advised: "Questions of vocabulary are always important in practical politics. The word socialist is still so foreign to most American ears that it is probably best to call yourself a radical democrat, and do whatever you can to bring about the establishment of a nationwide American Labor Party." On a similar track in 1996, Aronowitz averred: "There is virtually no effective practice of socialist agitation, no serious effort to propose socialist alternatives, no attempt to link the specific ideology of socialism to the changing economic and political context of late capitalism (on the strategic level) to the new social movements, there is no warrant, except sentimental bordering on religious faith, to hold on to the label [socialist] *as the universalist unifying ideology.*" Aronowitz thus proposes, as did Matthiessen, that "radical democracy" replace "socialism" in political agitation and organization.[36]

But in 1943 Mills felt that "radical" was not likely to win any popularity contests. When Dwight Macdonald brought up *The Radical Review* as a possible title for the new journal he was about the edit, Mills warned that it—and the title *The Left*—would alienate and estrange readers as well as potential academic contributors. So they settled for *politics* and, as Mills counseled, let the radicalism come out in the analysis.[37] As noted in chapter 5, Jesse Jackson, at the apex of his influence in the mid-1980s, tactically distanced himself from "radical" and certainly had no interest in "socialist."

Even Frances Fox Piven, who eulogized Miliband for having unqualifiedly called himself a socialist (not softened as "democratic socialist"), recognizes the "extraordinary difficulty," in this era of capitalist globalization, "of envisioning a socialist transformation."[38] During debates about how best to battle Thatcher, some socialists criticized their colleagues for transforming socialism into "an extension of liberalism."[39] But in the late 1980s one former British New Leftist doubted that "socialism was a word that could still be used" in Britain.[40] Chapter 1 argued that one aspect of the Americanization of cultural studies is the tendency to ignore its older socialist aims, to liberalize it, and to make it relatively safe for capitalism's universities. Indeed, if socialism is a "project" in America, it seems to be primarily a critical, textual, historical, and cultural project. In American universities one typically finds professionalized Marxist "critics," "theorists," and "historicists" more than faculty and students who conceive of themselves as socialist intellectuals and activists. Much academic Marxism has more to do with ways of reading and contextualizing—critical "politicizing"—than "political embodiment."

Some Marxist critics have charged, however, that various recent critical trends are symptoms of silently surrendering the project of transforming capitalism into socialism.[41] In the 1940s Michael Gold termed this surrender "futilitarianism."[42] The strength of this critique of critique is that it resituates capitalism—a system that shapes economic relations, political systems, emotional needs, and subjective forms—as a foundational problem and asks critics interested in its multiplicitous ramifications not to take it as an unalterable given and thus excuse it from critique.

What American cultural studies shows too little evidence of, even when influenced by Marxism and socialism, is redistribution studies—critiques of the redistribution of wealth, power, resources, and access that Riesman took a step toward in his 1950s and 1960s abundance studies. For Piven this is vital to socialist critique and planning: "[Miliband] understood socialism after all as essentially an extension of democratic arrangements to economic spheres, without which political democracy could not be realized."[43] Raymond Williams compellingly integrated cultural and redistribution studies in 1958, when he affirmed that Britain was "a nation, not a firm": "We now spend £20,000,000 annually on all our libraries, museums, galleries, orchestras, on the Arts Council, and on all forms of adult education. At the same time we spend £365,000,000 annually on advertising." He advocated reversing these allocations to regain "some sense of proportion and value." Williams upbraided taxpayers who begrudge state support for artists and scholars by reminding them that "we" all pay and that the world is for "us": "On your own—learn your size—you could do practically nothing." Arguing that a "socialist economy" is essential to a socialist democracy, he warned that capitalists were busy establishing "power which can survive parliamentary changes" and that "many Labour planners" have put "an abstraction called the public interest" in place of socialism.[44]

As Williams's skepticism about Labour planners suggests, many New Leftists favored support for movements even more than active engagement in the Labour Party.[45] And yet in much of its radical work British New Left cultural studies demonstrated more intellectual interest in producing knowledge about cultures of daily life and "the popular"—as a key to political transformation—than concentrating explicitly on issues of how to spur socialist activism and organization. The critical front, as Williams saw it in 1984, had become less keyed into movements, parties, and pickets, and more centered on "launch[ing] the widest public process of reconsidering and (where necessary) changing every popular assumption, habit and attitude."[46] Some forms of critical "politicizing" are understandable as responses to the sinking feeling that "there is no mass movement in the street."[47]

Numerous social theory books that were part of my early training in American studies made liberal, anarchist, socialist, and sometimes imaginatively quirky efforts to focus on and even plan the future. Paul Goodman and Percival Goodman proposed new ways of establishing economic relations, art, and community life in cities. Murray Bookchin's *Post-Scarcity Anarchism* (1971) reassessed the kind of America we could develop with new technological, economic, and ecological priorities and planning. Ivan Illich's books speculated on ways of reorganizing cities, transportation, and education. Buckminster Fuller expanded beyond architectural design into a global social vision of egalitarian resource use he termed "livingry-design" and "world planning." In the 1960s Robert Theobald proposed futures in which Americans would receive a guaranteed national income. More recently, Stanley Aronowitz and William DiFazio reworked and reproposed the idea. While Staughton Lynd's *Living Inside the Hope* (1997) and Howard Zinn's *You Can't Be Neutral on a Moving Train* (1994) combine autobiography, the history of activism, and gestures toward conceptualizing an "alternative" American future.[48]

Before the New Left took shape, George Orwell articulated the problem that some in the New Left would come to realize they faced: "To take a rational political decision one must have a picture of the future."[49] Orwell's point was indebted to a long tradition of socialist thought. In the early postwar period Thompson quoted Harry Pollitt's praise for William Morris's eagerness to paint "'the vision splendid'" and "'glimpses of the promised land,'" for they are "'missing from our speeches, our Press and our pamphlets, and if one dares to talk about the "gleam," one is in danger of being accused of sentimentalism.'" Thompson advised his colleagues to get the guts to be "utopian."[50] Mills, esteemed by Thompson, warned the Left not to make the words utopian and futile synonymous.[51] Wald regretted the relative absence of Marxism from American academic and cultural life in the mid-1960s because he "could not visualize a future for [himself], occupationally or personally, in the dominant culture."[52] Thompson, Williams, and Hall, in sync with Mills's emphasis on devising programs, exhorted the Left of 1968 to devise a "Socialist National Plan" and formulate not just "defence" but "detailed developments and proposals."[53]

At least through the 1930s many socialists could sketch the sort of social relations they wanted to establish through criticism and mobilizing. "If you were asked what was wrong, you knew," Norman MacKenzie wrote in 1958. "If you were asked what should be done about it, you produced a petition, a membership card, or a leaflet advertising the mass meeting, next Sunday afternoon." The 1930s socialism MacKenzie describes was not only a theory or a critique, it was an organized practice and a plan to bring into being a social, economic, political, and cultural system. By contrast, Mackenzie described the late 1950s in Britain as a time of "paralysis," "resignation," and drift for many progressives who tried to evade contradictions by retreating "into private worlds."[54] Since the Cold War assault on the Old Left and the explosion of movements and of the very idea of "politics" in the 1960s, a progressive future has been more challenging for many to imagine. Numerous students I have taught want not only a vision of a world worth struggling to get, but, like consumers, five easy steps to achieve it.

Proposing a future isn't easy, perhaps because we have quietly given up on expecting it of ourselves. In the early 1960s, William Appleman Williams deviated from conventional history-writing practice to conclude his now classic New Left study of America's imperialist "open door" foreign policy with proposals for "a radical but noncommunist reconstruction of American society in domestic affairs" and for the American support of "revolutions" abroad that will "transform the material world and the quality of human relationships." In one revealing moment the historian admitted that even if he persuaded many readers of the importance of this reconstruction, there was no organized way for them to become a group to voice and act on their dissent: "There is at the present time no radicalism in the United States strong enough to win power, or even a very significant influence, through the processes of representative government—and this essay rests on the axiom of representative government." Faced with this paucity of "radical" options in Kennedy's New Frontier, he felt compelled to invest the little hope he had in a dominant conservative ethics and reasonableness that might "act upon the validity of a radical analysis."[55]

A decade later the historian's postscript to his conclusion acknowledged that American conservatives did no such thing. Buoyed by the political and cultural developments of the 1960s, however, he singled out Chile's new socialist democracy as a model for the revolution that might occur not only outside but inside America. "Perhaps we Americans, whose votes have mattered increasingly less in recent decades, can restore the integrity of our own franchise through a similar display of self-determination."[56] (Shortly after, the Nixon administration abetted a military overthrow of President Salvador Allende's Chilean government, an authoritarian coup followed by decades of mass executions and atrocities.)

David Harvey does not underestimate how hard it is to establish imaginative political agency in late capitalism. Quoting Marx's famous formulation that it is "'not the consciousness of men that determines their being but, on the contrary, their social being that determines their consciousness,'" he comments: "How, then, can the human imagination, made so much of in *Capital,* range freely enough outside of the existing material and institutional conditions (e.g., those set by capitalism) to even conceptualize what the socialist alternative might look like?" Hence he identifies the major "task of dialectical and intellectual inquiry" as the imagining of "real possibilities and alternatives." Harvey's dialectical utopianism places the socialist accent not just on critique but on imagination. (The closing chapter of one of his recent books imagines what Baltimore could be like in a revolutionary future.)[57]

Along these lines, Fredric Jameson has suggested why Raymond Williams's understanding of socialism as a formation of energies and agency—not just as a political and economic structure—appears somewhat vague. The socialism that Williams cannot quite envision with specificity is much more "complicated" than capitalism. "To imagine the daily life and the organization of society in which for the first time in human history, human beings are fully in control of their own destinies makes demands on the mind which are forbiddingly difficult for subjects of the present 'administered world' and often understandably frightening to them."[58] By "renewal" of socialism, Hall had in mind—or did not quite have in mind—"a whole new conception of life, a whole new type of democratic socialist civilisation."[59] This vision would not be wholly defined by that which it criticized, but would see beyond such circumstances. Rustin has tried to be as specific as possible about the vision splendid and, like Hall, comes close to designating *quality of life* as a synonym for socialism that addresses not just "per capita income, consumption or individual choice," but also "people's enjoyment of and fulfillment in their work, participation in public life, roles of responsibility as active citizens, and contribution to a shared culture through arts, sports and other kinds of expression."[60] But Rustin does not begin to spell out how a government might help materialize this. Intriguingly, neither cultural studies nor American studies has many active and visible "practitioners" in the field of government reorganization.[61]

Activism Studies

In her preface to *Emerson's Emergence* (1989), Mary Kupiec Cayton notes how her book project shifted from a 1970s interdisciplinary emphasis on situating Emerson and his ideas in social and economic history—standard Americanist contextualization studies—to a 1980s critical inquiry informed by her own itinerant experience as a "temporary faculty member." Her guiding question became: "How do intellectuals have the power to act as transformative agents within society?"[62] A history of intellectual activism might discuss not only figures like David Montgomery, Noam Chomsky, Staughton Lynd, Howard Zinn, Angela Davis, E. P. Thompson, and Manning Marable, but also the history of efforts to develop alternative educational structures (histories of American workers' colleges, of union education departments, and of radical programs developed in schools, high schools, colleges, universities, tribal colleges, community centers). Books like *The Dissenting Academy* (1968)—edited by Theodore Roszak, and with essays by Chomsky, Lynd, Louis Kampf, and others—and like *The Cold War and the University* (1997)—with chapters by Chomsky, Montgomery, Zinn, Ohmann, R. C. Lewontin, and others—testify to the intellectual and political significance of this history.[63]

Sometimes academic activism has been an arduous, isolating endeavor. F. O. Matthiessen and Paul Sweezy both helped develop the Harvard Teachers' Union in 1935 to bring strength and solidarity to the struggle. Matthiessen served as the union's vice president and in 1940 assumed its presidency for most of the next decade. Sweezy recalls that Matthiessen-the-organizer encouraged "others to see that they had more to contribute than they themselves were aware of," acted "as a stern conscience to still others who might be tempted to evade the cares and obligations that go with responsibility," and was "the sort of person who makes an organization what it is." Matthiessen was especially grateful to the Harvard Teachers Union for introducing him to a wider arena of political action: "We also grew to learn the necessity of being better informed about what was taking place in the State House and gained experience in lobbying and testifying for or against various bills." He represented his union at the Boston Central Labor Union and at the American Federation of Teachers. Vincent Dunne, labor movement and Socialist Workers Party leader, admired Matthiessen's refusal to be "bullied or bribed." On at least one occasion the English department chair admonished a young colleague to shun this "evil man." Matthiessen, like Mills, found many of his colleagues retributive.[64]

His activism consistently spread beyond the campus. Matthiessen belonged to dozens of liberal-to-Left organizations, ably listed by the House Un-American Activities Committee, and walked door-to-door canvassing and campaigning for Henry Wallace's presidential candidacy on the new Progressive Party's ticket in 1948. He used academia—introducing himself as "Professor Matthiessen"—not to mention logic, knowledge, and integrity, to add distinction to his case. One Beacon Hill cocampaigner remembers: "His efforts to establish a rapport with people were always touching, so earnest yet just anxious and tentative enough to make it difficult as hell to talk with him on the backstairs of a stinking tenement, with kids scurrying at his feet and screams and radios in the background." He did it anyway. A friend observes that while many "union workers and officers ... found in him the most solid, reliable, and cooperative supporter they knew outside their own inner ranks," and although he despised "class barriers," Matty "sensed imperfectly the necessity of simply watching and listening and gradually getting to see what working people are really like—and then modifying his own behavior accordingly." Although Wallace's defeat was overwhelming, Matthiessen, Sweezy notes, "always approached political problems with a view to sharpening his own *actions*." For Matthiessen, backing Wallace was the ethical thing to *do*. He insisted: "I am concerned with finding the concrete issues upon which the forces of the left can unite, and with basing those issues upon a viable political theory." But the McCarthy freeze set in. His suicide note admitted: "I am exhausted."[65]

The 1960s could be exhausting, factious, and exhilaratingly eye-opening for academic activists activated by history. A blend of this is patent in the landmark volume edited by Louis Kampf and Paul Lauter, *The Politics of Literature: Dissenting Essays on the Teaching of English* (1972), a contribution to Pantheon's "antitextbooks" series. Its essayists developed politicized scholarship provoked by *for what?* and *for whom?* questions. The biographical blurbs reassessed achievement: "Paul [Lauter] was most recently fired from the University of Maryland, Baltimore County, allegedly for 'subversion of the grading system.' He now works for the United States Servicemen's Fund, a support organization for the GI antiwar movement. He has followed that route from college teacher to movement activist before: from Hobart College to the Mississippi Freedom

Schools in 1964; from Smith to the American Friends Service Committee and Students for a Democratic Society; from Antioch-Putney Graduate School to Resist." Kampf and Lauter note that "nearly all [their contributors] have committed acts of civil disobedience" and "several have been fired for political reasons." Not only has "political work" reeducated their "perceptions of social relations, of reality itself," far more than "professional criticism" it has revised their sense of why literature is worth reading. They situate "problems of pedagogy" in "problems of politics" whose "solution[s] are political." The book's authors understand the university not only as a subtle site of class reproduction but as a place of employment and literary knowledge fabrication that too often "diminish[es] people's desire or capacity to act for change."

Shortly after publishing his chapter for the volume, Bruce Franklin was sacked from Stanford. His blurb starts by announcing that he "is on the Central Committee of Venceremos, a multinational revolutionary organization in the San Francisco Bay Area." Franklin's chapter is supercharged by the recognition that his ostensibly nonpolitical literary training had systematically deflected him from reading "from the point of view of the oppressed." His "radicalization took place almost entirely outside [his] professional work" until "an increasingly intense contradiction began to develop between [his] political and [his] professional life." Franklin's prescient chapter highlights the exploitation of graduate student pedagogical labor as an issue.[66]

Ohmann, unlike Lauter, Franklin, and so many other activist academics, kept getting promoted—at Wesleyan. Ohmann relates how he moved from a typical 1950s "politics, beyond voting liberal, seemed irrelevant" academic posture to a 1960s intellectual rebel-with-a-cause stance. He became a tenured professor, provost, and then Interim Chancellor; an editor of *College English;* the vice president of the Modern Language Association; an FBI file subject; a counselor of draft resisters; a founder of RESIST and member of its steering committee; a member of the radical New University Conference; and a sponsor of the student-run course, "Toward a Socialist America." His 1950s post-Matthiessen Harvard schooling drilled in him "the imperative never to make a scene." Just a few years later he failed the test with flying colors—Ohmann was filmed on Walter Cronkite's CBS news program lined up in front of the Pentagon, divesting himself of a mock version of the draft card he had already turned in. Ohmann's upbeat narrative and tone bring out the pride, thrill, and relief—despite real risks—of standing up and being counted. Running through Ohmann's self-historicizing narratives is his feeling of gratitude for his reeducation and reconception of the academy's possibilities as a site for wide-ranging intellectual debate, ethical expression, and political action.[67]

Vietnam War–era "teach-ins," which inspired Ohmann and so many faculty and students around the country, asserted that the university was more than a certification factory, that students and faculty were citizens and had more than a professionalized bond with one another, and that critique should be developed for social justice's and social transformation's sake. Teach-ins challenged the confines of disciplinized discourse in the institutional classroom. However much Henry Steele Commager may have failed conceptually, in the eyes of some, by not fully recognizing the diversity of groups and conflicts that he homogenized as "the American mind," in 1965, when campuses were beginning to redefine their possibilities and responsibilities, this American studies historian not only defended the constitutional basis for teach-ins, he linked the right to criticize with the struggle to establish a free society. "We do not need to fear criticism, but the silencing of criticism. We do not need to fear excitement or agitation in the academic community, but timidity and apathy. We do not need to fear resistance to political leaders, but unquestioning acquiescence in whatever policies those leaders adopt." He used his academic prestige to help make such questioning reputable. That year the Marxist Eugene Genovese greeted his participation in the teach-in as a civic opportunity to speak of contradictions that he felt he could not address in his history classes: "The duty of all Americans is to expose and defeat those who are making our country the most hated country on earth." He advocated both the restoration of Vietnam to the Vietnamese and the restoration of America to the Americans: "We will have to uproot this social order and replace it with one that has no need to throttle anybody and, when we do so, then and only then will America have realized its promise of civilization and civilized values."[68] Teach-ins did more than "make a scene," they rewrote the scene.

Ohmann, Kampf, Lauter, and other members of the Modern Language Association's radical caucus established the *Radical Teacher* collective and journal in 1975 to carry on, energize, and better organize the work they believed in, conveyed in part by their subtitle: *A News Journal of Socialist Literary Theory and Practice*. In 1982 the collective emended this to *Socialist and Feminist Theory and Practice of Teaching*. In the mid- and late 1970s, when poststructuralism absorbed "theory" journals, the collective elected to further develop the political critiques of education and knowledge production that crystallized in the 1960s. Their open-ended, accessible, and usable socialism was not simply an intellectual project but an activist and organizing project. They explored not just new ways of theorizing working in schools, but tactics for implementing and institutionalizing this theorizing. The late 1970s and early 1980s saw the rise of the academic celebrity theorist. But *Radical Teacher* exhorted everyone involved in public and private education—from preschool to high school to community college to graduate school—to contribute. From the start the journal offered course descriptions, ideas about curriculum development, and tips about classroom practice, and it devoted special issues to emerging feminist studies, gay, lesbian, and sexuality studies, and to racial and ethnic studies initiatives, and to mass culture and cultural politics. But it also covered schools as integral parts of communities, and as workplaces. The inaugural issue addressed how institutions of so-called higher education were involved in higher exploitation of adjunct and part-time teachers. Early issues covered efforts to set up faculty unions and to create bonds between faculty and nonfaculty employees who were struggling to unionize or to strike.[69] Its analyses, reportage, reviews, and grassroots engagement have something like the spirit of the original *New Left Review.*

The issue of the relationship between cultural studies and activism surfaced on numerous occasions at the Illinois cultural studies conference in 1990, usually offstage, but one exchange between Andrew Ross and Fred Pfeil was intriguing. In response to Ross's critique of New Age Politics, Pfeil raised a question that emerged from his "own activist politics" and queried: "Is there something we can take from [New Age politics]?" Alas, the full text of his response to Ross was cut and the published version in *Cultural Studies* omitted what I took to be Pfeil's key point. Bearing in mind that New Agers are well organized, he asked, can activists concerned with cultural studies learn from New Agers' appeals, their cooperation, their social success? Is there a "disjunction," Pfeil wondered, between cultural studies and activism studies?

Ross's response acknowledges the gist of Pfeil's key query. He portrayed cultural studies as "activist ... and let's hope that it remains so." Paraphrasing Pfeil (the part not published), Ross agrees: "As you say, it is in the world of the activist ... that we find an articulate level of political consciousness." Yet Ross also notes the peculiar fact that cultural studies "has not taken, as its object, the culture of activist groups. Rather, it has been involved in looking at the protopolitical expressions of subcultures and countercultures that are not always politically articulate."[70] One might ask, then, building on Pfeil's remarks: why have sociological, historical, and critical investigations into forms of activism and political organization *not* been a prime concern of an "activist" (academic) cultural studies?

At times the attention paid to the matter of activism has prompted a demand for solutions that has been more censorious than productive. Although Thompson, Williams, and Hall have all been praised for their concrete political commitments, they also have been criticized for not clarifying precisely "what to do now." In *Out of Apathy* Thompson assured readers: "We are not (as no doubt we may be represented) aloof and academic critics. We have been in there in the defensive battles; we have all done our envelopes, canvassed, served on committees, marched and the rest."[71] A sympathetic reviewer of *The Poverty of Theory,* in which Thompson took on Althusser for "immobilizing" young British socialists, concluded: "Insofar as a view about political organisation can be identified in Thompson's writings, he seems to hope for some new independent formation of the left, spontaneous activism around particular campaigns, or perhaps a transformed and radicalised Labour Party." He admitted the relevance of these positions, but regretted that Thompson's "strategic perspective remains vague, beyond an a priori dismissal of any role for the Communist Party." And Perry Anderson went so far as to contend that Thompson, unlike Thompson's hero William Morris, put his concerns about socialist morality in place of considerations of socialist strategy (even in his 1955 book on Morris).[72]

One obituary for Williams eulogizes his refusal to separate his "ideological work from the daily struggles of the broad democratic movement": "He would be found on a night of a blizzard in Cambridge in 1979 chairing a meeting for Nape to put the case for dirty job strikers; or speaking on the prospects for the year 2000 to a packed audience at a Marxism Today 'Turning Left' event attended by 1500 students."[73] Yet in his enthusiastic review of Williams's *Politics and Letters* in 1979, Arnold Kettle proffered one criticism "in diffidence": "If I find something missing, especially in the directly political parts of the book, it is a sufficient sense of what actual political activity, the organising of people to change the world they live in, involves in practice. Raymond Williams is not afraid of politics and makes many shrewd observations about political issues and tactics: yet one does sense in his attitudes and language a certain distance from the practicalities of day-to-day politics and in particular a certain unwillingness to recognise (what I'm sure he does in theory) that it is political parties, not political ideas as such, that actually change society." Kettle, however, averred that political ideas and political practice are interdependent.[74]

In a demonstration of self-irony, Hall acknowledged that New Left intellectuals searched for a "historical movement" they never quite "found": "We were organic intellectuals without any organic point of reference; organic intellectuals with a nostalgia or will or hope ... that at some point we would be prepared in intellectual work for that kind of relationship, if such a conjuncture ever appeared."[75] As Hall's comment suggests, vagueness about political objectives may result from the uneasy sense that there is not always a clear practical and organized way of productively acting on critique—no long-term established movement that critique can help define, redefine, organize.[76]

British New Left cultural studies had an innovative though perhaps ambivalent commitment to organizing.[77] Hall explains that tensions between the early *New Left Review* editorial board and the clubs factored into his decision to resign as editor. A major concern was intellectual: "We hoped that the clubs would develop their own independent organisation, leadership and channels of communication (perhaps their own newsheet or bulletin), leaving the journal free to develop its own project. But we lacked the resources to bring this about, which exacerbated in the clubs feelings that they had no control over the journal, and in the editorial board that a journal of ideas could not be effectively run by committees."[78] Rustin notes that clubs in the North sometimes contested the London-Oxford-Cambridge concerns they found in the journals—a problem that would beset the *New Socialist* by the late 1980s.[79] The New Left's active link with the Campaign for Nuclear Disarmament, even more than its clubs, made it possible for it to appear to be a "movement."[80] Still, its relation to organizing did not change significantly: "Neither in this first phase nor in several subsequent attempts over twenty years (the *May Day Manifesto, Beyond the Fragments,* the Socialist Society) has it proved possible to maintain a territorially organized base for political activity for more than a year or two, and never on a genuinely national scale."[81] For a movement that sought to enlighten the Left on how best to use culture to organize, New Leftists found organizing quite a challenge.

Yet they did get involved in protests. "The Trafalgar Square Suez demonstration was the first mass political rally of its kind in the 1950s," Hall recalls, "and the first time I encountered police horses face to face."[82] Many members of the New Left were also active in the Campaign for Nuclear Disarmament's Aldermaston march.[83] In addition, they staged a propaganda campaign to intervene in debates about revising the Labour Party's Clause 4, its statement of commitment to socialism.[84] As mentioned in chapter 2, New Leftists contributed to the antiracist struggles surrounding the 1958 Notting Hill race riots, helped develop a Tenants' Defense League and community associations, and ran an "adventure playground" in the area.[85] Moreover, in the field of education they were instrumental in establishing the National Association of Teachers and contrived "new approaches to English" that were used in schools.[86]

For many years Hall has registered both support of and some skepticism of activism. In his effort to define the political-intellectual's "prime responsibility" to intellectually and strategically "arm" the movement and "the people," Hall attested: "Intellectuals have much to atone for in the labour movement: their lack of involvement in the struggle, their lack of centrality in active politics, often their divorce from the experiences and aspirations of ordinary working people."[87] Nonetheless, he has also insisted that one must not blindly reaffirm socialism, but instead address the hard analytical questions: "Will [socialism] happen? How can it happen? In the real world, as we know it? Does it look as if it's going to happen now more than it did a hundred years ago? And if it doesn't, why not? . . . . Who? When? With what? Under what agenda?"[88]

In his inaugural *New Left Review* editorial, Hall also took up this tension between prepolitical analysis and instant activism. He lauded the "impatience" of those "large number" of supporters who demanded "political activity" and have been disappointed "with the hesitancies . . . we have shown for organisation. This can be ignored no longer." Hall assigned value to the pressure to "'cease talking and begin doing.'" Even so, he swayed more "firmly" toward analysis. "The most urgent task for socialism today remains the clarification of ideas" because the Labour movement has suffered from a "poverty of ideas."[89] Here Hall sounded much like Matthew Arnold defending analytical "inaction" and quoting "Goethe's maxim, 'to act is easy, to think is hard.'" Hall warned against "abasing ourselves before the altar of *action*—at any price." While favoring pedagogy over action for action's sake, he advocated an "education" designed to generate "political activity in all its aspects." Hall saw this activist education as developing not so much in school as in "centres of socialist work and activity."[90]

While Hall in 1960 acknowledged that "making socialists" would involve persuading voters to vote socialist and trying to capture state power—something traditionally predicated on party involvement—his account of the New Left's nascent effort to shape the Labour Party's consciousness sounds much like the sort of pedagogical work that academic cultural studies has undertaken. The New Left clubs "set up exhibitions on cultural issues at Labour Party conferences. We mounted, for example, the first—and only?—exhibition at an annual Labour Party conference offering a political critique of commercial advertising."[91] Such an exhibit might teach Labour Party members much about how culture shapes desires and aspirations of voters. But did it show how that critical awareness could reshape the party's vision of its political-cultural mission and its appeal to voters?

In a 1996 interview Hall related that he and his early New Left colleagues "were in the light of the Stalinist experience, deeply suspicious of the bureaucratic apparatus of the political party." While he stands by this "antiorganizational" position—"we didn't want any structure, we didn't want any leadership, we didn't want any permanent party apparatus"—he also realized retrospectively that "the 'tyranny of structurelessness' was a problem for all 'new social movements.'"[92] In his reminiscences of the New Left, Samuel recounts that he came to appreciate the compensatory intellectual dimension of a political antiorganization whose intellectual labor was not wildly effective at planning and executing political transformation: "I think of Marx's 11th thesis on Feuerbach—the philosophers have only interpreted the world; the point is to change it—and then think also that one can have consolation from reversing it—if we can't actually change the world, the least we can do is to understand it."[93] It is interesting that Samuel grew up in a communist family and had wanted to be a Communist Party organizer.[94]

Much postwar critique is perhaps more comprehensively and resignedly prepolitical than political. By the time the New Left emerged, many socialists regarded socialism as an intellectual synonym for a field of critique rather than a political movement. Over time this critique became increasingly academic.[95] Thompson resisted the tendency to make academic critique the sole response to Left despair.[96] He aspired to do more than understand the world and dedicated himself tirelessly to antinuclear activism, especially in the 1980s. Censorious of the self-preoccupied theoreticist Left, he also maintained: "In my view the movements and the practices may now be well ahead of the theorists. In the peace and human rights movements of the 1980s, and their associated or supportive 'new social movements,' the third way emerged on a substantial scale not as theory but as real social forces: as a historical *fact.*" He reminded *New Left Review* that the kind of "intelligent observations and analysis" it sponsors needs to be "sustained by practices." Echoing William Blake on the insufficiency of "only analytics," he added: "Something more than analysis is called for in 1990."[97] Still, this "something more" remains as faintly sketched as it was in his final chapter on revolution in *Out of Apathy* and the closing chapter of *May Day Manifesto.*[98]

A wariness of state solutions—not only in Britain but in the Eastern bloc—accelerated the turn toward "cultural questions": "What is the alternative to capitalism? Socialism. What is a socialist culture? State control," Raymond Williams observed in 1960. "There are many good liberals, and many anxious socialists, who draw back if this is the prospect." Culture, for Williams and others, represented a reorganization of life, value, and significance that jaded political parties seemed to have too little interest in exploring as a resource for remaking the world. The New Left wanted its culturally lively clubs, Hall writes, to be "prefigurative of socialism itself ... an effective critique of the political practices typical of either the major parties or the left sects."[99] New Left intellectuals, however, as suggested in chapter 5, may have placed too much pressure on "culture" to function not simply like the space in which a reorganization of life could be imagined and celebrated, but as the magical motor of social change. The clubs may have functioned partly as substitutes for structural political change, just as culture served partly as a substitute for politics.

That said, Hall and his cohort were more complex than this facile substitution thesis suggests. At the conclusion of his lecture at the Illinois cultural studies conference, Hall seemed to draw on Thompson's *Poverty of Theory* in his statement that "there is all the difference in the world between understanding the politics of intellectual work and substituting intellectual work for politics."[100] It would be too extreme and pat to argue that some in the British New Left used what Mills termed the "cultural emphasis" to talk themselves out of conventionally political engagement as a benighted waste of energy. But Thompson's remarks about William Hazlitt suggest that the New Left's effort to reconceive "politics" both gained and lost "power" by not being more actively narrowly political: "The stance, or attack, of Hazlitt—as indeed of [Jonathan] Swift [on the monarchy]—is that of a writer who is not responsible for actually holding power. And his writing is full of contempt for power, a contempt for office, a distrust not only of aristocrats but of political parties and formations."[101] If this "stance" gives Hazlitt critical power, it also detaches him from the corrupt "power of the state." And if critique is disconnected righteously from endeavors to transform the situation or problem under criticism, it can become a compensatory value in its own right.[102]

Critique Incorporated: Academicizing

Angela Davis's reminiscences about studying at the Frankfurt School with Theodor Adorno and Jürgen Habermas are interwoven with the mid-1960s activism she shared with her fellow students. When not delving into Kant, Hegel, and Marx, she was protesting with members of the German Socialist League to oppose the U.S. war against North Vietnam and strategizing how to dramatize their point without being assaulted by the German police. Her thoughts absorbed not only Adorno's aphorisms but news of the explosive events and organizing taking place in Mississippi, Watts, Newark, and Oakland. After two years she opted not to write her doctoral dissertation with Adorno and instead to "contribute something concrete to the struggle" at home and pursue her work with Herbert Marcuse, who "had been practically pushed out of Brandeis [Davis's college] for political reasons" and then taught at the

University of California, San Diego. "The struggle was a life-nerve."[103] Her extracurricular activism activated a higher education than that which was available only in class.

The relationship between activist learning and academia has long been a fundamental issue for Staughton Lynd, who in his varied career has distinguished himself as an organizer, political intellectual, historian, teacher, and labor lawyer. In his reflections on his relationship with his father, Robert Lynd, Staughton recalls that the elder Lynd expected him to grow up "to be an American Lenin and a tenured professor at an Ivy League university." He offers a fascinating account of some of his father's early work. "Crude-Oil Religion" (1922) examined the power relations in one of Rockefeller's oil camps, in Elk Basin, Wyoming. It drew a published response from John D. Rockefeller. Lynd demanded that Rockefeller introduce a six day work week, erect a community center, guarantee labor's right to organize unions, improve workers housing, and pay extra for overtime. Lo and behold, the Rockefeller Foundation's Institute for Social and Religious Research developed a scholarly project on the religious life of an average American community and gave Lynd the opportunity to do it. Robert and Helen Merrell Lynd swerved from the religion angle and instead wrote their classic study of daily life, *Middletown*. Columbia hired Lynd, classified the book as his dissertation, and tenured him. The son asks, aware of how academia can bribe, pacify, and drain its scholar-teachers: "Lately I have wondered, who won? My Dad won because he and my mother wrote the book they wanted to write, and it was a spectacular success. But Rockefeller also won, because he did get my father off the shop floor: my Dad became a professor."[104] Staughton Lynd, after leaving academia for labor law, continued to publish books on both American history and political organizing, convinced that one does not have to be "a university teacher in order to do intellectual work" and skeptical of the academy's influence.[105]

Academe's influence is often subtle and hard to gauge. Mills considered university teaching "the only half-free way of life in the United States because, despite everything, it allows you freedom and a physical chance as it were, to write as you like." He rejoiced in his promotion to full professor because of the pay hike and "because it makes it more difficult [for them] 'to get at me' and makes me feel freer to write with less anxiety than before." The tenured college professor, he felt, is usually "threadbare" but "privileged," in part because his or her position within "the U.S. money trap" is "less noticeable" than it is for other professionals.[106]

Yet he envisioned being "trapped" in academia in Orwellian terms: being "'inside the whale.'" The university often turned its hired help into "professional entertainers" or "tired and routine people." At one university function in the 1950s, Mills had to deal with sociology grad students who typically would be working on something earth shattering like "The Impact of Work-Play Relationships among the Lower Income Families on the South Side of the Block on 112th Street between Amsterdam and Broadway." Hearing this Mills would "boom": "Why?" At times he was enraged by "the moral cowardice" that plagued American academics and intellectuals and blasted "professional acclaim": "Nothing is worth the continual feeling that you're not your own man." Two years before his untimely death, Mills toyed with the idea of leaving academe altogether.[107]

In the main Mills refused to play the role of "scared employee" or bribed employee and retained control over his conception of what he researched and wrote. In the mid-1940s he identified "the deepest problem of freedom for teachers" as "not the occasional ousting of a professor, but a vague general fear—sometimes politely known as 'discretion,' 'good taste,' or 'balanced judgment.'" Such controls structure the academicized ego. The tacit boundaries established by "academic gentlemen" gestate self-censorship and "self-intimidation" in intellectual workers to the point where some projects are not simply undoable, they are unimaginable. Foundations dangling research funds and travel grants help police the borders that Mills migrated beyond.[108] Universities distribute distinction, award recognition, and try to manage the self-judgment of faculty as well as students.[109] If the self-critical as well as critical capability of "academics" is principally produced from within the profession, what are the dangers of this?

Sweezy, denied tenure at Harvard, admits that his independent income sustained his radicalism and does not blame formerly radical activists for "adjust[ing] their ideas and values, political values and preferences, to the real possibilities." He remains intellectually grateful for being detached from an academia whose "academicism" funnels Marxist scholars "into doing pretty much Marxist versions of the academic specializations and fashions." His coauthor of *Monopoly Capital* (1966), Stanford economist Paul Baran, felt isolated as well as underpaid at an institution that found him and his radicalism an "embarrassment" in the McCarthy years and after: "Baran was a perfect example of one who needed more than just Stanford."[110] Baran, like Matthiessen and Mills, under pressure, died much too young.

Some of the most illuminating recent work on the origins of British cultural studies roots it in the postwar Workers Education Association movement in which Thompson, Williams, and Richard Hoggart taught for years. Williams declined a fellowship at Cambridge to accept the higher paying job of staff tutor for the Oxford Extra-Mural Delegacy. Thompson fought hard to get his post amid anticommunist discrimination.[111] This experimental venue freed up tutors, such as Williams and Thompson, to have students develop critical readings not only of literature but of newspapers and advertisements. "The sheer marginality of extramural work," Tom Steele writes, "which did not compete for grants with internal departments because of its separate 'Responsible Body' status, meant that any potential hostility to its work from internal departments became, instead, sheer indifference." Williams, Thompson, and Hoggart later tried to bring what they learned with their adult students to universities that years before would not have provided support for the development—or imagining—of such approaches.[112]

At the Illinois cultural studies conference, Hall related how the (now-defunct) Birmingham Centre had operated on a shoestring budget—academic openings for its graduates were scarce in the 1970s. He suggested that in well-funded American conditions academic opportunities—and, one must add, bribery—had affected the sort of theoretical work that was conceived. "It would be excessively vulgar to talk about such things as how many jobs there are, how much money there is around, and how much pressure that puts on people to do what they think of as critical political work and intellectual work of a critical kind, while also looking over their shoulders at the promotions stakes and publications stakes."[113] However "vulgar" it may have seemed, Hall broached that subject. In the United States it may be as common for radical prima donnas to gossip over who is getting job offers as any career-for-career's-sake academics intoxicated by the academicization of self-interest (a friend of mine dubs this "prestige grubbing").

If Raymond Williams approached cultural studies as "a practice, not a profession," it is hard to see how this would speak to many American academics whose sole field of practice is their profession.[114] Most American academics see "cultural politics" not as a dimension of a revised socialism, as Hall, Williams, and Thompson did, and perhaps not even as related to socialism. In the 1970s and 1980s the universities to a great extent superseded "movements" as the major sites for debates about progressive ideas. As noted in chapter 2, A. H. Halsey's glowing review of Mills fretted about this in 1959. In postmodern America, academic professional-managerial-class critique is usually a highly professionalized activity with professionalized objectives pragmatically tied to getting jobs, promotions, raising families, and paying off mortgages. Critique is partly a form of professional capital—career currency.

Wald is mindful of the American academic temptation and tendency to regard "one's career"—and, I would say, one's way of thinking—as "one's contribution to the movement."[115] Hall again addressed the academicization of political concern at the Illinois conference when he counseled cultural studies practitioners to live "with the possibility that there *could* be, sometime, a movement which would be larger than the movement of the petit-bourgeois intellectual."[116] Perhaps Hall should have said: "larger than the publishing and teaching ambitions of the professional-managerial-class academic."

Often I have heard academic theorists get put on the spot when anxious students ask about links among scholars, the production of knowledge, and activism. Theoretically progressive academics frequently protest that they are intellectuals, work hard, and leave the implementation of organized, concrete social change (outside of teaching students and publishing their interventionist books and articles) to others.[117] Scholarship and teaching can perform meaningful cultural and political work in manifold ways. Many academics would not feel comfortable doing any more than academic work, and many of their contributions should be valued. Still, I suspect that many undergraduates and graduate students would appreciate knowing about the history of connections among academics, academic programs, student organizing, and political movements.[118]

Especially during the last two decades, many graduate students have helped write an important chapter of that history in their campaigns to form graduate student unions. In a remarkable volume, which fuses labor studies, American studies, cultural studies, Left studies, and organizing studies, *Will Teach for Food* (1997), three Yale graduate students, Kathy Newman and Michelle Stephens (both American studies), and Corey Robin (Political Science), begin to explain how their efforts to organize their peers into a graduate student union—the Graduate Employees and Students Organization (GESO)—reeducated them and their comembers (www.geso.org). Members of GESO—and of graduate student unions elsewhere—have come to reread the so-called ivory tower as an ivory workplace, a corporate bureaucracy, and, more hopefully, a community institution. They have learned much about the tendency of professionalized individualism to be a disorganizing force and about the power made possible through collective agency. Some grad students, disenchanted with striving to join an increasingly managerial (and micromanaged) professoriate have chosen to become organizers rather than professors. Grad students under pressure aim not just to produce knowledge but to produce and disseminate knowledge about how to organize.

GESO concocted a term to describe the best they could hope for from many students and faculty: "soft support." It tried to persuade grad students not just to support but join the union. But GESO welcomed soft support from professors, grad students, and undergraduates—some of whom no doubt were immersed in reading critical theory, Marxist theory, feminist theory, Queer studies, African American studies, ethnic studies, American studies, cultural studies, political theory, radical sociology, and so on. Soft support might entail activities such as verbal defense of the union in formal and informal campus discussions, attending a rally, signing a petition on behalf of GESO, or witnessing the arrest of union members and activist allies engaged in civil protest.[119] *Will Teach for Food* made me wonder if there is a correlative for soft support: *soft critique*?

The modern university has long been a political space in which Right and Left have tussled to influence the fabrication, organization, and dissemination of knowledge. In the late nineteenth and early twentieth centuries Thorstein Veblen made a job tour of American universities, trying to earn a living without compromising his work. His sharp-edged analysis of the situation that plagued him became the first great study of the corporatization of the American university: *The Higher Learning: A Memorandum on the Conduct of Universities by Business Men* (1918).[120] One obituary of Raymond Williams appropriately commemorated his activism not only outside but inside an academy "increasingly threatened by Thatcherite attacks on intellectual liberty."[121] In this vein, Jameson has warned his colleagues on the Left not to degrade the social importance of "academic politics, and the politics of intellectuals, as a particularly 'academic' matter."[122] As Lauter puts it: "the professional is political."[123]

There has been a venerable tradition of American and British progressive intellectuals who have indeed reached beyond academia.[124] When *New Socialist* was founded in 1981, it presented its project as an alliance between Left scholars and politicians. The first issue's contents makes this patent: "Stuart Hall, professor at the Open University, on the riots," "Peter Townsend, professor at Essex University, explains why Labour needs an alternative social strategy," and so on. Its advertisement announced: "To be confident of these victories, we have to come out on top in the battle of ideas."[125] Many "new socialists" saw theory as more of a catalyst for political reorganizing than a sufficiently radical act in and of itself.

In the 1990s the Scholars, Artists, and Writers for Social Justice (SAWSJ) organization was established in America to better form alliances and dialogues among scholars, artists, and writers and union members (Web site: www.sage.edu/html/SAWSJ and www.sage.edu/SAWSJ/join.htm; e-mail: sawsj@lrrc.umass.edu). This endeavor has been supported by academic organizations already engaged in this work, such as the Labor Center at the University of Massachusetts, Amherst, which trains students to contribute to the labor movement (www.umass.edu/lrrc). SAWSJ's signatories include Tony Kushner,

Gloria Steinem, John Sayles, John Edgar Wideman, Dar Williams, Jack New-field, Janice Radway, and Robin D. G. Kelley. Conferences feature panels that showcase members of all of the groups that are involved and provide opportunities not just for mutual education but for learning about specific struggles in which members might lend their support. Panels address concerns such as "On Becoming an Organizer." Such organizations give scholars a framework in which activism goes beyond radical teaching, radical journal subscribing, and radical theorizing, historicizing, and politicizing in publications. These contacts also enable scholars to meet union organizers, researchers, and educators who are eager to share their insights and sense of mission with students. Scholars, artists, writers, and union members empower one another through a solidarity that generates confidence and commitment as well as knowledge.

The Holding Pattern: Politicians without a Party

Matthiessen lamented in his final years: "I am a socialist, though still without a party." And in 1960 Mills, for all his interest in proposing programs and policies, profiled himself as a "politician without a party, and within the American political context, without any talent for real politics, without opportunities to develop them, and with little inclination to do so." He concluded unashamedly: "The political demands that I put upon myself are now more or less satisfied by writing." It is noteworthy that Mills voted for Norman Thomas, the Socialist Party candidate, in every presidential election from 1928 to 1948.[126] Are many postmodern academic critics politicians without a party who—partly out of despair—are "more or less satisfied by writing"? And are they teaching students to be politicians without a party, politicizers whose "political demands" become mainly theoretical and historicizing demands? Is the unpartied Left—or academic Left—a dilemma, a possibility, or both?[127]

Sometimes Mills declined requests to speak at rallies because he saw his books and articles as significant "political action" on their own. Reversing Marx's dictum—and expressing sentiments that would resurface in Samuel's affirmation of consolatory understanding and theoretical socialism a quarter century later—Mills reported: "A friend of mine in Warsaw repeated to me what Marx said about philosophers not just interpreting the world but changing it. Then he added, 'We must, just now, reverse that: the point is to interpret it.'" At times Robert Lynd also found the consolation prize of understanding sufficient. In the mid-1950s he inscribed a journal entry reaffirming the significance of "try[ing] to know the score in [one's] lifetime": "The one ultimate indignity of life is to go over the hill into oblivion without at least understanding what is wrong with our time and why it is wrong." Lynd labored to advance critique not principally for professional or even intellectual reasons, but to try to "do what is decent, rather than simply drifting or cashing in on the times in which one happens to live."[128]

Yet Mills, like Lynd, kept asking *understanding for what?* Social critics, Mills warned, must not fixate on what seems to be their "powerlessness," dismiss utopian thinking, and in response offer "politically trivial" (and timid) the-smaller-the-better insights or proposals. Many scared, bribed, and alienated employees fetishize "understanding": "Simply understanding is an ideal of the man who has a capacity to know truth but not the chance, the skill, or the guts, as the case may be, to communicate them with political effectiveness."[129] Mills tested his resolve with the question: "Isn't [writing about politics and culture] a defaulting of the political obligations of every man today to act?"[130]

Still, much of Mills's writing suggests that not only "cultural activities" but critical activities can seem like "the only available form of opposition" in "the absence of opposition parties." One must not underestimate how disillusioned political intellectuals in the United States and Britain were with mainstream parties, "free world" governments, Communist states, and the labor movement in their turn toward culture and critique. With "direct party struggle" shut to most American, British, and Russian intellectuals, and with "merely local and ineffective 'politics'" inadequate, the critic, by way of compensation, may elect "to believe that problems are really going to be solved in *his* medium, that of the word." Mills did not naively "believe" in writing as a "solution" either to the problems at hand or to feeling "politically irrelevant," but he was happy to define writing as his most meaningful and enjoyable political activity. He admitted that his principled "politics of truth" may be a "politics of despera-tion," a prepolitical "holding pattern," yet "the only realistic politics of possible consequence ... readily open to intellectuals": "It is an affirmation of one's self as a moral and intellectual center of responsible decision; the act of a free man who rejects 'fate;' for it reveals his resolution to take his own fate, at least, into his own hands." Mills favored the remaking of a Left in which intellectuals would not surrender what they did best and loved most "to become work-ing-class agitators or machine-politicians, or ... play-act at any other direct political action."[131] Despite assertions like this, he never banished the thought that critical opposition could operate more as evasion than engagement.

If anything, Lynd intensified Mills's anxieties about critical evasion. Lynd, who had not published a book since *Knowledge for What?* in 1939, was at work in the mid-1950s on a never-to-be-completed study of power in America. At that time he wrote a punchy review of his younger Columbia colleague's *The Power Elite* in *The Nation.* Lynd, like Sweezy and others, scolded Mills for replacing the Marxist language and analysis of class with "elite theory." This focus on the reproduction of elites in different sectors produced a "top down" critique that, Lynd felt, let both elites and capitalism off the hook. But even more fundamentally he hinted, as did Philip Rieff, that Mills's book would be a popular success because Mills's "analysis—all this significant documentation and good thinking—was not intended to get anywhere" (soft critique).[132] For all its perceptiveness, Lynd's review exhibits how much political struggle had been narrowed and displaced on the critical arena, as if "politics" now depended on the theory one endorsed.[133] These two colleagues could have been staunch allies, coconspirators, perhaps coauthors. After he suffered his first major heart attack—the second killed him—Mills wrote Miliband: "Only one prof. of sociology at Columbia has sent me as much as a sorry you're sick card, Robt Lynd."[134]

But Mills, like Lynd at his best, held fast to the belief—as did Judith Williamson in her 1980s critique of consumer socialism—that ideas counted. When he published *The Causes of World War Three* (1958) and *Listen, Yankee,* best sellers both, many readers wrote him—their radical Miss Lonelyhearts—to ask what to *do.*[135] Readers hungered to become not just social thinkers but social agents. He encountered the implicit demand that his political-cultural studies become a kind of what to do studies.

Mills's responses to this demand, though activist in spirit, tended to be more analytical than concrete—more *Always politicize!* than *Always organize!* In fact, he was suspicious of dead-end organizations or organizing-for-organizing's-sake. Once a representative of a socialist splinter group asked Mills to sign a petition to have his organization removed from a government blacklist. Mills signed the petition but exasperated his visitor by disagreeing with his party line. Finally the socialist demanded to know what Mills did believe in. Mills, a trained motorcycle technician, looked up from his bike and replied: "German motors." When the baffled and irked socialist left, Mills said: "It's ridiculous to say those guys are a threat to the government. They've only got about 150 guys—how could they overthrow anything?"[136] The questions underlying this were: How is "overthrowing" doable and what does "overthrowing" even mean in the 1950s?

To his credit, Mills challenged intellectuals to be more forthright and specific about who they expect to do the "overthrowing." He acknowledged bluntly that intellectuals love to "create standards and point out goals" and then dump their analyses and recommendations on "other groups, other circles, other strata to realize them." Sounding like a speaker at a SAWSJ conference or a GESO rally, he exhorted intellectuals to "repossess our cultural apparatus" and engage in "direct action" in their own workplaces and "immediate milieu": "It is a mistake for us to swallow ourselves in some great, vague, abstract, political 'We.'" Yet what he may have had in mind for academic intellectuals remained somewhat fuzzy: "stop whining" about their "alienation" long enough to "form radical critiques, audacious programs, commanding views of the future" and "define and redefine reality" in the light of "utopian ideals."[137]

"Overthrowing anything" is especially difficult, perhaps, when Cold War states and parties have influenced one, as Hall put it, to favor antiorganization organizations. Miliband's requiem for Mills foregrounded his friend's antiorganizational bent. "He never belonged to any party or faction; he did not think of himself as a 'Marxist,'" Miliband wrote unapologetically, but with a critical eye. "He was on the left, but not of the left, a deliberately lone guerilla, not a regular soldier. He was highly organised, but unwilling to *be* organised, with self-discipline the only discipline he could tolerate."[138] Hans Gerth, Mills's coauthor on several projects, concurred: "Mills . . . had no talent for joining disciplined ranks of any sort. . . . He feared, possibly, to be 'boxed in,' to be decorated with proper labels, to be shelved and made harmless."[139] The Texas maverick was a radical form of American unpartied "individual." If Mills considered this a problem in any way—no solidarity—he claimed he had no regrets. Older American radicals, European communists, and the New York intellectuals once knew "'fraternity,'" he commented, whereas he did "not cry for it." Isolation "made [him] into an intellectual." If it brought "loneliness"—the isolation that tore up Matthiessen—more importantly it gave Mills the spunk to be "audacious and free."[140]

Mills often commended a socialism that, as Thompson observed, "entailed the decomposition of state power." But he really liked to label himself a Wobbly in "political ethos" and "spiritual conditions" rather than in "political orientation" and practice. Early twentieth-century Industrial Workers of the World—Wobblies—stood for One Big Union and No Big Bosses. In the late 1940s Mills interviewed a worker who recited a poem about a sheriff who, confronting a group of Wobblies, demanded that they identify their leader so he could make his arrest. They yelled: "We ain't got no leader / We're all leaders." Mills defined "Wobbly freedom" as freedom from bosses, "capitalistic or communistic," as only "taking orders" from oneself, as being "one's own boss at all times": "the opposite of bureaucrat."[141] His Wobbly disposition despised not just various parties and states but a "fully routinized" self-proclaimed Left establishment ("The Old Futilitarians") that "sets the key tasks, the suitable themes, and establishes the proper canons of value, taste, and reality." In his BBC address of 1959, he questioned the very existence of a U.S. Left and worried about Britain also. "Even if the Left wins state power, as in Britain, it often seems to its members to have little room for maneuver—in the world or in the nation."[142]

If Ohmann is correct that in the 1950s one of the greatest academic transgressions was "to make a scene," then Mills truly relished making a scene, not just in the university but in Left journal circles, because he took the imperative for radical social change to heart. The brilliant Irving Howe, whose acquaintance with Mills ended in the late 1950s, sketches a perceptive, preemptively self-critical, yet suggestively fearful portrait of Mills in that period. "In both his person and his writings Mills was a figure of power, a fiercely grinding sort of power that came down like a fist." He acknowledged that Mills "was ambivalent toward the New York intellectuals" and that, "not without some justice," these ex-partisans "had given up all hope of making their opinions matter and had settled into a mere routine of display." Mills was not content to enact socialism as intellectual bickering in journals, even if this represented a conflicted effort to restore intellectual prestige to socialist critique. Howe registers their anxiety that if Mills kept up his pressure, he might get them all in trouble-by-association. "He was exhausting, a man whose pressures of will never let up, often forcing other people, even those who loved him as I could not, into a rigidity of self-defense." Howe's resentment that Mills had not accepted his limits mingles with physical alarm: "Mills barged into New York at the very moment the intellectual Left was falling apart. Physically large yet fragile, he seemed a robber baron of intellect, one of those native radicals neither hardened by dogma nor softened by defeat nor—but this was rather serious—chastened by modern history."[143]

Translation: this "educated Cowboy of the Left" was not only hard to pin down as a nondogmatic American radical, he was too uncanonical to be dogmatically anticommunist. Mills was not of the European-immigrant urban Left. Howe concluded that Mills was "insufficiently bruised"—perhaps too strong for his own good and for the New York Intellectuals' good to display discretion as they had. In short, this overly earnest sociological "muckraker," running around "exhorting and declaiming," trying to shame the Left into serving as the "moral conscience" of society, was embarrassingly presumptuous. "To me, his outlook was an intellectual disaster; to him, mine must have seemed like the conservatism of a radical afraid to surrender familiar positions."[144]

Yet Mills's writings do not suggest exactly what he might have said to Radway's student Kevin, who asked: So what do we *do* with critique? Nor does Mills address in detail the concern: What does critique help make *doable*? Miliband, writing to Thompson in 1963, believed that Mills's sometimes desperate feelings of isolation on the Cold War Left partly accounted for his overinvestment in intellectuals and students as catalysts of social change in place of the traditional socialist focus on workers. Mills struggled not only with the absence of "a serious labour movement in the United States," but with "a barrenness of alternatives," and "that is why he took so warmly to 'the new left,' and was so disappointed with it and with the humanist revisionists. That is also why he took so hotly to the Cubans and Fidel Castro. He was looking for 'agencies,' and even tried to invent them." Yet a few years earlier, in 1956, Philip Rieff suggested that though Mills "must be ranked as one of the caretakers of the socialist polemical tradition," his militant but ultimately unthreatening critique is not directed toward agents or toward organizing agents: "He incites without hope; he offers not a single saving myth—no hope from the proletariat; nor from the engineers; and certainly not from a cultivated and responsible upper class."[145]

The 1960s, however, continued to complicate and enrich understandings of the potential to establish progressive agencies and organizations. Mills, who died in 1962, did not live to see the full power of the Civil Rights Movement, the New Left, and the antiwar movement, or the efflorescence of political movements that grew out of them. These movements changed American society in important ways—affirmative action, desegregation, equal voting rights, feminist solidarity, gay, lesbian, and transsexual organizing and legal intervention, and new productions of knowledge in the university. Ohmann argues that the university—not Left party development or Left culture—is "the site where movement gains have taken root most deeply." While Ohmann praises "the ferment around teaching" that led to "more democratic relations of instruction and better pedagogies," he also acknowledges that neither the movements nor the knowledge revolution in academe has brought about a "democratic revolution in the U.S." Academia, albeit not without many battles that still rage, helped make numerous sorts of studies—"black studies, women's studies, working-class studies, and gay and lesbian studies" for starters—not just doable but (more) "reputable."[146] Ohmann, Lawrence Levine, and others, including myself, do not underrate this work in progress. If citizens experience difficulty in finding a candidate and a party they can vote for with good conscience, they can indeed take courses, read books and articles, and subscribe to liberal-Left magazines and practice intellectual citizenship. But if the postmodern emphasis on critique and questioning—a valuable one in so many ways—centers more, as Lynd, Mills, and others urged, on producing knowledge about agency, organizing, programs, and planning, it will have to concentrate more specifically on what's doable and be more committed to moving beyond what Mills called a holding pattern.

The Scope of the Critique Project

I will close with a few clusters of considerations-in-progress that bring together some ideas and problems I will be contemplating over time. First, since the onset of the postwar period, Anglo-American critique has been shaped—in some cases stunted—by acute Left despair.[147] If the British New Left emerged at what many British socialists thought was perhaps the last moment when socialism still had some small chance of functioning as a popular political rallying point, the vast majority of American progressives assumed that that moment had passed in their country two decades before. Left futilitarianism often fosters the premise that the times are not propitious for substantive social change and that the best academy-based critics can do—as Mills, Samuel, and others have suggested, at moments in their lives—is try to "understand" what's what. In these conditions the battle too often becomes not Left against Right but Left internecine "critical" sparring. Left despair frequently informs the idea that capitalism is far too mighty a system—or system of contradictions—to transform.

Two resilient critics have tried to explain why even Left defeat is not a lost cause. "Even when social movements fail to achieve their own stated goals," George Lipsitz argues, "they send a message to people in other places about the potential for struggles and resistance. They provide tools for people to ask new questions, to settle old scores, to speak about parts of their lives that have been repressed and suppressed.... Martin Luther King Jr. lost most of the important battles he fought." Of course, King did not want to lose. "The question is," West reassures us, "Do you still have your integrity after you struggle? That's winning."[148] There is wisdom in these consolations.

Still, I find myself especially energized by Michael Moore's populist zest for fighting and strategizing even when the Democratic Party ("professional losers"), the Green Party, and progressives botch what should be smart campaigns to unseat regimes making a mess of America and the world. Apparently no one schooled Moore—a college dropout—in Left fatalism. He is driven to popularize and win. His persistent question is: "*So what do we do?*" And he is unfashionably optimistic: "True, we don't have the money and the media outlets they have—but we've got something better: We've got the people on our side." What would social critiques—and progressive popularizing strategies—over the last half-century have looked like if more of them had been propelled by this impulse?[149]

Second, in addition to cultural studies or cultural critique, it would be useful to think more about cultural design. Here the key question is not just something like *how does culture mystify and reproduce social contradictions,* but *how might culture be designed to better cultivate life?* This resonates with William Morris's "vision splendid" and the kind of utopian imagining one finds in Aldous Huxley's *Island.* By cultural design I do not simply mean utopian thinking. At stake is reimagining the possibilities not only of thinking and acting but of being—as Huxley might say, of being here and now. Older, sometimes ancient, discourses, some of which have been restylized, synthesized, and commodified by the New Age industry, have partly addressed such concerns. But this field should be of interest to political and critical progressives who see the wisdom of not being wholly fixated on and channeled by that which they criticize. If the aim is not only to overcome oppression and exploitation, but also to conceptualize how to devise a better quality of life, must not the political-cultural front in part be a life-enhancement front? One of Karl Marx's and Frederick Engels's most moving indictments of industrial capitalism's exploitative "use of machinery" and "division of labor" was that work "lost all individual character, and, consequently, all charm for the workman."[150] Life with *charm* is a social necessity. And in Leon Trotsky's vision splendid "life . . . will not be monotonous."[151] In harmony with such expansive concerns, Terry Eagleton has redescribed socialism not just as an economic and political reorganization of society, but as the politicization of love and of living well.[152] Those schooled from their earliest years in the domestication and psychologization of love and commitment may find it hard to apprehend the significance of this social conception.

Third, if progressive teaching can be viewed not just as a profession—institutionalized intellectualism—but a form of ethical stewardship and intellectual citizenship, how might the progressive teacher imagine students? Is he or she helping students to be not only theorists, critics, historicizers, contextualizers, and politicizers, but also citizens, activists, and creators?[153] Could it be productive to set up something like MoveOn.edu—interdisciplinary, multidisciplinary, and postdisciplinary Internet Web sites and e-mail lists for progressive teachers and students? Could this facilitate critical organizing and more? Harry Boyte and Nancy Kari stress the importance of building civic muscle. Most progressive teachers only encourage their students to develop critical muscle. In *Building America* (1996), Boyte and Kari want to reconceive work as "public work." They are fascinated by Lewis Mumford's proposal to establish a "public work corps" that would train youth to improve their world (and get used to the idea that it can be improved). Boyte and Kari make a case for redefining incentive as civic incentive, reconsidering agency as civic agency, and establishing new versions of community organizer Saul Alinsky's "schools of public life." They contend that too often "academic culture" has failed to grasp this pragmatic dimension of democratic education. For them democracy is not merely voting, occasionally volunteering, or spouting a nationalist ideology. Democracy is something one exercises, something one does.[154]

Jeremy Brecher and Tim Costello also recognize that too many American citizen-consumers—like so many deskilled industrial and service workers—have been critically deskilled. In 1976 Brecher and Costello celebrated the Sons of Liberty, the Nonimportation Associations, the Town Meetings, the Committees of Correspondence, and other grassroots organizations that sprung up to spearhead the American Revolution as direct actions and movements that offer strategic organizing lessons for the present. They hold that the vast numbers of "ordinary" Americans who are economically, politically, and culturally "managed" already have the agency to cooperate with one another to overthrow a minority rule. They insist that the majority of Americans can take control of their lives, labor, and knowledge development. Invoking Tom Paine, Brecher and Costello pitch their argument not on the basis of radicalism (although socialist critique resonates throughout their analyses), but on the grounds of American common sense. Their inspiring effort to provide *how to organize* guidelines, illustrated with anecdotes by veteran organizers, advances *organizing theory*, even if the upshot still remains vague and difficult to act on.[155]

As the twenty-first century takes shape the corporatization and micromanagement of the university have been accompanied not only by greater activism among undergraduates, graduate students, and faculty, but by more scholarship—of uneven quality, usefulness, and intellectual power—on activism and organizing.[156] I suspect that scholars who find this field of knowledge production compelling will need more to think with than a progressive civics discourse.[157] However, the social and democratic value that Mumford, Brecher and Costello, Robert Bellah and his coauthors, Boyte and Kari, Tony Bennett, and others put on *practicing* social and collective agency is crucial. Some observers have cast doubts on the disposition of American intellectuals shaped by privatized individualism to organize and form coalitions—doubts that the international antiwar marches of 2003 and progressive organizing during the presidential election of 2004 may have complicated. Perhaps the lesson and hope one takes from Zinn's *People's History of the United States* (1980, updated every few years) are that organizing, protests, and making commotions—not legislation alone, political parties alone, media coverage alone, education alone, publications alone, culture alone—accelerate change.[158]

Thinking critically about this range of fronts and strategies, it is vital to state again, as I did in chapter 5, that oversimple admonitions about the tendency of cultural politics to supplant concrete organizing can be perilously counterproductive: the incentive-building and organizing powers of culture remain urgent for progressives to fathom. Thomas Frank's *What's the Matter with Kansas?* (2004), like other recent books, suggests that lately conservatives have been better than progressives at "cultural studies" and mobilizing around cultural issues. Frank analyzes how conservative proletarian populism in Kansas has galvanized huge segments of the working class as righteous and self-sacrificing activist "martyrs" whose subjective and spiritual sense of meaningfulness is enhanced from feeling victimized not by government-sponsored corporate welfare or the growing maldistribution of wealth, resources, and access that systematically hurts them, but by abortion, the banning of school prayer, Darwinism, and gay marriage. These cultural issues help popularize categories through which conservatives formulate what constitute problems ("liberal elite" substitute for corporate elite as a problem) and solutions (grassroots Republican campaigns for electoral victory replace union-based struggles for economic democracy as a solution). Only if culture ceases to be central to the way people understand the world, their identities, and the contradictions that entangle them will it become peripheral to the formation of political explanations, motivations, and actions.[159]

Mills culminated his critique of *The Power Elite*'s critics by speculating: "What many reviewers really want, I think, is less of a program than a lyric upsurge—at least at the end. They want a big thump on the intellectual and political back. They want a sturdy little mood of earnest optimism, out of which we step forward all nice and fresh and shining."[160] While I have no lyric upsurge to offer, there are three basic intellectual as well as pragmatic responses to the *critique for what?* challenge: critique for analysis, organizing, and what Stuart Hall terms "hegemonizing."[161] Some critics, theorists, and scholars based in the academy will choose to focus on a production of knowledge that offers progressive analysis. Much of that analysis has been and will continue to be immensely valuable, politically and intellectually. And some within this group will endeavor to extend their scope of critique in ways sketched above, mindful of what the English playwright Harold Pinter observed in his 2005 Nobel Prize acceptance speech's blistering critique of U.S. and British imperial policies: "Many thousands, if not millions, of people in the United States are demonstrably sickened, shamed, and angered by their government's actions, but as things stand, they are not a coherent political force—yet."[162]

Afterword: On Culture

> Conventional wisdom agrees that political fiction is not art; that such work is less likely to have aesthetic value because politics—all politics—is agenda and therefore its presence taints aesthetic production.
> —*Toni Morrison, Foreword to Sula*

IN PHONETICS, THE BRANCH OF LINGUISTICS THAT ATTENDS TO THE SCIENCE of meaningfully articulated sounds, there is, I am told, something called a zero signifier—a sound that does not sound; or, more formally, an abstraction that accounts for other sounds without being a sound itself. In mathematics, irrational numbers, or surds, are much the same thing. In the human sciences, the incest taboo serves roughly the same purpose—to prohibit sex among those too close on the animal side of their nature is to mark off the point of intimacy where nature and culture digress. Though the taboo is commonly broken—constantly in fantasy, occasionally in practice—it remains the zero signifier that sets off the meaning of human nature from that of the animals. Incest is for dogs. Humans sniff and screw more discriminately—at least in principle.

In some ways, the model fits also the nasty intercourse between culture and politics. The crisis of the modern age might be said to be the repeated violations of the taboo on the commingling of culture and politics. If we screw our daughters we become dogs; if we politicize our culture, we become ideologues. Matthew Arnold, in *Culture and Anarchy* in 1869, remains the Lévi-Strauss of the taboo on cultural ruination. Culture can hardly save the masses, if it descends to the ordinariness of the common man. He may have had Marx's materialism in mind. The grand narrative of the modern, said now to be in decline, has been at its core the story of culture in the globalizing European diaspora.

215

Culture is the signifier of the human, from which comes all things good for man, than which none better than pure science (unless it is pure profit). This grand story of Culture—which is to say: the Modern West—takes the form of a tragedy. Politics slays the fair maiden, Culture, by despoiling her purity. Her death entails, thus, the poison that puts science into a coma.

The surd is the love hidden from contamination; for which the absurd is the improbability of it all. The classical nineteenth-century dream of pure culture as the zero signifier of human progress—hence of modern politics—has fallen through the hole in the night kitchen. The absurdity of the classically modern scheme rises on voicing of culture as not virginal but necessarily political. Surds become absurd to those who can hear smut they were taught as children. For those willing to learn a new scale, the surd is merely set differently.

Such is the strangeness of the times in which we think early in the 2000s. The varieties of cultural studies that came on the scene in the 1980s in the wake of the political revolutions of the 1960s are themselves a tribute to the complexities of the age. Quite apart from the academic study of culture, the so-called culture wars that began in earnest in the 1980s continue to violate the taboo in a most bestial manner. To grant the political power of culture is one thing; to make of culture a weapon is quite another. Whether the weapon is a holy scripture or the great books of the old days, the idea is to destroy those who would stray from the truth that Culture, in all its variations, is unmentionable beauty. Whether the dirty old men declaim from Mecca or the secular wing of University of Chicago, their intent is to silence new and unruly voices that, far from merely speaking truth to power, utter the significant truth that had been pressed down as the surd of modern life.

No less in the academy, where cultural studies has sent a panic through the old-guard that was, for a while, able to dismiss the French as evidently risible. But when cultural studies came to the fore for its brief but potent institutional life in Birmingham, the old timers thought it was enough to Sokal-ize this daring method. But then they learned that it was, in effect, a speaking in several tongues at once. Then and there, Marx and Freud, not to mention Derrida and Habermas, among others, came out of the silence to which their opponents had sought to confine them. By uttering their meanings all at once, allowing no room for bureaucratized compartments, cultural studies spoke power to truth.

Some still ask Richard Johnson's question long after it has been answered, "What is cultural studies, anyway?" But they ask it as the spent lover asks "Was it good for you?" If you have to ask, you already know. Thus in the more traditional academic domains, like sociology, you can find today the most bizarre sorts of activities that call themselves cultural sociology or, worse yet, the sociology of culture. What they stand for, however noble their efforts, is a pallid grasp on the original surd. One hears talent nonsense like the criticism that Foucault did not have a "strong research program". The plaint seems to be the one old guards of all ages have always thrown down. Whatever may be interesting in that *stuff*, it is not good science; hence it must be bad culture. This while the anthropologists who invented the game look on in amused contempt—they being, with the people in English and other of the new homes of cultural studies, among those with scant regard for the old surd.

A new surd has come to the fore. It is still culture, without the caps. But is the inversion of the older one. Culture, now, is the surd of politics in direct correspondence to the breakdown of its former significance. Culture is no longer, and never again will be, the Other to politics that saves the modern from having to acknowledge its unspeakable filth. Rather, culture is the zero signifier of postmodern politics. In the absence of a center, the voice loses its power to manage the system. Global politics after 1989 are the politics of voices proclaiming the social differences that attest to the absence of a center. The fainting of the weary dream of a coherently organized social order is the sound that cannot sound. Hence, the irony that tragedy has come to its end. Irony is the trope of a world in which the zero signifier is the former center, once merely silent, now beyond even a dog's hearing. The codgers strain to hear the ever more faint tones.

Charles Lemert

Notes

Abbreviations

FOM   F.O. Matthiessen Papers, Yale Collection of American Literature, Beinecke Rare Book and
        Manuscript Library
ML   Max Lerner Papers, Manuscripts and Archives, Yale University Library
DM   Dwight Macdonald Papers, Manuscripts and Archives, Yale University Library
VFC   V. F. Calverton Papers, New York Public Library

Notes for the Introduction

1. Blake, "The Marriage of Heaven and Hell," in *William Blake: The Complete Poems*, ed. Alice Ostriker (Harmondsworth, Middlesex: Penguin, 1977), 192. Hall, "Gramsci and Us," *Marxism Today* 31 (June 1987): 16–21, see 21. C. Wright Mills to his imaginary Russian correspondent, Tovarich, fall 1959, in Mills, *C. Wright Mills: Letters and Autobiographical Writings*, ed. Kathryn Mills with Pamela Mills (Berkeley: University of California Press, 2000), 277. Endnote references to Hall refer to Stuart Hall, to Williams refer to Raymond Williams, and to Thompson refer to Edward Palmer Thompson, unless it seems useful to include the first name or initial to be clear. Lisa Wyant guided me to Blake's poem.

2. Trachtenberg, "Introduction," in *Critics of Culture: Literature and Society in the Early Twentieth Century*, ed. Alan Trachtenberg (New York: John Wiley, 1976), 1–13, see 8.

3. Paul Goodman was on the same wavelength more than four decades ago, when he expressed frustration with the American Sociological Association's highly academicized caucus called the "Social Problems Approach" ("the sociologists did not have … [a] pragmatic involvement in the problem by which a solution might emerge; they were applying 'methods'"), but showed keen interest in a course on Community Dynamics taught by William Biddle at Earlham College in Indiana: "Here the method is for the professor and students to go into the problem area, to study and work with the people involved; they irradiate the problem from within, with such science and understanding as they have; and, in reported cases, solutions have emerged from their participation. Clearly this is both classical progressive education and classical pragmatic sociology" ("Utopian Thinking," *Commentary* 32 [July 1961]: 19–26, see 25).

4. See George Lakoff, *Don't Think of an Elephant! Know Your Values and Frame the Debate* (White River Junction, VT: Chelsea Green, 2004), 27–28.

5. Here I think of Perry Anderson's explanation for why his Marxism is one that mainly feeds off and criticizes previous work within the Marxist traditions: his and E. P. Thompson's "contrasting contributions to a common socialist culture have in many ways each involved restatements or criticisms of classical inheritances, whether values imagined by [William] Morris or [Christopher] Caudwell, or strategies devised by [Rosa] Luxemburg or [Antonio] Gramsci, more than innovative advance into unknown terrain. The reasons for this are not hard to seek: the absence of a truly mass and truly revolutionary movement in England, as elsewhere in the West, has fixed the perimeter of all possible thought in this period" (*Arguments within English Marxism* [London: Verso, 1980], 207).

6. Huxley, *Island* (New York: Harper and Row, 1968 [1962]), 80.

7. Tom Steele summarizes the expectations of many contemporary adult education students not unlike those taught by Williams, Thompson, and Richard Hoggart in Workers Education Association courses in the postwar period: "How does this help me to change the world I live in?" (*The Emergence of Cultural Studies: Adult Education, Cultural Politics and the "English" Question* [London: Lawrence and Wishart, 1997], 192).

8. On critical fuzziness—with Gramscian notions of cultural revolution in mind—see Ioan Davies, *Cultural Studies and Beyond: Fragments of Empire* (New York: Routledge, 1995), 115, 117.

9. Lynd, *Knowledge for What? The Place of Social Science in American Culture* (New York: Grove Press, 1964 [1939]): all quotations from this book will be followed by page numbers in parentheses.

10. At the outset of World War II, Lynd implied a progressive redefinition of patriotism. He attacked the "unstated" premise that Americans must agree to forego economic equality to sanction hype about political equality (voting) and warned that "capitalist economic power" threatens "the whole structure of democratic authority everywhere and always" ("The Structure of Power," *New Republic* 107 [Nov. 9, 1942]: 597–600, see 597).

11. George A. Lundberg's review of *Knowledge for What?* in *American Journal of Sociology* 45 (Sept. 1939): 270–74, quotes Lynd's "knowledge for its own sake" on 270. Robert MacIver, "Enduring Systems of Thought," *Survey Graphic* 28 (Aug. 1939): 496–97, see 497. Alexander Goldenweiser's review (under the headline "Theory"), *American Anthropologist* 42 (Jan.–March 1940): 164–66, see 165–66. See Lynd's rebuttal to MacIver, "Intelligence Must Fight," *Survey Graphic* 28 (Aug. 1939): 498–99, see 498. Max Lerner, "The Revolt Against Quietism," *New Republic* (July 5, 1939): 257–58, see 257 (claims), 258 (theory of social change, social iniquities).

12. Lynd adds: "The 'disillusioned reformer' is a man who has given up trying to create change in the hardest possible way, i.e., by piecemeal attack upon isolated symptoms" (111).

13. For a different reading of *Knowledge for What?* see Richard Wightman Fox's brilliant chapter on Lynd, "Epitaph for Middletown: Robert S. Lynd and the Analysis of Consumer Culture," in *The Culture of Consumption: Critical Essays in American History 1880–1980*, ed. Richard Wightman Fox and T. J. Jackson Lears (New York: Pantheon, 1983), 101–41. And for a view of the postwar Lynd—still pushing toward critical activism—see Lynd's pro-Marxist critique of C. Wright Mills's *Power Elite*, "Power in the United States," *The Nation* (May 12, 1956): 408–11. Lynd to Macdonald, March 31, c. 1945, DM.

14. Riesman, *Abundance for What? And Other Essays* (New York: Anchor, 1965 [1964]). Riesman questioned the American distribution of "abundance" to the military (290)—an "abundance" that many Americans never found in abundance (100)—and contemplated some of the salubriously "collective" (289) uses to which it could be put instead. He acknowledged

that his "proposals, here as elsewhere, are far from matching [his] critical diagnoses" (105). Clearly, Riesman was influenced by Lynd.

15. On ethical relativism see Riesman, "Some Observations on Community Plans and Utopia," *Yale Law Journal* 57 (Dec. 1947): 173–200, see 179. Riesman, *Abundance for What?*, 349. This "abundance" is now even more lopsided: 1 percent of Americans own 40 percent of the wealth. See Bertell Ollman, *How to Take an Exam ... and Remake the World* (Tonawanda, NY: Black Rose Books, 2001): "Between 1983–1997, the productivity of American workers went up 17 percent, while their share of the wealth they produced went down 3.1 percent. They made more, but got less" (7). "Of this new wealth, 85.5 percent has gone to the richest 1 percent of the population (268 of whom are billionaires), because they own 88 percent of all U.S. stocks and bonds" (8). "If these super-rich donated only 1 percent of their wealth, we could provide free primary education to every child in the world" (8). "Though it still produces far more wealth than any other country, the U.S. has fallen out of the top twenty on the UN's Quality of Life Index, which includes such things as literacy, life expectancy, infant mortality, social services, and average income. A recent World Health Organization study (June 2000) that graded countries on how well they met the health needs of their populations places the United States 37th" (8).

16. Martinson, "The Critics of C. Wright Mills," *Anvil and Student Partisan* 11 (Winter 1960): 13–16, see 16. Mills admired Riesman's meditation on planning, programs, and utopian thinking cited above, "Some Observations on Community Plans and Utopia" (1947). Riesman's article is an extended review essay on Percival Goodman and Paul Goodman's *Communitas: Means of Livelihood and Ways of Life* (1947) (see Mills to Hans Gerth, Sept. 26, 1948, in *C. Wright Mills,* ed. K. Mills with P. Mills, 122). For critical views of Mills, see Paul M. Sweezy, "Power Elite or Ruling Class?," *Monthly Review* 8 (September 1956): 138–50; Philip Rieff, "Socialism and Sociology," *Partisan Review* 23 (Summer 1956): 365–69; George Rawick, "The Powerful," *Anvil and Student Partisan* 7 (Winter 1957): 7–8; Tom Bottomore, "Charles Wright Mills (1916–62)," in *Encyclopedia of the American Left,* ed. Mari Jo Buhle, Paul Buhle, and Dan Georgakas (Urbana: University of Illinois Press, 1992), 470–71; Herbert Aptheker, *The World of C. Wright Mills* (New York: Marzani and Munsell, 1960).

17. Mills, "Culture and Politics," 236–46, see 245; "The Complacent Young Men," 387–94, see 393 in Mills, *Power, Politics and People: The Collected Essays of C. Wright Mills,* ed. Irving Louis Horowitz (New York: Oxford University Press, 1963). Mills to Bette and Harvey Swados, Oct. 10, 1956, 215 and Mills to William Miller, c. 1949, 136 in *C. Wright Mills,* ed. K. Mills with P. Mills. One of the finest volumes on the subject of America's failure to live up to its official image of itself as a bastion of freedom is Frances Fox Piven and Richard Cloward's collection of essays, *The Breaking of the American Social Compact* (New York: New Press, 1997). Also see the informative textbook by Elliott Currie and Jerome H. Skolnick, *America's Problems: Social Issues and Public Policy* (New York: Longman, 1997). Margaret Atwood's moving antiwar "Letter to America" updated Mills's critical project in its plea that Americans reconsider not just "what you're doing to other people but ... what you're doing to yourselves" (*The Nation* [April 14, 2003]: 22–23, see 23). Mills declared war on the Cold War partly because he saw it as "a showdown on what kinds of human beings and what kinds of culture are going to become the models of the immediate future, the commanding models of human aspiration" ("Complacent," in Mills, *Power, Politics and People,* ed. Horowitz, 393).

18. Mills, "Decline of the Left," 235 in Mills, *Power, Politics, and People,* ed. Horowitz. Mills to Harvey and Bette Swados, June 13, 1961, 332 and Mills to his imaginary Russian friend, Tovarich, Fall 1959, 280 in *C. Wright Mills,* ed. K. Mills with P. Mills.

19. Mills to Dwight Macdonald, March 10, 1950, DM.

20. Dan Wakefield, "Introduction," in *C. Wright Mills*, ed. K. Mills with P. Mills, 1–18, see 6, 10. Mills, "The Social Role of the Intellectual," 292–304, see 302, in Mills, *Power, Politics and People*, ed. Horowitz.

21. See editors' notes in *C. Wright Mills*, ed. K. Mills with P. Mills, 320.

22. There is much to be said about Matthiessen's interest in writing about women authors decades before much critical attention was focused on them (his first American literature book is on Sarah Orne Jewett, and his last published review is of a bibliography of her writings). Matthiessen, besides studying Jewett, also wrote on Margaret Fuller, Emily Dickinson, and Katherine Anne Porter. His socialist lens is evident in much of this criticism (which, it must be acknowledged, was sometimes sexist; for instance see Matthiessen's *The American Renaissance: Art and Expression in the Age of Emerson and Whitman* [New York: Oxford University Press, 1941], x–xi). Thus Matthiessen singled out Fuller's admission, inscribed in a letter not long before she drowned, that her revolutionary activities in Italy had made her "'an enthusiastic Socialist; elsewhere is no comfort, no solution for the problems of the times'" ("Margaret Fuller as Critic," in F. O. Matthiessen, *The Responsibilities of the Critic: Essays* by F. O. Matthiessen, elected by John Rackliffe [New York: Oxford University Press, 1952], 145–47, see 146). "Whitman," Matthiessen attests movingly, "was my first big experience, particularly *The Children of Adam* and *Calamus* poems, which helped me to begin to trust the body" (*From the Heart of Europe* [New York: Oxford University Press, 1948], 23). Henry Abelove has explored the influence that Matthiessen's positioning as a gay scholar had on his literary and political commitments ("American Studies, Queer Studies" in his *Deep Gossip* [Minneapolis: University of Minnesota Press, 2003], 56–69). Also see Leo Marx's "'Double Consciousness' and the Cultural Politics of F. O. Matthiessen," in his *The Pilot and the Passenger: Essays on Literature, Technology, and Culture in the United States* (New York: Oxford University Press, 1988), 239–60. Marx's chapter was originally written for the Monthly Review Foundation. Speculating on what it may have meant "to be a Harvard professor and a homosexual" in the 1930s and 1940s, Marx suggests that "the double life that [Matthiessen] and [Russell] Cheney felt compelled to live, and the many humiliating concealments and dissimulations it entailed" contributed to Matthiessen's incentive to engage in critical analysis (250). For background on Matthiessen, consult Giles B. Gunn, *F. O. Matthiessen: The Critical Achievement* (Seattle: University of Washington Press, 1975), Frederick C. Stern, *F. O Matthiessen: Christian Socialist as Critic* (Chapel Hill: University of North Carolina Press, 1981), William E. Cain, *F. O. Matthiessen and the Politics of Criticism* (Madison: University of Wisconsin Press, 1988).

23. See Matthiessen, review of Granville Hicks's *The Great Tradition* in *Atlantic Monthly* 152 (December 1933): 16, 18 and his review of V. F. Calverton's *The Liberation of American Literature* in *New England Quarterly* 6 (March 1933): 190–95. Also see Matthiessen, "'The Great Tradition': A Counter-statement," *New England Quarterly* 7 (June 1934): 223–34.

24. Matthiessen, *From the Heart of Europe*, 23, 45. Leo Marx notes that many English departments in Matthiessen's era derogated American literature "as a minor off-shoot of British high culture": "It is hard to remember how provincial, belletristic, and unremittingly genteel the reigning conception of our literature was before the publication of *American Renaissance*" (*Pilot and the Passenger*, 244). Paul Lauter reminisces: "American literature was regarded with some scorn even when I was in [Yale] graduate school in the 1950s" (*From Walden Pond to Jurassic Park: Activism, Culture, and American Studies* [Durham, NC: Duke University Press, 2001], 23). Lawrence Levine, speaking on the president's panel at the 1999 American Studies Association conference,

described the position of American literature in the early twentieth century as "colonial." He sees postwar American studies—which provided a refuge for the study of American literature and culture—as partly made possible by the decline of European cultural hegemony after World War II and the onset of the Cold War. Matthiessen's critical project was never strictly literary: it brought into its orbit the history of American painting, Federal Writers' Project road books, popular culture, labor struggles, and electoral activism (see Henry Nash Smith, "American Renaissance," in *F. O. Matthiessen [1902–1950]: A Collective Portrait*, ed. Paul Sweezy and Leo Huberman [New York: Henry Schuman, 1950], 55–60 as well as Sweezy and Huberman's bibliography of Matthiessen's writings, 148–54).

25. See L. Marx, *Pilot and the Passenger*, 248.

26. See L. Marx, *Pilot and the Passenger*, 253–56 (especially 254), 258–59.

27. Matthiessen was in no way mired sentimentally in one period. "The first awareness for the critic," he urged, "should be of the works of art of our own time. This applies even if he is not primarily a critic of modern literature." Paraphrasing T. S. Eliot, he stressed "the inescapable interplay between past and present: that the past is not what is dead, but what is already living; and that the present is continually modifying the past, as the past conditions the present." Challenging literary critics to know much more than their "own field," he emphasized not only the importance of history but of cultural anthropology, economics, and, of course, politics. And he had his eye on British Marxism. Matthiessen praised Christopher Caudwell's Whitmanesque conviction that one realizes oneself not in "opposition to society" but "through society." While acknowledging the "sweeping immaturity of many of [Caudwell's] judgments," he appreciated Caudwell's Marxist criticism for "asking the big questions about man in society that the school of close textual analysis has tended to ignore." Matthiessen was partly Eurocentric in intellectually productive ways. Thus he enjoyed reading French critics on Faulkner who, unlike so many Americans, saw beyond his sensationalism and valued his historical attention to "injustice to the Negro." He profited from "look[ing] back at America through French eyes" ("The Responsibilities of the Critic," in Matthiessen, *Responsibilities of the Critic*, 3–18, see 6, 7, 10, 8, 11, 10, 11, 12, 13).

28. Matthiessen, "The New Mexican Workers Case," *New Republic* 82 (May 8, 1935): 361–63, see 362. On McWilliams, consult Michael Denning's magnificent *The Cultural Front: The Laboring of American Culture* (New York: Verso, 1996), 449–54. Matthiessen and McWilliams were friends. McWilliams looked forward to throwing a party for Matthiessen when he was scheduled to visit his family (letter, McWilliams to Matthiessen, March 19, 1949, FOM).

29. Matthiessen, *From the Heart of Europe*, 192.

30. On Matthiessen's tendency to focus on "contradictions"—literary, cultural, political—see L. Marx, *Pilot and the Passenger*, 245. Marx regards this emphasis as a significant critical "turning point in American studies. It signaled the virtual disappearance of the older, complacent idea of our national culture as an essentially homogeneous, unified whole" (245).

31. See Matthiessen's copy of a letter he wrote to the editor of *Sewanee Review* pertaining to a symposium the journal published on the theme "What the Negro Wants" (FOM).

32. Saldívar, *Border Matters: Remapping American Cultural Studies* (Berkeley: University of California Press, 1997).

33. Howe, "The Sentimental Fellow-Traveling of F. O. Matthiessen," *Partisan Review* 15 (Oct. 1948): 1125–29, see 1125.

34. See Sweezy, "Labor and Political Activities," in *F. O. Matthiessen*, ed. Sweezy and Huberman, 61–75.

35. Matthiessen, "Needed: Organic Connection of Theory and Practice," *Monthly Review* 2 (May 1950): 11.

36. Why derogate Matthiessen as "defeatist" because he supported Henry Wallace and the Progressive Party in 1948 and took his life two years later? David W. Noble tends to dismiss Matthiessen's socialism in *Death of a Nation: American Culture and the End of Exceptionalism* (Minneapolis: University of Minnesota Press, 2003), 94–97.

37. Matthiessen's review of Brooks, *The Flowering of New England: 1815–1865* in *New England Quarterly* 9 (December 1936): 701–709, see 709.

38. Matthiessen, "Needed," 11. Matthiessen makes a similar point about the necessity of "international cooperation" among democratic socialists, communists, and progressives in *From the Heart of Europe*, 193–94.

39. L. Marx, *Pilot and the Passenger*, 241.

40. On Wallace, see Matthiessen's typescript of his "Seconding Speech," and on not conceptualizing American culture in narrowly national terms, see Matthiessen's typescript of an undated letter without an addressee (FOM).

41. L. Marx, "The Teacher," in *F. O Matthiessen*, ed. Sweezy and Huberman, 37–43, see 42.

42. For some recent discussions and debates about American studies, British cultural studies, and cultural theory by scholars within American studies, see the special issue of the journal *American Studies* 38 (Summer 1997) titled, *American Studies: From Culture Concept to Cultural Studies?* In particular, Barry Shank's "The Continuing Embarrassment of Culture: From the Culture Concept to Cultural Studies" (95–116) offers useful historical comparisons of approaches and trends within British cultural studies and American studies (especially its social science manifestations).

43. McDowell, *American Studies* (Minneapolis: University of Minnesota Press, 1948), 68, 91, 94, 92, 62, 43. Surprisingly, some critics of prewar and postwar American studies, who champion moving beyond the borders of the canon, tend to have taken a restrictive Great Books-Great Authors approach to historicizing American studies. While it is still possible, it would be enlightening to compile oral histories of American studies dating from the early postwar period. A valuable resource is the profiles of several major American Studies programs (including Amherst, University of Pennsylvania, Yale, University of Minnesota, George Washington University) in "Programs in American Studies" (ed. Robert E. Lucid), *American Quarterly* 22 (Summer 1970): 430–598. (In that same issue also see "Writings on the Theory and Teaching of American Studies," 412–17.) On the University of Minnesota American Studies Program see Noble, *Death of a Nation*. On the development of the American Studies Program at the University of California, Davis, see Jay Mechling, Robert Meredith, David Wilson, "American Culture Studies: The Discipline and the Curriculum," *American Quarterly* 25 (October 1973): 363–89 and Jay Mechling, "Some [New] Elementary Axioms for an American Cultur[al] Studies," *American Studies* 38 (Summer 1997): 9–30. My research raised questions in my mind about the range of interests students developed and acted on in American Studies programs. For instance, when Robert Bone, who became an illustrious contributor to the field of African American literary studies, was doing his doctorate in American studies at Yale in the 1950s (after he completed his B.A. in American studies there) he was also an editor of and frequent contributor to the impressive radical journal based in New York, *Anvil and Student Partisan*. His articles include a bold critique of the politics of the Yale English department: "God and the New Criticism at Yale: The New Conservatism and Cleanth Brooks," *Anvil and Student Partisan* 7 (Spring–Summer 1956): 23–24. He wrote this piece when he served as an instructor at Yale. My discussions with Alan Trachtenberg,

who was a graduate student in American studies at the University of Minnesota in the 1950s, suggest that there is indeed a history of American studies activism that has yet to be brought to light. Considering the paradoxes of "classic" American studies, Lauter concludes: "For some, American studies offered an academic framework to carry out the kind of left-liberal program associated with the wartime Office of Strategic Services and significant tendencies in this early CIA—anticommunist to be sure, but also antifascist and promotional of democratic liberal values associated with the kind of coalition FDR had assembled" (*From Walden,* 23). For some scholars, American studies was exclusively a pluralistic and open-ended way of studying history, literature, art, or sociology. While for other scholars, American studies may have permitted them to come as close as possible to engaging in a revisionary socialist historicizing studies adapted to the American scene. Despite evidence of its critical and political limitations and complicities, the history of nation-based American studies cannot be reduced to and then dismissed as what sometimes informed it: American exceptionalism. For two provocative analyses of American studies complicity with the U.S. Cold War government, see Sigmund Diamond, "Surveillance in the Academy: Harry B. Fisher and Yale University, 1927–1952," *American Quarterly* (Spring 1984): 7–43 and Michael Bérubé, "American Studies without Exceptions," *Proceedings of the Modern Language Association* 118 (January 2003): 103–13. Indeed, while I think he somewhat underplays the intellectual and cultural impact of socialism in America, I appreciate Leo Marx's critical view of American exceptionalism: "Among the advanced capitalist countries of the world the United States is 'exceptional' in the failure of its intelligentsia to take Marxism seriously, in the failure of socialism to gain a mass following, and in the absence of a working-class social- ist party" (*Pilot and the Passenger,* 256). Thinking strategically about the political efficacy of historical novels and their potential to rewrite dominant national myths, scholar and novelist Richard Slotkin—founder of the American Studies Program at Wesleyan University—writes: "American myths and the master narratives of American historians have tended to reify and reinforce the primacy of nationality as a way of organizing human society. Consequently, such narratives also privilege the ideologies and programmes of those classes whose interests are most fully realized in the politics of the nation-state" ("Fiction for the Purposes of History," *Rethinking History* 9 [June/Sept. 2005]: 221–36, see 228).

44. See Will Brooker, *Cultural Studies* (Chicago: Teach Yourself Books [NTC/Contemporary Publishing], 1998); the author's name appears neither on the cover nor on the spine of the book, only on the back cover. On the front cover the book appears to be titled: *Teach Yourself Cultural Studies.* Some recent cultural studies volumes include: *Cultural Politics in Contemporary America,* ed. Ian Angus and Sut Jally (New York: Routledge, 1989); *Rethinking Popular Culture: Contemporary Perspectives in Cultural Studies,* ed. Chandra Mukerji and Michael Schudson (Berkeley: University of California Press, 1991); Antony Easthope, *Literary into Cultural Studies* (London: Routledge, 1991); *Cultural Studies,* ed. Lawrence Grossberg, Cary Nelson, and Paula A. Treichler (New York: Routledge, 1992); Jim McGuigan, *Cultural Populism* (London: Routledge, 1992); *A Critical and Cultural Theory Reader,* ed. Antony Easthope and Kate McGowan (Toronto: University of Toronto Press, 1992); *The Cultural Studies Reader,* ed. Simon During (New York: Routledge, 1993); *Study- ing Culture: An Introductory Reader,* ed. Ann Gray and Jim McGuigan (London: Arnold, 1993); John Storey, *An Introductory Guide to Cultural Theory and Popular Culture* (Athens: University of Georgia Press, 1993); Fred Inglis, *Cultural Studies* (Oxford: Blackwell, 1993); *A Cultural Stud- ies Reader: History, Theory, Practice,* ed. Jessica Munns and Gita Rajan (London: Longman, 1995); *Cultural Politics: Class, Gender, Race and the Postmodern World,* ed. Glenn Jordan and Chris Weedon (Oxford: Blackwell, 1995); *What Is Cultural Studies: A Reader,* ed. John Storey

(London: Arnold, 1996); *Black British Cultural Studies: A Reader*, ed. Houston A. Baker, Jr., Manthia Diawara, and Ruth H. Lindeborg (Chicago: University of Chicago Press, 1996); *British Cultural Studies: Geography, Nationality, and Identity*, ed. David Morely and Kevin Robins (Oxford: Oxford University Press, 2001); *Media and Cultural Studies: Key Works*, ed. Meenakshi Gigi Durham and Douglas M. Kellner (Malden, MA: Blackwell, 2001); *Without Guarantees: In Honour of Stuart Hall*, ed. Paul Gilroy, Lawrence Grossberg, and Angela McRobbie (New York: Verso, 2000); *American Cultural Studies*, ed. Catherine A. Warren and Mary Douglas Vavrus (Urbana: University of Illinois Press, 2002); *Cultural Studies: From Theory to Action*, ed. Pepi Leistyna (Malden, MA: Blackwell, 2004). I cite other studies that belong in this category elsewhere. Books on the cultural turn include: Fredric Jameson, *The Cultural Turn: Selected Writings on the Postmodern, 1983–1998* (New York: Verso, 1998) and *Beyond the Cultural Turn: New Directions in the Study of Society and Culture*, ed. Victoria E. Bonnell and Lynn Hunt (Berkeley: University of California Press, 1999).

45. Jameson, "On 'Cultural Studies,'" *Social Text* 11 (Winter 1993): 17–52, 18 (indeed, this quotation is a section title in his essay). There are, it should be said, many Marxist practitioners of cultural studies. For an excellent, well-informed articulation and defense of cultural studies contributions, see Rita Felski, "Those Who Disdain Cultural Studies Don't Know What They're Talking About," *Chronicle of Higher Education* 45 (July 23, 1999): B6–B7. Felski's critique is focused on English departments—caught up in the culture wars—that misconstrue in various ways what cultural studies is and does.

46. In addition to works by Guenter Lenz, Paul Lauter, David Noble, John Carlos Rowe, and Donald Pease and Robin Wiegman that I cite elsewhere, recent volumes and articles on American studies include: *The New American Studies: Essays from Representations*, ed. Philip Fisher (Berkeley: University of California Press, 1991); *American Studies in Germany: European Contexts and Intercultural Relations*, Günter Lenz and Klaus J. Milich (New York: St. Martin's Press, 1995); Richard Pells, *Not Like Us: How Europeans Have Loved, Hated, and Transformed American Culture Since World War II* (New York: Basic, 1997). George Lipsitz, *American Studies in a Moment of Danger* (Minneapolis: University of Minnesota Press, 2001). Older volumes on American studies include: Robert H. Walker's *American Studies in the United States: A Survey of College Programs* (Baton Rouge: Louisiana State University Press, 1958) and *American Studies: Topics and Sources* (Westport, CT: Greenwood, 1976); Sigmund Skard, *American Studies in Europe: Their History and Organization*, vols. 1 and 2 (Philadelphia: University of Pennsylvania Press, 1958); *Studies in American Culture: Dominant Ideas and Images*, ed. Joseph Kwiat and Mary Turpie (Minneapolis: University of Minnesota Press, 1960); *American Studies in Transition*, ed. Marshall Fishwick (Philadelphia: University of Pennsylvania Press, 1964); Cecil F. Tate, *The Search for a Method in American Studies* (Minneapolis: University of Minnesota Press, 1973); *The Study of American Culture: Contemporary Conflicts*, ed. Luther Luedtke (DeLand, FL: Everett Edwards, 1977); Guenter H. Lenz, "American Studies—Beyond the Crisis?: Recent Redefinitions and the Meaning of Theory, History, and Practical Criticism," *Prospects* 7 (1982): 53–113; Gene Wise, "'Paradigm Dramas' in American Studies: A Cultural and Institutional History of the Movement," *American Quarterly* 31 (Bibliography 1979): 293–337.

47. For example, see Graeme Turner, "'It Works for Me': British Cultural Studies, Australian Cultural Studies, Australian Film," and the discussion that follows (650–53), in *Cultural Studies*, ed. Grossberg, Nelson and Treichler, 640–50. Also consult *Relocating Cultural Studies: Developments in Theory and Research*, ed. Valda Blundell, John Shepherd, and Ian Taylor (London: Routledge, 1993).

48. London, "How I Became a Socialist," reprinted in *Literature, Class, and Culture,* ed. Paul Lauter and Ann Fitzgerald (New York: Longman, 2001), 501–03, see 503. Gilroy, *The Black Atlantic: Modernity and Double Consciousness* (Cambridge, MA: Harvard University Press, 1993). As an undergraduate at the University of Sussex, Gilroy's subject was American studies. He then studied with Stuart Hall at the University of Birmingham's Centre for Contemporary Cultural Studies. Another key text that helped shape the transnational trend is Benedict Anderson, *Imagined Communities: Reflections on the Origin and Spread of Nationalism* (New York: Verso, 1983). "Rather than thinking about the proper places of ideas, and the proper ideas for places," cultural studies theorist Lawrence Grossberg recommends, "we need to begin to think about the ways in which ideas are articulated spatially, and spaces articulated theoretically" (*Bringing It All Back Home: Essays on Cultural Studies* [Durham, NC: Duke University Press, 1997], 301).

49. The transnationalizing of American studies is part of a collegiate as well as corporate transnationalizing trend. Some of America's elite universities are issuing declarations of independence from obsolete territorial concepts of "America." The elite transnational university cites proudly not only its international faculty, students, and alums, and its use of the Internet (marketing courses worldwide), its exchange programs (globalizing class identity formation), and its area studies as valuable investments in its transnational portfolio, it rewards transnational critics who bolster its intellectual status and sophistication. Corporate transnationalism, of course, needs universities to serve as well meaning "humanities" curators of cultural difference partly because a reassuring preoccupation with difference helps cover—and compensate for—capitalism's global standardizations. For intriguing comments on this multifaceted trend, see George Rupp, "A Global Perspective, Columbia University, The President's Report 1998–1999." At Wesleyan University more than half of the students now spend at least one semester abroad. If this internationalization of perspective and contacts can be read as a beyond-borders preparation for America's future corporate class, it can also lead to radical perspectives. For one example of this, see Dani McClain's (Columbia '00) class, gender, and economic analysis of her semester in Ghana (an analysis that encompasses not only Ghana but the United States and its foreign relations), "Broadened Horizons," *Columbia College Today* 26 (February 2000): 10–15. For a smart analysis of the linkage between the corporatizing and transnationalizing of state universities and the American studies preoccupation with "international nationalism" (105) see Bérubé, "American Studies without Exceptions," 103–13, especially 103–05. Some "new" transnational perspectives might not be altogether novel to members of the U.S. State Department, corporate expansionists, scholars of U.S. foreign relations, economic historians, socialist-internationalists (such as John Dewey, who long ago urged schools to teach migration studies), or readers of American journals such as *Monthly Review* (on Dewey, see Joel Pfister, *Individuality Incorporated: Indians and the Multicultural Modern* [Durham, NC: Duke University Press, 2004], 238). "National one-sidedness and narrow-mindedness [have] become more and more impossible," Karl Marx and Frederick Engels noticed in *The Communist Manifesto* (New York: International, 1948 [1848]), 12–13. Terry Eagleton also notes this perspective in *The Communist Manifesto,* but adds, usefully: "The nation was a way of rallying different social classes—peasants, workers, students, intellectuals—against the colonial powers which stood in the way of their independence. And it had a powerful argument in its favour: success, at least to begin with" (*After Theory* [New York: Basic, 2003], 11). Thinking about the progressive possibilities of this development in the early 1960s, Riesman hoped that a time would come when "every man's patriotism will be planetary" (*Abundance for What?,* 105). In 1979 Gene Wise observed that the "classic" American studies Old World-to-New World cross-culturalism was

beginning to move beyond efforts to examine how Americans adapted European ideologies and practices to encompass U.S. relations with "the new, post–World War II nations of Africa, the Middle East, Southeast Asia, and Latin America" ("Paradigm 'Dramas' in American Studies," 334). Many postwar American Studies Programs endeavored to address international concerns. For example, see Sydney E. Ahltstrom's profile, "Studying America and American Studies at Yale," *American Quarterly* 22 (Summer 1970): 501–17: "Most persistently discussed are the questions pertaining to the avoidance of a parochially United States–centered course of study" (517). On balance the postmodern American studies push to transnationalize its scope and projects—gaining momentum since the early 1990s—has opened some fresh historical fields, theoretical concerns, and political questions. Four particularly illuminating critical perspectives on the transnational turn are by a Marxist anthropologist, a Marxist literary theorist, an American studies historian, and an American studies literary historian: Roger Rouse, "Thinking Through Transnationalism: Notes on the Cultural Politics of Class Relations in the Contemporary United States," *Public Culture* 7 (Winter 1995): 353–402; Bruce Robbins, "Some Versions of U.S. Internationalism," *Social Text* 14 (Winter 1995): 97–123; Robert A. Gross, "The Transnational Turn: Rediscovering American Studies in a Wider World," *Journal of American Studies* 34 (Oct. 2000): 1–21; Shelley Fisher Fishkin, "Crossroads of Cultures: The Transnational Turn in American Studies—Presidential Address to the American Studies Association, November 12, 2004," *American Quarterly* 57 (March 2005): 17–56 (also see the two responses to her analytical overview). For an exemplary synthesis of Marxist, cultural studies, historical, and American studies transnational analysis, see Michael Denning, *Culture in the Age of Three Worlds* (New York: Verso, 2004), especially 1–72. Some practitioners, eager to rechart and retheorize the field in these ways, also appear to have felt obliged to be extremely critical of older American studies contributions bordered within the nation and its "myths." See Alan Wolfe, "Anti–American Studies," *New Republic* (Feb. 10, 2003): 25–32. Wolfe reviews three books that champion transnational American studies: *The Futures of American Studies,* ed. Donald E. Pease and Robyn Wiegman (Durham, NC: Duke University Press, 2002); John Carlos Rowe, *The New American Studies* (Minneapolis: University of Minnesota Press, 2002); Noble, *Death of a Nation.*

50. Wise, "Paradigm 'Dramas' in American Studies," 316–17.

51. Fredric Jameson, *The Political Unconscious: Narrative as a Socially Symbolic Act* (Ithaca, NY: Cornell University Press, 1980).

52. Kasson, *Amusing the Million: Coney Island at the Turn of the Century* (New York: Hill and Wang, 1978), 108, 109. A key theoretical text that examines mass-cultural subjection—a critical approach focusing on the top-down flow of power that theorists who stress agency within culture, including Tony Bennett, have sought to complicate—is Max Horkheimer and Theodor W. Adorno's classic, "The Culture Industry: Enlightenment as Mass Deception," in their *Dialectic of Enlightenment,* trans. John Cumming (New York: Seabury, 1972 [1944]), 120–67.

53. Bennett, "A Thousand and One Troubles: Blackpool Pleasure Beach," in Fredric Jameson et al., *Formations of Pleasure* (London: Routledge and Kegan Paul, 1983), 138–55, see 148, 144, 148, 154.

54. Alan Trachtenberg's insightful 1976 sketch of the significance of the writings of Randolph Bourne, Lewis Mumford, Waldo Frank, and Van Wyck Brooks highlights the complexity of this concern. Their work helped inspire the interdisciplinary formation of postwar American studies. Trachtenberg is quick to acknowledge that these critics "accepted, indeed carried further, the popular notion of America as an exceptional society in human history, with a destiny

peculiar to it." However, these proto–American studies intellectuals "address[ed] not only the nation but also the nation in its potential." And so "their 'nationalism' ... has to be taken in a special light—as a feature of their strategy for establishing themselves as mediators between a neglected tradition ('usable past') and a misdirected present." Trachtenberg also deems it important to point out that these early critics—like many postwar American studies scholars and many postnational critics of these postwar scholars—"did no more than adumbrate in vague outlines a social and political program commensurate with their program for cultural change." They turned their gaze toward culture—what Trachtenberg terms "cultural stud-ies"—while the socialism that roused their sympathies "remained for most of them a rather abstract possibility." In fact, they steered clear of any "political movement" and invested their hopes in critique and the arts. "Most of the writers here believed that socialism was the proper solution to certain problems, to inequality of wealth and social injustice. The change they hoped for ... was intellectual and moral, a change in consciousness, in culture. Unlike John Reed, who cast his lot with revolution and devoted the last years of his brief life organizing for the newly founded Communist Party, the critics of culture did not look to the working class as a source of change" (Introduction, in *Critics of Culture,* ed. Trachtenberg, 10, 9, 10, 11, 12, 11, 12). For me this critical tendency—at least as much as scholars' concentration on the nation—merits extended scrutiny. On this group also see Casey Blake, *Beloved Community: The Cultural Criti-cism of Randolph Bourne, Van Wyck Brooks, Waldo Frank, and Lewis Mumford* (Chapel Hill: University of North Carolina Press, 1990), including Alan Trachtenberg's "Foreword," xi–xiii, and Paul Buhle, "Lewis Mumford," in *The American Radical,* ed. Mari Jo Buhle, Paul Buhle, and Harvey J. Kaye (New York: Routledge, 1994), 221–28. Mumford was a leading organizer of an anti–atom bomb movement in 1946. As did E. P. Thompson from the 1950s through 1980s, Mumford wanted those involved to see that a larger critique of American power was at stake (see Mumford to Max Lerner, March 23, 1946, ML). Recent writings by Paul Lauter (*From Walden*) and George Lipsitz attempt to orient American studies in this direction. Lipsitz endeavors to explore key "links between American studies and social movements" (*American Studies in a Moment of Danger,* xvi). Also consult two recent collections of essays that have sought to high-light cultural studies as social transformation studies: *American Cultural Studies,* ed. Warren and Vavrus, especially see Catherine A. Warren and Mary Douglas Vavrus, "Introduction," 1–11 and Robert W. McChesney, "Whatever Happened to Cultural Studies?," 76–93; *Cultural Studies: From Theory to Action,* ed. Leistyna.

55. On the historical and political specificity of a British cultural studies that took shape within the British New Left, see Dennis Dworkin, *Cultural Marxism in Postwar Britain: History, the New Left, and the Origins of Cultural Studies* (Durham, NC: Duke University Press, 1997) and Davies, *Cultural Studies and Beyond,* 8, 122, 158, 161 (cites Alan O'Connor: 407).

56. Here I will mention just one book in each of these important fields that has influenced my thinking. On ethnoracial matters and cultural studies, see especially E. San Juan, Jr., *Racism and Cultural Studies: Critiques of Multiculturalist Ideology and the Politics of Difference* (Durham, NC: Duke University Press, 2002). On feminist studies, see *Teaching Feminist Activism: Strate-gies from the Field,* ed. Nancy A. Naples and Karen Bojar (New York: Routledge, 2002). And on queer studies, see *The Lesbian and Gay Studies Reader,* ed. Henry Abelove, Michèle Aina Barale, and David M. Halperin (New York: Routledge, 1993) and its superb bibliography.

57. Also see Davies, *Cultural Studies and Beyond,* 5.

58. This is a complex matter. Many intellectual contributions have had manifold political effects, even if they are not keyed into organized political movements. For instance, Davies

acknowledges that Perry Anderson hoped that the *New Left Review* he took over as editor in 1962–63 would "rewrite the agenda of British intellectual life" and "provide the theoretical foundations for 'a revolutionary practice within which culture is possible'" (*Cultural Studies and Beyond,* 13). To put it mildly, it came much closer to achieving the former than the latter (it did not succeed in either project). Yet the former—though not connected with the development of a political organization—was a major "political" achievement. If Anderson was more concerned with the advancement of Marxist theory in Britain and the world than in sparking social movements, the theoretical contributions he helped make available contributed to much political critique production and Marxist intellectual culture. On the other hand, to what degree can a journal—even Anderson's impressive version of *New Left Review*—build revolutionary culture? He "argued that if intellectuals attempted to build a socialist movement before the proper time—as the [first] New Left had—the results would be 'paralyzing confusions' and an 'unconscious creeping substitutionism'" (Dworkin, who paraphrases and quotes Anderson, *Cultural Marxism in Postwar Britain,* 114).

59. I thank my brother Jordan Pfister for this "Quotable Card," May 4, 2003.

60. See Paul Buhle's sketch on "Humor" in *Encyclopedia of the American Left,* ed. Buhle, Buhle, and Georgakas, 341–45. I am grateful to Richard Lowry for introducing me to the term "intellectual citizenship."

Notes for Chapter 1

1. For details about the manifesto, see Scott Heller, "Protest at Cultural Studies Meeting Sparked by Debate over New Field," *Chronicle of Higher Education* 36 (May 2, 1990): A10–A11. Hall, "Politics and Letters," in *Raymond Williams: Critical Perspectives,* ed. Terry Eagleton (Boston: Northeastern University Press, 1989), 54–66, see 66. Williams, *Politics and Letters: Interviews with New Left Review* (London: Verso, 1979). Hall recounted these political "interventions" in the Birmingham Centre in his conference paper, "Cultural Studies and Its Theoretical Legacies." *Women Take Issue: Aspects of Women's Subordination,* ed. Women's Studies Group (London: Hutchinson, 1978), 11. Centre for Contemporary Cultural Studies, *The Empire Strikes Back: Race and Racism in 70s Britain* (London: Hutchinson, 1982); Gilroy, *"There Ain't No Black in the Union Jack"* (London: Hutchinson, 1987), 12. Fry, "From (Sunlight) to Sin," in Lawrence Grossberg, Tony Fry, Ann Curthoys, and Paul Patton, *It's a Sin: Essays in Postmodernism and Political Culture* (Sydney: Power Publications, 1988). Johnson, "What Is Cultural Studies Anyway?" *Social Text* 16 (Winter 1986/87): 38–80, see 42.

2. O'Connor, "The Problem of American Cultural Studies," *Critical Studies in Mass Communications* 6 (Dec. 1989): 405–13, see 405; also see O'Connor's excellent bibliography. Editor [Stuart Hall], "Editorial," *New Left Review* 1 (Jan.–Feb. 1960): 1–4, see 1. *New Times: The Changing Face of Politics in the 1990s,* ed. Stuart Hall and Martin Jacques (London: Lawrence and Wishart, 1989). *Resistance through Rituals: Youth Subcultures in Post-War Britain,* ed. Stuart Hall and Tony Jefferson (London: Hutchinson, 1976); Stuart Hall, Tony Jefferson, John Clarke, and Brian Roberts, *Policing the Crisis: Mugging, the State and Law and Order* (London: Macmillan, 1978). Paul Willis, *Learning to Labour: How Working-Class Kids Get Working-Class Jobs* (London: Saxon House, 1977); Dick Hebdige, *Subculture: The Meaning of Style* (London: Methuen, 1979). Editor [Stuart Hall], "Editorial," 2–3.

3. Hall and Jacques, "Introduction," 11–20, see 13, and Hall, "The Meaning of New Times," 116–34, see 128, 128–29, in *New Times*, ed. Hall and Jacques.

4. Hall, "The 'Political' and the 'Economic' in Marx's Theory of the Classes," *Class and Class Structure*, ed. Alan Hunt (London: Lawrence and Wishart, 1977), 15–60, see 23. Hall, "Cultural Studies and the Centre: Some Problematics and Problems," in Centre for Contemporary Cultural Studies, *Culture, Media, Language: Working Papers in Cultural Studies, 1972–79* (London: Hutchinson and Centre for Contemporary Cultural Studies, 1980), 15–47, see 31. Johnson, "The Story So Far: And Further Transformations?" in *Introduction to Contemporary Cultural Studies*, ed. David Putner (New York: Longman, 1986), 277–313. Also see Hall, "Rethinking the Base/Superstructure Metaphor," in *Class, Hegemony, and Party*, ed. John Bloomfield (London: Lawrence and Wishart, 1976). Hall commented on Marxism as a problem in his conference paper, "Cultural Studies and Its Theoretical Legacies."

5. Johnson, "Culture and the Historians," in *Working-Class Culture: Studies in History and Theory*, ed. John Clarke, Chas Critcher, and Richard Johnson (London: Hutchinson and Centre for Contemporary Cultural Studies, 1979), 41–71, see 63.

6. Phases in the rethinking of "lived experience" can be seen in Centre for Contemporary Cultural Studies, *On Ideology* (London: Hutchinson, 1978); Centre for Contemporary Cultural Studies, *Working-Class Culture*; and *Making Histories: Studies in History Writing and Politics*, ed. Richard Johnson, Gregor McLennan, Bill Schwarz, and David Sutton (London: Hutchinson and Centre for Contemporary Cultural Studies, 1982); E. P. Thompson, *The Poverty of Theory* (New York: Monthly Review Press, 1978); Hall, "In Defence of Theory," in *People's History and Socialist Theory*, ed. Raphael Samuel (London: Routledge and Kegan Paul, 1981), 378–85; Johnson, "Histories of Culture/Theories of Ideology: Notes on an Impasse," in *Ideology and Cultural Production*, ed. Philip Corrigan, Annette Kuhn, and Janet Wolff (New York: St. Martin's Press, 1979), 49–77, see 75; Gilroy, *"There Ain't No Black in the Union Jack,"* 12; Hall, "Cultural Studies and the Centre." Also see Perry Anderson's critique of Thompson's concept of experience in his *Arguments within English Marxism*, 25–29, 57–58.

7. As Alan O'Connor has pointed out, many cultural studies texts are difficult to procure in the United States (published by Hutchinson). Anthologies not listed in *Books in Print 1990–91* are: *The Empire Strikes Back; Culture, Media, Language; Women Take Issue; On Ideology;* Gilroy's *"There Ain't No Black in the Union Jack"* is not listed either. Republished anthologies are: *Making Histories* (University of Minnesota); *Resistance through Rituals* (Unwin Hyman); *Working-Class Culture* (St. Martin's); *Policing the Crisis* (Holmes and Meier). (Since writing this chapter in 1990 and publishing a version of it in 1991, I was happy to learn of: *The Screen Education Reader*, ed. M. Alvarado et al. [London: Macmillan, 1989]. Moreover the University of Chicago Press republished Gilroy's important book in 1991 with a foreword by Houston Baker, 3–6.) O'Connor, "Problem of American Cultural Studies," 407. Cornel West's conference paper, "The Postmodern Crisis of Black Intellectuals."

8. Cary Nelson and Lawrence Grossberg also organized a Marxist theory conference in 1983, part of the proceedings of which were published in a book they edited, *Marxism and the Interpretation of Culture* (Urbana: University of Illinois Press, 1988). For a good example of Marxist cultural studies American literary history, see Cary Nelson's *Repression and Recovery: Modern American Poetry and the Politics of Popular Memory 1910–1945* (Madison: University of Wisconsin Press, 1989). Hall, "Cultural Studies and Its Theoretical Legacies."

9. Grossberg, *It's a Sin*, 8. An issue of *Journal of Communication Inquiry* 10 (1986) was devoted to the work of Stuart Hall, who was interviewed: "On Postmodernism and Articulation: An

Interview." See Grossberg, "Strategies of Marxist Cultural Interpretation," *Critical Studies in Mass Communications* 1 (Dec. 1984): 392–421. O'Connor, *Raymond Williams: Writing, Culture, Politics* (London: Blackwell, 1989) and Williams, *Raymond Williams on Television: Selected Writings,* ed. Alan O'Connor (London: Routledge, 1989). O'Connor, "Problem of American Cultural Studies," 407, 408, 407.

10. Bennett, "Putting Policy into Cultural Studies"; Grossberg, *It's a Sin,* 3; Mike Budd, Robert M. Entman, and Clay Steinman, "The Affirmative Character of U.S. Cultural Studies," *Critical Studies in Mass Communications* 7 (June 1990): 169–84, see 177–78; Gitlin, "Who Communicates to Whom, in What Voice and Why, about the Study of Mass Communications," *Critical Studies in Mass Communications* 7 (June 1990): 185–96, see 191–92.

11. Gilroy, "Cultural Studies and Ethnic Absolutism"; Turner, "'It Works for Me': British Cultural Studies, Australian Culture, and Australian Film"; Johnson, "What Is Cultural Studies Anyway?" 63; Robbins, "The Politics of Theory," *Social Text* 18 (Winter 1987/88): 3–18, see 11; Hall, "Cultural Studies and the Centre," 44.

12. Carolyn Steedman, "Culture, Cultural Studies and the Historians."

13. Patrick Brantlinger, *Crusoe's Footprints: Cultural Studies in Britain and America* (New York: Routledge, 1990), 3, 198.

14. Carby, "Schooling in Babylon," in Centre for Contemporary Cultural Studies, *Empire Strikes Back,* 183–211, see 197, 193, 194. Brantlinger, *Crusoe's Footprints,* 163, 11, 73; Hall, "The Emergence of Cultural Studies and the Crisis of the Humanities," *October* 53 (Summer 1990): 11–23, see 11, 12, 22.

15. Brantlinger, *Crusoe's Footprints,* 155.

16. Giroux, Shumway, Smith, and Sosnoski, "The Need for Cultural Studies: Resisting Intellectuals and Oppositional Spheres," *Dalhousie Review* 64 (Summer 1984): 472–86, 476. Brantlinger, *Crusoe's Footprints,* 26.

17. Brantlinger, *Crusoe's Footprints,* 27. Giroux et al., "Need for Cultural Studies," 476. Matthiessen and Ware quoted in Guenter Lenz, "American Studies and the Radical Tradition: From the 1930s to the 1960s," *Prospects* 12 (1987): 21–58, see 35, 33. Also see Philip Gleason, "World War II and the Development of American Studies," *American Quarterly* 36 (Bibliography 1984): 343–58. *Ideology and Classic American Literature,* ed. Sacvan Bercovitch and Myra Jehlen (New York: Cambridge University Press, 1986).

18. Giroux et al., "Need for Cultural Studies," 476. Brantlinger, *Crusoe's Footprints,* 48.

19. See Russell Jacoby's discussion of Marxism in the academy in *The Last Intellectuals: American Culture in the Age of Academe* (New York: Noonday Press, 1987), 124–30. Trachtenberg, "The American View of Life," *The Nation* (July 19, 1965): 42–45, see 44–45, 45.

20. Trachtenberg, *The Incorporation of America: Culture and Society in the Gilded Age* (New York: Hill and Wang, 1982), vii. For a twenty-years-later reassessment of Trachtenberg's classic, see several articles—originating in a Modern Language Association panel—published in *American Literary History,* especially Brook Thomas, "Culture, Society, and *The Incorporation of America,*" *American Literary History* 15 (2003): 732–37, and Alan Trachtenberg, "*The Incorporation of America* Today," *American Literary History* 15 (2003): 759–64. Also see Trachtenberg, "A Note on 'Myth and Symbol' as Cultural Criticism," in *Crisis of Modernity: Recent Critical Theories of Culture and Society in the United States and West Germany,* ed. Guenter H. Lenz and Kurt L. Sheil (Boulder, CO: Westview, 1986), 155, 151, 149, 148, 149, 153. Trachtenberg's vision of the American studies mission is somewhat different from Fred Pfeil's profile of his own Marxist cultural studies project. Like the American studies critic, Pfeil writes "within

the conditions and against the current of my own culture and time." Yet Pfeil takes pains to specify the adversary of his adversarial criticism as late capitalism. Pfeil's inflection is more on strategy than on prophecy, and he is consistently precise about what he would like to accomplish: "democratic socialism" (Pfeil, *Another Tale to Tell: Politics and Narrative in Postmodern Culture* [New York: Verso, 1990], 1, 2).

21. Williams, *Marxism and Literature* (New York: Oxford University Press, 1977), 113.

22. Recently numerous astute commentators on American studies, such as Paul Lauter (*From Walden*, 24) and Michael Bérubé ("American Studies without Exceptions," 107), have quoted Denning's rereading of the ideological Cold War significance of American studies.

23. Denning, "'The Special American Conditions': Marxism and American Studies," *American Quarterly* 38 (Bibliography 1986): 356–80, see 357, 358, 360, 364, 369, 360 (reprinted in Denning, *Culture in the Age of Three Worlds,* 169–91). There was no mention of Denning's article in Linda Kerber's American Studies Association presidential address, "Diversity and Transformation in American Studies," *American Quarterly* (Sept. 1989): 415–31; Robert Berkhofer, Jr., "A New Context for a New American Studies," *American Quarterly* 41 (Dec. 1989): 588–613; and Allen F. Davis, "The Politics of American Studies," *American Quarterly* 42 (Sept. 1990): 353–74. Gene Wise, "Some Elementary Axioms for an American Culture Studies," *Prospects* 4 (1979): 517–48; Jay Mechling, "Mind, Messages, and Madness: Gregory Bateson Makes a Paradigm for American Culture Studies," *Prospects* 8 (1983): 11–30. R. Gordon Kelly, "*The Social Construction of Reality*: Implications for Future Discussions in American Studies," *Prospects* 8 (1983): 49–58. For Denning's more recent reflections on American studies, cultural studies, and intellectual work on culture see his *Cultural Front* and his *Culture in the Age of Three Worlds,* especially 75–166.

24. L. Marx, "The Long Revolution," *Commentary* 32 (Dec. 1961): 517–23, see 517, 518, 520, 518.

25. L. Marx, "Notes on the Culture of the New Capitalism," *Monthly Review* 11 (July–August 1959): 111–16, see 116. L. Marx, "The American Scholar Today," *Commentary* 32 (July 1961): 48–53.

26. C. Wright Mills, "On the New Left," *Studies on the Left* 2 (1961): 63–72. John F. C. Harrison, "The Long Revolution in Britain," *Studies on the Left* 3 (1962): 80–85; Williams, "Ibsen, Miller and the Development of Liberal Tragedy," *Studies on the Left* 4 (Spring 1964): 83–97. Few scholars (for example, Allen Guttman and Warren Susman) published in both *American Quarterly* and *Studies on the Left*. The 1970s Althusserian moment in *American Quarterly* was more like an Althusserian paragraph: David Pace, "Structuralism in History and the Social Sciences," *American Quarterly* 30 (Bibliography 1978): 282–97. Under Janice Radway's tenure as editor, *American Quarterly* opened up by reintroducing book reviews. Thus in 1984 the journal reviewed Terry Eagleton's *Literary Theory: An Introduction* (Minneapolis: University of Minnesota Press, 1983) and Bryan Jay Wolf's synthesis of poststructuralism and American studies insights, *Romantic Re-Vision: Culture and Consciousness in Nineteenth-Century American Painting and Literature* (Chicago: University of Chicago Press, 1982). Elizabeth Long, "Women, Reading, and Cultural Authority: Some Implications of the Audience Perspective in Cultural Studies," *American Quarterly* 38 (Fall 1986): 591–612.

27. How different American studies was, Sklar realized, from *poverty studies*: Can one imagine an Ivy League senior getting elected to Phi Beta Kappa with a major in poverty studies? Robert Sklar, "American Studies and the Realities of America," *American Quarterly* 22 (Summer 1970): 597–605, 600, 599, 600. On the ideological role of American studies in this "international effort," see Gene Wise, "'Paradigm Dramas' in American Studies."

28. Berkhofer, "New Context for a New American Studies," 589, 597, 594.

29. Brantlinger, *Crusoe's Footprints*, 22.

30. Carby, *Reconstructing Womanhood: The Emergence of the Afro-American Woman Novelist* (New York: Oxford University Press, 1987), 7, 6. Hall, *The Hard Road to Renewal: Thatcherism and the Crisis on the Left* (New York: Verso, 1988), 41, and Gramsci is quoted on 42. On "conjuncture," see Hall, "Meaning of New Times," in *New Times*, ed. Hall and Jacques, 126, and Louis Althusser, *For Marx*, trans. Ben Brewster (London: Verso, 1977), 250, 9–12. Also see Janet Batsleer, Tony Davis, Rebecca O'Rourke, and Chris Weedon, *Rewriting English: Cultural Politics of Gender and Class* (London: Methuen, 1985), 3, 2. The authors, in their work on the 1930s, recognize that a historical study of media, schooling, and publishing cannot be narrowly understood as an inert "context" for various kinds of "literature" written within the conjuncture; rather these cultural forms and institutions played an "active role in determining the meaning and value of writing and reading." Their object of study became the operation of power within the social formation and, more locally, the study of "literature" itself as "one of the forces structuring the historical and ideological ensemble we were attempting to analyse."

31. See Lynn's review of T. J. Jackson Lears's magisterial *No Place of Grace* (1981), "Looking Backward," *New York Times Book Review* (January 10, 1982), 8. Slotkin, *The Fatal Environment: The Myth of the Frontier in the Age of Industrialization, 1800–1890* (New York: Atheneum, 1985); Wilson, *The Labor of Words: Literary Professionalism in the Progressive Era* (Athens: University of Georgia Press, 1985); Levine, *Highbrow/Lowbrow: The Emergence of Cultural Hierarchy in America* (Cambridge, MA: Harvard University Press, 1988); Lipsitz, *Time Passages: Collective Memory and American Popular Culture* (New York: Routledge, 1989); Denning, *Mechanic Accents: Dime Novels and Working-Class Culture in America* (New York: Verso, 1987), 75. Hall, "Deconstructing the Popular" in *People's History and Socialist Theory*, ed. Samuel, 227–40.

32. Laclau and Mouffe, "Post-Marxism without Apologies," *New Left Review* 166 (Nov./Dec. 1987): 79–100. Jameson nominates "socialism" as the overarching term to direct the "new social movements" toward "*total* transformation of society" in the discussion (358–60) following his "Cognitive Mapping" (347–57) in *Marxism and the Interpretation of Culture*, ed. Nelson and Grossberg: "Without the sense that the immediate [local] project is a figure for that social transformation, so that everybody has a stake in that particular struggle, the success of any local struggle is doomed, limited to reform" (360).

33. Davidoff and C. Hall, *Family Fortunes: Men and Women of the English Middle Class, 1780–1850* (Chicago: University of Chicago Press, 1987), 30. Also see C. Hall, "The Tale of Samuel and Jemima: Gender and Working-Class Culture in Early Nineteenth-Century England," in *Popular Culture and Social Relations*, ed. Tony Bennett, Colin Mercer, and Janet Woollacott (London: Open University Educational Enterprises, Milton Keynes, 1986), 73–92. Steedman, *Landscape for a Good Woman: A Story of Two Lives* (New Brunswick: Rutgers University Press, 1987); also see *Language, Gender, and Childhood*, ed. Carolyn Kay Steedman, Cathy Unwin, and Valerie Walkerdine (Boston: Routledge and Kegan Paul, 1985); Armstrong, *Desire and Domestic Fiction: A Political History of the Novel* (New York: Oxford University Press, 1987), 20; Poovey, *Uneven Developments: The Ideological Work of Gender in Mid-Victorian England* (Chicago: University of Chicago Press, 1988); Ryan, *Cradle of the Middle Class: The Family in Oneida County, New York, 1760–1865* (New York: Cambridge University Press, 1981); Martin, *The Woman in the Body: A Cultural Analysis of Reproduction* (Boston: Beacon, 1987); Scott, *Gender and the Politics of History* (New York: Columbia University Press, 1988), 48.

34. Barrett and McIntosh, *The Anti-Social Family* (London: Verso/NLB, 1982); Zaretsky, *Capitalism, The Family, and Personal Life* (New York: Harper and Row, 1976), 76, 128–29. Also see Richard Sennett's wide-ranging *The Fall of Public Man: On the Social Psychology of Capitalism* (New York: Vintage, 1978); Foucault, *The History of Sexuality, Volume I: An Introduction* (New York: Vintage, 1980). The Coward and Ellis book had its origins in the Language and Ideology Group at the Birmingham Centre: *Language and Materialism: Developments in Semiology and the Theory of the Subject* (Boston: Routledge and Kegan Paul, 1977); Burniston and Weedon, "Ideology, Subjectivity, and the Artistic Text," in Centre for Contemporary Cultural Studies, *On Ideology*, 199–229. Weedon, *Feminist Practice and Poststructuralist Theory* (New York: Blackwell, 1987).

35. On "structures of feeling," see Williams, *Marxism and Literature*, 128–35. For criticism of this concept, see Hall, "A Critical Survey of the Theoretical and Practical Achievements of the Last Ten Years," in *Literature, Society and the Sociology of Literature*, ed. Francis Barker, John Coombes, Peter Hulme, David Musselwhite, and Richard Osborne, proceedings of the conference held at the University of Essex, July 1976, 1–7; and Hall, "Politics and Letters," in *Raymond Williams: Critical Perspectives*, 62. On the Althusserian approaches, see Hall, "Cultural Studies and the Centre," 33. Weedon, *Feminist Practice and Poststructuralist Theory*, 82–83, 106. On authorship, see Janet Wolff's *The Social Production of Art* (New York: New York University Press, 1984) and *Aesthetics and the Sociology of Art* (London: George Allen and Unwin, 1983).

36. Johnson (on Barthes and form), "The Story So Far," 296. On literature as a force that institutionalizes subjectivity see Roland Barthes, *On Racine* (New York: Octagon, 1977), 171–72, quoted in Tony Bennett, *Outside Literature* (London: Routledge, 1990), 3. Johnson, "What Is Cultural Studies Anyway?" 62. Williams, *The Sociology of Culture* (New York: Schocken, 1981), 148–80. McRobbie, "Working-Class Girls and the Culture of Femininity," in *Women Take Issue*, ed. Women's Study Group, 96–108, and "Dance and Social Fantasy," 130–61, in *Gender and Generation*, ed. Angela McRobbie and Mica Nava (London: Macmillan, 1964). Radway, *Reading the Romance: Women, Patriarchy, and Popular Literature* (Chapel Hill: University of North Carolina Press, 1984). Johnson discusses "the subjective tug" of the romance genre in "What Is Cultural Studies Anyway?" 59. Elizabeth Long offers a superb survey and bibliography of feminist cultural studies projects in "Feminism and Cultural Studies," *Critical Studies in Mass Communications* 6 (Dec. 1989): 427–35.

37. Armstrong and Tennenhouse, "Introduction: Representing Violence, or 'How the West was Won,'" in *The Violence of Representation: Literature and the History of Violence*, ed. Nancy Armstrong and Leonard Tennenhouse (London: Routledge, 1989), 1–26, see 7. Armstrong and Tennenhouse, "The Literature of Conduct, the Conduct of Literature, and the Politics of Desire: An Introduction," in *The Ideology of Conduct: Essays on Literature and the History of Sexuality*, ed. Nancy Armstrong and Leonard Tennenhouse (New York: Methuen, 1987), 1–24, see 2.

38. Consult Joel Pfister, "Hawthorne as Cultural Theorist," in *The Cambridge Companion to Hawthorne*, ed. Richard Millington (Cambridge: Cambridge University Press, 2004), 35–59.

39. Jameson, *Political Unconscious*, 64. Poster, *Critical Theory of the Family* (New York: Seabury, 1980), 21, 14, 19. Foucault, *History of Sexuality*, 131, 123.

40. Stallybrass and White, *The Politics and Poetics of Transgression* (Ithaca, NY: Cornell University Press, 1986), 159, 193, 192.

41. Johnson, "What Is Cultural Studies Anyway?" 61. Spivak, *The Post-Colonial Critic: Interviews, Strategies, Dialogues*, ed. Sarah Harasym (New York: Routledge, 1990), 121. Anders Stephanson, "Interview with Cornel West," in *Universal Abandon? The Politics of Postmodernism*, ed. Andrew Ross (Minneapolis: University of Minnesota Press, 1988), 269–86, see 271.

42. See Ohmann, *Politics of Letters* (Middletown, CT: Wesleyan University Press, 1987) and "Thoughts on CS in the US" (manuscript, 1990). B. Ehrenreich and J. Ehrenreich, "The Professional-Managerial Class," 5–45, and "Rejoinder," 313–34, in *Between Labor and Capital*, ed. Pat Walker (Boston: South End Press, 1979); also see 12. West, "The Postmodern Crisis of the Black Intellectuals." For an excellent critique of Jacoby's book see Ohmann, "Graduate Students, Professionals, Intellectuals," *College English* 52 (March 1990): 247–57.

43. Hall, "Emergence of Cultural Studies and the Crisis of the Humanities," 17, 18.

44. *Building Bridges: The Emerging Grassroots Coalition of Labor and Community*, ed. Jeremy Brecher and Tim Costello (New York: Monthly Review Press, 1990). Pfeil, *Another Tale to Tell*, 9.

Notes for Chapter 2

1. Mills, "Complacent," in Mills, *Power, Politics and People*, ed. Horowitz, 392. Lynd, "Structure of Power," 599. Greene, *The Quiet American* (New York: Penguin, 2002 [1955], 24).

2. Thompson, "William Morris and the Moral Issues Today," in *The American Threat to British Culture* (London: Arena Publications, c. 1951), 25–30: all quotations from this chapter will be followed by page numbers in parentheses.

3. For a critique of the British Left and "first" New Left use of Morris, often focusing on Thompson, see Perry Anderson, *Arguments within English Marxism*, 157–207.

4. Thompson, "A Homage to Thomas McGrath," in his *The Heavy Dancers* (London: Merlin, 1985), 279–337, 291, 292, 292–93, 293.

5. Gilroy, *Black Atlantic*, 11. Also see Perry Anderson's comments on Thompson's blend of nationalist-internationalism, *Arguments within English Marxism*, 25–29, 57–68.

6. Steele quotes Hall as noting that in the late 1950s and early 1960s cultural studies was "'identified with the first New Left.'" Referring to Williams, Steele asserts: "He saw what he and others were doing was quite definitely not founding a new academic subject area but contributing to the process of social change itself" (*Emergence of Cultural Studies*, 15). Also see Lin Chun, *The British New Left* (Edinburgh: Edinburgh University Press, 1993).

7. Editor [Hall], "Editorial," *New Left Review* 1 (Jan.–Feb. 1960): 1–3. In 1986 Hall criticized "how the world dreams itself to be 'American'" (quoted in Dworkin, *Cultural Marxism in Postwar Britain*, 259).

8. On aspects of this shift, see Stephen Woodhams, *History in the Making: Raymond Williams, Edward Thompson and Radical Intellectuals, 1936–1956* (London: Merlin Press, 2001), 185; Steele, *Emergence of Cultural Studies*, 9, 20, 28, 200–204; Dworkin, *Cultural Marxism in Postwar Britain*, 57, 99. On the ideological spread of middle-class identity that erodes working-class consciousness and identity in America, see Ollman, *How to Take an Exam ... and Remake the World*, 18–19, 26.

9. Williams, "Walking Backwards into the Future," *New Socialist* 27 (May 1985): 21–23, see 22. Also see Williams's "Hesitations before Socialism," *New Socialist* 41 (Sept. 1986): 34–36, see 36. British socialists had long before expressed doubts of this sort about America. Harold Laski's *Democracy in Crisis* (Chapel Hill: University of North Carolina Press, 1933) criticizes "the disproportion in America between the actual economic control and the formal political power" and objects to a "constitution so organized as to minimize the power of [the]

popular will" (quoted in Lynd, *Knowledge for What?*, 68, 67). Matthiessen, like Laski and Lynd, favored the establishment of economic democracy in America.

10. Williams quoted in Michael Kenny, *The First New Left: British Intellectuals after Stalin* (London: Lawrence and Wishart, 1995), 107.

11. Williams, Thompson, Hall, *May Day Manifesto, 1968* (Harmondsworth, Middlesex: Penguin, 1968), 66.

12. Kenny writes that "some of the theoretical and methodological shifts registered by [the New Left] formation paved the way for the popularity of concepts such as hegemony, organic intellectuals and the war of position" (*First New Left*, 209).

13. Of course, for the British New Left transnational considerations were part of socialist critique. Nowadays transnational concerns—although often expansive in scope—sometimes stand in for socialist critique.

14. Read "Proposal for a New Journal to be called *New Monthly Review*" (FOM). See Christopher Phelps, "Introduction: A Socialist Magazine in the American Century," in the special issue *Fifty Years: Three Interviews: Paul M. Sweezy, Harry Magdoff, Ellen Meiksins Wood* of *Monthly Review* 51 (May 1999): 1–30, see 2–3.

15. See William Appleman Williams, *The Tragedy of American Diplomacy* (New York: Dell, 1972 [1962]), 270, also Alan Sinfield, *Literature, Politics and Culture in Postwar Britain* (London: Athlone Press, 1997), 93. On America's use of the Marshall Plan to weaken the power of the Communist bloc and curb the influence of the Communist parties of Western European countries, see Henry Pelling, *Britain and the Marshall Plan* (London: Macmillan, 1988), 125. For multidimensional perspectives on postwar America, see *A History of Our Time: Readings on Postwar America*, ed. William H. Chafe and Harvard Sitkoff (New York: Oxford University Press, 1983) and William H. Chafe, *The Unfinished Journey: America since World War II* (New York: Oxford University Press, 1995 [1986]).

16. See Peter Worsley, "Imperial Retreat," in E. P. Thompson, Kenneth Alexander, Stuart Hall, Alasdair MacIntyre, Ralph [Raphael] Samuel, and Peter Worsley, *Out of Apathy* (London: New Left Books, 1960), 101–40. The United States clamped down on "old imperialism" (106): "The supreme principle of U.S. policy—the unification of the non-Soviet world into an anti-Communist bloc—had been jeopardised by Britain's indiscretion in pursuing her private imperial interests.... . Go it alone imperialism was still possible and permissible, but only if it did not endanger the overall anti-Communist strategy" (104). The United States had the United Nations indict the aggressors (104). "By the time of Suez, the neutral, uncommitted, 'emergent,' ex-colonial world had become infinitely stronger. One could not afford to alienate it" (104). Of postwar accommodation, he writes: "Britain had, some time in the forties, passed on the White Man's Burden to the United States. The surrender had been all the easier in that it had been made in the name of anti-imperialism. The terms were negotiated by the same Labour Government that was acceding to Indian independence; the burden was passed on to a country which many still thought of as the country of Roosevelt, Henry Wallace, Wendell Wilkie—advocates of the right to self-determination of colonial peoples" (108). On the significance of the Suez conflict and the Soviet invasion of Hungary, see Woodhams, *History in the Making*, 140, 145, 148–49.

17. Williams, Thompson, and Hall, *May Day Manifesto*, 88, 39. Hall's 1990 comment is quoted in Dworkin, *Cultural Marxism in Postwar Britain*, 250.

18. See the Editorial, "Americans, Asians and Arabs," *New Statesman and Nation* 52 (Nov. 24, 1956): 653. On some of the momentous events of 1956, also see G. D. H. Cole, "Midway

Thoughts on Suez," *New Statesman and Nation* 52 (Oct. 27, 1956): 508–09; Anonymous, "An Empire Afraid," *New Statesman and Nation* 52 (Nov. 3, 1956): 536; Editorial, "The Return from Port Said," *New Statesman and Nation* 52 (Nov. 10, 1956): 573. America and its Arab allies effectively cut off Britain's oil supply until it got in line.

19. Editor [Hall], "Editorial": "The present form of nationalisation is not a socialist form: it does not give ordinary men and women control over their own lives" (1). For background on the Labour Party, the Left, and the New Left see *The Left in Britain 1956–68*, ed. David Widgery (Harmondsworth, Middlesex: Penguin, 1976); Arthur Marwick, "A Social History of Britain, 1945–1983," in *Introduction to Contemporary Cultural Studies*, ed. Punter, 19–46; Ralph Miliband, *Parliamentary Socialism: A Study in the Politics of Labour* (London: Merlin, 1972 [1961]); D. N. Pritt, *The Labour Government 1945–51* (New York: International, 1963), on the United States see 57–58, 61, 143–45, 196–99, 220–21, 314–15; Henry Pelling and Alastair J. Reid, *A Short History of the Labour Party* (New York: St. Martin's, 1996 [1961]); F. S. Northedge, *Descent from Power: British Foreign Policy 1945–1973* (London: George Allen and Unwin, 1974), on the United States, see 173–204.

20. Tony Barrow, "How the Beat Began," *The Beatles Monthly* (July 2000): 4–12, see 5. For Reyner Banham's reminiscence of the powerful impact of American popular culture in the postwar period, see Dworkin, *Cultural Marxism in Postwar Britain*, 85.

21. Matthiessen, *From the Heart of Europe*, 3, 14. In addition, Matthiessen wrote: "Tawney also recognized that the Jefferson revolution, magnificent as it was, fell short to the degree that it conceived of freedom and equality solely in political terms. Those terms must now be extended to our economic life" ("The Education of a Socialist," in *F. O. Matthiessen*, ed. Sweezy and Huberman, 3–20, see 18). Matthiessen, *From the Heart of Europe*, on Czechoslovakia and Britain, 176, 178. According to Paul Sweezy, Matthiessen liked "the feeling that the Czechs were finding a road to socialism that had been closed to the Russians, a road that involved not the denial or overriding of bourgeois freedoms but their preservation and extension to the sphere of economic relations; and that, while traveling this road, the Czechs were providing a really effective channel of communication, a bridge, between the socialist East and what was still progressive in the capitalist West" ("Labor and Political Activities," in *F. O. Matthiessen*, ed. Sweezy and Huberman, 61–75, see 72).

22. MacKenzie, "After the Stalemate State," in *Conviction*, ed. Norman MacKenzie (London: MacGibbon and Kee, 1958), 7–22, see 12, 13, 13–14.

23. W. A. Williams, *Tragedy of American Diplomacy*, 233. For a more detailed analysis of this consult R. N. Gardner, *Sterling-Dollar Diplomacy* (Oxford: Oxford University Press, 1956). Also see Tony Benn, "Britain as a Colony," *New Socialist* 1 (Sept.–Oct. 1981): 58–62, see 61.

24. Consult Sinfield, *Literature, Politics and Culture*, 95, also see 94.

25. Sweezy, "An Interview with Paul M. Sweezy," *Monthly Review* 51 (May 1999): 31–53, see 40. Williams, Thompson, Hall, *May Day Manifesto*, 138, 166, 138.

26. Williams, Thompson, Hall, *May Day Manifesto*, 138.

27. Williams, Thompson, Hall, *May Day Manifesto*, 182, 181.

28. Williams, Thompson, Hall, *May Day Manifesto*, 15, 182, 183, 16.

29. See Hall, "The 'First' New Left: Life and Times," in *Out of Apathy: Voices on the New Left Thirty Years On*, ed. Robin Archer et al. (London: Verso, 1989), 11–38, on G. D. H. Cole at Oxford, 15. Williams and Thompson studied at Cambridge. To better distinguish the original *Out of Apathy* (1960) from the later *Out of Apathy* (1989) titled in its honor, henceforth I will include the date of publication of the second volume when I cite it. For

an astute critique of the deradicalizing of much current cultural studies scholarship and a comparison of this work to the *Monthly Review* critical tradition, see Robert McChesney, "Whatever Happened to Cultural Studies?" 76–93, especially 82–86, in *American Cultural Studies*, ed. Warren and Vavrus.

30. Thompson, "Highly Confidential: A Personal Comment by the Editor," in *Warwick University, Ltd.: Industry, Management and the Universities*, ed. E. P. Thompson (Harmondsworth, Middlesex: Penguin, 1970), 146–64, see 153. Thompson taught history at the University of Warwick for a few years and was a visiting professor at Rutgers University.

31. Williams, Thompson, Hall, *May Day Manifesto*, 54.

32. Jameson, "On 'Cultural Studies,'" 50.

33. Williams, Thompson, Hall, *May Day Manifesto*, 133.

34. On this expansion, see Kenny, *First New Left*, 177.

35. Though some scholars, inside and outside the United States, contributed to a "cosmopolitan" American studies intent on studying America's position in the world's cultures and how such pluralist knowledge might ameliorate the United States. In particular, see Lawrence W. Chisolm, "Cosmopolitan Possibilities," in *American Studies in Transition*, ed. Fishwick, 298–313. Chisolm's critical world pluralism engages matters such as reorienting "American Studies toward comparative cultural history" (310), establishing "Centers of American Studies in the United States [that] would be models for centers in an international network" (313), and using this comparative knowledge not only to rethink America but reconsider "what it means to be a human being" (311). Chisolm's cosmopolitan American studies does not resemble the transnational socialist critique that members of the British New Left and many contributors to *Monthly Review* and other journals developed, but it does endeavor to internationalize the scope of American studies cultural analysis in provocative ways. Fishwick devoted one-third of the volume's essays to the theme "On Confronting the World" (197–329) and invited several non-American American studies scholars to contribute to the volume.

36. Hall, "'First,'" in *Out of Apathy*, ed. Archer et al. (1989), 29.

37. Williams, "Ideas and the Labour Movement," *New Socialist* 1 (Nov.–Dec. 1981): 28–33, see 31.

38. Hall, Samuel, Charles Taylor, "Then and Now: A Re-evaluation of the New Left," in *Out of Apathy*, ed. Archer et al. (1989), 143–70, 148.

39. MacKenzie, "After the Stalemate State," in *Conviction*, ed. MacKenzie, 19. And on "World America," see Alfredo Valladâo, *The Twenty-First Century Will Be American*, trans. John Howe (London: Verso, 1996).

40. Williams, Thompson, and Hall, *May Day Manifesto*, 184, 174, 65. MacKenzie also addresses this incorporation: "The aim is stability, a system in which the Establishment is tolerated because it no longer behaves like a ruling class at bay, and in which some of the claims of the working class are met because it does not seek to dispossess the Establishment altogether." William Morris, as paraphrased by MacKenzie, observed that "the Establishment ... can play a game of cat-and-mouse with reformers as long as they accept its rules for the game of politics. It does not require a policy: its purpose is to avoid change or to limit the extent of change when it is unavoidable" ("After the Stalemate State," in *Conviction*, ed. MacKenzie, 20). Davies notes that Williams composed the 1967 May Day Committee draft and that the many additional contributors to the published version—besides the three main authors—did not include any editors of the late 1960s *New Left Review* (*Cultural Studies and Beyond*, 17).

41. Hall, "The Supply of Demand," in Thompson et al., *Out of Apathy*, 56–97, 58.

42. Williams, Thompson, Hall, *May Day Manifesto,* 180.

43. Consult the debate between E. P. Thompson and Labour Party representative Michael Foot, "Where Do You Stand?" *New Socialist* 3 (Jan.–Feb. 1982): 4–9. Thompson doubted "Labour's credibility" as a force that would contest U.S. defense and foreign policy (5). Foot used the language of "revolt"—as if Britain and Europe were contemplating revolt against the U.S. Mother Country: "the whole European revolt … I think that revolt is going to succeed" (6).

44. For example, see A British Socialist, "The Growth of Bevanism," *Monthly Review* 3 (April 1952): 384–89; A British Socialist, "The Struggle within the Labor Party," *Monthly Review* 4 (Dec. 1952): 282–88; Political Economist Writing from England, "The Anglo-American Alliance," *Monthly Review* 6 (Sept. 1954): 174–80; Geoffrey Bing, "Britain, China, and the United States," *Monthly Review* 5 (Nov. 1953): 310–19; Editors, "What Every American Should Know about the Suez Crisis," *Monthly Review* 8 (Oct. 1956): 177–95.

45. Thompson, "Revolution," in Thompson et al., *Out of Apathy,* 287–308, see 307.

46. Benn, "Britain as a Colony," 61. Two years later, the United States invaded Grenada, a Commonwealth country, causing John Cox to note that the United States has employed military force on "215 occasions between January 1946 and December 1975" (Cox, "America Presents Arms," *Marxism Today* 27 [Dec. 1983]: 7–10). "President Reagan objected to the exclusion of American maize products from Spain and Portugal in consequence of their joining the Common Market," Frances Morrell pointed out. "He threatened to levy a 200 per cent duty on British gin, French and Italian wine, Dutch cheese, cognac, olives" (Morrell, "End of the Affair," *New Socialist* 47 [March 1987]: 22–23, see 22). Recently David Cannidine, a professor of history at the University of London, characterized Britain's effort since 1945 to play Greece to America's Rome—in a bid to seek "global influence"—as an "abusive" rather than a "special relationship." British involvement in U.S. military operations has served simply to lend legitimacy to U.S. imperialism ("A Special Relationship, or an Abusive One?" *New York Times* [November 22, 2003]: A15). In the mostly mediocre film *Love Actually* (2003), written and directed by Richard Curtis, a youngish prime minister, new on the job, actually stands up to the American president at a press conference and reclassifies their "special relationship" as an especially abusive one in which the U.S. power structure calls all the shots. Having enacted what must have been a fantasy for some postwar prime ministers, the British celebrate him as a hero.

47. Eagleton, *After Theory,* 225. Eagleton's efforts to conceptualize new (really, rather traditional) subjects that "theory" has supposedly overlooked or has not taken seriously (evil, biology, nature, human nature, religion, death, universal truths, social progress) often turns into a critique, sometimes an enraged critique, not just of American culturalism but of the Bush-governed United States—one key political condition that shapes Eagleton's socialist-humanist attempt to reroute theory in ways that he hopes will combat this fundamentalist force (104, 162–63, 185–88, 194, 203, 224–27).

48. Thompson, "Outside the Whale," in Thompson et al., *Out of Apathy,* 141–94, 172, 173.

49. Thompson, "N.A.T.O., Neutralism and Survival," *Universities and Left Review* 4 (Summer 1958): 49–51, see 50, 51, 51.

50. Thompson, "The Ends of Cold War," *New Left Review* 182 (July–August 1990): 139–46.

51. *Star Wars,* ed. E. P. Thompson (Harmondsworth, Middlesex: Penguin, 1985), 24.

52. Sartre, "Imperialist Morality," *New Left Review* 41 (Jan.–Feb. 1967): 3–10, see 9, 8.

53. Williams, Thompson, Hall, *May Day Manifesto*, 55, 58.

54. Williams, Thompson, Hall, *May Day Manifesto*, 53, 58, 67, 18, 107.

55. Williams, Thompson, Hall, *May Day Manifesto*, 67.

56. Williams, Thompson, Hall, *May Day Manifesto*, 76–77, 93, 77.

57. Hall and Fruchter, "Notes on the Cuban Dilemma," *New Left Review* 9 (May–June 1961): 2–11, see 7, 2. I do not mean to suggest that these critics held homogeneous views. See Mills to Harvey and Bette Swados, Nov. 3, 1956, in *C. Wright Mills*, ed. K. Mills with P. Mills. Mills appreciated Sweezy and Huberman's criticisms of U.S. policy toward Cuba. He considered Sweezy to be "doctrinaire," yet more "generous" (217) than many "liberal stuff" reviewers of his work. "Let's not forget that there's more [that's] still useful in even the Sweezy kind of Marxism than in all the routineers of J. S. Mill put together" (218). Also see Mills to Ralph and Marion Miliband, March 16, 1962. Just four days before he died, Mills suggested that "Leo [Huberman] and Paul [Sweezy]" come out to have lunch at his house with the Milibands (340). Fruchter, who was in his early twenties when he worked with Hall, went on to a career in progressive education. He has served as director of the Institute for Education and Social Policy at New York University, where he is professor of clinical education.

58. Hall and Fruchter, "Notes," 6, 8.

59. Hall and Fruchter, "Notes," 4, 7, 10.

60. Williams, Thompson, and Hall, *May Day Manifesto*, 96.

61. Inglis, *Raymond Williams* (London: Routledge, 1995), 214.

62. Hobsbawm, "Vietnam and the Dynamics of Guerilla War," *New Left Review* 33 (Sept.–Oct. 1965): 59–68, see 60, 63, 68. Hobsbawm, "The Pentagon's Dilemma: Goliath and the Guerilla," *The Nation* 201 (July 19, 1965): 33–38.

63. Thompson, "N.A.T.O.," 50.

64. Williams, Thompson, Hall, *May Day Manifesto*, 89.

65. Some New Leftists who got involved with the CND supported Nye Bevan in the Labour Party not only because Bevan had opposed making Britain a nuclear junior partner, but because in doing so, in Mervyn Jones's words, he refused to enact the typical "docile subservience to Washington." However, Bevan—hopeful of becoming foreign secretary if the party won office, which it did not—reversed his position. Yet again some members of the Left felt left out of Labour (Jones, *Chances* [London: Verso, 1987], 146).

66. Hall, "'First,'" in *Out of Apathy*, ed. Archer et al. (1989), 32. Also see Perry Anderson's class critique of CND, *Arguments within English Marxism*, 148.

67. Jones, *Chances*, 150.

68. Riesman and Macoby, "The American Crisis," *New Left Review* 5 (Sept.–Oct. 1960): 24–35, see 25.

69. Thompson, *Star Wars*, 11, 108, 10, 24. For a radical American critique, also see Bruce Franklin, *War Stars: The Superweapon and the American Imagination* (New York: Oxford University Press, 1988).

70. Thompson, *Star Wars*, 107, 119, 26, 148. Also see Williams, "The Politics of Nuclear Disarmament," *New Left Review* 124 (Nov.–Dec. 1980): 25–42.

71. Thompson, "Outside the Whale," in Thompson et al., *Out of Apathy*, 189, 157, 164, 159. On psychologization, Thompson writes: "Novels, plays and theses were written, displaying not only Communism but also radicalism as projections of the neuroses of maladjusted intellectuals" (168).

72. Thompson, "Outside the Whale," in Thompson et al., *Out of Apathy*, 168, 177, 183.

73. Hoggart, "Speaking to Each Other," in *Conviction*, ed. MacKenzie, 121–38, see 136, 138.

74. This was not a new development. See Henry Pelling, *America and the British Left: From Bright to Bevan* (London: Adam and Charles Black, 1956), which surveys aspects of Anglo-American relations—especially Left relations—from the Civil War to 1956. Pelling, for instance, quotes from Aneurin Bevan's *In Place of Fear* (1952). Bevan had risen from the occupation of miner to the Labour government's foreign secretary (1945–51). He was inspired by American radicalism. "'As I was reaching adolescence, towards the end of the First World War, I became acquainted with the works of Eugene V. Debs and Daniel De Leon of the U. S. A.... When I found that the political polemics of De Leon and Debs were shared by so loved an author as Jack London, the effect on my mind was profound. Nor was I alone in this. My experience has been shared by thousands of the young men and women of the working class of Britain.... From Jack London's *Iron Heel* to the whole world of Marxist literature was an easy and fascinating step'" (155).

75. See Francis Newton, "Lady Sang the Blues," *Universities and Left Review* 7 (Autumn 1959): 70–71; Machel Parsons, "John Cage," *New Left Review* 23 (Jan.–Feb. 1964): 83–86; Lee Russell, "Samuel Fuller," *New Left Review* 23 (Jan.–Feb. 1964): 86–89; Alan Beckett, "The New Wave in Jazz," *New Left Review* 31 (May–June 1965): 90–94; Alan Beckett, "John Lee Hooker," *New Left Review* 27 (Sept.–Oct. 1964): 81–84 (see his comments on Chuck Berry on 81).

76. Miller, "The Freedom of the Writer," *New Reasoner* 1 (1957): 115.

77. Harrington, "What the Hell *Is* Happening on the American Scene?" *New Left Review* 6 (Nov.–Dec. 1960): 54–56, see 55.

78. Samuel, "Born-again Socialism," in *Out of Apathy*, ed. Archer et al. (1989), 39–57, see 44. Hall, "'First,'" in *Out of Apathy*, ed. Archer et al. (1989), 24–25 (indigenous), 27 (SDS).

79. For instance, see Gabriel Kolko, "The American 'Income Revolution,'" *Universities and Left Review* 1 (Summer 1957): 9–14 and Dave Dellinger, "Cuba: America's Lost Plantations," *New Left Review* 8 (March–April 1961): 38–46. Irving Howe's *Politics and the Novel* was the second book—after *Out of Apathy*—published by New Left Books (later Verso). In his postwar phase Williams was interested in American intellectuals whose work was also important to the critical development of American studies: Lewis Mumford, Robert and Helen Merrell Lynd, and Ruth Benedict. Steele observes that in the postwar years Williams admired Mumford's *The Culture of Cities* (1938), the Lynds's *Middletown: A Study in Contemporary Culture* (1929) and *Middletown in Transition* (1937), and Ruth Benedict's *Patterns of Culture* (1934), which developed the anthropological notion that culture should be understood as the making of the whole way of life (*Emergence of Cultural Studies*, 195–96).

80. Phelps, "Introduction," 19. Monthly Review Press published the first U.S. edition of Thompson's *Poverty of Theory*. See Williams, "Class and Voting in Britain," *Monthly Review* (Jan. 1960): 327–34.

81. Samuel, "Born-again Socialism," in *Out of Apathy*, ed. Archer et al. (1989), 46. Hall, "'First,'" in *Out of Apathy*, ed. Archer et al. (1989), 24–25, 27.

82. Williams, Thompson, Hall, *May Day Manifesto*, 11, 140.

83. Davies writes, without elaboration: "As far as most people on the British left were concerned, the American influence started with Mills" (*Cultural Studies and Beyond*, 161).

84. See *C. Wright Mills*, ed. K. Mills with P. Mills: Mills to William Miller, March 14, 1957, 230; Mills to Ralph Miliband, May 1, 1958, 266; Mills to Miliband, August 1, 1957, 243;

Mills to Miliband, June 22, 1960, 290; Mills to Harvey and Bette Swados, June 13, 1961, 332; Mills to his imaginary Russian correspondent, Tovarich, 1959, 279. For awhile Mills viewed England as a refuge from an America where his life had been threatened (because of his support for Cuba) and as a cosmopolitan base. Miliband, write Kathryn Mills and Pamela Mills, "introduced Mills to members of the New Left in Britain and Europe in the late 1950s" (238). Yet Mills also wrote his publisher, Ian Ballantine, Oct. 2, 1961: "[England] *is* a foreign country to me" (337). Also see Mills to the editor of *Commentary,* spring 1957: "Since World War II any sound business ideology is likely to be relevant to international expenses as well as to domestic politics" (236). On Mills's internationalism and his battle against the Cold War, also consult "Decline of the Left" in Mills, *Power, Politics, and People,* ed. Horowitz: "[We need] viewpoints that are genuinely detached from *any* enclosure of mind or national- ist celebration" (235).

85. Dan Wakefield, Introduction, in *C. Wright Mills,* ed. K. Mills with P. Mills, 1–18, see 4. An anonymous obituary notice concurred in *Studies on the Left* 2 (1962): "It is an indict- ment of the current intellectual climate that [Mills] was more highly regarded and better understood in Europe than in this country" (6).

86. Mills, "Complacent," 388, 389, 390, 392, 393, 394, and Mills, "The Cultural Apparatus," 405–22, see 408 on inactionaries, both in Mills, *Power, Politics, and People,* ed. Horowitz.

87. Mills: "Cultural Apparatus," 420 and "On Knowledge and Power," 599–613, see 606; "Complacent," 329; "Cultural Apparatus," 408, 410 and "Knowledge and Power," 602–03; "Cultural Apparatus," 421 and "Knowledge and Power," 605–06; "Cultural Apparatus," 420 and "Knowledge and Power," 604–06; "Cultural Apparatus," 422; "Cultural Apparatus," 420 and also see "Knowledge and Power," 606; "Cultural Apparatus," 422; "Culture and Politics," 236–46, see 245 in Mills, *Power, Politics, and People,* ed. Horowitz.

88. Halsey, "Sociological Imagination," *Universities and Left Review* 7 (Autumn 1959): 71–73, see 72, 73.

89. Editor [Hall], "The American Scene," *New Left Review* 5 (Sept.–Oct. 1960): 17. Rustin, "The Relevance of Mills Sociology," *New Left Review* 21 (Oct. 1963): 92–106, see 102, 104.

90. Samuel, "Born-again Socialism," in *Out of Apathy,* ed. Archer et al. (1989), 42–43.

91. MacIntyre, "Breaking the Chains of Reason," 195–240, in Thompson et al., *Out of Apathy,* 223, 225, 224. Also see Kenneth Alexander, "Power at the Base," 243–86, in Thompson et al., *Out of Apathy.* Alexander praises Mills's critique of American union leaders who have sold themselves as tools of corporate management (285).

92. Miliband, "C. Wright Mills," *New Left Review* (May–June 1962): 15–20, see 15, 16–17, 17. Miliband notes: "It was altogether fitting that ... Castro should have sent a wreath to his funeral" (19).

93. Mills, "Letter to the New Left," *New Left Review* 6 (Sept.–Oct. 1960): 18–23, see 20, 18, 18, 18–19, 19, 21, 20, 21, 23.

94. See *C. Wright Mills,* ed. K. Mills with P. Mills, 315. Displaying his compassion and good sense, Mills also stressed Thompson's poverty and urged Castro to advance him and his family transportation funds (316).

95. *C. Wright Mills,* ed. K. Mills with P. Mills, 316.

96. *C. Wright Mills,* ed. K. Mills with P. Mills, 320.

97. Thompson, "Remembering C. Wright Mills," in his *Heavy Dancers,* 261–74, 273, 271, 274. Dworkin suggests that there may have been some intellectual tension and disagreement between Mills and Thompson over the matter of the working class as a principal agent of

social change and cites Thompson's dismissal of the idea of classlessness. Mills, however, never subscribed to the classlessness position, even though he renamed the classes at odds in American culture (for instance, redubbing the ruling class the power elite) (on this possible friction, see *Cultural Marxism in Postwar Britain*, 101).

98. Mills, "Letter," 22. Mills sought to conceptualize class clearly from the outset of his career. He asked Dwight Macdonald to appear with him on an American Sociological Association panel set up to address "class, status, and occupations of the 'new middle class'": "It is the first time, to my knowledge, that the whole issue of class has really been raised in such a dignified meeting" (Oct. 21, 1942, DM).

99. Thompson, "Highly Confidential," in *Warwick University, Ltd.,* 148. For some remarks about Thompson's five years at Warwick and his founding of a center for historical research see Davies, *Cultural Studies and Beyond,* 32–33. I thank Clive Bush, who taught at Warwick during the uprising, which he facilitated, for making the links between his friend and colleague Thompson's critique and earlier work by Veblen and Mills.

100. Rexroth, "Students Take Over," *New Left Review* 5 (Sept.–Oct. 1960): 38–41, 39, see 39.

101. Hall, "'First,'" in *Out of Apathy,* ed. Archer et al. (1989), 16.

102. Williams, Hall, Thompson, *May Day Manifesto,* 188. Also see Kenny, *First New Left,* 172–78. Thompson stressed: "What is at issue here is not just the government of one university, but the whole way in which a society selects its priorities and orders itself" (162).

103. Jenkins, "In Black and White," *Universities and Left Review* 1 (Winter 1958): 80–82, see 81.

104. Robert F. Williams, "Can Negroes Afford to Be Pacifists?" *New Left Review* 1 (Jan.–Feb. 1960): 44–46, see 46. Dave Dellinger, "Are Pacifists Willing to Be Negroes?" *New Left Review* 1 (Jan.–Feb. 1960): 46–47, see 47.

105. Hall, "'First,'" in *Out of Apathy,* ed. Archer et al. (1989), 30.

106. Birnbaum, "Foreword," in Thompson et al., *Out of Apathy,* ix–xii, see x, xi. On Birnbaum, see Dworkin, *Cultural Marxism in Postwar Britain,* 54. Perry Anderson employs the substitution-for-Marxism thesis to criticize Thompson's emphasis on morality in his history writing, especially in *The Poverty of Theory:* "For Thompson, in effect, history becomes essentially a pattern-book of moral examples, to be learnt and handed on for ethical imitation.... What he fails to see is that the reason why the founders of historical materialism were so chary of ethical discussions of socialism . . . is their tendency to become *substitutes* for explanatory accounts of history. Aggressively claiming to reinstate 'moralism' as an integral part of any contemporary culture of the Left, Thompson has forgotten the distinction which the term itself is designed to indicate in ordinary usage. Moral consciousness is certainly indispensable to the very idea of socialism: Engels himself emphasized that 'a really human morality' would be one of the hallmark's of communism, the finest product of its conquest of the age-old social divisions and antagonisms rooted in scarcity. Moral*ism,* on the other hand, denotes the vain intrusion of moral judgments in lieu of causal understanding." Anderson later praises Thompson for recognizing the power of William Morris's "moral imagination" and bringing these concerns to British Marxism (*Arguments within English Marxism,* 85–86, 160). He also admits: "The abuse committed by my rejoinder to [Thompson] over a decade ago was to reduce the profound continuity of this pursuit of a communist morality to a mere 'moralism'" (186). Anderson does not really address what Thompson does in so many instances: endeavor to explain the causes of actions and events *and* work out their moral significance.

The two aims are by no means mutually exclusive. Anderson goes on to hold that "what the past bequeaths the present is first and foremost a set of lines *of force* for transformation, not a gallery of model lives for imitation" (98). I am not quite sure how to define lines of force, but might "imitating"—or identifying with, or simply admiring—moral lives play some role in making "lines of force" forceful?

107. Thompson, "Revolution," in Thompson et al., *Out of Apathy,* 308, and Thompson, "William Morris," 28.

108. Hall, "'First,'" in *Out of Apathy,* ed. Archer et al. (1989), 32. Editor [Hall], "Editorial," 2.

109. For perspectives on transatlantic Left dialogues and contacts that preceded this, dating from the Civil War to 1956, see Pelling, *America and the British Left.*

110. O'Neill, *The Hairy Ape,* reprinted in *Eugene O'Neill: Complete Plays, 1920–1931,* vol. 2 (New York: Library of America, 1988), 147. Du Bois, *An ABC of Color* (New York: International, 2001 [1963]), 125, 204. Mary Harris Jones, *The Autobiography of Mother Jones* (Chicago: Charles H. Kerr, 1996 [1925]), 203. On Jones see Elliott J. Gorn, "Mother Jones," in *American Radical,* ed. Buhle, Buhle, and Kaye, 177–82. Paul Simon, "Mrs. Robinson," *Scarborough Fair* (album).

111. Adam Nagourney, "A Senator's Death and the Fight for Congress," *New York Times,* "Week in Review" section 4 (Oct. 27, 2002): 1, 5, see 5. Anonymous, "Top Anti-War Slogans," *The Onion* 39 (March 27–April 2, 2003): 1. In 1972 John Berger sketched another development that has inflected the popular response to politics in Britain and America: consumption functions as "a substitute for democracy," "takes the place of significant political choice," and "mask[s] and compensate[s] for all that is undemocratic within society" (Berger et al., *Ways of Seeing* (Harmondsworth, Middlesex: Penguin, 1979 [1972]), 149).

112. Piven and Cloward, *Why Americans Still Don't Vote: And Why Politicians Want It That Way* (Boston: Beacon, 2000), 3, 10, 8, 271. Also see Richard A. Cloward and Frances Fox Piven, *Poor People's Movements: Why They Succeed, How They Fail* (New York: Vintage, 1979 [1977]).

113. Zinn, "Beyond Voting" (1976) reprinted in his *Howard Zinn on History* (New York: Seven Stories, 2001), 59–61, see 60, 61. Zinn gave a talk at Wesleyan University on March 29, 2001, in which he underscored the importance of making a "commotion" to catalyze progressive social change. I like to think of the intellectual organization of this history and these strategies as commotion studies. Organizers Jeremy Brecher and Tim Costello also point out that efforts to effect change through conventional political and electoral means "have been notoriously unsuccessful" and add that "the main centers of power in our society lie beyond the control of elected politicians" (*Common Sense for Hard Times: The Power of the Powerless to Cope with Everyday Life and Transform Society in the Nineteen Seventies* [New York: Two Continents, Institute for Policy Studies, 1976], 5). They too favor grassroots, bottom-up movement politics (more on this in chapter 6). William Julius Wilson, director of the Joblessness and Urban Poverty Research Program at the John F. Kennedy School at Harvard, is also pessimistic about the Republican-Democratic closed system and recently has tried to give more concrete form to the sort of movements that can draw on the political strength of African Americans and sway the parties. Coalition politics, he maintains, is the only solution to party politics (*The bridge over the Racial Divide: Rising Inequality and Coalition Politics* [Berkeley: University of California Press, 1999], 117–28). Wilson, alas, does not explain how a national coalition—if it could be formed—could effectively apply pressure to the parties.

114. Moore, *Stupid White Men* (New York: Regan Books, 2001), 224–25. Moore tries to move beyond the dilemma: "Do you want to get fucked by someone who tells you they're going to fuck you, or do you want to get fucked by someone who lies to you, and then fucks you?" (245). On electoral activism see 25–28, 97, 171, 226–28, 243, 253–56.

115. Domhoff, *Changing the Powers That Be: How the Left Can Stop Losing and Win* (Zanham, MD: Rowman and Littlefield, 2003).

116. Gitlin, *Letters to a Young Activist* (New York: Basic, 2003), 111, 121. He adds: "This Left *is* ambivalent—as a matter of style, almost as a matter of principle. Many of its partisans are ambivalent even about participating in politics, which they see across the board—with some reason—as corrupt and 'irrelevant.' ... The Left despises the political party that most of its constituents vote for" (110). Moreover, the Left, like the Right, is often "quick to trash" those Democrats, such as Bill Clinton, who actually hold office (118). Gitlin, like Moore, who also makes this point, has no illusions about the ways in which Democratic Party politicians uphold many of the contradictions that wrack America (and do so under the banner of liberalism), yet he does point to a Left critical—and ideological—tendency (hardly a strategy) that does little to help defeat the Right. The Right is better at forging a strategic front even when it is ideologically divided: "The activists of the Right are .... not terribly interested in pure parties or theoretical refinement, not even in ideas or morals as such" (114). Also see 80–88, 97, 109, 113. For Gitlin the aim is not only to better theorize, but to better strategize and win power.

117. I borrow the term "unpartied Left" from Steele, *Emergence of Cultural Studies,* 27. Stanley Aronowitz notes: "Marx, Lenin, and Rosa Luxemburg had warned against a too complete reliance by working-class organizations on parliamentary and electoral processes, institutions that according to Marxist theory were perfectly suited to incorporation of working-class demands without yielding capitalist power" (*Roll over Beethoven: The Return of Cultural Strife* [Hanover, NH: Wesleyan University Press, 1993], 101). Perry Anderson's *Arguments within English Marxism* is highly skeptical of reformist parliamentarism and features provocative discussions about William Morris's antielectoral arguments (178–79), Morris's later support for electoral activism (182–84, 190), and Thompson's parliamentarism (193). Anderson also offers critiques of the Labour Party, parliament, and electoral strategies as structural manifestations of the capitalist problem (196, 205).

118. Matthiessen, "Education of a Socialist," in *F. O. Matthiessen,* ed. Sweezy and Huberman, 7. Matthiessen against the lesser of two evils, *From the Heart of Europe,* 194.

119. James, *American Civilization* (Cambridge, MA: Blackwell, 1993), 258. James wrote his draft of this book in 1950, but it was not published in his lifetime.

120. James, *American Civilization,* 258. Cole, *The People's Front* (London: Victor Gollancz, 1937). For more information on Cole's critical stance toward the Labour Party, his socialist internationalism, and his socialist morality, see Woodhams, *History in the Making* 164, 166, 181.

121. Miliband, "The Politics of the Long Haul," *Monthly Review* 10 (Feb. 1959): 379–91, see 389, 382, 391.

122. Williams is quoted in Dworkin, *Cultural Marxism in Postwar Britain,* 149.

123. See Woodhams, *History in the Making:* 149; 141; 158, 180, 181; 150, 156, 160–61; 162. Consult Dworkin, Cultural *Marxism in Postwar Britain:* 47–48; 50–53; 48; 49; 49, 132; 62; 67; 69; 63–64; 57.

124. Mills, "Complacent," 393; "Decline," 227, 228; 232; "Knowledge and Power," 609; "Cultural Apparatus," 416; "Culture and Politics," 242 in Mills, *Power, Politics, and People,* ed. Horowitz.

125. Editor, "Letter to Readers," *Universities and Left Review* 5 (Sept.–Oct. 1960): 72.

126. Editor [Hall], "Editorial," 3, and Hall, "'First,'" in *Out of Apathy,* ed. Archer et al. (1989), 35. For detailed discussions of Morris's developing politics, see E. P. Thompson, *William Morris: Romantic to Revolutionary* (London: Lawrence and Wishart, 1955) and Perry Anderson's chapter, "Utopias," in *Arguments within English Marxism,* 157–75.

127. Editor [Hall], "Editorial," 1. Hall's "as well" is crucial: "The humanist strengths of socialism—which are the foundations for a genuinely popular socialist movement—must be developed in cultural and social terms, as well as in economic and political" (1).

128. Williams, "Splits, Pacts and Coalitions," *New Socialist* 16 (March–April 1984): 31–35, see 34.

129. Williams "Hesitations Before Socialism," 34.

130. Thompson, "William Morris," in *American Threat,* 30.

131. Consult Hall, "Faith, Hope or Clarity," *Marxism Today* 29 (Jan. 1985): 15–19, see 16.

132. Rustin, "The New Left as a Social Movement," in *Out of Apathy,* ed. Archer et al. (1989), 117–27, see 120.

133. David Edgar, "Never the Old: Learning from the Sixties," *New Socialist* 38 (May 1986): 16–20, see 19.

134. Hall, "Face the Future," *New Socialist* 19 (Sept. 1984): 37, 39, see 37. Also see Williams, "Ideas and the Labour Movement."

135. Consult Hall, "Gramsci and Us," 20 and Roger Simon, "Gramsci: A Glossary of Revolution," *Marxism Today* 31 (April 1987): v.

136. Hall, "Faith, Hope or Clarity," 19. Hall writes: "To win the class argument, class and society wide issues have to be constructed together in a broad, popular strategy, advancing and winning converts on several fronts at once" (19).

137. Hall, "'First,'" in *Out of Apathy,* ed. Archer at al. (1989), 34.

138. Samuel, "Born-again Socialism," in *Out of Apathy,* ed. Archer at al. (1989), 50.

139. Miliband, "The Sickness of Labourism," *New Left Review* (Jan.–Feb. 1960): 5–9; Jones, "The Man from the Labour," *New Left Review* (Jan.–Feb. 1960): 14–17; Samuel, "The Deference Voter," *New Left Review* (Jan.–Feb. 1960): 9–13.

140. Hoggart, "Speaking to Each Other," in *Conviction,* ed. MacKenzie, 136.

141. Hall "Face the Future," 37.

142. Williams, "Culture is Ordinary," in *Conviction,* ed. MacKenzie, 74–92, see 91.

143. Samuel, "Doing Dirt on the Miners," *New Socialist* 42 (Oct. 1986): 12–16, see 16.

144. Hall, "Gramsci and Us," 21.

145. Mike Davis, "The Barren Marriage of American Labour and the Democratic Party," *New Left Review* 124 (Nov.–Dec. 1980): 43–84, see 83. On the Democratic Party's dealings with the Democratic Socialists of America, see Mike Davis, "The Lesser Evil? The Left and the Democratic Party," *New Left Review* 155 (Jan.–Feb. 1986): 5–36.

146. Riesman, "Some Observations on Community Plans and Utopia," 177.

147. Ralph Clifford, "We Need a Party," *Monthly Review* 8 (May 1956): 20–22, see 21. More generally see the readers and editors dialogue section in which this is included, "Problems of American Socialism" (13–23). Thompson Conley wrote C. Wright Mills that members of his Workers Party chose to rename themselves the Independent Socialist League because they held no electoral power. Rather than trying to put candidates up for office, they determined to concentrate their efforts on political education. In addition, the popular linkage of socialism

with Stalinism hurt them, and they wanted to get their organization excised from the attorney general's subversive list (April 26, 1949, DM).

148. Editors, "A Word to Our Readers," *Dissent* 1 (Winter 1954): 3–4, see 3.

149. Howe, "Does It Hurt When You Laugh?" *Dissent* 1 (Winter 1954): 4–7, see 7.

150. M. Rubel, "The Uses of the Word 'Socialism,'" *Dissent* 1 (Winter 1954): 10–11, see 11.

151. Lewis Coser, "Sects and Sectarians," *Dissent* 1 (Autumn 1954): 360–69, see 369.

152. See two untitled responses to Rubel's piece: Travers Clement, former national secretary, Socialist Party, *Dissent* 1 (Summer 1954): 286–87 and Sebastian Frank, a veteran European Socialist, *Dissent* 1 (Summer 1954): 287–89.

153. Gordon Haskell, "A Socialist Organization in the U. S. Today?—Yes!" *Dissent* 2 (Summer 1955): 271–78, see 271, 275, 273, 275, 277. Directly following Haskell's essay is Coser, "Lewis Coser replies," 278–79, see 278.

154. Rosenberg, "Marxism: Criticism and/or Action," *Dissent* 3 (Fall 1956): 366–75, see 369 and also 371.

155. Stanley R. Plastrik, "British Labour in Retrospect," *Dissent* 1 (Winter 1954): 75–91. Cole, "Socialism and the Welfare State," *Dissent* 1 (Autumn 1954): 315–31, see 331. S. P. [Sidney R. Plastrik], "British Labour's Defeat," *Dissent* 2 (Summer 1955): 198–200. William J. Newman, "British Labour's Self-Examination," *Dissent* 2 (Summer 1955): 264–68. G. L. Arnold, "British Socialism: Ferment and Polemic," *Dissent* 4 (Winter 1957): 70–75. Michael Walzer, "Hungary and the Failure of the Left," *Dissent* 4 (Spring 1957): 157–62. On the American scene, see Michael Walzer, "The Travail of the U.S. Communists," *Dissent* 3 (Fall 1956): 406–10, and David C. Williams, "How Liberals Survive in Washington," *Dissent* 4 (Summer 1957): 250–54. Compare two documents in Matthiessen's papers: a flyer for the newly organized *Partisan Review* (1937) and a brochure announcing the publication of *Monthly Review* (c. 1948). *Monthly Review* stated its interest in the transformation of America "from a capitalist to a socialist society . . . not only for Americans but for all mankind." *Partisan Review* enunciated its sponsorship of "revolutionary," "dissident," and "experimental" points of view that focused not on politics per se but on culture. Its aim was not so much the transformation of society as of "consciousness." It assured readers—well before the rise of Senator Joseph McCarthy—that it permitted "no commitments, either tacit or avowed, to any political party or group." This "Marxist literary monthly" defined Left as being nonaligned, uncommitted, "controversial." The restoration of "the integrity of the Left" seemed to warrant confining "politics" to culture and journals (FOM).

156. Editor [Hall], "Editorial," NLR 1960. For Hall's more recent views on some of these concerns, see Kuan-Hsing Chen, "The Formation of a Diasporic Intellectual: An Interview with Stuart Hall," in *Stuart Hall: Critical Dialogues in Cultural Studies,* ed. David Morley and Kuan-Hsing Chen (New York: Routledge, 1996), 484–503. Thinking about his position as a black Jamaican in relation to the Labour Party, its Englishness, its campaigns, and its constituencies, Hall acknowledges: "I was always reluctant to go canvassing for the Labour Party. I don't find it easy to say, straight, face to face, with an English working-class family, 'Are you going to vote for us?' I just don't know how to utter that sentence" (494). Yet it is noteworthy that he used the pronoun "us" in this sentence he cannot utter.

157. Ehrenreich, "Democrats and the Pot of (Electoral) Gold," *New Socialist* 18 (July–August 1984): 23–25, see 23–24.

158. On socialist "renewal," see Hall, "In Praise of the Peculiar," *Marxism Today* 31 (April 1987): vi–vii, see vii.

159. James, *American Civilization*, 274, 275.

160. On Matthiessen and Wallace, see Cain, *F. O. Matthiessen and the Politics of Criticism*, 107–114.

Notes for Chapter 3

1. Lynd, *Knowledge for What?*, 130. Mackenzie, "After the Stalemate State," in *Conviction*, ed. Mackenzie, 7–8. Žižek, *For They Know Not What They Do: Enjoyment as a Political Factor* (New York: Verso, 2002 [1991]), 273.

2. See chapter 1, "The Americanization of Cultural Studies." See C. Hall, "Missionary Stories: Gender and Ethnicity in England in the 1830s and 1840s," 240–70, and "Discussion," 270–76, and Steedman, "Culture, Cultural Studies, and the Historians," 613–21, and "Discussion," 621–22, in *Cultural Studies*, ed. Grossberg, Nelson, and Treichler: all quotations from C. Hall, Steedman, and the questions in response to their presentations are from this book and will be followed by page numbers from this book in parentheses.

3. Hall was not alone in learning the postwar version of this lesson about past and present. In 1958 Norman MacKenzie, an editor of *New Statesman*, underscored the importance of keeping the memory of socialist movements and practices alive while not being disabled by them. "Almost all our politicians, and most of the voting public, had their ideas and attitudes fashioned in a different age . . . . [Today] it is easier to fall back upon the old clichés. It is this that has given such an air of irrelevance to so much of British politics since 1945, that has made people less sure what ought to be done, and what can be done" ("After the Stalemate State," in *Conviction*, ed. MacKenzie, 12). "Conference Scrapbook," in *Out of Apathy*, ed. Archer et al. (1989), 129–41, see 134.

4. Hall, Samuel, Taylor, "Then and Now," in *Out of Apathy* (1989), 169 (born again), 170 (Heraclitus).

5. Mulhern, *Culture/Metaculture* (London: Routledge, 2000), 162.

6. Jameson, "On 'Cultural Studies,'" 18.

7. Steinberg, "Cultural History and Cultural Studies," in *Disciplinarity and Dissent in Cultural Studies*, ed. Cary Nelson and Dilip Parameshwar Gaonkar (New York: Routledge, 1996): all quotations from Steinberg's essay in this book will be followed by page numbers in parentheses.

8. Berger et al., *Ways of Seeing*, 11.

9. For some interesting historical analyses of this see *In Defense of History: Marxism and the Postmodern Agenda*, ed. Ellen Meiksins Wood and John Bellamy Foster (New York: Monthly Review Press, 1997).

10. The faculty and graduate students at the Birmingham Centre in the 1970s studied Benjamin and Weber as foundational resources for the development of a theoretically complex cultural studies. Hall writes: "We read Weber, we read German idealism, we read Benjamin, Lukács, in an attempt to correct what we thought of as the unworkable way class reductionism had deformed classical Marxism, preventing it from dealing with cultural questions seriously" (Chen, "Formation of a Diasporic Intellectual," in *Stuart Hall*, ed. Morley and Chen, 499).

11. Dorothy Thompson, "Introduction," in E. P. Thompson, *The Poverty of Theory: Or an Orrery of Errors* (London: Merlin Press, 1995): all quotations from this introduction will be followed by page numbers in parentheses.

12. In *Cultural Studies and Beyond,* Davies makes some provocative yet problematic assertions about the Thompsons's class stature. He acknowledges Thompson's immersion in activist—more than academic—culture, but also casts him as an independently wealthy "member of the left aristocracy of letters" and "the creative 'aristocratic' marabout of British intellectual life," whose "activism ... was made possible by an aristocratic lifestyle" (53). Thompson's activist campaigns, he reports, were "conducted from a farmhouse or a bishop's palace in Halifax, Lemingtom Spa, or Wick" (50). Yet he also quotes Dorothy Thompson as saying that they had little money when Edward began teaching for the Workers Education Association in 1948 (although family support prevented them from getting into "a situation in which lack of money could have been an absolute disaster'" [66]) and notes that Dorothy taught at Birmingham for several years during the 1970s (53). How detailed is Davies's knowledge of the Thompsons' life together—which they kept rather private? Offering what seems to be a crude materialist complicity critique, he appears to conclude that Thompson's radicalism was somehow automatically tainted because of his class: "Most of the people who helped to put together the cultural politics of Britain in the 1970s and 1980s did not operate from bishoprics in Worcester: they operated from tenement houses in Salford, Leeds or north London, or else tried to negotiate mortgages on slender salaries" (53). It may well be that Thompson's financial position, class instruction, and public school (32) as well as Cambridge background strengthened his social self-confidence and informed his "evangelical" (42) zeal, but I am in no way persuaded that the homes he lived in compromised his ceaseless efforts on behalf of the Left, labor movements, and antinuclear campaigns. If Thompson was so rich, why didn't he bail out the *New Left Review* financially in 1963 rather than surrendering it with a struggle to the independently wealthy Perry Anderson? Thompson, a complex figure, had enormous integrity and intelligence. On another matter, there is something in what Davies says about Thompson's view of history as the quintessential political discipline: "For Williams the issue was not English as an academic discipline (contrasted, for example, with E. P. Thompson's almost paranoid sense that history *was* the discipline) but that English was the frame that provided the base for going beyond" (59). Yet this overlooks Thompson's "cultural studies" range of interests in writing and reading poetry, writing literary criticism, teaching literature (which he did for the first few years he taught in the Workers Education Association) and contemporary critique. Thompson's degree at Cambridge was in English as well as history (a flexible combination made possible by the impact that World War II had on Cambridge's requirements for returning students).

13. See the E. P. Thompson interview in MARHO, The Radical Historians Organization, *Visions of History,* ed. Henry Abelove, Betsy Blackmar, Peter Dimock, and Jonathan Schneer (New York: Pantheon, 1983): 5–25, all quotations from this interview will be followed by page numbers in parentheses. I concur with Perry Anderson that Thompson's "works of history have ... been deliberate and focused contributions to theory" and that "every major, and nearly every minor, work he has written concludes with an avowed and direct reflection on its lessons for socialists of his own time" (*Arguments within English Marxism,* 2, 1).

14. For an astute analysis of Thompson's historical project—especially his consistent linkage of literature, history, and politics—see Henry Abelove's wide-ranging review essay on Thompson's *Poverty of Theory* in *History and Theory* 21 (1982): 132–42.

15. In 1985 Thompson approached his homage to C. Wright Mills not just as a historian but as a theorist. "There is a tension in his writing between the Marxist concept of 'class,' Weber's terminology of 'status,' and his own preferred language of 'structure' and 'elites,' which—while

fruitful in descriptive analysis—is never resolved on a theoretical plane" ("Remembering C. Wright Mills," 263).

16. Thompson and Althusser were not polar opposites. In *Cultural Marxism in Postwar Britain*, Dworkin observes: "Despite their vast difference, Athusser's and Thompson's projects were formed in common opposition to the ossification of Marxist thought that occurred during the Stalin era" (226). He also repeats Perry Anderson's point that both Althusser and Thompson had embraced Eurocommunism and "social democratic strategies" (233). Building on some of Hall's remarks, Dworkin notes that by 1978, when Thompson published *Poverty of Theory*, "the Althusserian onslaught in Britain and elsewhere was already beginning to recede, a result of an accumulation of critiques, including many from the crumbling ranks of theoretical practice itself" (232). I was privileged to see Thompson deliver his polemic against Althusser at the University of Sussex in 1977 and the heat of the debate seemed to be at full boil.

17. See Colin Sparks, "Stuart Hall, Cultural Studies, and Marxism," in *Stuart Hall*, ed. Morley and Chen, 71–101. During Hoggart's regime the center was not the theoretical hothouse it became in the 1970s: "The version of cultural studies which developed, increasingly focused around the Birmingham Centre, in the 1960s was thus one in which the explicit legacy of Marxism was more or less absent. If one examines the early self-published Occasional Papers of the Center, its Annual Reports, or the more formally published work it inspired, there is little evidence of the kind of intellectual upheavals that were imminent." Sparks characterizes Hoggart as untouched "by theory, let alone Marxism" (79).

18. Hindess and Hirst, *Pre-Capitalist Modes of Production* (London: Routledge and Kegan Paul, 1975): all quotations from this book will be followed by page numbers in parentheses.

19. Having gotten the spotlight with such claims, Hindess and Hirst followed up this book with another, *Mode of Production and Social Formation: An Auto-Critique of Pre-Capitalist Modes of Production* (London: Macmillan, 1977).

20. Thompson, *Poverty of Theory*, 5.

21. Samuel, "History and Theory," in *People's History and Socialist Theory*, ed. Samuel, xl–lvi, see xliii.

22. See Abelove's 1982 *History and Theory* review of Thompson's *Poverty of Theory*, 134.

23. Hall, "In Defence of Theory," in *People's History and Socialist Theory*, ed. Samuel, 378–85, see 381.

24. Johnson, "Thompson, Genovese, and Socialist-Humanist History," *History Workshop Journal* 6 (Autumn 1978): 79–100: all quotations from this article will be followed by page numbers in parentheses.

25. Johnson's and Stedman Jones's untitled letters are published in *History Workshop Journal* (Autumn 1979): 196–98 (Johnson's letter, the quotation is on 196) and 198–202 (Stedman Jones's letter, the references are to 198 and 199).

26. Samuel, "Editorial Note," in *People's History and Socialist Theory*, ed. Samuel, 376–78, see 377.

27. See Hall, "In Defence of Theory," Johnson, "Against Absolutism," 386–96, Thompson, "The Politics of Theory," 396–408, in *People's History and Socialist Theory*, ed. Samuel: all quotations from this Hall-Thompson-Johnson debate published in *People's History* will be followed by page numbers in parentheses.

28. On Johnson's appointment see Dworkin, *Cultural Marxism in Postwar Britain*, 220, and on the offices, see Davies, *Cultural Studies and Beyond*, 41.

29. Schwarz, "'The People' in History: The Communist Party Historians' Group, 1946–56," in *Making Histories*, ed. Johnson, McLennan, Schwarz, and Sutton, 44–95, see 44: all quotations from this book will be followed by page numbers in parentheses. No doubt, some dialogues between members of the Birmingham history department and the center were productive. For instance, a piece by the centre's Bill Schwarz on the Communist Party Historians Group's construction of "the people" includes grateful acknowledgment of Hilton's reading of the manuscript.

30. For a theoretically sophisticated update of this sort of critique of Thompson, see Michael E. Brown, "History and History's Problem," *Social Text* 16 (Winter 1986/87): 136–61. I am grateful to my colleague Henry Abelove both for lending me some of the Birmingham Centre's "stenciled occasional papers" from the History Series (from his collection) and for alerting me to the importance of considering the relationship between the center historians and the history department historians at Birmingham.

31. Raphael Samuel, "Afterword: History Workshop, 1966–80," in *People's History and Socialist Theory*, ed. Samuel, 410–17, see 410, 411, 410.

32. See Hall's comments about this phase in Chen, "Formation of a Diasporic Intellectual," in *Stuart Hall*, ed. Morley and Chen, 492–97. Also see Kenny's useful *First New Left*, 54–68. For a brilliant historical and political analysis of the production of Left critique in this period, see Sinfield, *Literature Politics and Culture*, especially 232–76.

33. These included: *Culture, Ideology and Politics: Essays for Eric Hobsbawm* (1982), ed. Raphael Samuel and Stedman Jones; *People's History and Socialist Theory* (1981), ed. Raphael Samuel; *Socialism and the Intelligentsia, 1880–1914* (1987), ed. Carl Levy; *Sex and Class in Women's History* (1983), ed. Judith L. Newton, Mary P. Ryan, and Judith Walkowitz; *The Progress of Romance: The Politics of Popular Fiction* (1986), ed. Jean Radford; and *Language, Gender, and Childhood* (1985), ed. Carolyn Steedman, Cathy Urwin, and Valerie Walkerdine.

34. See Bloch, *The Historian's Craft*, trans. Peter Putnam (New York: Vintage, 1953). Bloch wrote: "Misunderstanding of the present is the inevitable consequence of ignorance of the past. But a man may wear himself out just as fruitlessly in seeking to understand the past, if he is totally ignorant of the present" (43). And: "Some men will always specialize in the present, as others do in the Stone Age or Egyptology. We simply ask both to bear in mind that historical research will tolerate no autarchy. Isolated, each will understand only by halves, even within his own field of study" (47). Samuel mentions Bloch's advocacy of "present-minded" historical practice in his "Afterword: History Workshop, 1966–80," in *People's History and Socialist Theory*, ed. Samuel, 416. Editors, "History Workshop Journal," *History Workshop Journal* 1 (Spring 1976): 1–3.

35. Alexander and Davin, "Feminist History," *History Workshop Journal* 1 (Spring 1976): 4–6, the quotations are on 4.

36. Samuel and Stedman Jones, "Sociology and History," *History Workshop Journal* 1 (Spring 1976): 6–8, my summary refers to 7. This was seen as an important theoretical move in this period. Peter Burke notes that in the 1970s the great Marxist sociologist Tom Bottomore asked Burke (both taught at the University of Sussex) to write a book on "Sociology and History"—an effort that would extend Burke's interdisciplinary teaching on "Social Structure and Social Change." The outcome in 1980 was Burke's useful book, later revised and republished as *History and Social Theory* (Ithaca, NY: Cornell University Press, 1992), see vii. In the United States some inventive sociologists were exploring history in significant ways. For example, see Richard Sennett, *The Fall of Public Man: On the Social Psychology of Capitalism*, and Eli Zaretsky, *Capitalism, the Family, and Personal Life*.

37. Samuel, "Foreword," in *People's History and Socialist Theory,* ed. Samuel, xi–xiii, see xi.

38. Samuel, "Afterword: History Workshop, 1966–80," in *People's History and Socialist Theory,* ed. Samuel, 414, 415.

39. Samuel, "History and Theory," in *People's History and Socialist Theory,* ed. Samuel: all quotations from this essay will be followed by page numbers in parentheses.

40. Samuel tried to do here—historicize theoretical and historical work—what most cultural studies scholars did not do with their appropriations of Gramsci and Althusser in the 1970s and 1980s. Too many American cultural studies practitioners repeated this pattern in their decontextualization of British cultural studies work in the 1980s. Recent work has more successfully historicized cultural studies theorizing (for example, Davies' *Cultural Studies and Beyond,* Dworkin's *Cultural Marxism in Postwar Britain,* Steele's *Emergence of Cultural Studies,* Woodhams's *History in the Making*).

41. Hall, "Cultural Studies and Its Theoretical Legacies," in *Cultural Studies,* ed. Grossberg, Nelson, and Treichler, 277–86, see 282. Also see Chen, "Formation of a Diasporic Intellectual," in *Stuart Hall,* ed. Morley and Chen, for Hall's somewhat different account about mid-1970s feminism and the Centre: "Michael Green and myself [*sic*] decided to try and invite some feminists, working outside, to come to the Centre, in order to project the question of feminism into the center. So the 'traditional' story that feminism originally erupted from *within* cultural studies is not quite right. We were very anxious to open that link, partly because we were both, at that time, living with feminists. We were working in cultural studies, but were in conversation with feminism" (499). As feminism did take hold, teaching became more challenging for Hall: "[I]f I had been opposed to feminism, that would have been a different thing, but I was for it. So, being targeted as 'the enemy,' as the senior patriarchal figure, placed me in an impossibly contradictory position.... Living with politics is different from being abstractly in favour of it. I was checkmated by feminists; I couldn't come to terms with it, in the Centre's work.... I couldn't live part of the time being their teacher, and being their father, being hated for being their father, and being set up as if I was an anti-feminist man.... So I wanted to leave" (500). So he did, for the Open University.

42. Hall, "C. L. R. James," *History Workshop Journal* (Spring 1990): 214.

43. See "Eric Foner," interview in *Columbian Seventy-Three: Columbia College, Barnard College* (1973) (no other publication information): 43–45: all quotations from this interview will be followed by page numbers in parentheses.

44. Bruck, "Renegades and Troublemakers," *The New Journal* (March 2, 1984): 48–55, see 49: all quotations from this article will be followed by page numbers in parentheses.

45. See Staughton Lynd's autobiographical essays in his *Living inside Our Hope: A Steadfast Radical's Thoughts on Rebuilding the Movement* (Ithaca, NY: ILR Press, 1997). For the rest of this chapter, all endnote references to publications by Lynd will mean Staughton Lynd. Also see MARHO, *Visions of History,* ed. Abelove, Blackmar, Dimock, and Schneer, 149–65.

46. Lynd, *Living Inside Our Hope,* 25.

47. See Robert B. Westbrook, "C[omer] Vann Woodward," in *A Companion to American Thought,* ed. Richard Wightman Fox and James T. Kloppenberg (Cambridge, MA.: Blackwell, 1995), 745–46, see 746.

48. See Woodward's 1969 presidential address to the American Historical Association, "The Future of the Past," in his *The Future of the Past* (New York: Oxford University Press, 1989), 3–28. Excoriating both radicals and conservatives who import political agendas to history, he writes: "Those Americans who pursue the usable past have unconsciously assumed

a space-time continuum that confuses forbears with descendants and homogenizes time past with time present. Whether they are conservatives with friendly and affectionate feelings toward the past or radicals with cynical and iconoclastic attitudes, the resulting confusion is the same. A fatal betrayal of the craft would be to permit the profession of history to become inextricably entangled with the future of the past, the purposeful past of the rationalizers, the justifiers, and the propagandists" (23). By contrast, see his Yale colleague's presidential address to the Organization of American Historians in 1972: Edmund S. Morgan, "Slavery and Freedom: The American Paradox," *Journal of American History* 59 (June 1972): 5–29. Morgan, clearly influenced by the social movements of the 1960s as well as by new historical scholarship, acknowledged the challenge that radical historians interested in the contradiction of slavery posed to more mainstream historians who stressed the American foundations of liberty: "Colonial historians, in particular, when writing about the origin and development of American institutions have found it possible until recently to deal with slavery as an exception to everything they had to say. I am speaking about myself but also about most of my generation. We owe a debt of gratitude to those who have insisted that slavery was something more than an exception, that one fifth of the American population at the time of the Revolution is too many people to be treated as an exception" (5). His first footnote read: "Particularly Staughton Lynd, *Class Conflict, Slavery, and the United States Constitution: Ten Essays* (Indianapolis, 1967)." Morgan went on to offer a dazzling reading of landowners' anxieties about class conflict in colonial Virginia (conflict with a roaming population of newly freed but landless indentured servants) that led to the increased abduction, transport, and use of Africans as slaves to support the tobacco economy, the wealthy, and the potent rhetoric of universal liberty (universal for some). Morgan concluded by using his analysis of the past to suggest that it can help illuminate the "contradictions" of the present: "Thus began the American paradox of slavery and freedom, intertwined and interdependent, the rights of Englishmen supported on the wrongs of Africans. The American Revolution only made the contradictions more glaring, as the slaveholding colonists proclaimed to a candid world the rights not simply of Englishmen but of all men…. [This explanation] may perhaps make us wonder about the ties that bind more devious tyrannies to our own freedoms and give us still today our own American paradox" (29). Morgan did not—unlike the radical historians he lauded—endeavor to explicate the "ties" between contemporary "devious tyrannies" and "our own freedoms," or specify the new "American paradox." Morgan further developed his thesis in his classic study, *American Slavery—American Freedom: The Ordeal of Colonial Virginia* (New York: Norton, 1975).

49. See Lynd, "Historical Past and Existential Present," in *The Dissenting Academy,* ed. Theodore Roszak (New York: Vintage, 1968), 92–109, see 95.

50. Lynd, "Historical Past," in *Dissenting Academy,* ed. Roszak, 96.

51. Lynd, "Historical Past," in *Dissenting Academy,* ed. Roszak, 97.

52. Lynd, "Historical Past," in *Dissenting Academy,* ed. Roszak, 102.

53. Lynd, "Historical Past," in *Dissenting Academy,* ed. Roszak, 103, 104. For a similar discussion about planning the future, see Thompson's "Revolution," in E. P. Thompson et al. *Out of Apathy,* 287–308.

54. Lynd, "Historical Past," in *Dissenting Academy,* ed. Roszak, 109. Lynd published histories, activist tracts, and social planning works, and often synthesized them, as he did in his book with Gar Alperovitz, *Strategy and Program: Two Essays toward a New Socialism* (1973), which uses the labor and political movements of the 1930s to analyze the present and propose a future.

55. Lynd, *Living Inside Our Hope,* 115.

56. Lynd, *Living Inside Our Hope,* 116.

57. Lynd, *Living Inside Our Hope,* 117, 121, 114.

58. Lynd, *Living Inside Our Hope,* 112.

59. Thompson, "Homage to Thomas McGrath," 327, 329.

60. See Zinn and Barsamian's conversation about "How Social Change Happens," in Howard Zinn, *The Future of History: Interviews with David Barsamian* (Monroe, ME: Common Courage Press, 1999), 27–45. Also see Barbara Miner's interview with Zinn, "Why Students Should Study History: An Interview," in Howard Zinn with Donaldo Macedo, *Howard Zinn on Democratic Education* (Boulder, CO: Paradigm, 2005), 187–200.

61. Zinn, "'Who Controls the Past Controls the Future': Interview with David Barsamian," in Howard Zinn, *The Failure to Quit: Reflections of an Optimistic Historian* (Monroe, ME: Common Courage, Press, 1993), 3–21, see 9.

62. See Zinn, "The Politics of History in the Era of the Cold War: Repression and Resistance," in Noam Chomsky et al., *The Cold War and the University: Toward an Intellectual History of the Cold War Years* (New York: The New Press, 1997), 35–72, see 35.

63. Zinn, "'Who Controls the Past Controls the Future,'" 10.

64. Zinn, "Politics of History," 38.

65. Zinn, *You Can't Be Neutral on a Moving Train: A Personal History of Our Times* (Boston: Beacon Press, 1994), on this period in Zinn's life see 15–45, the quotation is on 26.

66. Zinn, *You Can't Be Neutral,* 24.

67. Zinn, *You Can't Be Neutral,* 32.

68. See the South End Press Collective's interview with Zinn, "A New Great Movement," in their *Talking about a Revolution* (Boston: South End Press, 1998), 113–24, see 114.

69. Zinn, "Marxism and the New Left," in *Dissent: Explorations in the History of American Radicalism,* ed. Alfred F. Young (Dekalb: Northern Illinois University Press, 1968), 357–72, see 360, 362.

70. Zinn, "'Who Controls the Past Controls the Future,'" 11. Similarly, Richard Slotkin notes that "To be construed as 'history' ... facts must be selected and arranged on some sort of plan.... All history writing requires a fictive or imaginary representation of the past.... Historians like to associate their field with the social sciences, but in fact the discipline is more like novel writing" ("Fiction for the Purposes of History," 222).

71. See Lemisch, "The Radicalism of the Inarticulate: Merchant Seamen in the Politics of Revolutionary America," in *Dissent,* ed. Young, 37–82, see 58. Also see Lemisch and John K. Alexander, "The White Oaks, Jack Tar, and the Concept of the 'Inarticulate,'" *William and Mary Quarterly* 29 (Jan. 1972): 109–34 and Lemish, "Listening to the 'Inarticulate': William Widger's Dream and the Loyalties of American Revolutionary Seamen in British Prisons," *Journal of Social History* 3 (Fall 1969): 1–29. See the interview with Hobsbawm in MARHO, *Visions of History,* ed. Abelove, Blackmar, Dimock, and Schneer, 29–46.

72. Lemisch, *On Active Service in War and Peace: Politics and Ideology in the American Historical Profession* (Toronto: New Hogtown Press, 1975): all quotations from this book will be followed by page numbers in parentheses.

73. Writing of the relationship between the American student New Left and the increasing visibility of radical historians, Peter Novick observes: "Both arose around 1960 in a climate characterized by the decline of McCarthyism, frustration with the mindlessness of politics in the Eisenhower years, admiration for the emerging civil rights movement in the South, the first stirrings of opposition to the nuclear arms race, and the turmoil in the Communist movement

occasioned by Khruschev's Twentieth Party Congress speech and the Soviet suppression of the Hungarian Revolution" (*That Noble Dream: The "Objectivity Question" and the American Historical Profession* [New York: Cambridge University Press, 1988], 418). On the American New Left, see *The New Left: A Collection of Essays*, ed. Priscilla Long (Boston: Porter Sargent, 1969); Christopher Lasch, *The Agony of the New Left* (New York: Alfred Knopf, 1969); Wini Breines, *Community and Organization in the New Left: 1962–1968: The Great Refusal* (South Hadley, MA: J. F. Bergin, 1982); and *"Takin' It to the Streets": A Sixties Reader*, ed. Alexander Bloom and Wini Breines (New York: Oxford University Press, 1995). Work by New Left–era radical historians has been collected in *Dissent*, ed. Young (1968); *Towards a New Past: Dissenting Essays in American History*, ed. Barton J. Bernstein (New York: Pantheon, 1968); *Past Imperfect: Alternative Essays in American History*, ed. Barton J. Bernstein; Blanche W. Cook, Alice K. Harris, Ronald Radosh (New York: Knopf, 1973).

74. Genovese, "Marxian Interpretations of the Slave South," reprinted in his *In Red and Black: Marxian Explorations in Southern and Afro-American History* (New York: Pantheon, 1971), 315–53, see 351.

75. Genovese, "On Antonio Gramsci," reprinted in his *Red and Black*, 391–422: all quotations from this article will be followed by page numbers in parentheses. For a more detailed discussion of some of these issues and related ones, see Anne Showstack Sassoon, *Gramsci's Politics* (New York: St. Martin's Press, 1980). Sassoon, who taught at Kingston Polytechnic when she published this book, does not mention Genovese's piece.

76. Williams, *Marxism and Literature*, and Hall, "Gramsci's Relevance for the Study of Race and Ethnicity," reprinted in *Stuart Hall*, ed. Morley and Chen, 411–40.

77. Genovese, "Staughton Lynd as Historian and Ideologue," reprinted in his *Red and Black*, 354–67, see 356.

78. Ellen Ross and Judith Walkowitz, "Raphael Samuel (1934–1996): An Appreciation," 275–79, and the anonymous piece (reprinted from the *Guardian*), "In Memory: Raphael Samuel," 280–84, in *Radical History Review* 69 (Fall 1997).

79. The Boston Collective, "Editors' Introduction," *Radical History Review* 19 (Winter 1978–1979): 3–5, the quotations are on 3.

80. Sue Benson, Jane Caplan, Ellen Ross, and Sean Wilentz, "Editorial," *History Workshop Journal* 22 (Autumn 1986): n.p.

81. See Michael Merrill and Michael Wallace, "Marxism and History," in *The Left Academy: Marxist Scholarship on American Campuses*, ed. Bertell Ollman and Edward Vernoff (New York: McGraw Hill, 1982), 202–42. Merrill and Wallace write the following about the American scene: "Whereas the previous generation of Marxist scholars—including, most notably, Herbert Aptheker and Philip Foner—had to work for much of their lives in relative academic isolation, the number of radical and Marxist scholars in the United States has increased tremendously since the 1960s. As a result, Marxists and radicals have begun, for the first time, to exercise some influence over the historical profession; for example, three of the last four presidents of the Organization of American Historians—Eugene Genovese, Gerda Lerner, and William Appleman Williams—have been leftists. This rapid growth in Marxist scholarship makes it difficult to encompass all that has been done in a short survey article such as this one" (215). Overall, their thirty-nine-page survey does give a fuller picture of radical historical work produced in the United States, especially since 1960, than one might infer from the American editors' comments in the *Special American Issue* of *History Workshop Journal*. Also see Richard Flacks, *Making History: The American Left and the American Mind* (New York: Columbia University Press, 1988), especially his chapter "Struggling for a Better Day: The Left Tradition in American History," 98–192.

82. Howe, "Notes on Mass Culture," *politics* 5 (Spring 1948): 120–123. Walter Benjamin, "The Work of Art in the Epoch of Mechanical Reproduction," translated by H. H. Gerth and Don Martindale, *Studies on the Left* 1 (Winter 1960): 28–46.

83. Thompson, "Preface," in Staughton Lynd, *Class Conflict, Slavery, and the United States Constitution* (Indianapolis: Bobbs-Merrill, 1967), ix–xiii: all quotations from this preface will be followed by page numbers in parentheses.

84. Montgomery, "Introduction," in Chomsky, et al., *Cold War and the University*, xi–xxxvii, see xvi. Also consult the interview with Montgomery in MARHO, *Visions of History*, ed. Abelove, Blackmar, Dimock, and Schneer, 169–83. And also see Natalie Zemon Davis, "A Life of Learning," *American Council of Learned Societies Occasional Paper* 39 (1997): "Smith College was an exhilarating place in the years right after World War II. Young women came there from all over the United States and beyond, and a significant number of them were on scholarships.... We were activists, the class of 1949, concerned about the rebuilding of Europe, supporting the new United Nations, and creating a lasting peace in the face of the atomic bomb. Even after events began to split us along political lines—the beginnings of the Cold War, the establishment of the Communist regime in Czechoslovakia, HUAC and the Hollywood Ten—hope for the future was not extinguished and friendships remained strong. The mood was in contrast with the silences that fell only a year after we graduated, with the start of the Korean War and the intensification of the Red Hunt.... Marxist socialism was a revelation when I heard about it in my freshman year.... I imagined a future where changed structures truly transformed human behavior.... I joined organizations like the American Youth for democracy, the Marxist discussion group, and the Young Progressives, not exactly mass movements at Smith" (4). The harsh political treatment that Davis's husband and she endured for their political convictions over the next decade served to sharpen, not squelch, her critical consciousness (9–11).

85. *History Workshop Journal* (which published Mary Ryan, Eric Foner, and other American historians) and *Radical History Review* (which published Thompson, Hobsbawm, and other British historians) were in sync with one another, while *New Left Review* and *Studies on the Left* were also attuned to one another (for instance, they both published the same article on the New Left by C. Wright Mills [1961] and a review of E. P. Thompson et al., *Out of Apathy* [1960]).

86. Higham, "The Construction of American History," in *The Reconstruction of American History*, ed. John Higham (London: Hutchinson University Library, 1962), 9–24. Also see Gene Wise's *American Historical Explanations: A Strategy for Grounded Inquiry* (Minneapolis: University of Minnesota Press, 1980 [1973]).

87. For an excellent collection of articles from the journal *History and Theory*, see *History and Theory: Contemporary Readings*, ed. Brian Fay, Philip Pomper, and Richard T. Vann (Malden, MA: Blackwell, 1998). Palmer, *Descent into Discourse: The Reification of Language and the Writing of Social History* (Philadelphia: Temple University Press, 1990). Palmer writes: "It is not necessary to accept all of Edward Thompson's views on the threat posed by what he referred to as the theoreticist, structuralist Althusserianism of the late 1970s to grasp that what he feared then, and thus polemicized against, has returned in a more diversified form in the late 1980s.... Althusserianism, if not quite dead, is certainly subdued; discourse rages on, and in many historical circles is, as they say, all the rage. Within the deconstructive community the disdain for 'history' bears a remarkable similarity to the contemptuous dismissals—from Hindess and Hirst, Balibar, and others—associated with the structural Marxism of Althusser" (199). For Palmer the disciples of discourse include Michel Foucault, Hayden White, and Joan Scott. Overall, the book—which is not without its rigidities—is a provocative read. Palmer's

endnotes cover work in history, historical theory, literary theory, and cultural theory. Very different readings of the use of "discourse" in history writing can be found in *Post-structuralism and the Question of History,* ed. Geoff Bennington and Robert Young (Cambridge: Cambridge University Press, 1987). For more recent critiques of postmodern shifts in history writing, see Martin Bunzel, *Real History: Reflections on Historical Practice* (New York: Routledge, 1997), and Willie Thompson, *What Happened to History?* (London: Pluto, 2000).

88. See "Symposium: Intellectual History in the Age of Cultural Studies," *Intellectual History Newsletter* 18 (1996): 3–69: all quotations from this symposium will be followed by page numbers in parentheses.

89. For historical discussions of this relationship, see two important review essays: Robert Darnton, "Intellectual and Cultural History," in *The Past Before Us: Contemporary Historical Writing in the United States,* ed. Michael Kammen (Ithaca, NY: Cornell University Press, 1980), 327–54, and Thomas Bender, "Intellectual and Cultural History," in *The New American History,* ed. Eric Foner (Philadelphia: Temple University Press, 1997), 181–202. Consult William Bouwsma, "From the History of Ideas to History of Meaning," *Journal of Interdisciplinary History* 12 (1981): 279–91.

90. Foucault, *The Use of Pleasure: The History of Sexuality,* vol. 2, trans. Robert Hurley (New York: Vintage, 1986), 6.

91. In 1962 Raymond Williams wrote: "We are used to descriptions of our whole common life in political and economic terms. The emphasis on communications asserts, as a matter of experience, that men and societies are not confined to relationships of power, property, and production. Their relationships in describing, learning, persuading, and exchanging are seen as equally fundamental" (quoted in Dworkin, *Cultural Marxism in Postwar Britain,* 93).

92. In the British New Left period one often finds the category of "achievement" invoked by scholars whose work helped set up cultural studies.

93. John C. Burnham suggests that the way early twentieth-century American bourgeois socialists interpreted people subtextually in terms of class interests helped set the ideological stage for bourgeois Freudian and pop psychological subtextual readings of instincts and the unconscious in the United States ("The New Psychology," in *1915, The Cultural Moment,* ed. Adele Heller and Lois Rudnick [New Brunswick: Rutgers University Press, 1991], 117–27, see 121).

94. Levine, *The Opening of the American Mind: Canons, Culture, and History* (Boston: Beacon, 1996), 20. Also see Loewen, *Lies My Teacher Told Me: Everything Your American History Textbook Got Wrong* (New York: Touchstone, 1995).

95. Matthiessen, *From the Heart of Europe,* 74.

96. Editors, "Language and History," *History Workshop Journal* (Autumn 1980): 1–5, the quotation is from 5. See the letter from Andy Durr written in response to Raphael Samuel's "History and Theory" (1978) editorial: *History Workshop Journal* 7 (Spring 1979): 209. Durr notes that he had worked in the engineering trade in the 1950s and 1960s and in the 1970s teaches "an Adult Education History Workshop at Brighton Polytechnic, and [serves] also as President of my local Trades Council." He is an avid reader of *History Workshop Journal,* but feels that the "History and Theory" essay has betrayed the commitment of the journal—stated in its inaugural issue—to publish work in clear language intended for everyone interested in history: "I found the last editorial by the collective a nightmare of long words and jargon.... The whole editorial smacked of a few academics talking to other academics; there are other journals for that. The subject of the 'History of Theory' is important—don't keep it to yourselves." He drew an interesting analogy based on his work experience: "[T]oolmakers have their own

words and jargon which is in common use in toolrooms in the country. If a toolmaker were to talk and interest 'ordinary people' in tool-making he would try to use everyday language." Could the toolmaker give a detailed talk on the intricacies of "his" craft without introducing the audience to some of the key names of toolmaking tools and techniques they did not know? Suppose the toolmaker was offering an adult education course on toolmaking? How long would it be possible or desirable to speak only in "ordinary" language?

97. See Colin Sparks, "The Evolution of Cultural Studies . . . ," reprinted in *What Is Cultural Studies?*, ed. Storey, 14–30. Sparks, who originally wrote his essay for *Screen Education* in the late 1970s, observed that work on cultural studies was intense at the Birmingham Centre (where he had studied), but added that "at the same time there are people beavering away at very similar problems, writing and researching and teaching, often in considerable isolation" (14). Some progressive American studies scholars who were developing critiques of culture and history in this era—such as Alan Trachtenberg, Warren Susman, Richard Slotkin, and John Kasson—were not, however, working in such institutional isolation.

Notes for Chapter 4

1. Thompson, "William Morris," 27. Batsleer et al., *Rewriting English,* 6–7. Their volume grew out of debates in the English Studies Group at the Centre for Contemporary Cultural Studies at the University of Birmingham in the late 1970s.

2. Aronowitz, *Roll Over Beethoven,* 227–28.

3. Michael Bérubé reassures readers that rigorous institutional critiques of the corporatization of the university and of the exploitation of academic labor, the championing of graduate student unionization, and the practice of cultural studies are in no way mutually exclusive with a love of literature in *The Employment of English: Theory, Jobs, and the Future of Literary Studies* (New York: New York University Press, 1998). Also consult *The Aesthetics of Cultural Studies,* ed. Michael Bérubé (Malden, MA: Blackwell, 2005). For an insightful analysis of shifts in English department preoccupations and the reimaginings—and critiques—of literary value from the 1950s to the present, see Phyllis Rose, "The Coming of the French: My Life as an English Professor," *American Scholar* 74 (Winter 2004): 59–68.

4. See Steele, *Emergence of Cultural Studies,* on Williams, 188–89, and on Thompson, 20–21, 144 on his training and interest in being a poet, 152 on teaching. Thompson admired the Marxist literary criticism of Christopher Caudwell, 152–53. On the postwar Workers Education Association perception of English as a "woman's subject" and the idea that teaching it required some political "apology" (188–89), Steele writes that it was productive for Williams to experience "the pressure . . . to find a social relevance for literature in its own right, not just as an annex of history or sociology" (189). He also argues that for Thompson "the 'literary' . . . occupies a special place in anti-hegemonic popular struggle and can't be dismissed as either part of the hegemonic cannon [*sic*], or merely highbrow decoration. Poetry belongs properly to popular culture" (162–63). For excellent discussions of Thompson's literary emphasis, see Henry Abelove's 1982 *History and Theory* review of Thompson's *Poverty of Theory,* 132–42, and John Goode, "Thompson and 'the Significance of Literature,'" in *E. P. Thompson, Critical Perspectives,* ed. Harvey J. Kaye and Keith McClelland (Philadelphia: Temple University Press, 1990), 183–203.

5. Hall is interviewed in Chen, "Formation of a Diasporic Intellectual," in *Stuart Hall,* ed. Morley and Chen, 498. Hall's "A Critical Survey of the Theoretical and Practical Achievements of the Last Ten Years," his contribution to the volume *Literature, Society and the Sociology of Literature,* ed. Barker et al., focuses on cultural and literary theory, 1–7. Also see *Representation: Cultural Representations and Signifying Practices,* ed. Stuart Hall (London: Sage in Association with the Open University, 1997). For an example of Hall's literary criticism see "Lady Chatterley's Lover," *New Left Review* 6 (Nov.–Dec. 1960): 32–35. Hall concludes about D. H. Lawrence's controversial and censored novel: "Is there any need to say that a society which had any notion at all of the value of literature would long ago have put [Lawrence's novel] back in place?" (35). Literature had a major impact on the events of 1956 that so influenced Hall and other New Leftists. In late 1956 British New Leftists savored an interview with Hungarian author Paul Ignotus in which he explained that the revolution the Soviets had just suppressed in his country—a bloody repression he had narrowly escaped—was a "national rising ... started by poets and novelists" ("Questions about Hungary," *New Statesman and Nation* 52 [Dec. 8, 1956]: 738). The appreciation of literature as a liberatory force is alive and kicking. Tariq Ali, a novelist as well as a radical social critic and editor of *New Left Review,* commenced his book-length analysis of the American-Anglo "recolonization of Iraq" by lauding the critical and affirmative powers of "untamed" Iraqi poetry. "They alert their readers to the punishments that befall those who remain silent and become accessories to murder." Their "acidic verses" indict Saddam Hussein and the American-Anglo occupation and Iraqi "jackals" complicit with it. Yet the poets "never allow themselves to become submerged in despair; they continue to hope" (*Bush in Babylon: The Recolonisation of Iraq* [London: Verso, 2003], 18, 24, 40).

6. On complicity as a critical preoccupation in contemporary Americanist literary studies, see Richard H. Brodhead, "After the Opening: Problems and Prospects for a Reformed American Literature," *Yale Journal of Criticism* 5 (Spring 1992): 59–71, see 68. For an illuminating effort to identify some of the problems with the complicity emphasis in reference to popular culture, see Colin Mercer, "Complicit Pleasures," in *Popular Culture and Social Relations,* ed. Bennett, Mercer, Woollacott, 50–68. Terry Eagleton reminds "those radicals for whom high culture is *ipso facto* reactionary" not to "forget that much of it is well to the left of the World Bank" (*The Idea of Culture* [Oxford: Blackwell, 2000], 52. Richard Slotkin, contemplating the historical novel, reconsiders narrative as a tactical resource for bringing about social change, not just as an ideological symptom: "People are evidently not mere victims of inherited myths and ideologies, but have an active role in transforming received culture. It follows that the forms and genres of culture, including narrative, are not a set of conceptual restraints but potentially a set of tools or instruments for dealing with a changing and troublesome reality" ("Fiction for the Purposes of History," 229).

7. Benjamin, *Illuminations,* ed. Hannah Arendt, trans. Harry Zohn (New York: Schocken, 1969), 257. Raymond Williams's masterful, materialist historical complicity critique is *The Country and the City* (London: Chatto and Windus, 1973). Eagleton, *The Significance of Theory* (Oxford: Blackwell, 1990), 33.

8. Benjamin is quoted and translated by Jameson, *Political Unconscious,* 281.

9. Eagleton, *Literary Theory: An Introduction* (Minneapolis: University of Minnesota Press, 1983), 207–08. Nationalist ideologies also must be reread in a global context. It "hasn't been all bad," writes Alan Sinfield sardonically, reflecting on "slow and uneven ... movement toward equality and social justice" in Britain since 1945, "especially if you disregard the fact that our relative wealth is premised on the poverty of most of the world" (*Literature, Politics, and Culture,*

xxii). Noam Chomsky is particularly adept at developing the concept of responsibility. He quotes Dwight Macdonald's quotation of a Russian death camp paymaster who, on learning that the Russians were going to execute him, objected: "What have I done?" Macdonald commented: "Only those who are willing to resist authority themselves when it conflicts too intolerably with their personal moral code, only they have the right to condemn the death camp paymaster." Chomsky elaborated (alas, his point is still relevant today): "The question 'What have I done?' is one that we may well ask ourselves, as we read, each day, of fresh atrocities in Vietnam—as we create, or mouth, or tolerate the deceptions that will be used to justify the next defense of freedom" ("The Responsibility of Intellectuals," in *Dissenting Academy,* ed. Roszak, 254–98, see 291).

10. John Brenkman describes the terrain of this knowledge: "the complex relations that derive from the uses that human beings make of one another in the satisfaction of their own needs, and the history of violence and injury embedded in those relations" ("Theses on Cultural Materialism," *Social Text* [Spring/Summer 1983]: 19–33, see 24).

11. Marcuse, *Negations: Essays in Critical Theory,* trans. Jeremy F. Shapiro (Boston: Beacon, 1968), 103.

12. Consult Dworkin, *Cultural Marxism in Postwar Britain,* 5. On the establishment of the Institute of Social Research, see David Held, *Introduction to Critical Theory: Horkheimer to Habermas* (Berkeley: University of California Press, 1980), 29–39. Perry Anderson also comments on "the aristocratic—or at times esoteric—cast of the work of Adorno and Marcuse, and its distance from active politics" (*Arguments within English Marxism,* 173).

13. Carl Van Doren writes: "Much of the best American literature has always inclined toward the left" ("To the Left: To the Subsoil," *Partisan Review* 3 [Feb. 1936]: 9). The American studies critic Daniel Aaron elaborated on this in the first sentence of his classic book: "American literature, for all of its affirmative spirit, is the most searching and unabashed criticism of our national limitations that exists, the product of one hundred and fifty years of quarreling between the writer and his society" (*Writers on the Left: Episodes in American Literary Communism* [New York: Columbia University Press, 1992 (1961)], 1.

14. Emerson, *The Collected Works of Ralph Waldo Emerson, Vol. 1: Nature, Addresses, and Lectures,* ed. Robert Spiller (Cambridge: Belknap Press, 1991), 147, 148.

15. Emerson, *Selected Writings of Ralph Waldo Emerson,* ed. Brooks Atkinson (New York: Modern Library, 1950), 452. For recent critiques of Emerson's complicity with social contradictions, see Mary Kupiec Cayton, *Emerson's Emergence: Self and Society in the Transformation of New England, 1800–1845* (Chapel Hill: University of North Carolina Press, 1989) and Christopher Newfield, *The Emerson Effect: Individualism and Submission in America* (Chicago: University of Chicago Press, 1996).

16. Liza Featherstone and United Students against Sweatshops, *Students against Sweatshops* (New York: Verso, 2002), 2, 99, viii. On students' views of capitalism as a producer of systemic economic and class divisions, see 94. Also see *No Sweat: Fashion, Free Trade, and the Rights of Garment Workers,* ed. Andrew Ross (New York: Verso, 1997). Thoreau, *Walden and Other Writings,* ed. William Howarth (New York: Modern Library, 1981), 21, 24, 31, 45. He published *Walden* in 1854.

17. Davis, *An Autobiography* (New York: International Publishers, 1988 [1974]), 131.

18. Sarton, *Faithful Are the Wounds* (New York: Rinehart, 1955): all quotations from this novel will be followed by page numbers in parentheses.

19. In his retort to Isabel, the professor revealingly links English with domesticity as fields of ideological seclusion: "You have like me deliberately chosen to shut yourself away from the

agonies of your time. Don't you say, It's none of my business? My business is my husband, my children" (*Faithful Are the Wounds,* 193).

20. There are many linkages between Sarton's Edward Cavan and F. O. Matthiessen: both were socialists who taught English at Harvard and committed suicide (in the context of harassments by anticommunism crusaders). On the biographical dimension of Sarton's novel, see Eric Mottram, "F. O. Matthiessen," in *The Penguin Companion to American Literature,* ed. Malcolm Bradbury, Eric Mottram, and Jean Franco (New York: McGraw Hill, 1971), 170–71. Also see George Abbott White, "Ideology and Literature: *American Renaissance* and F. O. Matthiessen," in *Literature in Revolution,* ed. George Abbott White and Charles Newman (New York: Holt, 1972), 430–500.

21. Ohmann, *English in America: A Radical View of the Profession* (Hanover, NH: Wesleyan University Press, 1996 [1976]), xiv, xiv, xvi. Also see Ohmann, "The Personal as History," in *The Personal Effects: The Social Character of Scholarly Writing,* ed. Deborah Holdstein and David Bleich (Logan: Utah State University Press, 2002), 335–356, see 345–46, 349–50.

22. Ohmann, "English and the Cold War," in Chomsky et al., *Cold War and the University,* 73–105, see 76–80. Ohmann points out that the one exception was the antinuclear movement. Ohmann, "Personal As History," 345.

23. Ohmann, *Politics of Letters* (Middletown, CT: Wesleyan University Press, 1987), 8. And Bertell Ollmann writes that universities "have become a combination of training centers, finishing schools, employment agencies and warehouses for temporarily unneeded workers—all at public (meaning 'noncorporate') expense" (*How to Take an Exam ... and Remake the World,* 60).

24. For quotations that exemplify Cold War Anglo-American humanism's role in representing the communist bloc as too standardizing to nurture individuality, see Sinfield, *Literature, Politics, and Culture,* 89, 102, 104, 111–12. Also see Sarton, *Faithful Are the Wounds:* in the Harvard professor's exchange with Isabel, he dismisses Cavan's socialism as "anti-individualistic" (197) (interestingly, the postwar professor points to Britain as proof that socialism standardizes people). "The rich inwardness of the personal life, of which literature is the supreme exemplar," Eagleton argues, is "a view equivalent in the literary sphere to what has been called possessive individualism in the social realm ... it reflects the values of a political system which subordinates the sociality of human life to solitary individual enterprise" (*Literary Theory,* 197).

25. Hilden, *When Nickels Were Indians: An Urban, Mixed-Blood Story* (Washington, DC: Smithsonian Institution Press, 1995), 114. Stuart Hall, Raphael Samuel, Charles Taylor, "Then and Now," in *Out of Apathy,* ed. Archer at al. (1989), 163, 163–64, 152.

26. Trachtenberg, Foreword, in Joel Pfister, *Staging Depth: Eugene O'Neill and the Politics of Psychological Discourse* (Chapel Hill: University of North Carolina Press, 1995), xi–xiii, see xii. What is politically "objectionable," Terry Eagleton maintains, is not the news that "Alexander Pope was a Tory or Balzac a monarchist," but the ways in which "privileged group[s]" have tried to appropriate much literature as a self-legitimizing "spiritual badge" (*Idea of Culture,* 52). Louis Kampf, Ohmann's coconspirator in the Modern Language Association's radical caucus, helped lead a rebellion that got him elected president of that organization in 1970, shortly after he lambasted that "Chamber of Commerce" for being incorporative and complicitous: "The MLA's power lies in its strong stomach, in its capacity to digest almost everything, thus giving it institutional sanction." He called upon the literature teacher "to be true to his literary calling" and "court conflict." Kampf warned that "the study of literature must not become a haven for refugees from the pressures of the moment" ("Scandal of Literary Scholarship,"

in *Dissenting Academy,* ed. Roszak, 43–61, see 52, 51, 57, 59). Here Kampf allied himself with some postwar social critics who repudiated literary contributions to the affirmative reflex as an evasive reflex. For example, in *Universities and Left Review,* Michael Harrington criticized Saul Bellow's *Henderson the Rain King* (1959) for exhibiting an American literary tendency to sell "modern affirmation" in the face of evidence—in society and in the literary work itself—that undercuts it as wishful mystification. "When a contemporary novelist attempts the positive, he is regularly overwhelmed by his own immediate perception of the contrary" ("Saul Bellow's American," *Universities and Left Review* 7 [Autumn 1959]: 72–73, see 73). E. P. Thompson sympathized with Thomas McGrath's poetic struggle in a Vietnam War–era America that yielded "few affirmative evidences capable of carrying authentic symbolic power." McGrath believed that "the poet, in revealing human potential, is the vector of ... 'a view of life ... in a sense truer than the life we see lived all around us.'" But he also recognized that the yearning for "affirmative evidences" must not gloss over contradictions that thwart this potential, for then poetic truth becomes poetic evasion ("Homage to Thomas McGrath," 326). It is important to note that Kampf, like McGrath and Thompson, also saw some literature more affirmatively and strategically as "the sign of a creative act which expresses personal, social, and historical needs. As such it constantly undermines the status quo" ("Scandal of Literary Scholarship," in *Dissenting Academy,* ed. Roszak, 61). Nevertheless, it is requisite to consider: Affirmation for what and for whom?

27. Terry Eagleton offers the reminder that "culture is not inherently political at all"; it "become[s] political only when" it is invented and deployed within "a process of domination and resistance" and thus turns into "terrains of struggle": "The ultimate point of a politics of culture is to restore [cultural practices to] their innocuousness, so that one can sing, paint or make love without the bothersome distraction of political strife" (*Idea of Culture,* 122–23). Ohmann, *English in America,* xviii.

28. Mills, "Decline of the Left" in Mills, *Power, Politics, and People,* ed. Horowitz, 231.

29. Mills, "Knowledge and Power," 601, and also consider "Cultural Apparatus," see 408 on the politics of cultural work, in Mills, *Power, Politics, and People,* ed. Horowitz. Consult Mills's Canadian Broadcasting Corporation speech "To What, Then, Do We Belong?" (1954), 183–87, see 187, and Dan Wakefield, "Introduction," 6, in *C. Wright Mills,* ed. K. Mills with P. Mills.

30. Mills, "Cultural Apparatus," in Mills, *Power, Politics, and People,* ed. Horowitz, 406. Mills to his imaginary Russian correspondent, Tovarich, 280 and 280–81, and Mills to William Miller, 1952, 174, 174–75, in *C. Wright Mills,* ed. K. Mills with P. Mills.

31. West, "Postmodern Crisis of the Black Intellectuals," in *Cultural Studies,* ed. Grossberg, Nelson, and Treichler, 689–96, see 695. Also see West, *The Ethical Dimensions of Marxist Thought* (New York: Monthly Review Press, 1991). Here West observes that "black music" can be a form of "cultural equipment" that helps one "cope" "with the absurdities, anxieties, and frustrations, as well as the joys, laughter, and gaity of life"; it can provide "insights" into "existential and visceral levels" not addressed by "the Marxist tradition" (xxvii). Marxist critique is preoccupied "with improving the social circumstances under which people pursue love, revel in friendship, and confront death" (xxvii). Nonetheless, it does not offer "wisdom" that might guide one "how to live one's life day to day" in contemporary circumstances (xxviii).

32. Rose contributed an untitled paper to a panel organized by Scott Saul, "Rhythms of Social Change," at the Scholars, Artists, and Writers for Social Justice Conference (SAWSJ), Yale University, April 17, 1999. Sounds, quite apart from lyrics, can signify protest, cultivate *attitude,* generate solidarity.

33. See West's interview with Wynton Marsalis, (113–40, see 129–30, 135) and West's interview with former U.S. Senator Bill Bradley (35–61, see 45), in West, *Restoring Hope: Conversations on the Future of Black America,* ed. Kelvin Shawn Sealey (Boston: Beacon, 1997).

34. Levine, *Black Culture and Black Consciousness: Afro-American Thought from Slavery to Freedom* (New York: Oxford University Press, 1977): all quotations from this book will be followed by page numbers in parentheses.

35. Levine, "The Folklore of Industrial Society: Popular Culture and Its Audiences," *American Historical Review* 97 (Dec. 1992): 1369–99, see 1375, 1377; the final quotation is from Levine, "Levine Responds," 1427–30, see 1429. Aronowitz observes that Richard Hoggart's *Uses of Literacy* (1958) "sought to prove that it was not a lack but a set of affirmative attributes that marked the working class off from the middle class it was supposed to have become" (*Roll over Beethoven,* 89). Here Aronowitz refers to forms of working-class affirmation shaped by the working class. At the same time, might even this affirmation be considered in part managed affirmation, incorporated affirmation, compensatory affirmation?

36. Zinn, *You Can't Be Neutral on a Moving Train,* 201.

37. See South End Press Collective's interview with Zinn, "A New Great Movement," in their *Talking about a Revolution,* 113–24, see 117.

38. Anderson's film is quoted in Sinfield, *Literature, Politics, and Culture,* 262.

39. G. Miller, "Questions of Agency in Cultural Studies," Wesleyan University, unpublished essay.

40. See South End Press Collective's interview with LaDuke, "Power Is in the Earth," in their *Talking about a Revolution,* 67–79, see 77.

41. Lears, "Making Fun of Popular Culture," *American Historical Review* 97 (Dec. 1992): 1417–26, see 1418.

42. Bloom, *The Closing of the American Mind* (New York: Touchstone, 1987), 201.

43. Entin, one of my former Wesleyan American studies students who is now on the faculty of Brooklyn College, City University of New York, observed this in his reading of an earlier draft of this chapter.

44. For a discussion of the significance of agency for E. P. Thompson, Stuart Hall, and British cultural studies, see Dworkin, *Cultural Marxism in Postwar Britain,* 3, 52, 57, 61, 116, 147–48, 260.

45. Williams, *Politics and Letters: Interviews with New Left Review* (London: Verso, 1981), 39, 151.

46. Hall, "Praise of the Peculiar," vii.

47. Hall, "'First,'" in *Out of Apathy,* ed. Archer et al. (1989), 31. Perhaps Anderson tried to make up for lost time with his impressively theorized chapter on "Agency" in *Arguments within English Marxism,* 16–58. As he notes, E. P. Thompson had focused on the concept of agency in his work "since his early writings" (18). Historians, especially radical historians, tended to explore this concept long before many critical theorists did so.

48. Woodhams, *History in the Making,* 179.

49. Huggins, *Harlem Renaissance* (New York: Oxford University Press, 1971), 91, 254. Allegra Jones, another student, noted that corporations often individualized consumers' imagining of agency, empowerment, and "choice" as an internal experience tied not to democratic participation and social transformation but to the consumption of products.

50. West, "Postmodern Crisis," in *Cultural Studies,* ed. Grossberg, Nelson, and Treichler, 691.

51. James Wong, in his seminar essay, advised: "Agency Studies must incorporate, and to a certain extent be incorporated into the dominant discourse." The Wesleyan University unpublished seminar papers (1999) I quoted from are Pablo Morales, "Handbook," Morgenstein, "Agency Inc.," [Allegra] Jones, "Handbook on 'Agency Studies,'" Levenson, "Toward an Agency Studies," and Wong, "Agency Studies Manifesto."

52. P. Miller, *Errand into the Wilderness* (New York: Harper, 1964 [1956]), 8–9, and Bercovitch, *The American Jeremiad* (Madison: University of Wisconsin Press, 1978).

53. Morales, "Handbook."

54. Sinfield, *Faultlines: Cultural Materialism and the Politics of Dissident Reading* (Berkeley: University of California Press, 1992), 174, 146–47, 164–65. Similarly, Eve Sedgwick offers a critique (itself somewhat "paranoid") of the limitations of critique manufactured by "paranoid" new historicism: "While its general tenor of 'things are bad and getting worse' is immune to refutation, any more specific predictive value—and as a result, arguably, any value for making oppositional strategy—has been nil" ("Paranoid Reading and Reparative Reading; or, You're So Paranoid, You Probably Think This Introduction Is about You," in *Novel Gazing: Queer Readings in Fiction,* ed. Eve Kosofsky Sedgwick [Durham, NC: Duke University Press, 1997], 1–37, see 20).

55. Porter, "Are We Being Historical Yet?" *South Atlantic Quarterly* 87 (Fall 1988): 743–86, see, 781.

56. Ohmann, *English in America*, xxii, xxiii.

57. See the South End Press Collective's interview with Albert, "But What Are You For?" in their *Talking about a Revolution*, 1–12, see 7.

58. West, "The Dilemma of the Black Intellectual," *Cultural Critique* 1 (Fall 1985): 109–24, see 121. Foucault, one might add, forty years after Marcuse, contributed some of the most astute analyses of affirmation (affirmation through "sexuality") as a strategy in the formation of modern bourgeois identity: "the deployment of sexuality ... has to be seen as the self-affirmation of one class rather than the enslavement of another: a defense, a protection, a strengthening, and an exaltation that were eventually extended to others—at the cost of different transformations—as a means of social control and political subjugation" (*History of Sexuality*, 123). West's comments call for a reevaluation of the extent to which certain kinds of critique—even extensions of what Marcuse might term "negative" critique—contribute to "bourgeois" class affirmation and political evasion in the academy.

59. Aaron, *Writers on the Left*, Cohen, *Making a New Deal: Industrial Workers in Chicago, 1919–1939* (New York: Cambridge University Press, 1990), Denning, *Cultural Front*.

60. Lipsitz, *Rainbow at Midnight: Labor and Culture in the 1940s* (Urbana: University of Illinois Press, 1994), 14.

61. Gitlin, *Letters to a Young Activist*, 50–53, 66, 68, 76. Also, I am indebted to Joseph Entin, formerly a graduate student union (GESO) organizer at Yale, for suggesting that I peruse Kate Bronfenbrenner et al., *Organizing to Win: New Research on Union Strategies* (Ithaca, NY: ILR, 1998), a volume that does indeed offer some useful insights into the establishment of "organizing culture."

62. See the South End Press Collective's interview with Ehrenreich, "On Political Ecstasy and Marble Rolling," in their *Talking about a Revolution*, 27–38, see 32, also see 33. On the difficulties of organizing: "Politics has been reduced to lifestyle issues, and how do you think this affects organizing today, especially of youth? For example, the whole post-feminism scenario, in which being a feminist today is wearing the right kind of shoes, or reading a certain kind of 'zine—which is pretty different from talking about patriarchy and women in general" (34).

63. Williams, "Culture Is Ordinary," in *Conviction,* ed. Mackenzie, 92.

64. Stanley Aronowitz with Rachel Reidner and David Tritelli, "Writing, Pedagogy, and Activism in the Human Sciences: An Interview with Stanley Aronowitz," *Minnesota Review* 50–51 (Spring and Fall 1998): 101–111, see 111.

65. Thompson, "The Long Revolution," *New Left Review* (May–June 1961): 24–33, see especially 33. On the debate between Thompson and Williams, see Dworkin, *Cultural Marxism in Postwar Britain,* 104–105, 107, 120–21. Needless to say, Thompson is not alone in his efforts to affirm struggle. Since the 1950s singer, actor, and activist Harry Belafonte, for example, like Thompson, has sought out cultural and critical ways of assigning "great glory and great dignity and great power and great beauty" to social struggle (consult Cornel West's interview with Belafonte in West, *Restoring Hope,* 1–34, see 33).

66. Hall, "Praise of the Peculiar," vii.

67. Jones's reflection on the Left and art is in "Conference Scrapbooks," in *Out of Apathy,* ed. Archer et al. (1989), 135–36, see 136. F. O. Matthiessen, writing as a socialist critic in the late 1940s, characterized literature's "chief gift" as its capacity to enhance "our sense of living" ("Responsibilities of the Critic," 17). Also see *Left Polititics and the Literary Profession,* ed. Lennard J. Davis and M. Bella Mirabella (New York: Columbia University Press, 1990).

Notes for Chapter 5

1. See West's interview with Bill Bradley in West, *Restoring Hope,* 61. Winona LaDuke has gone on tour with the feminist folk duo, Indigo Girls, and addressed "Native environmental and community issues." She notes: "I think that the tours mean that the message about Native communities gets to an audience that wouldn't necessarily hear it. And that in itself is powerful. By and large, Indigo Girls fans are young, white women in their early 20s.... The downside? Does it feed into the mythology that reality is about superstars?" See the South End Press Collective's interview with LaDuke, "Power Is in the Earth," in their *Talking about a Revolution,* 68. The Rock the Vote campaign elicits help from groups like the Dixie Chicks ("Chicks Rock! Chicks Vote!") to help register voters and form "street teams" that show up at musical and educational events to encourage young people committed to "freedom of expression" to "take back our country." If Rock the Vote seems surprisingly vague about what needs to be "taken back," at least its Internet store offers a "Rock Star Babydoll" and "Script Logo Beanie" to display hip youthful enthusiasm.

2. Lemisch, "I Dreamed I Saw MTV Last Night," *The Nation* (Oct. 18, 1986): 361, 374–76, see 374, 376, 375.

3. Jesse Jackson's Rainbow Coalition, largely sidelined by the Democratic Party in the mid-1980s, contributed to setting the political-cultural stage for Lemisch's remarks.

4. See letters by Francis Shor, Ernie Lieberman, Maurice Isserman, and Richard Flacks in *The Nation* (Dec. 13, 1986): 658, 673–74. Anyone who has been to a Pete Seeger concert knows that he wants his "audience" to participate in music-making. This participation—this expectation—may indeed seem "uncool" to audience members socialized as consumers. Seeger's aim, judging from a concert he gave at Wesleyan University a couple of days after September 11, 2001, is to relate to the gathering as collective creators of a movement culture.

5. Lemisch, "The Politics of Left Culture," *The Nation* (Dec. 20, 1986): 700, 701, 702, 704, see 700, 702. Seeger, of course, has long embraced a range of Left causes that go beyond class critique, including antiracist campaigns and environmental work.

6. Jordan Pfister, my brother, has noted that in recent years MTV has taken on some overtly political issues. For instance, it criticized the rape of women at the 1999 Woodstock rock festival; some of its DJs condemned homophobia while still playing the songs of hip hop artist Eminem, some of which contain homophobic lyrics; and it urged young people to vote in the 2000 presidential elections.

7. Gitlin, "The Anti-Political Populism of Cultural Studies," in *Cultural Studies in Question*, ed. Marjorie Ferguson (Thousand Oaks, CA: Sage, 1997), 25–38, see 26.

8. Swados, *A Radical's America* (Boston: Little, Brown, 1962).

9. Quoted in Simon Frith, "John Lennon," *Marxism Today* 25 (Jan. 1981): 23–27, see 23.

10. Jones, *Autobiography of Mother Jones*, 73, 195, 10. Also see 145–47 on her use of sentiment—babies in court—and theatricality—singing in jail—to help incarcerated female protestors win their liberty.

11. Fox quotes from the Lynds' *Middletown* in "Epitaph for Middletown," in *Culture of Consumption*, ed. Fox and Lears, 126.

12. Leon Trotsky was suspicious of how dominant classes that could afford the "privilege of enjoyment" universalized and mystified it, when in fact "the manner and content of their enjoyment was always determined by the whole structure of the rest of society and suffered from all its contradictions" (Trotsky, *Literature and Revolution*, trans. Rose Strunsky [Ann Arbor: University of Michigan Press, 1960 (1924)], 151). On aspects of this concern—and of some matters I broach in the next few paragraphs—see Colin Mercer, "Complicit Pleasures," in *Popular Culture and Social Relations*, ed. Bennett, Mercer, and Woollacott, 50–68.

13. Consult Eagleton's review of Hobsbawm's autobiography (*Interesting Times: A Twentieth-Century Life* [New York: Pantheon, 2003]), "The Life of the Party," *The Nation* (September 15, 2003): 29–31, see 31.

14. See Mills to his imaginary Russian correspondent, Tovarich, 1959, in *C. Wright Mills*, ed. K. Mills with P. Mills, 278–279, see 278, 280.

15. Alan Wald with David Titrelli and Sharon Hanscom, "The Formation of an Activist Scholar: An Interview with Alan Wald," *Minnesota Review* 50–51 (Spring and Fall 1998): 125–42, see 130, 135, 140.

16. Hall, "'First,'" in *Out of Apathy*, ed. Archer et al. (1989), 34.

17. Hall, "The Culture Gap," *Marxism Today* 28 (Jan. 1984): 18–22, see 19. Hall, Samuel, and Taylor, "Then and Now," in *Out of Apathy*, ed. Archer et al. (1989), 148.

18. Editor [Hall], "Editorial," 2.

19. Hall, "Face the Future," 37, 39.

20. Editor [Hall], "Editorial," 1–2.

21. Hall, "Culture Gap," 18.

22. Editor [Hall], "Editorial," 2.

23. Editor [Hall], "Editorial," 2.

24. Samuel, "Born-Again Socialism," in *Out of Apathy*, ed. Archer et al. (1989), 44.

25. Williams, "Freedom and Ownership in the Arts," *New Left Review* 5 (Sept.–Oct. 1960): 53–57, see 54.

26. Williams, "Ideas and the Labour Movement," 33. Also consult Williams, "Splits, Pacts and Coalitions," 31–35.

27. For Hall's comments on Williams's concept of the "long revolution," consult, "Culture Gap," 21.

28. Hall, "Notes on Deconstructing 'the Popular,'" in *People's History and Socialist Theory,* ed. Samuel, 227–40, see 239. Also see Hall, "Popular Culture and the State," in *Popular Culture and Social Relations,* ed. Bennett, Mercer, Wollacott, 22–49.

29. Hall, "Culture Gap," 20.

30. For an analysis of the Labour Party's decline in the 1970s and early 1980s, see Daniel Kogan and Maurice Kogan, *The Battle for the Labour Party* (London: Kogan Page, 1983 [1982]).

31. Aronowitz, *Roll over Beethoven* (1993) and Lawrence Grossberg, *We Gotta Get out of This Place: Popular Conservatism and Postmodern Culture* (Durham, NC: Duke University Press, 1992). In *Cultural Studies and Beyond,* Ioan Davies registers similar impressions about cultural studies conferences such as the one at the University of Illinois. He sees them as occasions in which a globe-trotting cultural studies "avant garde" (140) stages "critical theory … performances for the academic cognoscenti" (140) that tend to decontextualize, universalize, and thus depoliticize cultural studies (159).

32. Shortly after the conference, one of its organizers, Cary Nelson, issued a "cultural studies manifesto" in which he echoed some of Stuart Hall's worries about cultural studies in America: "[Cultural studies] needs … to question its recent fetishizing of 'fandom.' A ritualized, unreflective confession of fandom has become almost a requirement in some American cultural studies circles. Being a fan is not a prerequisite for doing cultural analysis" ("Always Already Cultural Studies: Conferences and a Manifesto," in *What Is Cultural Studies?,* ed. Storey, 273–86, see 281).

33. On the politics of hipness, see Thomas Frank's "Hip Is Dead" *The Nation* (April 1, 1996): 16, 18–19; "Alternative to What?" in *Commodify Your Dissent: Salvos from the Baffler,* ed. Thomas Frank and Matt Weiland (New York: Norton, 1997), 145–63; "Hip as Official Capitalist Style," in his *The Conquest of Cool: Business Culture, Counterculture, and the Rise of Hip Consumerism* (Chicago: University of Chicago Press, 1997), 224–35.

34. For some perspective on this, one might compare Rebecca Mead, "Yo, Professor," *New York* 27 (Nov. 14, 1994): 48–53 and Elaine Showalter, "The Professor Wore Prada," *Vogue* (Dec. 1997): 80, 86, 92.

35. Dan Wakefield, "Introduction," in *C. Wright Mills,* ed. K. Mills with P. Mills, 6 (and 10 for Mills's amusing encounter with Lionel Trilling in his motorcycle cap). In this volume also peruse Pamela Mills, "My Father Haunts Me," xxi–xxiii, see xxii. Consult Robert Westbrook, "C[harles] Wright Mills," in *Companion to American Thought,* ed. Fox and Kloppenberg, 457–58: "Mills played up the role of the rebellious Texan. Commuting to Morningside Heights on his BMW motorcycle, he adopted the pose of the sociologist as leather-jacketed Wobbly, which horrified many button-down Columbia professors and endeared him to a later generation of radicals" (457).

36. Mills, "Decline of the Left," in Mills, *Power, Politics, and People,* ed. Horowitz, 234.

37. Hall, "'First,'" in *Out of Apathy,* ed, Archer at al. (1989), 16: in this section all quotations from Hall will be from this edition unless otherwise noted and indicated by page number in parentheses.

38. Samuel, "Born-again Socialism," in *Out of Apathy,* ed. Archer at al. (1989), 39: in this section all quotations from Samuel will be from this volume unless otherwise noted and indicated by page number in parentheses.

39. Wesleyan University Queer Alliance poster, May 2001: "So darn cool." But another Queer Alliance button, which focused on responsibility rather than hipness, read: "Silence is complicity."

40. "Conference Scrapbook," in *Out of Apathy: Voices,* ed. Archer at al. (1989), 138–39, 139.

41. Rustin, "New Left as a Social Movement," in *Out of Apathy,* ed, Archer at al. (1989), 117–27.

42. Cultural studies critical debates about "the popular"—how to theorize it, how to strategize in relation to it—are legion. For instance, see Tony Bennett, Colin Mercer, and Janet Woollacott, eds., *Popular Culture and Social Relations,* their seminal Open University text published in 1986.

43. Widgery, "The Rise of Radical Rock," *New Socialist* (Nov.–Dec. 1981): 34–37, see 35 (Hobsbawm and Widgery quotes).

44. David Edgar, "Never the Old," 18.

45. Lash and Urry, "The Shape of Things to Come," *New Socialist* 45 (Jan. 1987): 12–15, see 13.

46. Widgery, "Rise of Radical Rock," 35. For a sweeping critique of the theoretical tendency to rearticulate strategic socialism as strategic pleasureism, see David Harris, *From Class Struggle to the Politics of Pleasure: The Effects of Gramscianism on Cultural Studies* (New York: Routledge, 1992).

47. This sort of linkage is not unusual on either side of the Atlantic. I am reminded of a poster advertising Rethinking Marxism's 4th International Gala Conference, held at the University of Massachusetts, Amherst, titled, "The Party's Not Over: Marxism 2000." The poster reproduces Diego Rivera's "Dance in Tehuantepec" (1935), which depicts Mexicans dancing.

48. Quoted in Simon Frith and John Street, "Party Music," *Marxism Today* (June 1986): 28–32, see 30.

49. Hall, "Culture Gap," 20.

50. Hall, "Culture Gap," 22.

51. Hall and Jacques, "People Aid: A New Politics Sweeps the Land," *Marxism Today* 31 (July 1986): 10–14, see 11. There is something to this. The Republican administration and its media supporters took umbrage at the Dixie Chicks' criticism of George W. Bush, while performing in London, during the U.S. invasion of Iraq in March 2003, not because they said anything different from millions of people protesting in demonstrations or from thousands of commentators protesting in print around the world, but because that country-rock group is the best-selling female musical group in the history of the music industry, and they have the attention and interest of millions of consumers worldwide. Moreover, like Bush, they are Texans.

52. Elms, "Ditching the Drabbies," *New Socialist* 38 (May 1986): 12–14, see 12, 14. (Wilde was certainly far more socialist than many designer "socialists.") However much one may feel that Elms trivializes politics, style is very much a political concern. For example, see: John Berger's classic "The Suit and the Photograph," reprinted in his *Selected Essays,* ed. Geoff Dyer (New York: Vintage, 2001), 274–78; Dick Hebdige's 1979 classic, *Subculture;* Angela McRobbie, "Second-Hand Dresses and the Role of the Ragmarket," in her *Postmodernism and Popular Culture* (London: Routledge, 1994 [1996]), 135–54; *Chic Thrills: A Fashion Reader,* ed. Juliet Ash and Elizabeth Wilson (Berkeley: University of California Press, 1992).

53. The author of "Designer Bolshevism" (1986) admitted: "Whether Designer Socialism is really a politics which is alive to aesthetics, or is actually just the aestheticisation of politics (a rose by any other name), depends on where you stand." Has politics, the author queried, been "safely trivialised into a squabble over something called 'style'?" *New Socialist* 44 (Dec. 1986): 2.

54. For the past few years *The Nation* has sponsored an "Annual Seminar Cruise"—the first one was to the Caribbean—to allow the magazine's editors, contributors, famous progressive figures (such as George McGovern), and "well off" readers to mingle and strategize how to make the world a better place (just as radical professors do at elite university receptions), *The Nation* (Aug. 10–17, 1998): 29. The second trip was "Alaska Waits!" *The Nation* (Aug. 9–16, 1999): 35. Some readers have been quite critical of this development.

55. Michael Rustin took issue with the paradigm of post-Fordism that Hall and Jacques advocated as fundamental to a comprehension of New Times. The Fordist assembly-driven capitalism that Gramsci analyzed in the 1920s and 1930s, the New Times argument went, had been displaced by new information technologies, new organizations of work, new sorts of work (the ascendancy of the service sector), new political constituencies, and a new more expansive globalizing of capitalist forces, labor pools, and markets. Rustin contended that post-Fordism accounted for some but not all of the ensemble of capitalist strategies, systems, and government aid. The continuities connecting pre-Fordist, Fordist, and post-Fordist developments, he argued, suggested that Britain was enmeshed in not-altogether-new times after all. Moreover, the more-visible-than-ever state-supported powers of the Thatcherite ruling class testified to the ongoing relevance of the category of class in socialist critique. Rustin, "The Trouble with 'New Times,'" in *New Times,* ed. Hall and Jacques, 303–20, see 305, 308, 317, 319 (on diversity of capitalist strategies), 310, 319 (not-altogether-new times), 310, 311 (relevance of class analysis).

56. Williamson, "The Problems of Being Popular," *New Socialist* 41 (Sept. 1986): 14–15, see 14.

57. Rustin, "New Left as a Social Movement," in *Out of Apathy,* ed, Archer at al. (1989), 120–21.

58. Williamson, "Problems of Being Popular," 14. She adds: "If it is patronising to suggest that living entirely within popular culture is a diminishing experience, it is equally patronising to sit around with a degree in literature deciding that people don't really want to read Dickens, or Lawrence, or Shakespeare or whatever. The same applies to Left writers who may read Gramsci and Foucault in private, but don't think their readers could cope with them.... Have we nothing more to say than 'people' like it?" (15).

59. Williamson, "Problems of Being Popular," 15.

60. See the South End Press Collective interview with Ehrenreich, "On Political Ecstasy and Marble Rolling," in their *Talking about a Revolution,* 29, 30. In the same volume, see the interview with Winona LaDuke, "Power is in the Earth": "Take responsibility for history. Recognize that sometimes things take a long time to change.... You've got to have a 50-year or 100-year plan" (77).

61. Frith and Street, "Party Music," 32.

62. Might this be termed designer individualism?

63. Hall, "Culture Gap," 22.

64. Samuel, "Doing Dirt on the Miners," 14, 16. *Billy Elliott* (directed by Stephen Daldry, 2000) is an ideologically complex film about this strike and a striking miner's son's desire to dance. I will make only two points that speak to Samuel's critique. First, if the film portrays "masculinity" as a repressive construct that the boy must redefine to gain respect for his passion to dance, it also tries to give some sense of why the workers see the reproduction of certain styles of "masculinity" as exigent for class survival within harsh conditions of systemic exploitation. As police sirens scream outside the gym, the son, Billy (whose name his father pronounces *ballet*), rebels against learning how to box. His father scolds him for refusing to fight back—something

he gradually does, albeit on behalf of his drive to dance. The film demonstrates why a new more expansive politics such as that which Hall champions must emerge. Liberation must be understood not only in terms of economic and political transformation but also as emancipation from hegemonic gender, sexuality, and racial ideologies. Second, more problematically, the film suggests that the working class is so outnumbered that their cause is futile. Billy's father, brother, and other miners finally support Billy's bid to study at the Royal Academy not just so that he can truly "express" himself, but so that he can escape from the mines. His local dance teacher exits the cage-like inner fence within the gym to wish him luck at the Royal Academy and then resignedly reenters it to continue her class. Soon after, Billy's father and brother walk into the reopened mine, squeeze into the front of a caged elevator packed with men, and descend—buried alive. *Billy Elliott* makes their loss seem not only overwhelmingly tragic but inevitable. By contrast, years later the adult Billy flies through the air in the leading role of Matthew Bourne's all-male version of *Swan Lake*—symbolizing the ascent of new political subjects who seem to seek emancipation more through cultural than through conventional politics. Also see Alex Callinicos and Mike Simons, *The Great Strike: The Miners' Strike of 1984–5 and Its Lessons* (London: Socialist Worker, 1985).

65. Thompson, "William Morris," 30.

66. Kavanagh, "Ideology," in *Critical Terms for Literary Study*, ed. Frank Lentricchia and Thomas McLaughlin (Chicago: University of Chicago Press, 1990), 306–20, see 313.

67. Mulhern, "The Politics of Cultural Studies," in *In Defense of History*, ed. Wood and Foster, 43–50, see 48. As I noted in chapter 1, Tony Bennett has argued that cultural studies has become too cultural in its frame of reference, obsessed with "sleuth-like searching for subversive practices where you'd least expect to find them" ("Putting Policy in Cultural Studies," in *Cultural Studies*, ed. Grossberg, Nelson, and Treichler, 23–34, 32).

68. Eagleton, *Idea of Culture*, 76–85, 111, 129.

69. Rustin, "Trouble with 'New Times,'" in *New Times*, ed. Hall and Jacques, 320, 313.

70. Gitlin quoted in Mulhern, *Culture/Metaculture*, 158, 159, and see 169. Mulhern is critical of 1980s cultural studies work—such as that of John Fiske—that celebrates "television and shopping" as "theaters of subversion" ("Politics of Cultural Studies," 50). Gitlin also objects: "One purports to stand four-square for the people against capitalism, and comes to echo the logic of capitalism" ("Anti-Political Populism of Cultural Studies," in *Cultural Studies in Question*, ed. Ferguson, 32).

71. Whatever validity this criticism may have, it must not elide the U.S. history of dissident intellectuals, artists, workers, feminists, antiracists, sexuality activists, environmentalists, and others who have formed coalitions and sparked social movements. Michael Denning explores chapters in this history in *Cultural Front*. Gitlin's critique is a heated response to an American cultural studies that was beginning to resemble a more theoreticist version of Bowling Green's American Popular Culture Association. Not everyone interested in "cultural studies" was so limited in their critical scope. More recently, Gitlin has overgeneralized: "We like to argue about the political significance of movies and TV shows, not about the politics of pensions and living wages" (*Letters to a Young Activist*, 109). But here he overlooks the power of movies and TV to structure the preoccupations of Americans so that sometimes they pay less heed than they should to "the politics of pensions and living wages." Many social and cultural critics—perhaps outside the undefined "we" to which Gitlin refers—see the importance of examining a full range of contradictions, mystifications, and ideological concerns that make America tick. Their subjects of critique encompass living wages, pensions, movies, TV, and, thankfully, much else.

72. Gitlin, "Anti-Political Populism of Cultural Studies," in *Cultural Studies in Question,* ed. Ferguson, 37. Lipsitz, "Academic Politics and Social Change," in *Cultural Studies and Political Theory,* ed. Jody Dean (Ithaca, NY: Cornell University Press, 2000), 80–92, see 83. Also see Davies, *Cultural Studies and Beyond,* 123. Corporate-consumer-therapeutic capitalism has made "changing yourself" the object of huge industries. "Changing oneself" is often sold as doable in lieu of "changing the world," which is encoded as undoable. Still, it would be a categorical mistake to sever "changing oneself" from "changing the world," because historically the former project—however incorporated forms of it have been—has led to or been involved in the latter larger project. Sometimes "opposition" has been or has begun as an opposition of one. What qualifies as "oppositional"? "Oppositional culture" is not enough of an opposition, Eagleton is convinced: "[It] has withered each time as the political forces which underpinned it were defeated. It has learnt enough from this experience to know that the success or failure of radical critique is determined in the end by one fact alone: the fortunes of a broader political movement" (*Idea of Culture,* 86). Eagelton does not state the evidence on which he based this judgment, but cultural studies might indeed rethink its possibilities as a multipolitical alliance studies.

73. See Paul Gilroy's critical comparison of the Rock Against Racism movement and the Greater London Council's antiracism campaigns in "Two Sides of Anti-Racism" in his *"There Ain't No Black in the Union Jack": The Cultural Politics of Race and Nation* (Chicago: University of Chicago Press, 1991 [1987]), 114–52, especially 150–51. To again use Cameron Crowe's terms, Gilroy, more than Gitlin, it seems, apprehends "the buzz" and its political potential as an organizing force. For a provocative critique of Gitlin, see Henry A. Giroux, "Rethinking Cultural Politics: Challenging Political Dogmatism from Right to Left," in his *Impure Acts: The Practical Politics of Cultural Studies* (New York: Routledge, 2000), 16–38.

74. Michael Bérubé lists a few of the agencies and laws that have an enormous impact on Americans' lives and that have been affected by or in some cases brought into being by organized agitation: the Food and Drug Administration, the Occupational Safety and Health Administration, the minimum wage laws, the National Labor Relations Board, the Clean Air and Water Acts, the Individuals with Disabilities Acts, and the Voting Rights Act ("American Studies without Exceptions," 112).

75. As Michael Denning notes, "We should not, in our justifiable anger at the trivialization of cultural studies and cultural politics, give up the sense that there are forms of cultural politics that are irreducible to the politics of the workplace, the state, or the household" (see "What's Wrong with Cultural Studies?," in his *Culture in the Age of Three Worlds,* 147–66, especially 161–66, the quote is on 166). For some critical perspectives on and examples of cultural activism, see *Cultural Resistance Reader,* ed. Stephen Duncombe (New York: Verso, 2002). At times Gitlin does not simply see cultural politics as trivial, he actively trivializes it.

76. See Francis Beckett, "Compare Blair with Attlee: One Failed, One Succeeded," *Guardian* (Dec. 6, 2000), www.guardian.co.uk/Archive. For an argument against this respectability thesis, see Miliband, *Parliamentary Socialism.*

77. Jackson's politics were formed in a country in which religion—more influential than MTV—structures and disseminates notions of morality and justice. Still, Jackson's hegemonizing savvy did not overcome racial barriers to win significant Democratic Party backing for the coalition or his presidential bid. A decade later Cornel West, sounding something like Thompson in his evangelical mode, also affirmed that it is strategic to develop "moral channels through which … rage can flow" that "reflect a broad moral vision, a sharp analysis of wealth and power" (see West's interview with Harry Belafonte in West, *Restoring Hope,* 29). On this

matter former U.S. Senator Bill Bradley, also interviewed by West, and sounding something like Jackson, advised that progressives have got to put "morality out there. . . . But morality isn't enough. . . . We are the only society that is sufficiently multiracial, multiethnic, to be a world society. And if we intend to lead the world by the power of the example of our pluralism, then we've got to do a better job here at home" (in West, *Restoring Hope*, see 51). Also see Adolph L. Reed, Jr., *The Jesse Jackson Phenomenon: The Crisis of Purpose in Afro-American Politics* (New Haven, CT: Yale University Press, 1986). Also see Terry Eagleton's criticisms of the tendency of the Academic Theoretical Left—which he helped shape—to transplant discourses of morality with emphases on "style" and "politics" (*After Theory*, 140–73, especially 140–43).

78. And in response to the question, "Do you consider yourself part of the left?," Winona LaDuke explained that she was far more "conservative" than "radical" in her views about the modern "immensity of cultural, technological, social, and ecological change": "Most Native people are very conservative. . . . They say when you make a decision today, consider the impact of your decision on the seventh generation from now." See the South End Press Collective's interviews with Marable, "A Humane Society Is Possible through Struggle" (81–94, see 90), Chomsky, "There Are No Limits to What Can Be Done" (22), and LaDuke, "Power is in the Earth" (74), in their *Talking about a Revolution*.

79. Shortly after the 2004 presidential "election" Moore, intriguingly, appeared on the David Letterman talk show impeccably groomed—hatless, shorter haircut, and dressed in a suit and tie. Perhaps this can be read as his latest hegemonizing costume, suited to new conditions.

80. "Our bravest organizers (I do not include myself in this company)," Gitlin recalls, perhaps oversimply, about the 1960s New Left, "plunged into darkness not because it was stylish or because they were proud possessors of a theory that assured them that they were destined to win but *because they decided to overcome fear,* period." The payoff question is: How and why did they decide, and what can we learn and unlearn from this? Contemplating the range of motivations that propel youth to organize, Gitlin overgeneralizes (it seems to me) that "anger" drove activism in the 1960s, whereas "compassion" stimulates the organized protest of more recent times (*Letters to a Young Activist*, 27–28, 46). Thinking back to the 1960s and observing my students today, I see admixtures of these motivations—and others—at work.

81. See *The Nation* 273 (July 2, 2001): 13, 15, see 15.

82. A historical note on what is possible: in 1976 several Wesleyan students obtained faculty support to establish a student-run course (originally a tutorial) that became titled "Toward a Socialist America." By the late 1980s the course lost some momentum and was retitled "Critical Issues in Contemporary Society," which Richard Ohmann has described to me as a "mild" version of the activist studies initiative that preceded it. This course disappeared altogether by the mid-1990s.

83. John Colapinto, "The Young Republicans," *New York Times Magazine* (May 25, 2003), section 6, 30–35, 58–59, see 32, 34, 35, 59. In mid-February, 2003, however, President George W. Bush's dismissal of the unprecedented and dramatic worldwide protest of millions to the American-British threat to invade and occupy Iraq demonstrated a Republican willingness to bracket questions of legitimacy and hegemony-building, at least for the moment. Bush's brash dismissal brought to mind one of Noam Chomsky's more skeptical Reagan-era warnings about not confining progressive struggles to the battle for hegemony. "Public opinion is of no more concern to elite groups that control the state apparatus than security, survival, 'human rights, the raising of living standards, and democratisation,'" he concluded. "Not only the people of Latin America, but also those of the rest of the world, including the United States, are 'an

incident, not an end'" ("The Evil Empire," *New Socialist* 34 [January 1986]: 11–15, see 15). Perhaps Bush's more recent response to Ariel Sharon, prime minister of Israel, qualifies this somewhat. On the front page of the *Guardian,* Bush's headlined rejoinder to Sharon's claim to be "a man of peace and security" was: "I know you are a man of security. I want to work harder on the peace part.... I said you were a man of peace. I want you to know I took immense crap for that" (*Guardian: International Edition,* June 4, 2003, 1). Bush's main concern here seems to be "taking immense crap." For "taking immense crap" can lead to losing an election and the economic, political, and cultural clout that goes with it. Who is learning from whom, after all? One scene in Michael Moore's documentary, *The Big One* (1998), shows Moore with strikers in several cities marching to the soundtrack of Queen's 1980s pop anthem "We Will Rock You." Five years later the U.S. army blasted the same song to whip up troops at rallies that launched the invasion of Iraq. For an insightful analysis of conservative hegemonizing strategies, see Thomas Frank, *What's the Matter with Kansas? How Conservatives Won the Heart of America* (New York: Metropolitan, 2004). Also see Thomas Frank's *New Consensus for Old: Cultural Studies Left to Right* (Chicago: Prickly Paradigm Press, 2002).

84. Liza Featherstone and United Students against Sweatshops, *Students against Sweatshops,* 10, 103.

85. For information about the Rolling Thunder Down Home Democracy Tour, I have consulted the Public Broadcasting Station's Web site, pbs.org. This yielded various descriptions of the festival and Web sites linked with the wonderful coverage I had seen on Bill Moyer's PBS show *Now* (February 6, 2004). I am grateful yet again to Lisa Wyant for having me watch this show.

86. Dean appeared on the NBC television show, *Meet the Press,* May 22, 2005. Lakoff, *Don't Think Like an Elephant!,* 87, 43, 3–45 (on framing). Frank, *What's the Matter with Kansas?*

Notes for Chapter 6

1. Stevens, see his album *Tea for the Tillerman,* A and M records, 1970. McWilliams, *Brothers under the Skin* (Boston: Little, Brown, 1943), 48. McWilliams here makes reference to the failure of American theorists to think through a major wartime liability—the "Negro question" (48). He urges that a global perspective be taken to reform it. Rieff, "Socialism and Sociology," 366.

2. See "1997 American Studies Association Election" pamphlet distributed by the ASA.

3. Rexroth: "Students Take Over," 39. Ohmann, "Some Changes across Thirty-Five Years," in his *Politics of Knowledge: The Commercialization of the University, the Professions, and Print Culture* (Middletown, CT: Wesleyan University Press, 2003), 42–46, see 46.

4. Glaspell quoted in Pfister, *Staging Depth,* 198.

5. Foucault, *Use of Pleasure,* 8.

6. Aronowitz, "Writing, Pedagogy, and Activism in the Human Sciences," 103.

7. "An Interview with Paul M. Sweezy," 36.

8. Miliband, "C. Wright Mills," 17. Mills understood scholarship and critique as two intellectual practices by means of which one established a reflective life, not merely a career: "Scholarship is a choice of how to live as well as a choice of career" ("On Intellectual Craftsmanship," the appendix in Mills, *The Sociological Imagination* [New York: Oxford University Press, 1959], 195–226, see 196).

9. L. Marx, *Pilot and the Passenger,* 245.

10. In 1929 Lewis Mumford wrote V. F. Calverton that no ideas, not even "revolutionary" ideas, should be "protected" from scrutiny (Mumford to Calverton, VFC).

11. Linda M. Rodriguez and Adayna Gonzalez were members of my "Cultural Studies and American Studies" junior seminar (Spring 1998).

12. Williams, "The Writer: Commitment and Alignment," *Marxism Today* 24 (June 1980): 22–25, see 25.

13. See Mills to Ralph Miliband, June 22, 1960, 291; Mills to his imaginary Russian correspondent, Tovarich, 1957, 250, 248; Mills to William and Virginia Miller, probably 1949, 132 in *C. Wright Mills,* ed. K. Mills with P. Mills. While Barbara Foley is dismissive of the inflationary political value that academics assign to "critical thinking," she emphasizes that "a critical and truly thinking working class is intolerable to the present order" (Barbara Foley with Noreen O'Connor and Rich Hancuff, "Theory and Practice: An Interview with Barbara Foley," *Minnesota Review* 50–51 [Spring and Fall 1998]: 113–22, see 118).

14. Historicists, more than many historians who devote themselves to archival research, often endeavor to conceive of historical thinking as a branch of critical theory. Often "historicism" is something that members of English departments do while members of history departments write history. American studies, ideally, synthesizes the two. Needless to say, some historians (discussed in chapter 3) are expert theoretical historicists and some literary critics excel as historians. See Paul Hamilton, *Historicism* (London: Routledge, 1996).

15. For an excellent example of American studies and cultural studies fused and conceptualized as meaning production studies, see Teresa L. Emert, "The Crisis of Representation in Cultural Studies: Reading Postmodern Texts," *American Quarterly* 38 (Winter 1986): 894–902. For a fine example of cultural and communication studies as meaning production studies, see Graham Murdock, "Cultural Studies: Missing Links," *Critical Studies in Mass Communication* 6 (Dec. 1989): 436–40. Murdock writes about media industries: "These industries do not simply make commodities; they make available the repertoires of meaning through which the world, including the world of commodities, is understood. The task for theory is to conceptualize the relation between these two sides of the communication process—the material and discursive, economic and cultural—without collapsing one into the other" (136).

16. For a cautionary critique of brands of constructionism that efface biology—elements of biological determinism—see Barbara Ehrenreich and Janet McIntosh, "The New Creationism: Biology under Attack," *The Nation* (June 9, 1997): 11–16 and the responses in the "Exchange" section, *The Nation* (Aug. 25/Sept. 1, 1997): 2, 51–52 (this includes Ehrenreich and McIntosh's reply).

17. See South End Press Collective's interviews with Albert, "But What Are You For?" (2, 3, 6, 9) and LaDuke, "Power Is in the Earth" (77) in their *Talking about a Revolution.* Sainphor quoted in Liza Featherstone and United Students against Sweatshops, *Students against Sweatshops,* 67.

18. I thank Kate Gordon (Wesleyan '94) and Paul Ching (Wesleyan '93) for these timely letters.

19. It might be useful for teachers of progressive critique, to offer another example, to be aware that the Worker Education Extension Center at Queens College, City University of New York, coordinates the New York Union Semester, during which students intern with a labor union or union-affiliated organization in New York City and take courses in labor studies at Queens (www.qc.edu/unionsemester). In *Steal This Book* (New York: Grove, 1971) Abbie Hoffman,

attuned to the importance of better organizing, helpfully included an appendix that lists and describes "Organizations That Serve the People," 284–87. What might a section on "Critiques That Serve the People" look like?

20. Quoted in Richard Johnson, "Reading for the Best Marx: History Writing and Historical Abstraction," in *Making Histories,* ed. Johnson, McLennan, Schwarz, Sutton, 153–201, see 185.

21. Brecht is quoted by Tony Bennett in his "Putting Policy in Cultural Studies," in *Cultural Studies,* ed. Grossberg, Nelson, and Treichler, 31.

22. Mills to Gerth, September 26, 1948, in *C. Wright Mills,* ed. K. Mills with P. Mills, 121–22.

23. Aronowitz, *The Death and Rebirth of American Radicalism* (New York: Routledge, 1996), 191.

24. Wald, *The Responsibility of Intellectuals: Selected Essays on Marxist Traditions in Cultural Commitment* (NJ: Humanities Press, 1992), 218–19. Cornel West, also interested in "concrete" actions, has criticized some "disciples of Jacques Derrida and Michel Foucault" for illuminating the "subtle relations of rhetoric, knowledge, and power" while "remain[ing] silent about concrete ways in which people are empowered and what can be gained by such resistance" (*Ethical Dimensions of Marxist Thought,* xxii). Also see Cornel West, "On Fox and Lears's The Culture of Consumption," reprinted in West's *Prophetic Fragments* (Grand Rapids, MI: William B. Eerdmans/Trenton, NJ: Africa World Press, 1988), 188–92.

25. McLennan, "Class Conundrum," *Marxism Today* 28 (May 1984): 29–32, see 29.

26. Buhle, "America: Post-Modernity?" *New Left Review* 180 (March–April 1990): 163–78, see 165.

27. Thompson, "William Morris," 29.

28. Hall,"Gramsci and Us," 19.

29. Hall, Samuel, Taylor, "Then and Now," *Out of Apathy,* ed. Archer at al. (1989), 152, 163, 163–64.

30. Howe, for instance, concludes: "I could not help thinking that if some of us ever end our days in a 'corrective labor camp' it might well be because of the equally good intentions of intellectuals like F. O. Matthiessen." Also: "As a political thinker, Matthiessen is sentimental and befuddled, but not naive" ("Sentimental Fellow-Traveling of F. O. Matthiessen," 1129, 1126). See Matthiessen's brief and very restrained response, "L'Affaire Matthiessen," *Partisan Review* 15 (Nov. 1948): 1256: "The fact that your review of my book *From the Heart of Europe* was virtually indistinguishable from the one in *Time* should be of more concern to *Partisan Review* than it is to me."

31. Lynd to Macdonald, March 31, c. 1945, DM. Sniping still thrives. See Bernie Mazel's letter bemoaning some vitriolic Left crossfire that *The Nation* had recently published, "How About Some Civility," *The Nation* (Sept. 28, 1998): 2. He writes: "I guess the left (if I may use that antiquated term) will always be reserving their strongest blows for one another while Newt [Gingrich] and his pals continue to be reelected."

32. Anderson, *Arguments within English Marxism,* 128.

33. See L. Marx, "The Teacher," in *F. O. Matthiessen,* ed. Sweezy and Huberman 43. Quoted from Mills's letter to Harvey Swados, November 3, 1956, in *C. Wright Mills,* ed. K. Mills with P. Mills, 217. On March 18, 1952, Mills wrote to Norman Thomas the following appraisal of his former friend, Dwight Macdonald: "I hold quite firmly to certain now old-fashioned beliefs, including socialist and humanist and certainly secular ideals; I do not think Dwight is capable

of fixing his beliefs in any warrantable way.... Dwight has made a fetish of confusion and drift, which is now his charming style and serves for such trademark as he has" (DM).

34. Hall,"Gramsci and Us," 21 and Williams, Thompson, Hall, *May Day Manifesto, 1968,* 66.

35. Hall, Samuel, Taylor, "Then and Now," in *Out of Apathy,* ed. Archer et al. (1989), 149.

36. Aronowitz, *Death and Birth of American Radicalism,* 195. Also see Aronowitz's critique (and appreciation) of Ernesto Laclau and Chantal Mouffe's post-Marxist, promovementism, antiessentialist classic, *Hegemony and Socialist Strategy* of 1985, "Theory and Socialist Strategy," *Social Text* 16 (Winter 1986/1987): 1–16.

37. See Mills to Macdonald, October 10, 1943, and also see Macdonald to Mills, October 16, 1943 (DM).

38. Piven, "Reflections on Ralph Miliband," *New Left Review* 206 (July–Aug. 1994): 23–26, see 25. Also see Piven, "Is It Global Economics or Neo-Laissez Faire," *New Left Review* 213 (Sept.–Oct. 1995): 107–114: As a "practical political project" to enhance "working-class power" the "socialist project is foundering" (107).

39. James Curran (editor), "Last Word," *New Socialist* 51 (Summer 1987): 56. Curran is critical of this tendency, which he attributes to Roy Hattersley and others: "[They] ought to admit that this is really a liberal utopia they have in mind, and that from this point of view socialism is essentially an extension of liberalism—but liberalism without the traditional illusions and limitations, such as its instinctive resistance to state action, its attachment to capitalism and private property" (9).

40. Lindsay Anderson, "Conference Scrapbook," *Out of Apathy,* ed. Archer et al. (1989), 140.

41. Slavoj Žižek, "Multiculturalism, Or, the Cultural Logic of Multinational Capitalism," *New Left Review* 225 (Sept.–Oct. 1997): 28–51, see 46. Aidan Rankin writes of "new elitists": "For them, the collapse of the Berlin Wall has invalidated all aspirations beyond those of the acquisitive society. The only remaining task is to make that society more 'inclusive,' more 'gender-neutral'" ("Christopher Lasch and the Moral Agony of the Left," *New Left Review* 213 [Jan.–Feb. 1996]: 149–55, see 152).

42. Gold, "A Bourgeois Hamlet of Our Time," (*New Masses,* April 10, 1934) reprinted in *New Masses: An Anthology of the Rebel Thirties,* ed. Joseph North (New York: International, 1969), 219–24, see 219.

43. Piven, "Reflections on Ralph Miliband," 23, 24.

44. Williams, "Culture is Ordinary," in *Conviction,* ed. MacKenzie, 89, 90, 91. A bumper sticker, which I sighted in New Haven in March 2004, read: "U.S. Spends More in 5 Hours on Defense Than in 5 Years on Healthcare." This information is worth popularizing.

45. Tim Wohlforth, "The Sixties in America," *New Left Review* 178 (Nov.–Dec. 1989): 105–123, see 113, 123. Movement activism, he adds, has often taken up a great deal of time that many Americans do not have. On New Left movementism also see David Caute, *The Year of the Barricades: A Journey through 1968* (New York: Harper and Row, 1988).

46. Williams, "Splits, Pacts and Coalitions," 34.

47. Though for the American Marxist Barbara Foley, this disadvantage doubles as an advantage: "We might as well be part of a movement that is about the business of attacking the whole system, and proposing an alternative" ("Theory into Practice," 117).

48. Yet Robert Bellah and his coauthors, Richard Madsen, William M. Sullivan, Ann Swidler, and Steven M. Tipton, bemoan the fact that the individualized Americans they interviewed lack

a political vocabulary of the "good life" and visions of "ways to coordinate cooperative action with others" (*Habits of the Heart: Individualism and Commitment in American Life* [Berkeley: University of California Press, 1985], 20, 24). Consult Percival Goodman and Paul Goodman, *Communitas: Means of Livelihood and Ways of Life* (Chicago: University of Chicago Press, 1947) and Paul Goodman, *Utopian Essays and Practical Proposals* (New York: Random House, 1962); Murray Bookchin, *Post-Scarcity Anarchism* (Berkeley: Ramparts, 1971); Ivan Illich's *Energy and Equity* (New York: Harper and Row, 1974) and *Deschooling Society* (New York: Harper and Row, 1971); Buckminster Fuller, *The Buckminster Fuller Reader,* ed. James Meller (Harmondsworth, Middlesex: Penguin, 1972 [1970]); *The Guaranteed Income: Next Step in Socioeconomic Revolution?,* ed. Robert Theobald (Garden City, NY: Anchor, 1967 [1966]) and Robert Theobald, *An Alternative Future for America II: Essays and Speeches* (Chicago: Swallow, 1970); Aronowitz and DiFazio, *The Jobless Future: Sci-Tech and the Dogma of Work* (Minneapolis: University of Minnesota Press, 1994). See Perry Anderson's comments on why Marx and Engels eschewed futurism or utopianism, *Arguments within English Marxism,* 170–71. But for a review of Marx's writings that focuses on the values he hoped a communist society of the future would cultivate see Nilou Mobasser, "Marx and Self-Realization," *New Left Review* 161 (Jan.–Feb. 1987): 119–28. Curiously, Margaret Mead once proposed that history departments be replaced by "Chairs of the future" (quoted in Goodman, "Utopian Thinking," 19).

49. Williams, untitled review of Bernard Crick, *George Orwell: A Life,* in *Marxism Today* 25 (Jan. 1981): 28–29.

50. Thompson, "William Morris," 29.

51. Mills to his imaginary Russian correspondent, Tovarich, winter 1956–57, in *C. Wright Mills,* ed. K. Mills with P. Mills, 224.

52. Wald, "Formation of an Activist Scholar," 133.

53. Williams, Thompson, Hall, *May Day Manifesto,* 184.

54. MacKenzie, "After the Stalemate State," in *Conviction,* ed. MacKenzie, 11. This trend is long-standing. In 1998 Noam Chomsky criticized the "big efforts to make people feel helpless" ("There Are No Limits to What Can Be Done," in South End Press Collective, *Talking about a Revolution,* 24).

55. W. A. Williams, *Tragedy,* 311–12. Also see the interview with William Appleman Williams in MARHO, *Visions of History,* ed. Abelove, Blackmar, Dimock, and Schneer, 123–46.

56. W. A. Williams, *Tragedy,* 311–12.

57. Harvey, *Spaces of Hope* (Berkeley: University of California Press, 2000), 203, 206, 257–81. Frederick Engels also captured the historical difficulty that early nineteenth-century utopian thinkers necessarily experienced: "The solution of the social problems, which as yet lay hidden in undeveloped economic conditions, the utopian attempted to evolve out of the human brain" (*Socialism: Utopian and Scientific* [New York: International, 1998], 36).

58. Jameson, *Postmodernism; Or, The Cultural Logic of Late Capitalism* (Durham, NC: Duke University Press, 1991), 336.

59. Hall, "Praise of the Peculiar," vii.

60. Rustin, "The Politics of Post-Fordism: Or, The Trouble with 'New Times,'" *New Left Review* 175 (May–June 1989): 54–78, see 68. The aim of "the sociological imagination," Mills wrote, is to produce ideas and work that have a "chance to make a difference in the quality of human life in our time" ("On Intellectual Craftsmanship," 226).

61. *Cultural Studies and Political Theory,* ed. Jodi Dean employs cultural studies to expand political scientists' conception of what constitutes politics, but this interesting volume, published

in 2000, does not dwell on political-electoral issues. In contemporary conditions it is crucial to try to imagine what kind of "polity" would be needed to produce free "subjects of politics"—as emancipated and emancipating citizens (consult Andrew Ross, "New Age Technoculture," 531–48, and "Discussion," 548–55, in *Cultural Studies*, ed. Grossberg, Nelson, and Treichler, see 549–50). Legislation cannot address some of what needs to be changed in American attitudes and ideologies. Yet legislation can be a powerful force. Voting rights and bus desegregation acts, for example, which were the result of civil rights movements' struggles that put pressure on political parties, had wide-ranging effects on race relations.

62. Cayton, *Emerson's Emergence*, ix–x.

63. *Dissenting Academy*, ed. Roszak and Chomsky et al., *Cold War and the University*.

64. Sweezy, "Labor and Political Activities," 61, 63, 65, and Vincent R. Dunne, comments, 103–05, see 104, and Matthiessen on engaging in a wider arena of action in "Education of a Socialist," 8, all in *F. O. Matthiessen*, ed. Sweezy and Huberman.

65. Sweezy, "Labor and Political Activities," 75, 70, 71, and John Rackliffe, "Notes for a Character Study," 76–92, see 85–86, 87, 91 in *F. O. Matthiessen*, ed. Sweezy and Huberman.

66. Kampf and Lauter, "Introduction," 3–54, see 9, 10, 6, 50, and Bruce Franklin, "The Teaching of Literature in the Highest Academies of the Empire," 101–29, see 106, 112, 120 in *The Politics of Literature: Dissenting Essays on the Teaching of English*, ed. Louis Kampf and Paul Lauter (New York: Pantheon, 1972). See Lauter's blurb (415–16), Franklin's blurb (414).

67. Ohmann, "Personal As History," in *Personal Effects*, ed. Holdstein and Bleich, 340–45, 340. Also see Ohmann, "Teaching and Studying Literature at the End of Ideology," in *Politics of Literature*, ed. Kampf and Lauter, 130–59, and his activist blurb on 416, in which he profiles himself self-ironically as "'the well-known proletarian metacritic.'"

68. Commager, "The Problem of Dissent," 219–24, see 224, and Genovese, "American Imperialism Confronts a Revolutionary World," 224–29, see 229, in *Teach-Ins: U. S. A. Reports, Opinions, Documents*, ed. Louis Manashe and Ronald Radosh (New York: Praeger, 1967). Reread Commager's classic in the light of his critique cited above, *The American Mind: An Interpretation of American Thought and Character since the 1880s* (New Haven, CT: Yale University Press, 1950). On some of the tensions between the orientations and practices of socialist intellectuals, such as Genovese, and New Left radicals see Genovese, "On Being a Socialist and a Historian," in his *In Red and Black*, 3–22. For astute remarks on the significance of the anti–Vietnam war movement in Britain and America see Perry Anderson, *Arguments within English Marxism*, 152.

69. For key editorial statements about the journal's project see "Editorial," *Radical Teacher* 1 (1975): inner cover, 36; "Editorial," *Radical Teacher* 2 (1976): 2; "Radical Teacher: 10th Anniversary Editorial," *Radical Teacher* 31 (1986): 30–31; beginning in 1982, issue 22, the journal published first on the inside back cover and soon after on the back cover of issues its "radical teacher definition." A particularly moving article by a high school teacher who was fired from a conservative, suburban New Jersey high school for agreeing to be the faculty advisor for a student-run and student-conceived "Young Left" club, which provided students with a provocative countereducation, is Robert Bruno's "'The Young Leftists,'" *Radical Teacher* 39 (1991): 30–31. Kampf, Lauter, Bertell Ollman, Ira Shor, and many other contributors offered descriptions of courses or guides to how to situate traditional survey courses or conventional courses in a Marxist critical framework. For a few examples of articles devoted to theory in the service of strategy see Ollman, "What Is To Be Done—the little things," *Radical Teacher* 41 (1992): 30–33; Jack Weston, "Do Radical Teachers Have a Progressive Effect?" *Radical Teacher* 11 (1979): 10–11; Mark Maier, "Workers Control in the Classroom," *Radical Teacher* 21 (1982): 23–25. Two exhortations: "Public School

Teachers—Write Articles, Please!!!" *Radical Teacher* 34 (1988): inner cover and "Elementary and Secondary School Teachers—Write Articles, Please!!!" *Radical Teacher* 35 (1988): inner cover. On the exploitation of adjuncts see Lauter, "Retrenchment—What the Managers are Doing," *Radical Teacher* 1 (1975): 27–35. Just two early pieces devoted to academic organizing: Mary Vaughn, "Part II: Organizing from the Bottom Up," *Radical Teacher* 5 (1977): 17–19 and Elisabeth Young-Bruehl, "Report on a Strike at Wesleyan University," *Radical Teacher* 11 (1979): 31–33. The addition of the word "feminist" to the journal's subtitle reflected accurately the collective's perdurable commitment to contributing to and disseminating feminist pedagogy and critique. *Radical Teacher* contains gems by Ohmann, Kampf, Lauter, and many other editorial board members and contributors that should be collected in a multivolumed *Radical Teacher* reader. On matters pertaining to academic labor, the corporatization of education, and progressive pedagogy, also see the exciting journal *Workplace: A Journal for Academic Labor.* Its online version (www.louisville.edu/journal/workplace) contains a section on "Breaking News" and "Labor Links."

70. Pfeil's and Ross's exchange in "Discussion" (of Ross's "New Age Technoculture"), in *Cultural Studies,* ed. Grossberg, Nelson, and Treichler, 550.

71. Thompson, "At the Point of Decay," in Thompson et al., *Out of Apathy,* 3–15, see 15.

72. Robbie Gray, "E. P. Thompson, History and Communist Politics," *Marxism Today* 23 (June 1979): 181–87, see 186–87. Anderson, *Arguments within English Marxism,* 176–207, especially 176, 186. Thompson overlooks, he says, Morris's "strategic imagination" (185). Anderson endeavors to outdo Thompson as a strategist (204). This is also a contest between Anderson's *New Left Review* (which Thompson attacked) and Thompson (a founder of the *New Left Review* that preceded Anderson's tenure as editor): "The divisions between Thompson and *New Left Review* ... rooted in different formations, can best be seen as contrasted emphases on morality and strategy" (206).

73. Margot Heinemann, "Left's Man of Letters," *Marxism Today* 32 (March 1988): 9.

74. Kettle, review of Williams, *Politics and Letters,* in *Marxism Today* 32 (March 1988): 9.

75. Quoted in Fredric Jameson, "On 'Cultural Studies,'" 24.

76. On this dilemma also see Nigel Harris, "The Loneliness of the Left," reprinted in *The Left in Britain 1956–68,* ed. Widgery, 231–34. Harris, originally in *International Socialism* (Summer 1967), observes poignantly: "The problem for the traditional Left is not just the lengthening list of errors and omissions by the Labour Government ... but the whole meaning of social democracy in the absence of a popular movement. This makes the loneliness of the Labour Left much greater than ever before. Then they could argue, rightly or wrongly, that forces existed within and around the Party that, if only given control of the leadership, could create a new society. But there are no forces there pressing for the new society, and the Left becomes no more than the people of which it is composed, and precious few of them" (233).

77. The histories of British and U.S. cultural studies, and even the history of academic activism, to an extent are histories within the history of what Raymond Williams and Alan Sinfield respectively describe as "middle-class dissidence" (in more modern times, professional-managerial class dissidence). See Williams, *The Long Revolution* (London: Chatto and Windus, 1961) and Sinfield, "Middle-class Dissidence," *Ideas and Production* 9 and 10 (1989): 11–29. Rustin has criticized the professional-managerial-class British New Left for embracing intellectual and cultural concerns while allowing its ties with the labor movements and Labour Party to loosen ("New Left as Social Movement," in *Out of Apathy,* ed. Archer et al. [1989], 117–27). He has also questioned how much British New Left cultural studies—its journals,

publishing ventures, forty or so clubs, coffee houses, cultural activities—accomplished in its mainly intellectual and cultural efforts to catalyze political change. Its clubs flourished in large cities, especially London, and in university towns. "The founding of a left-wing coffee bar in Soho (the Partisan) suggests the desire of the New Left to make a congenial home for itself in the capital city, rather than a determination to win over its citizens" (121). Yet he underscores the importance of making culture a central critical concern in mass-societies so influenced by the "service, information and people-processing industries" (126).

78. Hall, "'First,'" in *Out of Apathy*, ed. Archer et al. (1989), 38.

79. Rustin, "New Left as a Social Movement," in *Out of Apathy*, ed. Archer et al. (1989), 121–22.

80. Rustin, "New Left as a Social Movement," in *Out of Apathy*, ed. Archer et al. (1989), 122.

81. Rustin, "New Left as a Social Movement," in *Out of Apathy*, ed. Archer et al. (1989), 122.

82. Hall, "'First,'" in *Out of Apathy*, ed. Archer et al. (1989), 18.

83. Hall, "'First,'" in *Out of Apathy*, ed. Archer et al. (1989), 30.

84. Hall, "'First,'" in *Out of Apathy*, ed. Archer et al. (1989), 30.

85. Hall, "'First,'" 30, and Samuel, "Born-again Socialism," 54–55, both in *Out of Apathy*, ed. Archer et al. (1989).

86. Samuel, "Born-Again Socialism" in *Out of Apathy*, ed. Archer et al. (1989), 54.

87. Hall, "Faith, Hope or Clarity," 16.

88. Hall, Samuel, Taylor, "Then and Now," in *Out of Apathy*, ed. Archer et al. (1989), 160.

89. Editor [Hall], "Editorial," 1.

90. Editor [Hall], "Editorial," 2. Keeping such questions active, he and his fellow New Leftists have conceptually linked this intellectual work to political organizing. The 1960 *New Left Review* advertisement for *Out of Apathy* reads: "Rejecting alike the philosopher's passivity, the salesman's ritual and the politician's soup kitchen, the contributor's [*sic*] plead for a total offensive leading to a humane and democratic socialist revolution—not in the 21st century, but NOW, as a serious immediate policy" (*New Left Review* 4 [July–Aug. 1960]: n. p.). Then again, Hall does not "endorse the picture of the continually engaged militant activist" who after living politics for a few years gives up "exhausted and disillusioned" (Hall, Samuel, Taylor, "Then and Now," in *Out of Apathy*, ed. Archer et al. [1989], 168). Arnold, *Culture and Anarchy: An Essay in Political and Social Criticism* in Matthew Arnold, *Culture and Anarchy with Friendship's Garland and Some Literary Essays,* ed. R. H. Super (Ann Arbor: University of Michigan Press, 1965), 227.

91. Hall, "'First,'" in *Out of Apathy*, ed. Archer et al. (1989), 30.

92. See Chen, "Formation of a Diasporic Intellectual," in *Stuart Hall,* ed. Morley and Chen, 495.

93. Hall, Samuel, Taylor, "Then and Now" in *Out of Apathy*, ed. Archer et al. (1989), 149. Alexander Cockburn makes a similar point in his homage to Paul Sweezy: "Like all great teachers, he gave us consolation as well as the burden of such knowledge." His next point is optimistic, yet vague: "If you know what's happening you're in a position to figure out how to do something about it, and that's always uplifting" ("Understanding the World with Paul Sweezy," *The Nation* [March 22, 2004], 8).

94. Consult Dworkin, *Cultural Marxism in Postwar Britain,* 54–55.

95. Davies sums up his view of the politics of the Centre for Contemporary Cultural Studies at Birmingham: "As a political agenda … cultural studies had no visible agents or actors, no

networks, no commandeering heights of the economy: it operated by secreting itself into the body politic, a samizdat of computers, publishing houses, venues, which bent and reformed themselves. If it existed as a political force, it was guerilla war against the political centre, or else as the avant-garde of the nomadic cultural elite" (*Cultural Studies and Beyond,* 44).

96. On postwar New Left despair, see Dworkin, *Cultural Marxism in Postwar Britain,* 45.

97. Thompson, "Ends of Cold War," 142, 144.

98. Also see Perry Anderson's comments on the vagueness of Thompson's notions of revolution in *Arguments within English Marxism,* 190–94. Anderson's critique is followed directly by his exposition of the post-1962 *New Left Review's* (under his editorship) notion of revolutionary strategy, which he terms "something harder and more precise" (194) than what Thompson offers. His summary description, however, is not "precise" enough to delve into how "the dissolution of the existing capitalist state, the expropriation of the possessing classes from the means of production" (194), "canceling the legitimacy of … parliamentary machinery," "the creation of organs of socialist democracy" (195) can be initiated. Equally vague, though admirable, is his suggestion that the "socialist movement" (is it big enough?), for "its short-term political practice," "should consciously seek to link the immediate demands of the working class to this ultimate objective by the formulation of transitional goals calculated to unbalance the established order, and to weld together all oppressed groups and strata against it" (195). Anderson seems to invest a great deal of agency in a "socialist movement" that has not yet developed anything like the social power he would like to see it possess.

99. Hall, "'First,'" in *Out of Apathy,* ed. Archer et al. (1989), 31.

100. Hall, "Cultural Studies and Its Theoretical Legacies," in *Cultural Studies,* ed. Grossberg, Nelson, and Treichler, 286.

101. Thompson and Foot, "Where Do You Stand?" 9.

102. Perhaps the New Left's great achievement was the cultivation of what Rustin termed a "radical intellectual culture" or "subculture" unfettered by doctrinaire "formulae" or "organizational discipline"—largely for "constituencies … in certain professional occupations [such as] teaching, social work, architecture, acting, journalism, film-making, even science" ("New Left as a Social Movement," in *Out of Apathy,* ed. Archer et al. [1989], 125, 124). This managerial-and-service-class "movement of ideas" had academic roots, hence it is not surprising that its greatest "popular" success, notwithstanding many academic struggles, was probably in the universities. Yet the achievement of an intellectual, later academic, radical subculture has been much more limited than the goals first envisioned by the New Left.

103. Davis, *An Autobiography* (New York: International, 1988 [1974]), 142–43, 145.

104. S. Lynd, *Living Inside Our Hope,* 19, 24, 24–25. Also see Richard Fox's account of Robert Lynd's critique of Rockefeller in "Epitaph for Middletown," in *Culture of Consumption,* ed. Fox and Lears, 108–16.

105. S. Lynd, *Living Inside Our Hope,* 21, 25, 26.

106. See *C. Wright Mills,* ed. K. Mills with P. Mills: Mills to Harvey Swados, September 23, 1956, 213; Mills to Hans Gerth, probably April 1956, 201; Mills to his imaginary Russian correspondent, Tovarich, 297.

107. See *C. Wright Mills,* ed. K. Mills with P. Mills: Mills to his imaginary Russian correspondent, Tovarich, 251; Mills to Walter Klink, March 13, 1961, 328; Mills to Ralph Miliband, June 22, 1960, 290; Mills to Hans Gerth, Feb. 15, 1952, 172. Mills, "Decline of the Left," in Mills, *Power, Politics, and People,* ed. Horowtiz, 233, 234. Dan Wakefield, "Introduction," in *C. Wright Mills,* ed. K. Mills with P. Mills, 12. On Mills's inclination to interpret receiving acclaim by academic liberals as a failure counterbalanced by Mills's reluctance to romanticize failure,

also see Mills to Lewis A. Coser, c. 1955 or 1956: "The success of such a book would in a way be a failure. But that is not to say that failure is not also a trap" (196). Nonetheless, Mills had been as canny about moving from the University of Maryland to Columbia, getting outside offers to improve his position at Columbia, sizing up publishers and securing advances, applying for fellowships and arranging for lectures in interesting places, as many a "careerist" academic of his day. If he derogated winning "acclaim" from "liberal types" as a sign of political-intellectual failure, he also fumed over publishers' readers' reports and reviews that trashed his work, and was proud when *Listen, Yankee: The Revolution in Cuba* (1960) sold several hundred thousand copies around the world. The whale partly shaped how he viewed himself and his success, even as he made its shaping power visible and fought it. So too the whale partly influenced Robert Lynd. Richard Fox writes of Robert and Helen Merrell Lynd's *Middletown* (1929), funded by the Rockefeller foundation: "The Institute of Social and Religious Research would not have permitted programmatic advocacy in the manuscript, but even if it had, it seems unlikely that the Lynds would have been more specific. For one thing, at this stage of his life, Lynd was extremely anxious to establish himself as a social scientist. When he objected to Harcourt's use of [H. L.] Mencken's 'dirty novel' remark [on the book jacket], he did so not on moral grounds but because 'such publicity does not help me professionally'" (127). Fox then points out that the book netted him two offers of tenured professorships, one from the University of Michigan and the other at Columbia (which reclassified the study as his doctoral dissertation as a means to hire him). "It was only after professional security had been bestowed upon him that Robert Lynd took an active interest in the political implications of his work" (127).

108. Mills, "Social Role of the Intellectual," in Mills, *Power, Politics, and People,* ed. Horowitz, 297.

109. See Pierre Bourdieu, *Homo Academicus,* trans. Peter Collier (Stanford, CA: Stanford University Press, 1988 [1984]).

110. "An Interview with Paul M. Sweezy," 41, 53, 45.

111. On Williams, see Woodhams, *History in the Making,* 75. On Thompson, see Steele, *Emergence of Cultural Studies,* 144–50.

112. Steele, *Emergence of Cultural Studies,* 136, also see 191.

113. Hall, "Cultural Studies and Its Theoretical Legacies," in *Cultural Studies,* ed. Grossberg, Nelson, and Treichler, 285–86. For more than a decade Elizabeth Powell has drawn brilliant illustrations for the covers of *Radical Teacher.* One cover illustration cleverly pictures the power relations built into some areas of American academic knowledge production. It shows two Vikings leading an army on their way to conquer: "My feeling is that robbery, pillage and plunder are basically young men's games. I figure when I get older, I'll parlay them into a nice endowed chair of political science somewhere" (*Radical Teacher,* Winter 1993).

114. Graeme Turner, *British Cultural Studies: An Introduction* (New York: Routledge, 1990), 68.

115. Wald, "Formation of an Activist Scholar," 126. For more of Wald's remarks about this matter, see Rachel Riedner and Noreen O'Connor, "Activism and the Academy," *Minnesota Review* 50–51 (Spring and Fall 1998): 55–62, see especially 58.

116. Jameson, "On 'Cultural Studies,'" 24; see Hall, "Cultural Studies and Its Theoretical Legacies," in *Cultural Studies,* ed. Grossberg, Nelson, and Treichler, 288.

117. Aronowitz generalizes: "Most left-wing academic intellectuals stay outside organizations of the ideological left" (*Roll over Beethoven,* 130).

118. On some of these issues consult Mark Edelman Boren, *Student Resistance: A History of the Unruly Subject* (New York: Routledge, 2001), especially 201–49.

119. Kathy Newman, "Poor, Hungry, and Desperate? or, Privileged, Histrionic, and Demanding? In Search of the True Meaning of 'Ph.D.,'" 81–123, see references to soft support on 105 and 113, and Corey Robin and Michelle Stephens, "Against the Grain: Organizing at Yale," 44–79, in *Will Teach for Food: Academic Labor in Crisis*, ed. Cary Nelson (Minneapolis: University of Minnesota Press, 1997). Also see 3, 25, 88, 91 (university as workplace), 49, 53–54, 65, 70 (faculty complicity), 57–59, 62–64, 67, 77–78, 100 (how-to-organize strategies). Also see *Steal This University: The Rise of the Corporate University and the Academic Labor Movement*, ed. Benjamin Johnson, Patrick Kavanagh, and Kevin Mattson (New York: Routledge, 2003), which contains a section of essays grouped under the title "Organizing"; Bill Readings, *The University in Ruins* (Cambridge, MA: Harvard University Press, 1996); Kevin Mattson, "New Year, New Organizing: Efforts on Campuses," *The Nation* (Oct. 5, 1998): 17.

120. See Veblen, *The Higher Learning: A Memorandum on the Conduct of Universities by Business Men* (New York: B. W. Huesbsch, 1918). Mills corresponded about having "to 'save' two instructors" at Columbia in 1957, near victims of his department's "sociological brawl" (Mills to Lewis and Rose Coser, Oct. 29, 1957, in *C. Wright Mills*, ed. K. Mills with P. Mills, 257). For a savvy historicized view of the current situation see Richard Ohmann, "What's Happening to the University and the Professions? Can History Tell?" in his *Politics of Knowledge*, 85–123. For critical perspectives on the role universities play in the American power structure, also see Christopher Newfield, *Ivy and Industry: Business and the Making of the American University, 1880–1980* (Durham, NC: Duke University Press, 2003) and John A. Howard and Bruce Franklin, *Who Should Run the Universities?* (Washington, DC: American Enterprise Institute for Policy Research, 1969).

121. Heinemann, "Left's Man of Letters," 9.

122. Jameson, "On 'Cultural Studies,'" 17.

123. Lauter, *From Walden*, 10.

124. See Eric Cheyfitz's criticism that academics such as Cary Nelson and Michael Bérubé tend to focus political struggle overmuch on the university in his "The End of Academe: The Future of American Studies," in *Futures of American Studies*, ed. Pease and Wiegman, 510–35.

125. See *New Socialist* (Sept.–Oct. 1981): 3, 38–39.

126. Matthiessen, "Education of a Socialist," in *F. O. Matthiessen*, ed. Sweezy and Huberman, 19. Also see Vincent Dunne's comments on Matthiessen: "'I envy you, Dunne,'" Matthiessen admitted. "'You have a political party. Probably that's what I need. I'm a socialist, too'" (*F. O. Matthiessen*, ed. Sweezy and Huberman, see 104). Dunne belonged to the Socialist Workers Party. Mills to his imaginary Russian correspondent, Tovarich, Summer 1960, *C. Wright Mills*, ed. K. Mills with P. Mills, 303; K. Mills notes her father's proclivity to vote for Norman Thomas, 41 and 120. In addition, see Eric Foner, "Richard Hofstadter: Columbia's Evolutionary Historian," *Columbia* (Fall 2005): 37–42. Hofstadter and Mills were good friends as well as eminent colleagues at Columbia. Hofstadter's response to the McCarthy-era assault on progressivism and Adlai Stevenson's failed presidential campaign in 1952 left him disillusioned about active politics. The historian's articulation of this resembles some of Mills's statements: "Although my interests are still very political, I nonetheless have no politics" (40).

127. For some insightful comments on the writing and theorizing of Marxism within a modern and postmodern climate of political despair—despair that is partly a response to the collapse of seriously oppositional parties—see Dworkin, *Cultural Marxism in Postwar Britain*, 137.

128. Quoted in Fox, "Epitaph for Middletown," in *Culture of Consumption*, ed. Fox and Lears, 141.

129. Mills, "Social Role of the Intellectual," in Mills, *Power, Politics, and People*, ed. Horowitz, 299, 300.

130. On peace rallies, see Mills to Russell Johnson, Dec. 15, 1958, 270; Mills to his imaginary Russian correspondent, Tovarich, 1960, 294, 295, in *C. Wright Mills*, ed. K. Mills with P. Mills.

131. Lest his self-affirmation seem too idealistic, he also depicted himself as an "ambitious," "impersonal egotist" who "feels most truly alive only when ... researching and writing," activities that have "interfere[d] with [his] attempts to be 'a decent human being.'" Nonetheless, the research and writing that kept him alive and indecent were directed toward developing and thinking about what could be done with "political initiative" in a society that had made "centers of political initiative less and less accessible." Mills to his imaginary Russian correspondent, Tovarich, Summer 1960, in *C. Wright Mills*, ed. K. Mills with P. Mills, 304. Mills, "Cultural Apparatus," 416, "Social Role of the Intellectual" 304, 294, and 293, "Decline of the Left" 235 and 234 in Mills, *Power, Politics, and People*, ed. Horowitz.

132. Lynd, "Power in the United States," *The Nation* (May 12, 1956): 408–11, see 409. Sweezy, "Power Elite or Ruling Class?," 138–50, and Rieff, "Socialism and Sociology," 365–69.

133. Mills retorted in a review of his reviews without naming Lynd: "One [reviewer] borders on an obstinate silliness over words like 'capitalism' and 'class'—words that have become clichés by which True Radicals try to retain the insurgency of their political adolescence yet avoid thinking freshly about what might be going on in the world today." Mills hinted that this criticism, perhaps like its author, was outmoded ("Comment on Criticism," which originally appeared in *Dissent* [Winter 1957], is reprinted with helpful footnotes that identify the reviewers that he criticized in *C. Wright Mills and the Power Elite*, compiled by G. William Domhoff and Hoyt B. Ballard [Boston: Beacon Press, 1968], 229–50, see 244).

134. Mills to Ralph Miliband (Jan. 25, 1961) in *C. Wright Mills*, ed. K. Mills with P. Mills, 325.

135. Wakefield, Introduction, in *C. Wright Mills*, ed. K. Mills with P. Mills, 2–3.

136. Wakefield, Introduction, in *C. Wright Mills*, ed. K. Mills with P. Mills, 14.

137. Mills, "Decline of the Left," in Mills, *Power, Politics, and People*, ed. Horowitz, 232–33.

138. Miliband, "C. Wright Mills," 15, 16–17, 17, 20. In response to the Soviet invasion of Hungary in 1956, Mills affirmed that he was critical of Marxism as well as "dominant" forms of liberalism and that "way down deep" he was "a goddamned anarchist" (Mills letter to Swados, November 3, 1956, in *C. Wright Mills*, ed. K. Mills with P. Mills, 217–18).

139. Gerth, "C. Wright Mills, 1916–1962," *Studies on the Left* 2 (1962): 7–11.

140. Mills to his imaginary Russian correspondent, Tovarich, Fall 1957, in *C. Wright Mills*, ed. K. Mills with P. Mills, 250, 251, 252. Miliband's profile of Mills resembles Clarence Darrow's sketch of Mother Jones: "The real leaders of any cause are necessarily individualists.... Mother Jones was always doubtful of the good of organized institutions" (Darrow, "Introduction" to the 1925 edition, in Jones, *Autobiography of Mother Jones*, 5–8, see 7).

141. Thompson, "Remembering C. Wright Mills," 265. Referring to his book in progress, *The New Men of Power: America's Labor Leaders* (1948), Mills effused: "That'll go right on the title page.... just the right irony for a book on labor leaders" (Mills to Ruth Harper, June 7, 1947, 105) and Mills to his imaginary Russian correspondent, Tovarich, Fall 1957, 252 both in *C. Wright Mills*, ed. K. Mills with P. Mills.

142. Mills, "Decline of the Left," 226, 221, 222 in Mills, *Power, Politics, and People*, ed. Horowitz.

143. On Mills's admiration for James Agee's tendency to express "great indignation," see his "Sociological Poetry," *politics* 5 (Spring 1948): 125–126, see 125. On Howe's later generational

clashes with the New Left, consult Mark Levinson and Brian Morton, "Irving Howe," *New Left Review* 202 (Nov.–Dec. 1993): 111–116.

144. Howe, *A Margin of Hope: An Intellectual Autobiography* (New York: Harcourt Brace Jovanovich, 1982), 243, 243–44, 244, 245. Mills, "Knowledge and Power," in Mills, *Power, Politics, and People*, ed. Horowitz, 611. In "Homage to Thomas McGrath," Thompson, thinking of McGrath, depicts a specifically American radicalism as: "not that of 'populism' but of the most radical—sometimes socialist, sometimes anarcho-syndicalist—and the most militant anti-capitalist affirmations within Labor-Farmer, Wobbly, and early American Communist traditions" (320). He quotes McGrath: "'In the '20s the Left had many of its origins further west than New York, and out there some of us had been living with the dark side of American experience for a long time. In the late '30s and even more the '40s the Left got corralled in the Eastern cities. And I think some of the writers were unprepared for the late '40s and '50s because they had taken in too much of the Popular Front and watered down their radicalism'" (320). Mills's "The Conservative Mood" appeared as the second long essay—after Howe's "Stevenson and the Intellectuals"—in the first issue of *Dissent* in winter 1954. Mills's "Knowledge and Power," quoted above, first appeared in *Dissent* 2 (Summer 1955): 201–12. And Mills's smart "'The Power Elite': Comment on Criticism"—in which he defends the need to make social judgments—was published in *Dissent* 4 (Winter 1957): 22–34.

145. Miliband to Thompson, October 7, 1963, excerpted in Michael Newman, *Ralph Miliband and the Politics of the New Left* (London: Merlin, 2002), 68. Also see 85–87, 116, 340. Rieff, "Socialism and Sociology," 366.

146. Ohmann, "Personal As History," in *Personal Effects*, ed. Holdstein and Bleich, 351, 348, 349. Dworkin also recognizes that the academy can be a safe haven: "The New Left cultural and political debate .... was kept alive by the emerging field of cultural studies, which in the 1960s transformed New Left cultural politics into a program of politically engaged academic research" (*Cultural Marxism in Postwar Britain*, 116). In addition, see *Left Academy*, ed. Ollman and Vernoff. Also consult Bruce Robbins, "Tenured Radicals, the New McCarthyism, and 'PC,'" *New Left Review* 188 (July–August 1991): 151–57.

147. For many reflections on the effects of Left despair see *The Left in Britain 1956–68*, ed. Widgery, especially Harris, "The Loneliness of the Left," 231–34.

148. Lipsitz, *American Studies in a Moment of Danger*, 61. Consult West's interview with Bill Bradley in West, *Restoring Hope*, ed. Sealey, 35–61, see 60.

149. Moore, *Dude, Where's My Country?* (New York: Warner, 2003), 203, 204, 213.

150. Marx and Engels, *Communist Manifesto*, 15–16.

151. Trotsky, *Literature and Revolution*, 254.

152. Eagleton, *After Theory*, 122, also see 169–70.

153. See Howard Zinn, "Historian as Citizen," in his *Howard Zinn on History*, 202–209 and Ohmann, "Teaching Literacy for Citizenship," in his *Politics of Knowledge*, 124–35.

154. Boyte and Kari, *Building America: The Democratic Promise of Public Work* (Philadelphia: Temple University Press, 1996), 114, 113, 147, 205. Their provocative question is: "What forms of education, popular organization, relationships, and cultural practices cultivate the confidence, spirit, and skills that citizens need for effective action and participation in governance?" (7).

155. See their concluding chapter, "Action," in Brecher and Costello, *Common Sense for Hard Times*, 201–29. As Stuart Hall and many others have stressed, what and who makes a movement move and why it moves is not static. For a complex historicized analysis of the

social movement that manifested in the coalition protest against the World Trade Organization in Seattle in November 1999 and of the ways in which this movement differs from the movements of 1968, see Michael Denning, "A Global Left?: Social Movements in the Age of Three Worlds," in his *Culture in the Age of Three Worlds*, 35–50. For a wide-ranging historical study in this field see Charles Tilly, *Social Movements, 1768–2004* (Boulder, CO: Paradigm Publishers, 2004).

156. Some recent books of varying quality bill themselves as "handbooks" of activism, such as: Earthworks Group, *You Can Change America* (Berkeley: Earthworks Press, 1993); Randy Shaw, *The Activist's Handbook: A Primer for the 1990s and Beyond* (Berkeley: University of California Press, 1996); Thomas Harding, *The Video Activist Handbook* (London: Pluto, 1997); and *The Future Is Ours: A Handbook for Student Activists in the 21st Century*, ed. John W. Bartlett (New York: Henry Holt, 1996). More and more academic books try to link scholarly work and activism, such as: Lauter's *From Walden to Jurassic Park: Activism, Culture, and American Studies* (2001); *Teaching Feminist Activism: Strategies from the Field*, ed. Naples and Bojar (2002); Zinn, Part I "On Activism" in *Howard Zinn on History*, 9–41; T. V. Reed, *The Art of Protest: Culture and Activism from the Civil Rights Movement to the Streets of Seattle* (Minneapolis: University of Minnesota Press, 2005); *Rhyming Hope and History: Activists, Academics, and Social Movement Scholarship*, ed. David Croteau, William Haynes, and Charlotte Ryan (Minneapolis: University of Minnesota Press, 2005). See Gitlin's distinction between "activist" and "organizer" (the latter is "someone who moves people into action and doesn't just rouse them for a particular occasion") in *Letters to a Young Activist*, 4. Duke University Press now advertises books under the category "Activism" (see Spring and Summer 2005 catalogue, 42).

157. I would not suggest that American cultural studies reconfigure itself—in any facile way—as American civics studies. Stanley Aronowitz and William DiFazio usefully describe what a focus on "citizenship" may obfuscate. "Marx's critique of the relation of power to domination erased the very idea of polity since it could be shown that 'citizenship' was an ideology that masked what should have been evident: that the individual as the subject of politics had not yet emerged—indeed, could not emerge until the relations of production were decisively transformed" (*Jobless Future*, 357). Yet "citizens" and "workers" are by no means mutually exclusive social constructions of identity.

158. See Bennett, *Culture: A Reformer's Science* (London: Sage, 1998) and for a briefer overview of some of Bennett's positions, see his "Useful Culture," in *Relocating Cultural Studies*, ed. Blundell, Shepherd, and Taylor, 67–85. On these matters also consult *American Cultural Studies*, ed. Warren and Vavrus and *Cultural Studies: From Theory to Action*, ed. Leistyna. For intriguing examples of current discourses on why the Left seems hard to organize (reminiscent of Miliband's profile of Mills as a "lone guerilla" uninterested in organizational discipline and of Hall's depictions of the British New Left as an anti-organizational organization), see Gitlin, *Letters to a Young Activist*, 109–11, 116–21, and Eagleton, *After Theory*, 40. Gitlin, bringing to mind Matthiessen's challenging door-to-door campaigning on behalf of Henry Wallace's presidential bid, writes of his experience on the American New Left: "I would rather have written poetry than knocked doors in poor neighborhoods" (116). Why not follow Matthiessen's lead and learn to do both? Of course, this is what Gitlin and others recommend. Zinn, *A People's History of the United States* (New York: Perennial Classics, 2003 [1980]), for example, see 510–11, 523. Both Zinn (635–36) and Ohmann, "What's Happening to the University and the Professions? Can History Tell?"

in his *Politics of Knowledge,* 112–23, study new exploitations of the professional-managerial class (for instance, managed medicine) and suggest that these conditions may provoke cross-class progressive alliances. The antiwar marches of 2003 drew astonishingly diverse groups to the campaign.

159. Frank, *What's the Matter with Kansas?,* 4, 5, 10, 75, 84, 120, 122, 208, 234, 251.

160. Mills, "Comment on Criticism," in *C. Wright Mills and The Power Elite,* compiled by Domhoff and Ballard, 249.

161. Conservative activists have put this into practice.

162. Pinter, "The Nobel Lecutre: Art, Truth, and Politics," reprinted from the *Guardian,* December 7, 2005, by www.truthout.org, January 1, 2006, 6. I am indebted to Lisa Wyant for focusing my attention on the importance of Pinter's speech.

Index

About the Author

Joel Pfister is Professor of American Studies and English and Chair of the American Studies Program at Wesleyan University. He is the author of three books including *Individuality Incorporated: Indians and the Multicultural Modern* (Duke University Press, 2004) and is coeditor of *Inventing the Psychological: Toward a Cultural History of Emotional Life in America* (Yale University Press, 1997).

CULTURAL STUDIES / HISTORY / SOCIOLOGY

GREAT BARRINGTON BOOKS
an imprint edited by Charles Lemert

CRITIQUE FOR WHAT?
Cultural Studies, American Studies, Left Studie
JOEL PFISTER
Afterword by Charles Lemert

Critique for what? Fortunately, some of the most provocative self-critical intellectuals, from the postwar period to the postmodern present, have wrestled with this question. Joel Pfister crisscrosses the Atlantic to take stock of exciting British cultural studies, American studies, and Left studies that challenge the academic critique-for-critique's-sake and career's-sake business and ask: critique for what and for whom? historicizing for what and for whom? politicizing for what and for whom? America for what and for whom?

Pfister's historical research convenes New Left revisionary socialists, members of the unpartied Left, cultural studies theorists, American studies scholars, radical historians, progressive literary critics, and early proponents of transnational analysis in what amounts to a lively book-length strategy seminar. British political intellectuals, featuring Raymond Williams, E. P. Thompson, Stuart Hall, and Raphael Samuel, and Americans, including F. O. Matthiessen, Robert Lynd, C. Wright Mills, and Richard Ohmann, help readers reconsider what links the critical project to social transformation, activism, and organizing. Eager to prevent cultural studies from lapsing into cynicism studies, Pfister thinks creatively about the possibilities of using as well as developing critique in our new millennium.

Joel Pfister is Professor of American Studies and English and Chair of the American Studies Program at Wesleyan University. He is a coeditor of *Inventing the Psychological: Toward a Cultural History of Emotional Life in* including *Individuality* (2004).

Critique for What?

978-1-59451-226-1

67878860

5269114U

99999   K   USED

2 901594 512260

Paradigm Publishers
3360 Mitchell Lane
Boulder, CO 80301
U.S.A.
www.paradigmpublishers.com

Cover photo: Mike Newland, 2007